Praise for “

This book is, first

deals with many a

true story of a tough fight battling this disease, its many faces and its deceitful progression.

But, it is also a book about awakening, surrendering and finding a way out.

Filled with empathy and educational importance.

Wonderfully written and beautifully executed.

Peter Nilsson

BSc Medical Biology and Chemistry

This is a strong narrative that should be of interest to most people. A book that even youngsters ought to read, so that they never become seduced by romanticized descriptions of narcotics or alcohol.

(Citation from booklet #12121088)

Pia Holmström, Reader, BTJ, the Swedish Library Service

Lotten's book “I Only Wanted to Dance” is an honest and well-written book about the progression of addiction and, most of all, about the painful path into a balanced recovery. Lotten gives life to the addicted parent's role and also portrays her love for her child. The narrative ought to be of solace to other parents and of benefit to social workers in search of solutions to help the children of addicts.

The book moved me deeply, I cried about some and was gladdened by the others of the phases in Lotten's life.

Everyone who comes into contact with addiction, whether within the family or in a professional capacity, has something to learn from Lotten's story. The book is all the more readable thanks to its strong narrative style and vivid language.

Thank you, Lotten, for having the courage to share your and your child's life with us. Best regards to you both!

Eva Edstedt,
Former Manager at Malin's Minne

About the Author

Lotten Säfström, born May 16th 1966 in Borlänge, Sweden, is an author, lecturer and publisher.

She is based at her own company, Salto De Vita.

Her life's work is to be part of the widespread movement of people around the world who are trying to learn what causes addiction and, most importantly, how to create a life-style that makes staying free of mind-altering substances more attractive than relapsing.

In her own words: "It is very important for professionals to research the physical and psychological hows and whys of this deadly affliction. For the victims in the wake of substance-abuse, though, a crucial thing is learning how people who have this disorder can begin to live a life where relapse does not become an option. Victims of addiction are also the children, relatives, friends and those devastated by crimes committed by abusers of alcohol and other drugs. We already know how to diagnose this deadly, and in so many ways, harmful disorder in the very early stages of its progression. Now, an even stronger focus needs to be put on continuing to implement this knowledge, in order to develop further the strategies that will decimate the awfully high numbers of those who suffer because of addiction."

Lotten is also an advocate for bringing education about healthy emotional development into school in order to give future generations a ground-breaking head start in personal health and adult responsibility.

The authors' books "I Only Wanted to Dance" and "Now the Dance has Begun" are written with the intention of relaying support, solace and hopefully inspiration to those living, caring for or working in the proximity of people with an addictive disorder.

Her literary works may also be of interest to people who have found the desire to give up that lifestyle and will, possibly interest those who are still suffering from active addictive patterns.

These books are written for adults but, with adult supervision, teenagers can benefit from reading them too.

I Only Wanted to Dance

by

Lotten Säfström

Salto de Vita

Published by Salto De Vita, 2016

info@saltodevita.com

Proofreading: Suzannah Young and Katja Hjelm

Cover Illustration: Limpo Rocha

Typesetting: Nanna Salemark

Print: Booksfactory, Poland, 2016

ISBN: 978-91-983173-0-5

Beloved child!

My spirit soars at the sight of you.

I love you. All the time.

I hope love, joy, courage and dedication

will continue to grow within you and, therefore,

always be yours to share.

Gratefully and forever yours!

Foreword

As I sit here, watching the pale blues and pinks of sunrise colouring the skies over Malmö, resting my gaze over the rooftops, a familiar surge of awe fills me.

My bustling city with its boundless diversity of people, from all over the world.

The beauty of our Earth.

My heart swells at the sensation of belonging.

The fact that I am sitting here awakens the humble numbness in me at having cheated death.

Gratitude blends with it, when I hear the sounds of my child behind her closed bedroom door, the typical sign of a teenager's need of privacy.

In my heart, deep in the silence of my innermost being, the knowledge of how close it had got awakens the horror of how I had nearly been lost to her.

What would have become of my child?

Too many of my friends and loved ones have perished.

Few find a way out of the destructivity of addiction and co-dependency.

I pursued the lie of something or someone outside myself being what would make life vivid.

Following that impulse was, in fact, generating the absolute opposite.

Addiction, the Destroyer of the innumerably Many.

To think then of the even higher numbers of those harmed in its wake.

Generation upon generation.

Miraculously I survived to tell this tale.

One

Mother refused to let me have a soda. She was so impossible, it was infuriating! I decided to run away.

I packed two bags full of comic books, my most valued possessions, and got dressed. I dragged the stuffed-full bags, huffing and sweating through the half meter-deep snow to my best friend's house. She and her family were also our closest neighbours, living 50 meters away from our house. I had to make the journey twice. It was heavy for a three-year old! My decision weighed sadly on my heart, but I gritted my teeth, braced myself against the sobs that were making my throat ache, picked up the last bag and said a silent farewell.

We played for what felt like forever before my friend's mother came in and told us that it was time for supper. When I was told what we were going to have, it was something that I definitely did not like. I wanted "real" food, so when my mother called and wanted to speak to me I agreed to come home. Looking back, I can see that deep inside, subconsciously, I had come to a fork in the path of my personal development - whatever happened, I would do my utmost never again to feel hurt the way I did that time.

Having to trudge back home with all that heavy baggage was unbearably humiliating. Twice!

Outside factors were never going to break me again!

No one talked about what had happened, at least not as far as I can remember, and if someone did I can bet it was nothing that really got to me.

That was the first time I remember consciously choosing to walk the path of the outsider.

The second time was a situation when my father said:

"You just can't think like that Lotten!" I was a little older then but not much since we still lived in Sweden. My reaction was without afterthought, immediately discarding what he had said. I remember thinking something like:

"Well, that's exactly what I can do. Actually, it's what I just did and that is precisely what I intend to keep doing, and you can't do anything about it!"

But I didn't say it out loud. Again, I cannot remember if we talked any more about whatever it was and, if we did, it was in a very normal way and most probably nothing that I would have paid any mind to. At this very early age I was already very accomplished at subtly defying and silently disregarding the input of others – always wary.

No one got to poke my insides. No one was allowed to disturb me.

No one had anything I needed.

Or so I thought. Of course those were the biggest lies.

Since my outlook and struggle to be untouchable always collided with my fellow humans, I constantly had to create explanations in my mind to strengthen my illusion of being different. And so my armour hardened. My choices and my sorrow were buried deeper and deeper. A toughening that turned into a jailor, imprisoning the loving little girl that was me. The strangeness of interacting with others brought about typhoon-like, chaotic and painful feelings inside me. This mental isolation-chamber became an instinctive means of shelter. A reaction of self-preservation.

The last of the three events happened when my grandmother on my mother's side was visiting.

I had taught myself to read at the age of four but I was not allowed to read after a certain time at night. A sound decision made by my parents, or perhaps it was the nanny. To me, this seemed like a huge lack of respect and immensely unfair. I protested but quickly realised that it was in vain and let the argument drop I complied, as far as anyone knew, but since my resolve not to be trampled on was as fresh as ever, I automatically started brainstorming for a way to satisfy my desire to read.

One day, the opportunity arose. I had found a way out of my fenced existence.

Granny arrived and soon I asked her for a gift that I knew would make her very happy. It was a little model church with a tiny lightbulb inside. Her religious heart swelled with joy and the gift was already mine on that very first day. I kept it at my bedside and, after bedtime, sneaked it with me under the covers so I could read for as long as I pleased, or stay awake.

The satisfaction I experienced from taking this course of action embedded in this little girl the idea that I had without a doubt taken the correct course of action. I was perfectly capable of catering for my needs and I did not have to accept being held back. Sidestepping the interference of others was obviously a winning path to freedom. I had once again found a solution by myself, which proved that I did not need to follow rules to be leading a fulfilling life.

As a young child I did have friends and had a fairly good relationship with my parents, my two younger siblings, relatives and the nannies who took care of and lived with us. My mother told me later in life that I was a very easy-going child. I think it was partially due to my always being preoccupied with planning my next course of action and trying to steer clear of others who wanted to meddle in my business. My mind was always busy making plans of how to silence what I only can describe as an inner emptiness, a hole that constantly shouted loudly to be filled. I developed methods, to get rid of these strong and unintelligible yearnings. Unaware that the cocoon I peered out from was not the way everyone else experienced the world.

I remember being very busy with the whats and whatnots that could make me happier. I was a little child and all these plans were very spontaneous and never truly malicious or outright defiant. For instance, I used to pack my knapsack and stroll along the gravel road outside our house.

Never too far, but far enough to experience the freedom and excitement of adventure. This was innocent but, in hindsight, to me these excursions felt like lifelines.

It was in these moments I felt truly relaxed. I didn't have to playact interaction with others which to me was an indescribably difficult web, one that was excruciating and drained my energy. Communicating and conducting social relations didn't come naturally to me, not as far back as I can recall. I was always very aware of how I did something, what I did and when I did it and was also aware of the deciding how, whether and why I should do anything at all. A sensation that always stood out was the notion of being lonely, as much when I was with those closest to me as when I was in a crowd.

A feeling of being alone instead of lonely would arise when I was left to my own devices and I knew that I was not going to be disturbed. In that state of mind I felt much more content. If I could have, I probably would have chosen to lead my whole life alone, but life does not work that way, does it?

·

As a person I always interact with other people. Even having made an active choice not to I am still making that choice with them as a factor in the equation. Always aware that they are there. I thought I could manage without and yet always having them.

An observer looking at my life situation from the outside would think I had all the requisites for a good foundation in life. My mother was a famous fashion designer, my father was highly educated and very ambitious, my grandparents were very committed to their grandchildren and we had tightly-knit bonds with our relatives. We did "real" family-stuff, like celebrating traditional holidays, spending time together outdoors, traveling and socializing with other families. We were frequently visited by our grandparents on our father's side. On our mother's side, my grandmother would come down from time to time whilst grandfather would stay up in the north to take care of their house. We also went to their houses often. Leaving our house and traveling was important in spicing up my existence. The adventure would be full-time then and I didn't have to create escapades since I was in the middle of one.

My father's parents lived in a townhouse in an idyllic part of Sweden called Dalarna in the small town of Borlänge, in central Sweden. That is where the painted horses, Dalahästar, one of the most recognised Swedish tourist symbols, come from. The family let us roam freely in the neighbourhoods and the limits were naturally set by distance and roads. I had many special spots

I could take off to and always managed to keep myself busy.

The utmost sensation of freedom I experienced as a small child was when we visited my mother's parents in a tiny village towards the southern part of Norrland, the most northern county, where they lived in a tiny village called Betåsen in Ångermanland. It was a beautiful place along the river of Ångermanälven and just inland from the World Heritage Site, Höga Kusten (The High Coast). It was a great adventure to travel up there. Several times, our parents even sat us by ourselves on the train to be met by our grandfather at the junction up north, there changing to the mini-train taking us to our destination – Betåsen Station, which was opposite our grandparents' house.

Big and white on the edge of the woods, the size of the house made it a place of peaceful relaxation indoors and outside I was glad to wander about by myself, well aware of the vastness of Norrland. There were few social and physical boundaries to tie me down and this was perfect for me since I was always able to find my own, private sanctuaries. The closeness to my siblings was also much less stifling here since they could also move around more freely due to the lack of dangers in the tiny village.

Here I felt I could let my guard down the most. My grandparents were always busy with their chores and we were seldom in each other's way in the large house.

This was where I laid the foundations for an inner sensation of security, a sense of being safe and calm, that I often fell back on during the gruelling mental illness and devastating existence of the future to come.

As I described before, my grandmother was a religious person. Every night, she had us recite a children's prayer. She lay in her room next to ours and shouted to us to speak up so she could hear that we were actually praying. So I grew up shouting a prayer at the top of my lungs until she was content. Afterwards I kept on praying for a while silently and, as time went on I kept up this type of reflecting, developing a growing feeling of contentment doing so. I am very grateful for this routine having been imparted on me as a natural thing to do. Throughout everything, I've always used this as a tool to look back at my day, to contemplate grinding decisions I need to make and to dissect and assess what I have already done. Somehow, prayer helps and, early on, this became an intrinsic part of who I am. A base for my faith was created – a spirituality that is real, free and true, not bound by taboos. The feeling of unconditional love I experience during these moments of stillness have carried me through my entire life.

But despite this, I remained emotionally incapable of coping with the fellow humans surrounding me. I developed approaches in contacts with others that were both conscious and, unconscious and instinctive. Now I can see that mostly I reacted with a sort of spontaneous behaviour. It was like any other impaired person's enhanced development of senses that others wouldn't have a need for.

Again, in hindsight, I can see that I learned to read people. It was an unconscious act and since I was so young I learned to do it with the perfection of any small child learning the art of communication. I realised this only after several years of total abstinence, recovering from alcohol and other drugs. When interaction became too strenuous, I learned to withdraw with tact or simply just shut down - by wearing a false but seemingly sincere smile and responding in the correct manner. I learned the sign language used by an emotionally and socially disconnected and impaired person. The sensitivity that allowed me to read people and the resourcefulness of a child made this skill-set, copying human behaviour, superior to that of any graduate from the finest acting schools in the world.

This therefore went unnoticed by those around me. Who could know that I wasn't in contact when my responses mimicked exactly what one would expect to be hearing and seeing? 'Charming' was a word often used by my family to describe me as a child. Charming, easygoing and self-confident. Not a problem child at all. I fitted in instinctively to avoid stirring up conflict.

In addition to this, it was as if I never went through the natural phase of growing out of needing everything to be about me. After the first few years of expressing my wants to the surrounding world for survival I stagnated. I kept on existing in the realm of the three-year-old where everything around me existed to fulfil my every impulse and everything beside that was unknown, unchartered. My development near enough halted as my experience of my surroundings was often scary and queerly inexplicable.

I lived in a world where I switched between being on the outside looking in or in a cocoon looking out, studying how others behaved and interacted. Unaware of this but always in a state of readiness.

Once, we were at a dinner party and I stayed at the table when the other kids ran off to play. I sometimes liked to sit and listen to grownups, studying them when they socialised. Especially if the mood was one where I felt I could sit undisturbed. They sat savouring their drinks, no one overly drunk, but as any child did, I noticed the change in their personalities. After a while, I reflected about them getting a bit raucous and sentimental and was just about to leave the table when a woman addressed me in an uneasy tone:

"Stop looking at us like that! It feels as though you're looking right through us!", she cried.

I understood that my presence made her feel very uncomfortable about. My parents immediately asked me to leave the table and I gladly removed myself, since the woman had touched me deeper than anyone else had in a long time. To have been seen and noticed in that direct manner was something I'd almost never had happen to me before. My own family and relatives were used to my ways and didn't react as this person had done.

It was somewhat of an awakening, an insight into other people having integrity and I was much more cautious after this incident. I let my fear of being detected rule my behavioural patterns even more and my innermost desire to be a part of humanity became more muffled. The gap of 'me versus them' that most children learn to bridge, was in my case a ravine which I impulsively widened instead. The natural, sound sense of belonging and cooperating never became a natural part of my growing up. Self-centredness remained the uneasy ground I tread in the world.

This was about as far as I could relate to being in a satisfactory emotional state and I was very happy.

Two

When I was five years old my father got a job in Amman, the capital of Jordan, and including our nanny the whole family moved abroad. To be thrown out into the unknown and thus making all my waking hours into a constant adventure, even in my home, was a dream come true. This became a golden rule for my continued walk in life. This was full-time excitement, which was the same as contentment to me. In Sweden, I had already moved house three times. The first time was when I was four months old.

We left Borlänge, the town where my father and I were born, for Gävle and then, after a year there, my parents bought a house on the outskirts of town. From there, we moved to Amman in Jordan. Within Amman we continued to change homes. After a couple of months, we went from a flat in a building with housing for those employed at my father's workplace to a much fancier and larger midtown apartment with a huge terrace. Later, we moved into an even larger, ground floor, four bedroom apartment with a big garden. We also changed nannies. The only two constants were the family and the school.

I was five when I started in first grade at the English International School of Amman. I have been told that I was exceptionally quiet at home during the first month of my schooling. I was going through an intensive learning process - learning English by listening and watching. Digesting the way a child does when introduced to something completely alien. My parent's English was poor in those early days abroad and this was my first and inescapable exposure to being spoken to solely in an alien language.

It was beyond strange at the beginning when I didn't understand a single word people said. I was lucky to have another Swedish girl in my class who helped the teachers and me by translating what was needed. This crutch was only allowed at the very start and then only sparsely. Translation was only allowed when deemed absolutely necessary since this was a school with very high demands on its' pupils. The school system was strict, and employed routine penal methods such as being sent to stand in the corner and even getting smacked with either a ruler or a stick depending on the severity of the offence. As I was focused on fitting in and going unnoticed, I steered clear of these disciplinary methods, except for once when I got put in the naughty corner in second grade.

Another method used by the teachers was that we were not allowed to use an eraser. This was to let the teachers get a clear understanding of the pupils' needs so that the necessary education could be given. I was a fast learner and comfortable with the challenges within this type of education.

In Sweden, I had never gone to a daycare centre like most children do, so this was my very first contact with teachers and children in a group setting. I was very comfortable with the school work and because of that the "crowded" classrooms didn't bother me too much, but as usual my co-existence with others was only superficial and quite energy-consuming. My strong impulse for privacy, for isolation, was limited by the scheduled, enforced routines of the school day. I would often wander off by myself during the breaks and let my imaginative mind thrive.

Within the school walls, we had a schoolyard with swings, hopscotch squares and ballparks but there was also an area beyond the walls, out back. This was a huge, undeveloped expanse of sand where the more obedient children could take their lunch-boxes during the midday break. I liked it when we got to go there and used to walk alone, spinning vivid, exciting tales. I remember one in particular. It took place at the top of the tall wall that rose behind the building of my classroom. I kept fantasizing about being a fearless tightrope-walker who had managed to escape beyond the walls of a prison by balancing on the barbed wire that stretched along the top of the wall. In my mind-game, I was wild and beautiful with a scar across my cheek bearing witness to my fearless and independent personality.

Through my lively imagination, I created colourful

and intense escapes like this one from the rigid school routine. I filled the days with excitement just as I had back in Sweden and, in time, this developed into more intricate scenarios. These solitary games overlapped each other and, combined with the challenge of my education, my days were filled with endless activity. I thrived!

I devoured all that I learned and soon found myself reading English fluently. Then, after the turmoil of our emigration and getting used to this very different country and culture, my new schedules and the English language, I could thankfully find my way back into the much less disturbing world of words.

There were only six small classes in the school and my need for solitude grew stronger than ever. The strain of socializing was much more tangible now and the small school-library became my sanctuary. There were entire walls of books that were mine to rummage through and freely pick and choose from! This was a wondrous discovery. Now I had comics, books and schoolwork to fill my existence instead of incomprehensible feelings. It was Heaven on Earth. To be able to escape into the lands of written adventures, kept in suspense and never knowing how the tale would play out was incredible bliss. This secluded and orderly desertion from life has always followed me. At different stages in my life, it has even reached the point of becoming an almost suffocating addiction, but always, always appeared safer than the alternative of the real world.

Every morning, we had assembly in the main room and said the Lord's Prayer together. Learning this new prayer was enriching for me, but this wasn't the case for everybody. There was a boy who had another religion and he used to just mouth the words. He was found out and then made to stand in front of the whole school and say the words aloud. The humiliation of this struck me deeply. To force someone into performing such a degrading act! It was in front of all the other children and most importantly it went against his own spiritual belief. This became a seed towards my firm belief in freedom and equality for all the various faiths and religions, including if a person has none. Also, unfortunately, this situation fuelled a very long and deeply rooted contempt towards authority figures in religious, spiritual and atheistic matters.

However, over all, the English International School of Amman was a very good school for me and I turned out to be a very good learner. It was here that my love of writing was born. My inner world was expanding.

There was a lot to see and do in Jordan. The cities, the beautiful desert landscapes, many well preserved Roman and other ruins, the Dead Sea and the whole culture that through the eyes of a child was both natural and exotic. There are two well-known archeological sites in Jordan – Jerash, in the north just outside Amman and Petra, a Nabataean burial-site in the south. In those days, these places were rather deserted and at times my family and I were the only ones roaming the ruins. We visited both quite often and those excursions were exquisite fertilisers for my imagination. There was always an adventure waiting around the next corner.

We also visited the refugee camps. The 1948 UN act that gave away large areas of already populated lands in neighbouring Palestine had forced many to leave their homes and many of these individuals had come to Jordan. The misery of the living conditions in the camps sank into me, a child uncoloured by the political aspects. It shook me to seeing the difference between my homes and those shabby shacks, the people's evident lack of kitchens and the insufficient sanitation facilities. I got a rude awakening to the injustices of our world. During the years in Jordan I became uncomfortably aware of the Western people's systematic looting of other countries' natural recourses, also their using underpaid local people to carry out exhausting manual labour, and rarely giving them any possibility of advancing within the companies. A global mindfulness emerged in me then and has been with me ever since.

I never became a political activist. From the start,

I internalised the feeling that self-serving and closed minds with a total lack of empathy were what drove those in power, the few who own the Earth. These few people were not able, or even willing, to master the art of responsibly managing our planet's resources. This short-sightedness, a symptom of their faults, drives them solely to take action that exhausts the Earth instead. This dawned on me very early on and became an uncontested view. The sorrow and futility of caring for the future of my world began at an early age and turned slowly but surely turned into a hatefulness that haunted me for a very long time. This process drew power from my illusion about being alien. I withdrew further and further from participating in the ventures of humanity.

***

We often visited Aqaba by the Red Sea. After a short time in Jordan, my parents started leasing a hotel on the seaside. Parallel to we children going to school in Amman and our father still working there, the family became hotel managers on the Southern coastline. We were often there and I discovered a new, most grand arena for adventures – the sea. We had a new nanny and this one taught me how to swim. The sea in Aqaba was unexploited at this time and our parents let us swim and snorkel unhindered in these fabulously rich waters filled with spectacular coral and creatures in wondrous shapes and colours. I experienced an enormous freedom in that environment. During my life since I've had sporadic dreams of being deep in the ocean, breathing under water. Those dreams were often a means for my subconscious mind to get a breather during the most deadly and terrifying times of my severe addiction.

The years when I was five to eight years old were the most harmonious of my life. There was so much of the new and the adventurous that I could fill my emptiness with, where my social life ought to have prospered, and I was as near contentment as I had ever known. Emotionally, I was the way I was but the extreme stimuli from my surroundings busied me, and therefore my emotional life wasn't as exhausted with the effort of being.

This is how I remember my early childhood. Shut off from others but very resourceful and drawn to seeking out excitement. When I lay in bed at night, drifting off to sleep, the sequences of the past day would flutter through my mind, but they seldom related to the people I'd had around me. I would lie there spinning the situations in my mind and weaving them into the most breath-taking scenes, mostly resembling movies, filled with extravagant characters and daring strings of events. Uncomfortable, normal or calming thoughts were brushed aside as soon as they popped up or at best used as raw materials to be overwritten with the spectacular. I drifted on an artificial theme of life.

With the gift of hindsight, I now know that my parents were on a slow path towards their divorce. The escalating wilderness of my fantasies and the rich adventures I undertook in the real world might partially be due to this event looming on the horizon. Most probably I was picking up on their feelings, a discomfort stirring under the surface of our outwardly happy and successful family unit. Fictive action used as a defence against a painful reality.

Nevertheless, I still refer to the first eight years of my life as being the most joyous part of my entire childhood.

Three

My mother was made to drink one small glass of red wine every morning when she was a child. My grandmother worried about her daughter being pale and wine was said to be good for the blood. When we had dinner parties at our home, once or twice a month, my siblings and I would be served a little wine stirred in water with a bit of sugar with the meal and no one in our family considered this inappropriate in any way. I was five or six when this happened the first time. Instantly I found that it was something I liked - and much more than candy. It wasn't so much the taste, even though I liked that too, it was the mind- and mood-altering effect it had on me. The calm and relaxation I experienced was revolutionary to me. Of course I didn't pour it by myself in the beginning but I dearly looked forward to being served and I asked for a sip from time to time when the grown-ups had it.

I made the first premeditated choice to drink from a wine bottle without supervision when I was eight. We were at home, alone with our nanny, and I took the opportunity when she lay soaking in the bathtub. The bottle was open but recapped on a counter in the kitchen. I remember wanting the effect. I knew that I had to be sneaky about it but as soon as I had started on the bottle there was no stopping me. I managed to empty more than half of it before the nanny came and stopped me.

I didn't get sick but was very dizzy and euphoric and was immediately helped to bed. If the nanny talked to me about this afterwards, I don't remember. I do know that I was twelve before sneaking alcohol became a more regular habit so she most probably did reprimand me.

I told my mother about this incident recently and she was shocked – my parents had never been told. Not that I think it would have made any difference in regard to my future addiction. As soon as I had gotten alcohol into my system the first time I was lost to it and I believe this would have happened even if I'd delayed my debut until the Swedish legal age of eighteen.

The state of completion that alcohol instilled in me at the beginning gave me a surge of utopian well being. Under its' intoxication I felt safer than ever before. It was as if a significant part of me which I had lacked before had suddenly grown itself. Under normal circumstances, I was always tense and my thoughts were subconsciously and continuously focused on how to act or be able to slip away unnoticed. With this drug in my body I could suddenly just be! Even sitting in the company of others, my mind would actually ease off and I could even feel relaxed. To get some alcoholic beverage in the company of the adults now began to seem important in a more intentional manner. I put myself in situations where my chances to get a taste increased.

In my eighth year it also became more and more apparent that my parents had problems in their marriage. I couldn't shut it out any more. My feelings erupted uncontrollably sometimes and emotional grindings little by little overtook my guarded poise. One day when we were playing at the hotel our parents came and fetched us. We were to go home and talk about something important. We never used to leave the hotel in the middle of the day. The way they talked and their behaviour must have warned me of impending doom because I cried in the car on the way to the house, and I almost never cried. The pain was almost unbearable. To feel powerlessness over this situation, the pounding understanding that there was nothing I could say or do to make them change their minds triggered a shutdown. I repressed my feelings with all my might, but of course there was no way of banishing the feeling of sheer abandonment that speared my insides and infested my innermost self. My defences against the hurt built frantic barriers that quickly thickened.

I was nine when they went separate ways. The three of us stayed with our father. Our parents had decided that the standard of living we were used to would be best kept up at his house. It became difficult to commute so we moved full time down to Aqaba where my mother also lived.

Since we didn't speak much Swedish at home and all

our schooling had been in English our father decided that we should be given a new kind of tutoring. He employed a Swedish teacher for us and our classroom was furnished in a small house on the hotel grounds. At the same time our last nanny moved away. It was a difficult time I was now embarking upon. We had always had the nannies to turn to but now there was no one. I was truly fortified in my isolation.

In time both my parents remarried. None of these pairs of grown-ups ever got along with the other. I became more and more hardened and seemed to be absolutely unreadable to those around me: they only seemed to see what I wanted them to. The sorrow and loneliness I felt was too ungraspable and painful to bear, relentlessly never releasing their grip on me.

The emotionally blocked little girl grew into a bigger child and now I was acting according to an even more consciously self-serving mentality. Bitterness slowly crept into my heart. This was how I trod through my tenth and eleventh years. The foundation for my teens laid out. During the last years in Jordan I seethed with this new, darker viewpoint of life. When it was time to move back to Sweden one day it was with my father and his new spouse whilst my mother stayed with hers in Jordan. I was eleven years old.

The house we'd had when we moved abroad had been

sold. During the weekdays my siblings and I lived with an aunt in Borlänge where we went to a public school during a few weeks until the summer holidays. At the weekend, the whole family stayed in one of my step-mother's family homes. My sense of alienation developed into larger proportions due to missing my mother and longing to go back to Jordan. I was also being bullied at school, being left out and called an immigrant as my Swedish wasn't the local dialect and words often escaped me. The school system was also very different from what I was used to. There was no discipline and no extra help in the classroom for those who had difficulties keeping up. Instead, the school-world was suddenly filled with favourites, invisibles and rejects.

I also heard the teacher being called names, even to her face. In the classroom there was often bullying. Since I was unsure about many words, I kept asking for them and other things to be explained so I got my fair share of taunting. I felt wretched and out of place from day one.

It was also a culture and climate shock. This was a most natural reaction but I can also see my disproportionate tendency for flight in the extremely painful longing not to be where I was. For the first time I allowed myself to openly show unfiltered feelings of the strong distaste I had for the world around me. Since I didn't have a healthy ability to handle my feelings, these emotional swellings overtook me. These emotions had thrived in hiding, in the inner spaces of my being, but now other people became aware of my loathing. Due to my inability to identify and express feelings I couldn't tell those around me what was troubling me. What they saw was the "perfect", ever so charming Lotten radically change into this unreachable, angry and arrogant personality. A personality that I knew very well, having nourished her for so long. In situations of my choosing, situations where I knew no one could penetrate my fortress, I lashed out and let my distaste take on an unmistakably fiendish air. The family chose to name these outbursts "early teenage mood-swings" and for my part they were welcome to as long as I got to release these strangling, all but maddening, storms of unmanageability.

Soon we moved again within Sweden and lived in Malung for a year. There I made friends, became physically active with swim-practice five times a week, and after practice I began shoplifting candy.

My dad found me out and sent me to the school counsellor. It was wonderful! For the first time, I got to talk about my feelings, my longing for my mother and Jordan. I was also going through a very hard time at home and this woman gave me tremendous support. This was an important piece of the puzzle toward decoding the incomprehensible codes of co-existence and communication with my fellow human beings.

After that year we moved again. Now to Nora, a small picturesque town further south, and there I never resumed that kind of therapy.

I was now in seventh grade and the new school was a little better than the two previous ones. I wasn't learning, enjoying and burying myself in schoolwork as I had in Jordan, but at least here I could muster more inspiration since the teachers and pupils were noticeably more involved in the learning process. It was a relief. I needed to have stimulation at school. In my class I had a cousin on my stepmother's side and she became a wonderful friend of mine. The bonus of having friends and an active lifestyle outside school was beginning to form itself into a new oasis. I had become older and the sense of alienation had grown stronger. Being as lost as I was had brought about many clashes with people during this period in Sweden and all those events were prime fertilizers for developing my defence tactics. Other people were not to be trusted and I fought ardently not to let anyone move me. More and more I became ironclad with self-confidence but with less and less self-esteem. Evolving only in seclusion and self-centredness.

During the holiday between seventh and eight grade we left for Saudi-Arabia. When the summer vacation came to an end I started at the American International Community School of Riyadh. It was wonderful to be back in an English-speaking environment and to live in a warm climate. But Saudi was a country that really didn't suit a young girl inclined to spend a lot of time alone in wild, unchartered adventures.

As most foreigners do in Saudi we lived inside a compound. There were large compounds but ours was a very small one with only six families and ten or so single men, and to me this felt terribly cramped and isolated. I had to have a male driver take me wherever I wanted to go outside the camp. Taking a walk outside the compound was not done without a male person to accompany you.

The school milieu was tinged with a culture of superficial glamour and competitive achievement. There were sharp contrasts between the English restraint, the Swedish introversion and the American outward assertiveness. I kept myself to myself with a Swedish friend, sports and studies.

School work was immediately stimulating and fun again, just the way I liked it, but my home conditions and the cooped-up residential issue made life outside school and sports-practice seem like purgatory and I couldn't stand it. I held out for a school-year before I asked my father if I could move to a boarding school, back "home" in Sweden.

Other children whose parents lived in Riyadh and already went to such schools came to Saudi for their holidays and through them I had gathered information about which of the schools would suit my agenda. I wanted to go to the slackest one. During the year in Saudi, my tasting of alcohol at home had increased so the luring tales of parties and alcohol-fuelled bashes that I heard of taking place at one of the most notorious schools helped me make the choice. This also seemed to be a school where it seemed most likely that there would be the least parental involvement possible. The choice was made from these criteria and I started in the ninth grade. So, within a few months of the idea being born, I had bolted free. As usual, it was very clear to me that I seemed to be the one most capable of fulfilling my needs.

Now my drug of choice could finally take its' rightful place, moving out of my longing fantasies into being a major part of my life.

Fourteen years old and I was set free.

Four

Logically, I cannot force the blame of my escalating drug abuse on my parents' letting go of me too early. The fact is that most children who attend boarding schools manage to conduct their lives without becoming severely addicted to drugs. A sense of sorrow, perplexity and bitterness can hit me sometimes though. Especially now that I have a daughter of my own and when I meet youngsters in their early teens. I realise that they are actually no more than children.

Despite this, the bitterness for what happened to me passes quite quickly today. I remind myself that addiction being regarded as a disease is a very new insight for the human race, even though the fact has existed throughout our entire history. This classification is still unknown or unaccepted by many people. The drug abuser is often stamped as having a low sense of morale, maybe combined with a mean streak. We forget that these traits often develop after the dependency has taken root. We also tend to forget that there must have been a disorder that caused this unhealthy abuse of mind-altering substances in the first place. I felt the drugs brought me normalcy. And in the beginning they did.

The diagnosis is still being mapped and, even in professional research on it, not everyone shares the view that a disturbance existed before the drug-abuse started.

But most of the addicts living in sobriety that I have listened to, people who have lived through it and have begun to recover, share similar experiences - that the affliction at the core of our disease was there before we started using. My parents and other adults in my proximity cannot have had any inkling about this.

I also realise that, for adult parents in our society, personal development issues are many and occur during various phases in life. Being a parent and an independent individual is difficult.

The most important thing that I remind myself of is of my sophisticated ability to read and instinctively manipulate the people around me. I was extremely skilled at using words and acting, if ever so subtly, in order to further my plans. I was a badass at mixing logical reasoning with spontaneous deliberation, easily weaving conversations with truth and lies. All to disperse any doubts and effectively hiding my true objectives. I was not a see-through child.

My parents loved me and they did what they in their hearts believed to be best for me. Of this I am wholeheartedly certain. They sent me off to boarding school with soaring hopes for my future since I had gotten almost straight A's in the American school.

I was given a single room. It was a small one on the second floor with a bed and a desk that were bolted to the floor.

To me, this confined space was Heaven on Earth. In time, I became an expert at changing even this room's décor since it was, as ever, very important for me to always change the world around me. There were no facilities for swim-practice in the little town and neither did I resume the basketball-practice I had gotten into in Saudi. Instead I started smoking cigarettes.

In total, twenty junior high-school pupils, including me, lived in my dormitory. For the most part, we were children whose parents were abroad but there were also those who had their homes in Sweden. It was an intimate environment and I was extremely grateful to have my own room.

Living like this was a new experience and I remember the first time I was hugged by another kid there. I stood straight and stiff as a rod, feeling the emptiness inside being hit with painful flashes of fear. Hugging was something I wasn't used to from home, not since my mother and the nannies had moved away. I was starving for attention and warmth. At home the atmosphere had been very reserved and I had not been in touch with my mother for long periods of time.

I adapted quickly though. I liked hugging and staying up talking and listening. These new friends became my extended family, in-so-far as I was able to interpret relationships that is. Even in these intimate surroundings I was still ridden with the false sensation of being apart.

There were a couple of factors in my notion of being different that stood out. For one, I was a year younger than my classmates since I had begun my schooling a year ahead of the Swedish school system. I also had ideas of how happy all the other children's homes must be as opposed to my own. In that belief, I created a scenario in which everybody else was spoiled with love and genuine happiness. That "truth" misled me and made my fear and alienation grow. I existed, as always, in isolation and self-centredness and so also in this company, but, as always, looked like the popular and self-assured one in the group.

My time in Saudi had made me a hardworking student but in Sweden I started to prioritise differently. I had so much sorrow and resentment about how life had turned out the last few years and my revolt against the establishment continued. For example, in French I had an A++ from the eighth grade. In my new school, the French teacher picked me as her favourite. But I had finally found others that I tried to identify with and resented being treated differently, so I drove my grades plunging down to an E- when I graduated that year. I still had an average of B- but that wasn't for having put any effort into my schoolwork.

I despised the societies of this world and told myself that I didn't want to become like the grown-ups I had met in my life. Not like anybody I had ever seen anyway.

My arguments for not taking part in the world grew stronger and more watertight with every passing day. In my interpretation of reality my own satisfaction came first, as always gaining strength from all these home made theories.

My father often said:

"You think too much Lotten."

And I would think:

"Yeah, yeah fool. Luckily someone does!"

I took very little of what others thought of me to heart, if it didn't suit my agenda. But all the well meant opinions and advice were of course stored in my brain, but from storage to actual usage was a totally different matter. I could act contrary, even if I saw that it was constructive criticism, just because it came from the wrong person or just because the advice was in conflict with what I had already decided to do, despite it being harmful. Angry, spiteful and reckless – what I disliked about others was actually what I was becoming myself.

We, the junior high school pupils, attended the local school and there I began getting to know kids who lived in the small village. Not everyone from the boarding school did this. For me it was a means to an end in my pursuit of alcohol and, later on, other drugs. The main reason, which I admitted to myself, was that I would be able to attend the "parties"- the word I used to cloak my early ventures into addiction. It took time to get to know people and until then the pubs in the village supplied what I wanted by letting us youngsters frequent their establishments and spend our generous allowances at their tables.

One evening during the spring semester, I sneaked out after curfew and went to see an older acquaintance who had liquor at home. I was already drunk after a night on the town and when I got to this house I asked for an Aspirin. I had never mixed drugs before but suddenly a strong urge took hold of me, driving me to get more intoxicated. I was given a tablet and then I poured vodka on top of that. I only have fragmented memories of what happened later that night and not a single one of how I got home. I awoke when the house-mistress knocked on my door as usual to summon us to breakfast. She opened the door to check that I was getting out of bed. This was shortly before lunch-time since we always got to sleep in during the weekends. She gave me a brief glance and then shook her head and shut the door behind her. I was lying in my own vomit.

No one brought this up afterwards. I was told that I had gone to another friends' house with a few others. Around 3 a.m., he'd had to carry me to my dorm, sneaking me back into my room, after I had fallen and hit my head badly on a radiator in his room. I became very scared. I remember thinking that I could easily have died that night and that I would probably put myself at great risks again if I kept on using alcohol. I could even have died from choking on my own vomit. Or what if the blow to my head had been worse? Who knew what could have happened to me!

I decided to stop using alcohol.

Five

I saw him on the bus and, I swear, his sharp blue eyes shone perfectly at me. It was almost creepy. He had long, wavy hazel-ish blond hair, was dressed in everyday clothes but the way he carried himself made him look like the coolest cat I had ever seen. I was hooked. Instantly. From having never seen him before, I immediately started asking around and soon found out that he lived just outside the closest larger town from us. My closest friend knew who he was and told me that there was a party coming up that he was supposed to be going to. She also warned me that he and his friends were doing hashish but I was hypnotically focused on meeting him and just shook it off.

I was very unaware of what narcotics were. We had never talked about such things at home and I don't recall taking special note of information given in school or the media. The same goes for alcohol. It seems strange, since drugs are such a devastating factor in so many people's lives and so important for young people to be aware of. If anything, alcohol and narcotics sounded exotic to my ears and the boy's charisma drove me straight to gathering information about him and how to make it possible for us to meet.

I had never acted this focused on any partner relationship issues before. I'd had one serious boyfriend earlier and also a few alcohol-related "sexual" encounters but those had more or less just happened without any sober choice being made. This time, I had to do a lot of planning and steering of people such as my house mistress and my aunt who was my guardian in Sweden. In the end it worked out and was supposed to be "sleeping over at a friend's house". I counted the days with rising anticipation.

Johan was late. I had almost given up and was upset, all but accusing my friend of having tricked me into going when he suddenly came walking up the driveway.

I hadn't had any alcohol, still frightened by what had happened when I had become unconscious recently. Despite this, I dared approach him. I think he said something about having a girlfriend but that didn't deter me at all. I was going to have him and that was that. Only a few weeks had passed since I had quit the use of alcohol when I became Johan's girlfriend. I was fourteen.

Before I began using hashish, I'd snuck around with alcohol and was used to acting deceptively to get my buzz. Alcohol is a legal and socially accepted drug so my sneaking had mostly been due to my being underage and, because of this, the hiding and lying were already habits. Now with using an illegal substance I tuned out much further and faster from society and in a more distinctly deliberate way. Using narcotics meant that

I started moving in circles of criminally active people. The justifications for my impulsive actions hardened my inner strongholds which became much stronger now. This mode of existence suited my personality perfectly.

The effects of hashish are, amongst others, a heightening of the senses and the dulling of a person's ability to truly connect with others. It makes you more or less paranoid, dampens your emotional alertness significantly and is extremely addictive. So this drug was really my thing, working as a completion of the kind of traits I was drawn to. To fill the empty inner space, where relationships with other people should have thrived, the hashish became that special something to fill this void with after the alcohol had scared me so.

Another benefit was getting to know others who were like me. Well, actually it wasn't the people that ruled these bonds, it was the drugs. But the acquaintances weren't altogether false either. Most of us had the same reason for hanging out. We cared for each other in a way that was caring as we had defined it. We met as often as we could and at any cost. The school and the world of grown-ups became irrelevant. We were the ones who had understood the lie of the land and the attraction of hanging out with these friends overtook all my other obligations. Being together with them smoking pot, talking about the world, listening to music and doing drug-related business felt like the most important activities

I'd done in my entire life. The intoxication, the way we related to each other and the adventures we experienced together grabbed me like nothing else ever had. We had codes and taboos as in any family. I had found my clan and it was a feeling I shared with the others in the gang.

We were a bunch of youngsters who were somehow adrift, each on their own in life. None of us seemed to have any deep connection with our parents, other grown-ups or friends who didn't use alcohol or other drugs. We turned to, raised and listened to each other. The norms we created sprung from how teenagers interpret the world and that was what we grew up to respect. Topping that off with a social disorder evolving through the first phases of addiction made for a recipe for disaster. It had been the same for the others when they had joined these kinds of circles and the same for the innumerable pre-addictive youths before us. It was us against the world. The drugs, the theories and the intimacy in these ties glued us together. This was how I paved my way towards adulthood.

I don't remember my first hash pipes. I remember laying off the alcohol in the beginning, being in love with Johan and that the hits of hash made me very differently drugged from how I was used to being with the alcohol. The world was kind of shut out and then filled up with a swirling echo of completeness. It was also very exciting and cool to be around this drug, it turned you into a villain of sorts. We smoked a lot. There was always money and access to it even though we were so young.

I had already shown that I was neglecting schoolwork and except for the normal pep talks to step up my efforts no one really reacted all that much to me getting even sloppy. These reprimands fell off me like water off a duck's back. I had found what was optimal for me and anyone else or the legal parameters surrounding this drug could just go mind their own business very much staying out of mine. I was a part of something now and my relentless search for adventure, satisfaction and seclusion in this strange world had acquired an even more stable platform.

During my first holiday from the boarding school I stayed with Johan and his parents at their house a lot. That summer, I ventured on my first smuggling trip to Christiania in Copenhagen, at fifteen years old. After that I began selling hashish on a small scale. I considered this a completely defendable course of action since the world was such a corrupt place. I defended it to myself by reasoning that if I could use, buy and have so much fun with this substance I had to be able to stand up for it all the way. Of course it was also a means to finance my own consumption. I also embarked on this risky business with something called the "noble code" among hippies. I did not sell to people who were too young, I did not rip off our customers and always bought the better quality even if it cut profits - the better quality being more expensive to buy, but the price for my buyers in turn had to the same market prices.

I had been so lost in the world before I found an identity in this lifestyle. I was starved of the respect we kids showed each other, even though it was faulty, but I didn't know that then. This factor made anything anyone would have to say about my lifestyle most difficult to try to talk me out of. My old friends tried but their words said nothing that even began to dissolve the bonds I had formed with my addiction and the people surrounding it.

My first year at senior high school began and now the boarding school's private faculties became my only tuition and I changed dormitories. I got to live with a girl who was new to the school and it went rather well. I had gotten used to the intimacy of having so many people around me all the time, but I think this was mainly due to the fact that I always had a means of escape close at hand. I took every opportunity to be alone and had distinct opinions on everything, even when what I said was off the top of my head. Hashish fuelled a lot of euphoric "insights" and half-baked theories. In that way, it affected me the same way my drug of choice had. Putting the world to rights over a glass of wine... In hindsight it all just looks embarrassing when reality sets in. The difference being that, as an addict, I did not wake up and have to regret the day after, and I definitely was not able to admit that the drugs had a reality-altering effect on my mind. I pursued my ideas forcefully and held these theories as truths day after day, strengthening my views that it was the rest of the world that was misled.

I created a collage that I hung on my wall with pictures of wars, starvation, rich versus poor, pollution, global warming, yes, the whole kit of unjustifiable issues that torment the citizens of our planet. But for me to get involved in any kind of reformation activities from within society seemed to me just as pointless as the injustices themselves. All I wanted was to point out that the world was inhabited by disappointing and duped people. In this, I began to cultivate resentment towards my God. How could this be allowed to happen? It all seemed without meaning. More and more I rejected what the school and my "ordinary" friends and family stood for. I was polite as usual but never shared anything real about myself or contributed other than sparsely to discussions. Only the friends in the gang got to know some small part of who I was.

Even I couldn't see where my ache and misplacement was rooted, so how would anyone else be able to?

In the middle of all this breaking free I had to ask for help.

I had begun to have nightmares about what my situation at home had been like before I moved out. The vulnerability I had experienced there had begun to wear me down. In my mind, I tried to get rid of the situations that were haunting me. I theorised, thinking my way through the angers towards those involved, but to no avail, the dreams just kept coming. Thoughts and feelings began hunting me even in my waking hours. I couldn't stand that these people could taunt me despite the fact that I had left them and was supposed to be free now. After a while, I realised that I had to get help, so I went to see the school counsellor.

At last I was able to talk about everything that had happened in my family. I had all the facts clear and the counsellor agreed with me about the dysfunction, just as many people had done before both outside and inside the family. But looking at the obvious madness and knowing of the acknowledgement from others didn't take away my anguish or help with the nightmares. The relief I felt was in the counsellor's office, in the moment. It helped me see everything more clearly but the emotional drainage continued. I went often to these sessions but it was still taking an enormous toll on me.

I just couldn't bear carrying that much resentment. It took too large a portion of what sparse energy I had, what with my already suppressed, undeveloped emotional tools. Logically and truly I saw that it all came down to the shortcomings of those involved which had made the living situation unbearable at home. Despite this clear chain of reasoning and understanding it all intellectually, the torment didn't cease. Since the theoretical approach to the problem wasn't enough I had to turn to the spiritual side of things in the end. It was my only hope. Finally I had to ask my God to help me.

I prayed and looked intensely inwards, asking for the answers being as meditatively silent as I could. The theoretical part of my insights slowly started to rest in the feelings about what had happened. Out of this, an unexpected understanding, or rather a sensation of seeing the whole picture, followed. What had happened was not in any sense alright. As if by a miracle I suddenly understood, was able to set my boundaries to protect my integrity based on that understanding and, finally, I was relieved of the bad dreams. They actually never returned.

Empathy for our family was born, which brought with it an ability to set up sound and strict limits in my interactions with them. I could never explain or prove how using spirituality worked on this problem, but through this and many other experiences of how things turned out when I practiced using that part of being human, I became convinced that looking inward and searching for a spiritual solution would inexplicably work. That is, when I remembered to apply that method. My resentment towards my God cooled off a little after that.

I don't remember much from that year in school. Hashish exhausts the memory function and dulled me very much. In the end, I didn't like the effect this drug had and after eight months of abstinence I took up my drug of choice again, but now I used beer instead of wine and stronger spirits. For me, beer was a kind of "soft alcohol" and I reasoned that if used it in moderation I wouldn't risk unconsciousness again. The difference in the effects of the two drugs became very apparent to me as I slowly awoke from the sameness of cannabis. This pattern became a winning concept for me through my life. When the alcohol started to wear my body down and the emotional results didn't match up to my expectations, I changed drugs for a while. Since I never really enjoyed the way narcotics affected me, those periods were only count-downs until I could resume my liquoring again.

Johan moved into his own apartment and, soon after, I moved in too, even though I still attended the boarding school. I took the bus back and forth on weekdays. How I managed to manipulate anybody to allow me to live in with a boy at the age of fifteen, I don't clearly remember, but since I was a champion at coaxing people it doesn't surprise me that much. Homework and getting involved in school projects were hardly things I engaged in now. What I valued was getting intoxicated, developing my home life with my boyfriend and the gang, doing business with drugs, listening to music, and of course, last but not least, elaborating my theories about the state of the world in grand and intricate webs.

That is what it is like to be stuck in addiction. Nothing new actually or truly develops on the inside of a person, it is mostly talk and sometimes external factors like drugs, events, money or housing might change.

Another graduation came up and I didn't spend any of it with my biological family. The cycle of addiction continued, varying only in that we moved the base of drug sales to the beach and the gang hung out under the blue sky of that extraordinarily warm summer. One evening towards the end of the holiday we made spaghetti bolognese at home and I suddenly realised that this was the first time we had eaten inside in several months. Candy, pizza, beer and pot had been the bulk of my consumption that summer. The fundamental part of a healthy existence being eating nutritious foods and drinking pure water and juices was something that eluded me for decades to come.

I began my second year in senior high school and, even though it was never my primary choice of drug, I had become a seasoned user of hash. I brought smoke to school and sometimes I used it with trusted friends. Once a girl I didn't know tagged along when we were going to light up. I asked the friend who had brought her along if we could really count on her keeping our secret and was assured that we could. A couple of weeks later I was called to the headmaster's office.

It turned out that this girl had a good relationship with her parents and she had told them that I had given her a smoke. There and then I couldn't blame anyone but myself and deep down I could actually acknowledge feelings of envy and admiration for her. I understood that it would have taken a lot of courage to admit such a thing at home. For me it would be unthinkable. In the uproar that followed, I used the technique of neither admitting nor denying what I had done.

An assembly of the school administration in the area and our faculty was set up with me at the centre of it. There were at least ten grown-ups questioning me and they got nowhere but I was unquestionably guilty and was given two choices. Either I would move in with a family living in the village or I could terminate my contract with the boarding school and move wherever I pleased. Obviously I chose to live with Johan. Somehow it was organized so that I started at one of the public schools there. I was at least reprimanded by being forced to leave urine samples with the nurse at the new school so I had to quit smoking hashish. At least for the time being.

In all of this, I cannot remember any form of communication with my parents. Most probably I did talk to them sometimes but that life was far from what I valued in those days and it has utterly slipped my mind. The outcome of the whole matter was that I ended my private schooling without being expelled and that was the end of that. Looking back, unthinkable and scary are the words that come to mind. Even so, as I have said before, it doesn't surprise me all that much given my uncanny ability to control my fellow humans, putting forward my case in a shimmer of deceptive conclusions. No one could foresee the coming disaster of so haphazardly letting me go. If the disease of addiction had been more known to mankind, I think someone would have seen the signs clearly in this young girl, but alas, that was not the era I grew up in.

At sixteen years old I had now flown the nest completely and was all but cut off from all contact with the adult world. This was my realtime launch into the Wild Wild West.

And the world continued to be a very strange place indeed.

Six

The first two weeks in my new home were tough. Going through abstinence from hashish, I had an internal, gnawing anxiety and was unable to do anything in the bathroom but tinkle for the first two weeks. I sold off what pot there was during this time and only saved one gram of some extra good quality stuff for Christmas. I suspected that I had been let off too easily from the business at the boarding school so I took the extra precaution of closing down my business. One evening towards the end of the second week, the doorbell rang and Johan opened the door without checking the peephole first.

I was sitting on the sofa in our one-room apartment, chatting with a couple of customers who had dropped by to get some smoke. Since I didn't have any to sell we had been speculating about who they could call instead. Johan opened the door and eight men stormed in. Three were uniformed police officers and, two were in plain clothes but clearly in command. The other three seemed to be civilians and I had a weird feeling about them. One of these carried a camera with which he soon started taking pictures.

Johan panicked and started arguing loudly, whereupon one of the uniforms drew his gun while another put a firm hand around Johan's throat. In this scuffle, all the men were drawn into the kitchen where the action took place and I, quick as lightning, saw my opportunity and snatched the small piece of hashish we had and threw it over the balcony. In a second I joined the others and turned to one of the plain clothed and more mature officers saying:

"Would you ask him to put down the gun, please? The guy is just scared."

It turned out that I had addressed an inspector from the narcotics division and he answered me in an almost confidential note:

"Yes of course. It's not always easy to keep these rookies in their place," and he smiled, winking at me and defused the whole situation immediately.

Our guests sat goggle-eyed and quiet as mice on the sofa until they had to give their names, were checked out and, as they were unknown to the legal system, they were sent off with a warning about choosing better things to do with their lives than frequenting suspected criminals.

Johan was the first to be interrogated and the plain-clothed inspectors sat him down in the kitchen. I was kept under guard in the other room and watched the dog sniff everywhere without detecting any scents of note. The uniforms searched the combined bed and living room area and soon found all our scales and asked me what they were for.

"We weigh aquarium fish," I responded. They just

shook their heads and sealed them all in plastic bags. I asked another officer what the guy with the camera was up to and was told that this was standard police procedure and that he was the officer who documented the raid.

When they were done with Johan, he came into the room and I tried to communicate to him that I had already gotten rid of our Christmas-piece but he didn't understand my signals and ran straight for the bookshelf, grabbed the vase where the hashish had been and bolted out on to the balcony. He had planned to swallow it. This resulted in the dogs finding the piece in the yard. I hadn't been able to swallow the hash since I had to leave samples at school.

It was my turn to be questioned. I kept a clear head and stayed calm during the whole thing. Everything turned crystal-clear and my brain was working at top speed. When they asked me how long I had been using hash, who in these circles I could tell them about and how long we had been selling, I denied everything. I also denied any knowledge of the piece they had found in the yard.

In this situation I didn't feel any aggression or hostility towards the police except about what I had deemed as unnecessary violence against Johan. In the cat and mouse game of the police and thief roles, we all only did what society expected us to do – they were mean and fishing and I was innocent and uncatchable.

To admit anything to the police would have been unthinkable. I was unshakeable and the session was soon over since they noticed that I didn't waver. I answered consistently and showed no insecurity about their presence. They commented that the apartment was filthy and that was what I took to heart in this whole ordeal and I actually did more cleaning afterwards, but all else had the water on the water-off-a-duck's-back-effect on me. I shut myself off and reasoned it all away. As usual.

I've never really hated the police. My position on cannabis at the time was that I firmly believed that as opposed to the legal substance of alcohol, hashish would be the better choice for some people. Too many couldn't handle using alcohol since it too often triggered dangerous and deep dark sides in people. Being rendered unconscious, the vomiting when the body rejected the poison, uncontrollable mood swings that too often resulted in violence or other dramatic outbursts, children that were mistreated due to grown-ups' irresponsible drinking habits, people having sex when they hardly knew how they got there and so forth. Despite alcohol being my drug of choice, I ignored the terrible ways that hashish affects you as a human being. As always the chameleon highlighting any facts to blend in with my agenda for the moment. I kept my resolve de jour freshly burning in any given moment. All to keep up a confident posture.

When they finally left, we went through our home which had been turned inside out. We found three grams of smoke behind some stuff in a cupboard. The dog hadn't been able to detect it, probably because the apartment was impregnated from the vast amounts of hashish that had been used there. Everything must have reeked of the scent, poor creature. I guessed it had gone smell-blind in there.

The camera guy and his two friends turned out to be reporters from one of the two biggest local daily newspapers. A picture of our room was posted in the middle of the front cover and we thanked our lucky stars that Johan's parents only read the other one. I contacted the editorial staff and was told that if we were going to sue them we would have to reveal our names publicly and neither Johan nor I were willing to do that. They had probably relied on us backing down. This weakened my trust further and confirmed my theories about this world being a corrupt and untrustworthy place.

This incident became my only conviction concerning drugs – 0.5 grams of hashish. I was a juvenile so my family got a letter about it. I don't remember if my father said anything to me on the matter. No punishment or change was forced on me, that I would have remembered, and I continued to live with Johan.

I quit school a few weeks before the end of the second year in senior high school. I wasn't into such things as planning for the future. "Being" someone in the eyes of the established system was something I despised. My focus was on satisfaction in the moment and that got all my attention. Just like a very small child only focusing on getting their basic needs seen to. A teenager with a very small world instead of expanding my horizons as other youths did and in complete denial of being the one who was pinned down.

We were very different, Johan and I. During our relationship I became more talkative and he grew more silent. I was drawn to the wild aspects of life while he got himself a regular job. As some young people who have had enough of rebelling, he started to cool off. That was not an option for me.

One evening, after a fight, he refused to talk it out and went to sleep on the couch instead. I decided that I'd had enough. I remember writing in my diary:

"Now a new life begins!"

It was a painful separation. We had been a couple for two and a half years. We had been intensely attached through these years of burning youth. Even in "ordinary" people's lives those years are incredibly intensive. For us who had shared a lifestyle within a closed-off, criminal grouping filled with secrets and tactics, our bonding had been immense. But I just couldn't stay when this all seemed to be moving toward normalcy. I didn't want a safe existence. As always, adventure and the unknown lured me more.

A short while before our separation I had resumed saying the Lord's Prayer which I had learned at the English school. Shortly after having been liberated from the nightmares about my family, I had stopped praying. Now that life with Johan had become more and more insecure and the drugs never gave any real relief, I turned again to the spiritual part of me which had given results back then by resulting in me getting a respite from my emotional fatigue.

The first time I resumed praying was that evening when I lay alone in Johan's and my bed and without warning, I suddenly had an intense spiritual experience. It rushed through me and was a penetrating insight of everything being in order, that everyone was where they should be and that love between all in existence was the glue that made the relationship between everything alright. It is difficult to explain. These visions were loaded with feelings that hit me like a tidal wave of love and understanding. I can still feel its' backwash to this day. This was a big step on the journey to search for meaning in life which I have been on throughout, as we all are. It also turned out to be a life-buoy that saved me many times, holding me back from venturing too deep in the deadly depths of addiction.

Another thing that gnawed at me was an underlying feeling of sorrow about being addicted to alcohol and other drugs, about being dependant on something external, something chemical, to make me (to fake me) happy. I was seventeen years old when these thoughts started to emerge and yet I continued to use for many, many years ahead.

Throughout the years of active addiction, I traversed lots of borders that I had set out for myself. Already when I was a small child I remember taking a vow never to start using nicotine. Letting myself down like this in life, creating justifications as I went along, crossing the lines and nurturing the destructive cycle, in time led to this behaviour seemingly starting to feed on itself with the inconsistencies and the lies. The dependence on mind-altering substances took over whatever ideals I'd had before. If I, for instance, had taken the spiritual revelation to heart, I would have had to break off from my addiction but, somehow, that never came up as a feasible alternative. To have my whole worldview punctured, to doubt the ideas I used to allow myself to follow the mad impulses – it was unthinkable. The soundness and purity of the spiritual bombardment lived on inside though and it literally carried me through some very rough patches on the hellish road all the way, until I found my sobriety. With these experiences stuffed in my heart I started to pack my things, mostly clothes and music records.

I got my own apartment. In the eighties there was no shortage of them where I lived so I was able to move in within the week. I began hanging out with the gang that was closest to the one we had mainly belonged to. Daniel was the one that I knew best there. He and I had always had a special friendship. Daniel's ex and Johan had always felt left out when he and I started talking and joking. Now we were both single and we had a really good time without there being any thoughts of starting anything but a friendly relationship, but after two months I suddenly realised that I was in love. We became a couple and this lovers' relationship was very different from my previous one. Each of us was, for better or for worse, just as wild and carefree as the other.

Daniel was a romantic, high-spirited and adventurous young man. He wooed me, complimented me and often came bearing small gifts. As we already knew each other very well, our relationship was laid back and friendly. We were able to "play" together. It felt so right that already a month in we decided to move in together.

A few weeks after we had moved in together we went to the countryside to visit my best friend Lena and to sleep over for a couple of nights. Her parents were traveling and we had the huge house to ourselves. It was the middle of May on my eighteenth birthday and there, Daniel proposed to me. I said yes immediately! We were completely right for each other! Over the moon and as crazily in love as couples you read about in love stories, except of course that the common denominator was focused on drugs and banditry instead of beautiful dreams of life-long health and plans of family.

The next day, we had promised to help Lena's parents weed the garden. Daniel, Lars, a friend from the gang, Lena and I kept at it all day. When we were done we split a bottle of wine and smoked a couple of pipes on the lawn admiring our day's work. It was a warm pre-summer day and I remember musing over the fact that I had never as comfortable and happy with anyone before as I was with Daniel. Our connection was so relaxed and natural. I even got a feeling of being grown-up in a way that I could like. The feeling of being apart was such an integrated part of me that when I got these rare moments of connecting with another person, even if in short bursts like this one, I could relate to the value of being together with another.

We cooked and had dinner together. I missed not having more alcohol but knew that we had more pot and even the thought of being with the others, and especially Daniel, soothed me. The guys said they would take the canoe out for a while and we waved them off from the kitchen calling after them to put on the life-vests. Lena and I continued to clear away the dinner table when suddenly Daniel sneaked up behind me. He grabbed me around the waist, lifted me up and kissed me.

"I love you!" he whispered.

I kissed him back and could from the bottom of my heart say it back. Then the boys disappeared down to the lake.

We continued to clean, talking and Lena put on some music and turned up the volume so that we could hear it above the sound of the vacuum cleaner and my dish-washing. The song was by a well-known Swedish singer, Lill Lindfors, and this was one of her biggest hits "Musik ska byggas utav glädje". It streamed out of the speakers and we were singing along joyously when I glimpsed a movement in the corner of my eye just by the kitchen door. I turned around and there stood Lars soaking wet. He was in a crouched position and mumbled the same words over and over again. I couldn't hear him properly because of the loud music, but whether it was his posture or a powerful intuition doesn't matter – I knew.

I called out for Lena who heard the anxiety in my voice and came running. I was frozen for a few seconds and unable to approach Lars so she did. I don't remember what was said but suddenly I moved with great speed right past them and ran the hundred meters down to the waterside and all the time thinking the same words:

"Don't be afraid Daniel, this isn't the end. Do not be afraid! You exist, there is no death – don't be afraid!"

The words just came out like that, it was instinctive and, wether or not there is an afterlife it gave me a strong feeling of comfort to keep repeating the words over and over. Lena found me and almost dragged me back to the house. Lars sat huddled on a chair, still repeating the same words and now I heard what he said:

"The canoe capsized n' he's drowned... The canoe capsized n' he's drowned..."

Now I could go up to him and I hugged him for a long, long time.

I was stunned. I continuously directed my thoughts to Daniel. Rescue teams of people came, the firemen, ambulances, the police. One that stood out was a nurse who came a little later when they had realised that there were only youngsters at home. She gathered us, put us in a car and we rode with her into the nearest village where she got tranquillisers for us. I think it was a police car that took us all. Lars stayed at the house for the first night. Lena's parents were contacted and would be arriving early the next day. The three of us slept on mattresses snuggled close together on the floor of Lena's room. I kept up my mantras to Daniel in my mind, I prayed to my God and in the sound from the wind chimes on the terrace outside Lena's room I imagined getting soothing replies. My pain in this sorrow was unbearable but I summoned the love we'd had and all the magical moments I had shared with him and let those memories take over the awful truth of what was happening, quieting the torment of it all.

This internal process was as intense as the focus I could muster to do it. I realised I would have to go through this pain for a long time coming. It was beyond nightmarish.

I was allowed to stay with Lena and her family for a week afterwards. Then I had to return to our apartment. My brother who had recently moved to the boarding school was there waiting for me and he supported me those first days. He was two years younger than me but he was still a pillar in my wrecked reality as best he could be.

Since my parents were abroad, I only had contact with them over the phone. We spoke once or twice about what had happened and then never mentioned it again. I suppose I needed their comfort but they assumed I had things under control as I always said I did. By now I was far gone from seeking them out as parents so I let them go and continued alone in my search of more stable ground.

Lars and I met daily and we went to Daniel's mother's house several times but there I felt like a villain of sorts having been there when the accident happened. At the funeral, his ex-girlfriend sat with the family and I could understand that. Daniel and I had lived outside the norms of society far more than his ex and he had and

I assumed that they saw me as a part of him being gone. At least those were the thoughts that the young girl that was me had about it.

Now I wanted to disappear as never before. I couldn't stand being in our apartment. I missed him so much. I decided to terminate my contract and leave without knowing where to go. I just knew I had to get away.

I had not been in contact with social services before but I had heard of friends who had gotten help from them. I didn't just want to up and leave everything in the flat so I went to their offices and told them that I needed help emptying the place and also that they could throw away or make use of the furniture and anything else there was as they pleased.

"But where are you going then?" somebody asked.

I answered quite truthfully that I didn't have the faintest idea but that it would surely work out. I was very curt and decisive. I had a vague picture of some kind of pilgrimage straight out into the world but I did not mention that to these people. Apparently I didn't have to – it turned out that they saw and understood. After leaving the keys on the counter and a note with the address I was just about to walk out the door and literally keep on walking straight out into the great beyond when someone called me back.

I was asked to wait for a moment and then showed

into a room with a couch and an armchair where I was soon joined by a woman who kindly asked me to tell her why I'd come to take such drastic measures. Since I had opened up about difficulties during my school years I now noticed an underlying need to talk to someone outside the circle of friends. I hadn't realised this during the weeks that had passed in anguish and shock. I told her, but only well extracted truths. I never mentioned alcohol or hashish. What her conclusions were I could only guess.

What happened after this conversation was very kind of them. I was told that I could stay with the family of one of the social workers for a while so that I could get my bearings in all that had happened. I was over eighteen, the legal age to choose for myself in Sweden, and surprisingly, even to myself, I accepted with a feeling of relief. Somewhere deep inside, I understood that I was walking a slippery path and would need to heal for a while before I set out on my journey. Because leaving on my pilgrimage was still a certainty if anything in the world was.

It was all set up very quickly. I went with them to my temporary home that very same day. I remained there for what was left of the summer and then started at a school in the village where I finished my senior high school diploma in a single year. It was a tough period with much sorrow to deal with.

When the apartment was emptied, they told me that

they had found dynamite hidden in the closet. I had no idea that Daniel was into that kind of thing and I had thought that he shared everything with me. Now he fell off the pedestal I had put him on. It helped me on the way to getting my perspective on things – maybe we hadn't been completely perfect for each other after all. Weapons have never been my thing. Hurting myself through using intoxicants was one thing and harming others by selling the stuff was another, but dealing with or handling weapons was always undoable for me. My love for Daniel didn't waver but the shimmering perfection of us that I had built a picture of in my mind became more realistic. I was able to feel angry with him and that was good.

The year at the school was the year in my adult life that I used the least drugs. Sometimes I went into the town where I had lived and met up with Lena and a few other friends but I didn't see anyone from the gangs. Us girls went to bars and the only drug I used during this year was alcohol and then only sparsely. It was a year of intense mourning.

I turned to my God for guidance and solace instead of going into counselling again. The spiritual experience I'd had had touched me so deeply that neither then nor now do I believe in death after leaving the body. This became a huge conflict in the grieving process – I prayed for death while knowing that there was no such thing. When the longing to be granted leave of this life became overwhelming, I turned to spiritual methods and I felt comforted in a miraculously soothing way. I recall a feeling of being embraced until I came out on the other side. In the calmer periods my faith in life having meaning was strengthened by this focus and subconsciously strengthened me to hold on when the surges of unmanageability surfaced again.

One day in the middle of winter, the emotional strain was especially draining so I decided to take a long walk despite a raging snowstorm. I trudged along the roadside into the village, praying and reflecting intensely. I remember feeling that I wouldn't be able to cope much longer. The grief was immensely tiring. A sudden inspiration made me think of visiting the tiny village library, get a loan card there and borrow a book. To a bookworm like me there was no place that could compete with a library when I was in need of serenity. The silence and the books themselves had always provided me with a safe haven without ever asking anything in return. Standing inside the warm lobby I wondered what I would like to read. I had never read philosophy before but suddenly I found myself standing in that row.

"Okay," I said under my breath, "help me now, please God," and I closed my eyes and stretched out a hand, pulling out the first book I touched. What followed was uncanny – I turned a few pages and skimmed through a few paragraphs and what came to me was almost frightening. On the page was described exactly what had happened to me that evening when I was lying in bed, one of those last days with Johan, praying for the first time in ages.

It was as if I had found home ground, not as forcefully as I had with the alcohol but I had a similar sensation of belonging. I felt love tingle through my system and I quickly borrowed everything by this author.

The most difficult highs and lows were soothed in this feeling of belonging and I was given the courage and strength to go on.

This philosopher, Martinus, was definitely not a sectarian. Without a doubt I would have turned and run in the other direction if that had been the case, me still being a person who did not want to join in with anything. The writings gave me solace and did not threaten or discard anything as far as I could discern. Whether my own experience had been induced by my drug habits, been pure madness or sprung from a survival instinct didn't really matter to me anymore. The important thing was the comfort I found in this event and now in this reading which I anyhow gave only a moderate space in my life. Later I found another philosopher that I liked, Jiddu Krishnamurti, who also had an attraction due to the fact that he also spoke far from all kinds of sectarianism.

In these reading sessions, I found much support and

intellectual stimuli that I had not found elsewhere. After a few years, I stopped turning to these books but the words followed and carried me during the escalating insanity of my life to come.

An interesting aspect of this spiritual search were the thoughts on drug abuse that these writers offered. The simple truth that all drugs shut a person off from reality. This is self evident. I had this fact clear as an intellectual insight during my whole addiction but the repulsion I experienced towards acknowledging certain feelings, my inability to stop using and the seclusion that follows with drug abuse lured me stronger than any logical conclusions ever could. Intellectual understanding is not the same as being intelligent.

The thought of living in a false state of mind when affected by alcohol only drove me to use again in an even more frenzied manner, trying to silence and shut out this truth. In the bigger picture, these facts and the spiritual aspect of my being were large pieces of what brought me to my knees and to hit rock bottom in the end. To choose the destructive path instead of the human and evolutionary one was extremely painful deep down. A life with intoxication made for endless, priceless moments lost to a chemical imitation of living. This truth was never negotiable to me. Not really, not at the core of things. And still I couldn't bring myself to quit. The disease is very clear to me when looking at how it always got the upper hand despite everything I "knew".

The year at school and my time in this village came to an end and the year of grieving too. Stronger, I moved on but did not go on the pilgrimage. I had calmed down a bit, mostly thanks to turning to my God in the passing of these difficult days.

My mother moved back to Sweden from Jordan and after a short interval trying to live with a guy I had met, I moved to Gothenburg where she and my siblings now lived together. I stayed with them for a short while until I found a boarding room in the centre of the city. There I lived directly above an organisation, FMN, – Föräldraföreningen Mot Narkotika - "Parents Against Narcotics".

Another process took off, giving birth to reflections on what I was actually doing with my life. I could see that I used drugs very sparsely now and concluded that I didn't have any problems with addiction. I made a decision not to expand my network of contacts and only bought pot very expensively on the streets. I used alcohol several times a week but only to the degree of getting a little tipsy. The putting of so much thought and effort into the hows, ifs and whens I should use drugs ought to have alerted me to my having an addictive personality. I believed that I was being moderate and sure, I was compared to how it had been before, but every day was a trial of sorts. Keeping myself grounded and worriedly peering out from the inner emptiness. I would have preferred being plastered all the time.

I became a faithful customer at the best, well-stocked alternative bookstore instead and poured a lot of money into that kind of literature, going to weekend courses nationwide and attending lectures on varying alternative-living subjects. Dedicated, or rather obsessed, and on my normal course towards something meant to fill my vacuum.

These quests didn't quench my yearning for the effect of drugs but instead tried to take their place. As always, I was stuck in judging the state of the world without getting involved in any form of methods to change either myself or what I considered being wrong.

The way we humans value different occupations and services held a huge part of my antipathy. To let people who work in health and educational positions, which are needed as key foundations for life itself, be vastly less valued than entertainers and athletes that we have solely for recreational purposes was one thing that angered me immensely.

My reasoning led me to theories about us living in a camouflaged feudal society where positions, resources and money are still passed on through legacy or conquest. The fact that those who own our planet don't have the devotion to, or even know the first thing about, tending to and looking after our world's resources in a responsible manner became the fuel for the oven that baked my alienation further. Since there was a lot of truth in these theories I let them lead me out of societies and their business. The increasing watertightness of these patterns of ideas empowered my continued flight. In the same way that I manipulated my fellow humans I fought to deceive myself with these worldly and "spiritual" pieces of my homemade puzzle. The worst issue for me was actually my drug abuse, but this was a truth which I forcefully silenced as soon as any bells threatening my addiction went off.

At work I never made any friends. I went on in my own bubble and went through the motions as if it were all a necessary evil. I would rather get into arguments with my colleagues if I noticed that they were performing their tasks sloppily. The first job in Gothenburg was on a hospital ward for old people with Alzheimer's. I quit when I found it too tiresome and the others were sitting around and having, in my opinion, too many coffee breaks. I didn't stay and fight for the rights of the elderly but just fled, as usual.

My next workplace was within home-care in inner city Gothenburg, close to my home. The group leader liked to play cards and she actually encouraged the staff to finish off their errands for the old people quickly so that the employees could join her at our office to gamble and drink coffee. I was hired by the hour and was assigned to the most difficult clients whose homes had fallen into disrepair with dirt and filth covering the floors and bathrooms. These elderly people had gotten used to having a bag of food put just inside their front door and nothing else. I went to the highest social welfare administration office in the city and demanded a meeting at the workplace about the lack of morale among the staff.

Up until the meeting I was threatened by my colleagues as soon as they learned of what I had done. When the meeting at last took place the whole matter was swept under the carpet by the administration representative and by the workgroup. I quit on the spot. Yet another event that I readily hoarded with my other resentments towards society. My final departure from the insanity of it all drew closer and this became a real "eye-opener" when I later in life justified the "choices" I had made.

A few years later, I met the woman from the administration office and she apologised to me. She told me that after this meeting she had resigned from her position, which was a job quite a way up the ladder. When she hadn't been able to stand up for me against the pressure of the workgroup she had realised that she wasn't fit for her role. She expressed the shame she had felt for the outcome of the meeting. This was a very nice gesture which I saved deep in the heart of my being in a small treasury of humane deeds, the contents of which were an important part of what helped me find my desire to stop using alcohol and become a part of reality in the end.

But for now it was time to make a change again. I had occasional contact with Lena who now lived in Stockholm and I asked her if I could crash on her couch for a while until I found my own place in the capital and she said yes. Said and done, I terminated my lease, packed all my stuff into a backpack and took off.

I was now twenty years old and very much in the belief of being in charge of my life.

Seven

I thought I knew what it would be like to live with girls my own age. It could have been taken straight out of a utopian teen film. We would talk, laugh, eat, booze but only getting a little bit tipsy, maybe go wild with a joint or two now and again, go out visiting the clubs and generally make the town vibrate with our very presence. Several of my friends from boarding school lived in Stockholm and they also featured in these dream scenarios. Of course I hadn't reckoned on my tendency to withdraw in these utopian social get-togethers and it turned out that in real life I perceived the others as being strange and different from me, as usual. They seemed to connect and have special bonds that I wasn't able to tune into. It was as if I was stuck inside myself and could only be an observer in the midst of their interactions. Actual contact - as always - eluded me. I had a way of being and a lot of charisma that sent out a signal of self-confidence, a young woman with wholesome self-esteem who at the same time appeared tough. This illusory person was who even I believed myself to be.

Those attitudes only filled my brain: simmering under the surface was an emptiness and a sensation of being utterly lonely - mostly feelings of being scared and astray hummed under the layers of my urbane image. Companionship was always a lost cause. As soon as vulnerability managed to creep through my lines of defence, the veil went up and with forceful and all but instinctive focus I searched out some way to oppress this intolerable weakness, either through occupying my mind or through purely physical reactions like using alcohol, going on adventures or working out. I rationalised the awkward feelings by thinking along the lines that those relationships were shallow and they should keep themselves to themselves. Me, I would get to know other people since they couldn't possibly understand me. I would find something far more true and meaningful to do with my life!

The theories of how useless relationships with other people were, were of course projections on my part - but about this I was absolutely clueless. Projection was one of my favourite words and I spent vast amounts of time analysing and judging other people as being self obsessed, well, at least whenever I wasn't caught off guard silently wishing that I could have that unattainable reality of belonging. That threatening yearning that always lurked in the corners of my mind.

I lived with Lena for a few months and quickly got a job at a retirement home. I soon tired of it but surprisingly held on until I found another job. I wound up in a café where I stayed on for quite a while. I was out in the big wide world now with bills to pay and dreams of my own apartment to keep me well-behaved. The flat we shared was in Stockholm city centre which was ideal for me in my dependency on exterior commotion. Alcohol was often an ingredient during the evenings and the hashish slowly but surely appeared as the alternative for me when boozing was threatening to get too heavy. Safe in chemical companionship again, the dream of the utopian youthful girlish escapades was never realized. The fact that human interaction was cut off for me as long as I used mind-altering substances was far from my understanding.

After a while, I found a one-room flat through a family contact and got a temporary lease. It was also in the city centre and this move was an enormous relief. I had suffered emotionally during this period of crowded living quarters and also about being in a position of dependency on my friend. In addition to that, there was the strain of my mental seclusion and the masking of that reality behind attitudes of gleeful independence. I was in dire need of my own place where I could drop the facade completely. I was always most at ease when I was by myself.

But this only lasted a short time. There was a guy in the picture, Hasse. We didn't have a romantic relationship when he moved in or when he moved out either. During the month or two that we lived together nothing happened at all. However, I did believe that I was in love with him the whole time. It was a strange affair. I had known him since the years with Johan. Ever since I'd moved to Stockholm I had felt a strong attraction to him but never made a single attempt to seduce him or tell him how I felt. It might have been the grief and the fact that I was still missing Daniel mixed in with the unpleasant memories of my break-up with Johan. In any case, to take any steps forward in this infatuation seemed far too intense and I just couldn't muster the energy. Later I learned that he hadn't ever had any inkling about my feelings.

We did many wild things during this short period. Everything was in a foggy existence fuelled by alcohol and pot. Now I had found another person who was drawn to the wild and crazy and finally I could breach the boundaries that I had forced myself to stay behind for so long. It was an immense relief to get completely plastered and stoned in a manner that had been unthinkable ever since I had woken up in my own vomit five years earlier.

Once when we were out biking, I fell off so many times that I counted 38 bruises afterwards. That day I had even snorted whiskey. I remember an elderly couple stopping their car asking if they could give me a lift home but I only laughed and declined peddling madly along, practically falling down the road. A death-defying tour if ever there was one but it was so liberating, so soothing, so cleansing to be "home" again. To let the drugs take control and not have to feel anything troubling me at all. I asked myself why I had let so much time pass, putting up with so much strain. This was the part of me, the pause and sense of belonging I had lacked for so long. It was as if a fundamental piece had wandered off unnoticed and now, with its' radical and much-noticed return, it awakened me from struggling through an eternal bad dream. The troubles of all the what's and who's were subdued and I was cradled in a honeymoon where all my doubts concerning the relationship between myself and drugs and addiction were vaporised and, without thinking twice about my doubts, I sent them out of the door with a physical sense of relief.

Hasse was told to move out after I had come home and seen him with his new girlfriend there. I gave him some time to find a new place to stay. My obsession with him was still there but instead of allowing myself to feel saddened, I hardened my armour against other people and my true self even more. The longing for connection ached inside me but more and more I evolved towards the extremely secluded person that would leave all illusions of healthy relationships behind her.

Again I found myself in a circle of people whose common reason for hanging out was drugs. Under the pretence of intellectual and adventurous endeavours, the alcohol and pot kept us all busy. We met very often and after a while a new process took off inside me. It became clearer and clearer that I didn't even belong with these people. Earlier, the feeling of being different had simply existed unquestioned as the way I was but now it surfaced as an insight and the pain increased with this acknowledgement.

I think my sense of being an outsider became stronger in this group of people who had, like me, very strong personalities. I had always been somewhat of a leader in my circles and now, suddenly I was one of a crowd and I didn't like to have to assert my position. The feeling of being special closed in on me. Being unique, as we all are, was something that I could relate to intellectually but my self-centredness blew the truth of that fact out of proportion, distorting uniqueness into there being something extraordinarily exceptional about me. I wanted to be at the centre of things and in this social circle it was impossible. I stood at a fork in the road of life and was only able to follow the impulse of going in the direction of isolation. The deception of self-centredness only lit up the street lights that lured me towards existing apart.

The process leading up to the final decision became a painful and extended one. The suffering that would come with the outcome was probably what made it so difficult. On some subconscious level, my being must have suspected the damage and hurt I would inflict on myself if the choice I made was the grim one of severing my ties with people.

We were a tight-knit group for two years. I remember my thoughts going haywire trying to understand what was happening to me in relation to these people. Out of pure self-preservation the theories crept to my rescue as usual. They went deeper and deeper, strengthening my barbed-wire defences against the others, pushing me to react in the way I was accustomed to doing. Terrible as it seems, being separate was known territory for me and therefore it appeared deceptively safe.

In the rearview mirror, I see that all the energy the young possess to spend on laying the foundations for their career, building friendships, experimenting with romantic ties, finding out what their hobbies and interests are - I also put into creating my place in the world. I spent colossal amounts of time in thought deliberating on which bonds to sever and which to reinforce. I sat quietly listening as they talked about their careers in the music business, as club entrepreneurs, dabbling in journalism, sales and so on and so forth. I sat through discussions about the world and our society. Slowly, over the course of almost a year, my resolve grew and when I finally made my decision it was based on an idea that had been "thoroughly thought through" and I had embedded these theories in my thought patterns.

I would not be a part of the vicious circle that was the

cause of our world's degeneration. In the end it felt as if a weight had been lifted from my shoulders concerning the whats and whys and ifs of what I was going to be when I grew up. The notion of being wise and superior returned. Since I was to have no part in the ruthless devastation committed by our planets' owners, my standpoint became something I could defend with head held high. I had already gone against many of the moral codes I had set up for myself in my childhood. Now I smoked cigarettes, used excessive amounts of alcohol and narcotic substances, I sold drugs on and off, shoplifted and was often dishonest. Living in Sweden made the choice of criminal activities another viable alternative to me due to the slack punishments and comfortable jails compared with many other countries. I would make my living on my own terms which was an easy enough thing to pledge to do with the frame of reference being Sweden in the booming 80's when there were endless jobs and opportunities to be had.

Working had begun to tire me again. I started to want money without having to put in too much effort and so I began stealing in a more organised fashion. I defended this by not taking from hard-working individuals but from the business sector of society, those having more money than they needed and if they inadvertently happened to be overly victimised I calculated coldly that they would be insured.

I wandered around in Stockholm and inside my head an intense hunt for ideas was in progress. Suddenly it came to me. I had found a commodity that would be extremely easy to steal and then sell without any greater effort. I often bought books in antiquarian bookshops and now I began stealing pricey books in one and selling them on to another. For a small risk and very little strain, I could get a neat sum of money in just a few hours. My looks and sets of social skills worked very well for me in this line of villainy. No one could believe that I was a thief and it was easy to be amicable with the staff in the stores since I hardly deemed myself one either. I pictured a romanticised version of a Bonnie without a Clyde, a female Robin Hood of sorts, taking from the established exploiters of my planet and giving to the poor and unfairly treated me.

I didn't tell the others in my circle of acquaintances about this goldmine. Most of them would have looked down on me for it. They were mostly normal in their dreams and pursuits, living and climbing within the ranges of acceptable livelihoods. I was not prepared to walk some lukewarm path as they did with a lot of talk about changing the system from within, something we could sit and discuss critically for hours on end. To me there was only the black and the white. I coined the expression "co-hell-ision", as opposed to the coalition of man, describing the ways of the world according to my views and deemed the others wimps. Today I can see that somewhere deep down I was jealous of their resolve in pursuing attainable dreams, making wholesome choices for their future selves, but as usual, so that I could keep some kind of sanity, balancing dangerously on my destructive impulses, I had to keep walking straight ahead with my theories held high.

Four of us got together in the early summer to make a journey to the annual music festival in Roskilde, Denmark. It was while I was on the verge of leaving this circle. My closest friend was working with a guy who could borrow a car. I had never met him until they picked me up outside my apartment. The others had already been picked up so I wiggled myself into the middle of the backseat and the new guy, Simon, greeted me by drawing his sunglasses down a bit and looking at me in the rearview mirror saying:

"Hi".

Now it happened again. Yes, his eyes, I promise you, they shone at me. I was instantly deeply moved but there was a great obstacle hindering me from following my first impulse which was to have him. He and my closest friend had recently spent a night together and I knew that even though they hadn't continued dating she was still attracted to him. This was a line I couldn't cross.

Apparently he viewed their 'thing' as a one night stand and this became very obvious as he continued flirting unashamedly with me. I had never experienced a guy making the first move – I was always the one who had chosen. Also, I was, even though the feelings were waning, infatuated with Hasse who was also on this trip. I shut off the vibrations with determination, as far as was humanly possible. We stopped at Freetown Christiania. Both Simon and I had been there several times before. We bought as much as we thought we would need, which was quite a lot since all of us were excessive consumers, and then we drove on. We arrived a day early and the first night was spent in a parking lot on a highway restroom area where we had stopped to take a shower but then managed to smoke ourselves senseless and had to stay overnight crashing in a sweaty, cramped bundle in the roomy sedan. The next day we drove the 20 kilometres on to the festival area.

It was 1987 – I know this because I googled the year one of our national poets and singers Cornelis Vreeswijk performed his last concert there. A concert which I missed because I was passed out on a small patch of grass in a fork in the middle of the festival centre. I had smoked huge amounts of pot and drunk lots of beer. This was the primary goal of every day and a big part of the plan in going to this event at all. This was what I valued in making it a "memorable" happening. Sadly the music was secondary.

On the evening of the first day we were running out of pot. So much for the calculations of the previous day's shopping. Simon, Hasse and I got in the car and drove back to Christiania to replenish our supplies. It turned into a trip that I'll never forget. Simon turned on the charm, which was one of his primary skills. Being a master at manipulation myself I saw through his routine with unfiltered clarity. With an inward smile and instinctive barriers against his seductive charms I had a conversation with him that evolved into an unexpected oasis from the isolation I was in the middle of cementing toward the others on this trip. It actually felt like the first sane conversation I'd had in my entire life. I can't recall exactly what we talked about but I know we talked all the way there and all the way back. I was taken aback by the enjoyable feeling of communicating with another adult, the memory of that sudden revelation is as clear to me today as if it happened yesterday. As is the work I put into resolutely resisting the strong romantic undertones. Lingering thoughts of Hasse and the complication with my friend's feelings toward Simon stopped me from entertaining any such notions. A friendship was what this was going to be.

When we got back to Stockholm Simon's and my relationship continued to be platonic but a most breathable zone for me in our circles which he now joined. I had almost made my decision to withdraw from my connections with the others before our trip and now I showed up only physically, not participating mentally or emotionally anymore. I volunteered nothing of myself. It was similar to how I had existed as a small child when I had studied the interactions of those around me, judging them, although now my behaviour was more evolved and tightly woven into my personality. I was consciously analytical and it was becoming more and more emotionally costly to shut the others out.

The only person I had any exchange with was Simon and this feeling grew stronger during the course of that summer. After three months I concluded that there would be no further development between my friend and Simon. I had begun to see my infatuation with Hasse for what it was and I had gotten over him. I took a more rational than emotional decision to initiate a relationship with Simon. The connection we had was very intellectual and the friendship we had had deepened over the course of these months. This, mixed with the charms of the man, made for a platform where I could muster the courage to get into a relationship again. Firstly, I spoke to my friend about it to ensure that there would be no hard feelings if I went ahead and she ensured me that it was all good. Then I literally lifted the bedcovers one night when we were sleeping over at a friend's house.

We didn't have sex during that first night together but the intimacy I experienced with him was up until then unexperienced for me.

Seventeen years of an intense, insane and, for both Simon and me, almost suicidal roller-coaster of life now set off.

Eight

As usual, every day, the availability of drugs was the most important thing for me to see to and, in Simon I had once again found a kindred spirit in this rut. We also had the friendship we had developed since Roskilde. We shared an intellectual cynicism, had a similar sense of humour and were both very goal-oriented. We completed one another on most levels – thus being a perfect match for moving steadily away from socially acceptable forms of living. Very driven and stubborn and on the whole agreeing upon the subject of the misled human race, we joined forces at the frontier against the world. Now I had found my Clyde, except for the robberies and weapons which were unthinkable for us both. From the very start, the relationship was very turbulent and we left each other many times during the years to come but always found our way back to each other after one or the other backed down and we reunited as the allies we were. The first separation came after only four or five months.

Simon had children and, considering my direction in life, I had difficulty consenting to my role as a step-mother. The lawlessness and the addiction drove me to terminating my lease, leave Simon and move back to Gothenburg. The last words I said to him before I left were:

"Take care of your family. Strengthen your ties with your kids."

I moved in with my mother and my siblings again.

My mother helped me get into home care for the elderly in the evenings and the wages were good. I refused to speak to Simon who called asking for me all the time. A couple of months passed but he was constantly in my thoughts. In the end I couldn't stand it and accepted his call. I knew what would happen if I heard his beautiful voice, listened to his logical reasoning and let him work his charismatic charm on me so accepting the phone-call was the same thing as getting on the train. Within a few days I was back in Stockholm and now we moved in together. This time it lasted longer.

Simon sublet an apartment in midtown Stockholm. Living with him was a new experience. I had a hard time coming to terms with working again and in the beginning he said it was okay if I stayed at home. He made a lot of money from his job. I remember staying in the flat, smoking lots of hash and hoarding a growing unease about what to do with my life. I stole books from time to time, sold some drugs but that didn't feel very good since I still had his children in mind. I believe I had a mild form of psychosis and the days were woven into each other while I became more and more paralysed and troubled. Simon tired of seeing me in such a heavy mood and helped me out of this state by hotly telling me off and listing his ultimatums – I had to get myself a job and until I'd found one I had to spend at least five hours away from the flat each day. I listened and knew he was right. I had to get my act together.

I found an employment office where I could get different day jobs, often lasting only one day but sometimes it could lead to more. It was perfect for me and my addiction to have this changeability. I would get in line with older alcoholics and other people leading vagrant lifestyles. There was a queue system and when my ticket was called out I was assigned to a workplace, often in a restaurant or cleaning work. The job would sometimes include a meal and after the day's labour I was paid in cash. I was a good worker and soon a large shopping mall in the city near Stockholm Central Station offered me employment. It took me three minutes to get from my home to work. It didn't take long before I discovered that I felt much better. Working brought me out of my stunned state of mind.

I didn't make friends among my colleagues, as usual, and arranged to have work hours in the evening and at the weekend when the pay was better and therefore allowing me to work as little as possible. I got to do varying tasks, moving around, mostly on the checkout and this met my desire for new scenery perfectly. I was actually content for over a year before the feeling of stagnation began eating its way up to the surface. The gnawing thoughts of being degraded and submitting to employment slowly began to overtake the satisfaction and the safety of the monthly pay checks. That I was meant for higher purposes was a vague notion that I could brood endlessly about, but I hadn't the foggiest idea of what that purpose could be. I had kept my criminal activities going on the side and, as always, money ran out as quickly as it flowed in. My addiction, the club life and transportation in the capital was costly.

That year I crossed yet another line – I began dabbling in amphetamines. The doses were small and not so frequent but it brightened up the humdrum routine of deafening my senses with alcohol and hashish. I used this narcotic in such small doses that I still slept at night and it took the edge off the other drugs, helping plant my feet on the ground. I also tried cocaine a few times but that substance never spoke to me at all. When some people start using either of these narcotics they become obsessed and they overtake want for any other drug, rather quickly becoming the drug of choice, but this never happened to me – it was always alcohol that made me feel most connected, comfortable and at home.

I moved out after a big row with Simon and broke up with him again. I went for what was meant to be a brief visit to Hasse who had moved out to the countryside. Instead we became a couple. I stayed and got jobs as a housemaid on different farms. It lasted almost two months. Then I ended it and went to live with my father who was in Sweden for a short period of time and I got a job in Nora, the small idyllic town where he lived. Again Simon found out where I lived and I really started missing the special bond we had had. I found my own in apartment in Stockholm, subletting through an old acquaintance. Simon and I got together again and now we isolated ourselves from both the old and newer circles we'd been moving in since we became a couple. Both of us worked – him with his profession and I at the daily employment office again.

We attended lots of parties and went on wild adventures but the romantic charm of using drugs was gone now and - as it turned out – it was gone forever. It turned into a necessary evil. All the time. Buying, seeing to the steady supply, keeping customers happy and being dependent on dealers and liquor stores, always, always this assessing of how I was feeling, how to manipulate my mood swings – dosing up and down, rear and centre and planning, planning, planning... It was a grim existence. I was sick and tired without realizing that I truly and thoroughly was just that, sick and tired - body, mind and spirit.

I had a change of scenery again. I found a job at a Christian health centre in central Sweden, deep in the forests of Närke. I reasoned that I would get my addiction under control, getting distance between me and the old ruts I got stuck in and, in gaining a new perspective, I would get a fresh angle on life. So I broke up with Simon, or perhaps it was the other way around - I can't recall who ended it this time - but off I was with all my possessions in my backpack.

Being an enemy to all religions, I really had chosen a strange place to move to. There was a sect mentality about the place and among most people who worked there. People not looking you in the eyes as they spoke to you, children shunning everyone they didn't know and they held closed church meetings and prayer sessions. The area was very big and the health centre was located in an entire village which had been bought by this church to house both the staff and in many cases their families. Most of the inhabitants were committed to the order and also worked there. As my impulse always drove me I didn't make friends among the staff or otherwise in the village. I lived and worked isolating myself from the community. When I think about it, I realise the people there might have been as friendly as any others and it was just my attitude and charred emotional state that made others keep their distance from me.

I stayed on for a few months but in the end it was too much of a strain to be isolated without the relieving effects of drugs and I was sorely missing their quieting effects on the stress of being so close to other people. It was an especially tense experience in an environment as intimate this one. I called Simon and we agreed that I should come and live with him again.

This time we set some ground rules based on mutual respect regarding our personal lives and choices. We each agreed to see to the rent and our individual expenses. We also committed, as maturely as we were able, to working seriously on building an "adult" relationship this time around.

We started up an operation making and selling bootleg liquor in addition to our incomes from work. Like everything else we undertook, it had to be excessive. We borrowed a distiller that could manage 80 litres and poured the fluid several times through activated carbon and filters to polish the flavour of the drug. The result was a very clean and high quality alcohol which led to a steadily growing number of customers in private homes as well as in professional establishments. One thing that I'd understood since my early teens was that hard liquor and I didn't get along so all the produce actually went into sales.

This was the kick-off into our future dealings with drugs and we were good at it. We kept a strict budget, were consistent about delivering a high quality substance and didn't cheat our customers and so the business boomed. I had some experience with partnering in business since my time with Johan but a new partner wanted for new methods and we learned how to deploy the tasks between us into a smoothly running operation. The profit wasn't exceedingly high but we got a good start at learning how to do business as a team. There was also a thought behind it of keeping a low profile - if we were caught with this lesser quantity of liquor, the punishment wouldn't be harsh enough to put us in police custody or, worse, in prison.

Simon was between jobs and tried my way of getting odd jobs around the city. We got into one of the best known restaurants in Stockholm and stayed on there for quite a while. We both had the looks and the capacity to hold on to positions if we chose to. We dabbled in part-time jobs for an exclusive members' club and also arranged a few high-end theme parties and such well payed projects. We could have stayed on for longer but always chose to move on before things got too settled. I also increased my intake of the three drugs that figured in my life at this time.

When everything was moving along at a nice pace and we were making good money: we suddenly had to move out of the apartment. We found a flat but there was a drunk, some acquaintance of the last tenant living next door who disturbed us, constantly knocked on the door and windows in the middle of the night so we couldn't stay there and we didn't even pay the rent. Now I asked an old friend of mine from the Johan days and we moved in with him that same day.

This friend was much farther gone than us in his addiction and he had diabetes. Here was my first trial with needles – yet another boundary I had told myself I would never break. After alcohol this was the best "kick" I had ever felt. My usage of amphetamines became an almost daily habit now, even though I still kept my dosage very low and it never lured me the way liquor did. I still slept at night and got my old job back at the shopping mall in the city centre. I only held on to it for a few weeks: the more lucrative business of selling drugs took over and this became my sole income for a long time. We paid my friend for the rent in drugs plus doing all the shopping and cleaning in the apartment. We stayed on for more than a year and during this time I drew further and further away from all things normal.

I had reached a new high in staying clear of the "co-hell-ision" of the world.

We moved out when another couple moved in and this was the final sprint toward homelessness. We literally moved out-side. I was burned out at this point, both of using and selling drugs. We discussed not getting a new place and not having to pay rent. No sooner said than done – we moved into the basement of the building were we had been subletting in the city centre before. We had kept a key that went to the basement there.

To defend actual homelessness made me evolve to, as of yet, unseen heights of theoretical defences concerning my choices in life. Well, not choices as a sane person would define choosing: rather it could be defined as following impulses. Instinctively following that which furthered my "freedom" to use mind-altering substances without others being able to get in-between.

For me, who had grown up in luxury and abundance, there was a rather loudly nagging aversion with regard to living in such a shoddy manner, but to second-guess this decision was simply not done. As soon as the queasy feelings emerged, I would oppress them with military discipline and mental raw surges of strength. I couldn't back down now. In a way, living like this was the ultimate reach of all the excuses I had concocted about my life style up to now - I had to live up to them. For 24 hours of every day I was on guard and held my doubts at bay. Constructing armour for this new, raw existence. I was a master at deceiving myself, shutting down emotions that threatened the validity of my following these spontaneous impulses. With the help of mostly alcohol, even this way of life soon normalised itself.

To be without a home affected my ability even to consider

a serious working career. It was impossible without a bed, kitchen and bathroom. I still got day jobs now and then and in between them I sold hashish in the parks of Stockholm. The basement was our most frequent sleeping place but we also made do with stairwells, trains and other hideouts. I ate at work, in restaurants, on a bench or wherever I was sleeping at the time. Showering was done at friends' houses or at the train station. Yet I told myself I was freer than I had ever been. Now I believed I lived for the day and only used my money to get to be the way I most wanted to be – intoxicated. That drugged state overrode all the difficulties and dangers of being a homeless person.

The drugs mixing with my delusions, grossly affecting my sanity, made me think that I truly had the whole wide world at my feet.

Nine

I remember celebrating Christmas by stealing from the neighbourhood grocery store where we had been regulars since we'd been living two doors down. After raiding the store, we went to nearby Vasaparken, a park where Stockholm's illegal drug-trade was done back then. That evening the snow glistened and it was a calm Christmas Eve. We only had one customer, a yuppie in his forties who complained about the relatives gathering at his home. He described a vivid scene of them all imposing on his space and disturbing the peace, being loud and drunk at the dinner table. In my mind, an unwanted image emerged. It was an image of warmth, togetherness and a straight-out-of-a-story-book, glittering Christmas-tree. A vision that brought on a sudden pang of longing. Instantly and resolutely I tried to shut it out, desperately painting it over with contempt, despising this man's deceptive life-style and his slavery to this terrible world. Me, I was free of having to sneak around and never had to grovel to anyone, anywhere.

Try as I might to cover up the sadness that had surfaced it still oozed, deep down. It was still true. It took a lot of subconscious effort to keep up this harsh attitude.

Living in the basement worked out for a few months. In our "home" we had a thick, wide mattress, linen, running water that actually went down into a drain so we could drink and keep basic hygiene down there. We even had a television set.

It was also possible to lock ourselves in – our nook was in a ventilation shaft with a thick door that had a handle on the inside so no one could open it from the outside. I could sleep without having to worry about being unpleasantly surprised by intruders in the middle of the night. Daytime was spent wandering in the city when I wasn't working. I got to know every cobble-stone in town and soon this life too began to reek of routine. A turning point came in the form of a very humiliating event.

One night, we found an open front door leading into an apartment-building in the central borough of Södermalm. We were very tired that evening and the effects of the drugs we had taken had begun to wear off. The garbage disposal room was open and didn't smell all that bad so we decided to sleep there for the night. I had never slept as scruffily as this before. I experienced a feeling of being degraded but we had "each other and freedom" as the song went in my head and I tried to laugh it off.

We lay there holding each other and I was nearly dozing off when the door suddenly opened. There was a guy about my age, wholesome and clean, mumbling something about how we couldn't sleep there. I, who had already felt that it was beneath me to sleep in a waste-disposal room reacted emotionally in full attack mode. My conviction about the whole of Earth being everyone's birth right and us all being victims of an outdated and segregated ownership-system overtook me. I didn't exactly shout at him but in a very condescending tone of voice I stated how Simon had actually been born in this part of town and that for us to be allowed to sleep in their precious waste-disposal room was not too much to ask. The poor guy was very polite and humble but stood his ground and Simon hooked my arm in his and we left without me being able to make much of a bigger deal about it. But it hurt. A lot.

Mariatorget subway-station was still open so we sneaked through the turnstile and got on a train so we could sleep there instead. The incident became a wake-up call for me. Simon was very highly educated and I came from a well-off family. I didn't want to end up in similar, or worse, places again. I told Simon about the thing I had going with stealing antique books which I'd had long before we met. Until then I'd kept this secret as a way out for myself, but as our relationship had been steady for quite a long time, plus the fact that I realised we had to make a radical change - and soon - I shared my profitable scam with him. We decided to raid the nearby shops over the next few days to get enough money to buy a car to live in. No sooner said than done, and within a few days we were the proud owners of a used SAAB. Simon was inventive and something of a handyman so he altered the seats so that we could easily rig up a comfortable double bed at night. We picked up our stuff, the bed clothes and the TV which worked just fine on the car battery.

Now life was renewed again and with a small radiator that we could plug into unguarded power sockets we were happily satisfied with our new housing conditions in varying parking spaces around the Greater Stockholm area.

This happy solution came to an abrupt end. We woke one night to being shone at with flashlights. It was the police wondering who we were. We both had ID and they checked our listed address which was in Stockholm, still at one of our previous addresses. We were both taken aback but managed to tell a synchronized story of how we had locked ourselves out of our apartment and had spare keys at a relative's, which we were picking up the next day.

When we had planned living this way we had agreed on keeping the interior of the car very clean and tidy as a precaution in case situations like this arose but the police became a bit suspicious when they saw the elaborate bedding arrangement. We made a show out of shrugging it off as a perfect camping setup and they reluctantly left after telling us to leave the car park.

The next night we stayed on the opposite side of town and in the middle of the night we were awoken by the same procedure, and by the same policemen. This was uncanny because even back then, the late 1980s', Stockholm was quite big with its' populace of one million souls. Incredible. We both took this as a sign that Stockholm had been sucked dry for our purposes. It was time to put the wheels we'd bought to use. We contacted one of our narcotics suppliers and with the trunk packed with drugs, we headed for Gothenburg.

On the way down we turned off the highway and onto a smaller road so that I could take a dose of amphetamine. We drove several kilometres without meeting a single car so in the end we just pulled over by the roadside. I was just about to fix the dose when we saw a police car drive over the ridge a couple of hundred metres behind us. Without showing how stressed out I became, I hurriedly hid the syringe and straightened out appearances, both of myself and the interior of the car before they drove up alongside us. We repeated under our breath the "drive by, drive by, drive by"-mantra, but that didn't happen. They stopped their vehicle in front of us, got out and walked to Simon's side of the car. Perfect police work. Now acting was called for, employing a high level of drama technique – we had a lot of illegal drugs in the car for God's sake.

Simon rolled down the window and to the question of what we were doing there we answer that we were tired travellers in sore need of relaxing off the motorway for a bit. We kept up this theme with carefully calibrated exchanges of words and eye-contact, balanced with proportionately amounts of smiling and probably a bit of light laughter in there somewhere. The officers returned to their car after having checked Simon's driver's license. Giving them a friendly nod we answered their waving goodbyes as they drove off, most probably both feeling satisfied that they had done a good job and with a positive spirit of having dealt well with these citizens. I had thanked them for being so vigilant and even checking road users in these remote parts of the countryside.

In situations like these, I was at the top of achievements in performing the life I led. All my senses quietened down and everything became crystal-clear. My thoughts and the acting in the moment were peaking in efficiency and my outside only showed exactly what I wanted my scrutinisers to see. It was, undisputedly, acting at its best. There were no margins for error, and so improvisation was given its' truest form of expression, this in front of an unrivalledly critical and professional audience. It was very strenuous. Of course we celebrated their leaving when we saw the car disappearing round the next bend but it was a shallow victory. Deep down, I never would have wanted to have to be in such a situation at all. But still, it was the life I had picked for myself and the life I kept defending ad absurdum.

We arrived in Gothenburg and found a parking lot looking down on the part of town where my mother lived. It was a beautiful place. I felt the surge of adventure and was overwhelmed by the freshness of this emotional breather, revelling in the experience of doing something new again. It was late and we made our bed for the night. Spring had arrived and matched how I felt – thriving in the apprehension of new possibilities. Probably as close as I could come to an "ordinary" person's feelings about new developments career-wise or moving into a long dreamed-of home.

Here in mother's corner of the world I had never gotten involved with people who were like me so we had a mission ahead of us in getting to know addicted people in order to support ourselves. In this, Simon was more of a go-getter than I. I felt resistance toward doing illegal business so close to my family. But, as with so many other boundaries, this one dissolved rather quickly when I pondered the advantages of having a network here. We lay awake for a long time that night talking about how we would proceed. When I fell asleep it was with a calm assurance that we would be able to pull this challenge off as well.

The next day, we bought lots of beer and went to sit in a park with the local drunks. We were more than welcome after we had invited those who wanted to for a smoke of pot with us and within a day or two we had met a guy who wanted to sell hashish for us. Finding a sales-person was the best solution since we didn't know anyone locally to sell the drugs to. Within a few days though, we realized that this guy had huge difficulties handling the business. He used too much for himself and kept lending or giving the hashish to the customers. We decided that we would hang out at his place and take care of the dealings instead and that he would get an amount of drugs for us using his place. I was not going to be cheated out of our profits. This turned out to be a great turn of events since we got to know lots of people. Soon, another person turned up who we learned was a reliable dealer and he took over the commerce and soon the stash was gone.

At this stage, we started commuting several times a week to Christiania in Denmark to purchase and then smuggle hashish back into Sweden. We drove back and forth along the west coast of Sweden making the trips memorable by finding beautiful places to sleep by the sea. We had reached our goal of creating a completely "new" lifestyle and business was booming. It was an achievement I could use to mentally soothe the toughness and dangerous aspects of smuggling.

It wasn't only across the border between countries that the smuggling was done, it also had to be smuggled out from Christiania. We had solid contacts inside the free-town but in the end it was up to us to get it out of there – hashish is illegal in Denmark. I will not describe how we went about doing this but I can say that we were meticulously careful in handling the whole process from leaving Gothenburg to getting back. There was no room for error. I often got very drunk and even in this there was a plan – stupid drunk Swedish tourists in Copenhagen. Simon was genuinely tired of me when I was in a drunken stupor with my drug of choice and this undoubtedly helped us many times in getting through the checkpoints. With careful deliberation we ran, almost honestly, with the "long-suffering husband dead-tired of his piss-drunk wife"-routine when walking through customs. He often got sympathetic glances from compassionate customs officers.

I was 24 years old when we started smuggling and we kept this up for about two years. We were never caught. Evidently we had our looks and manipulative talents working for us but it still feels unreal that we pulled it off that many times. Once I got too drunk and we got into a real argument, almost going separate ways in Copenhagen. When I walked through I had just tucked the pot inside my pants – something I never used to do. For the first time they directed me to the counter – this had never happened before and as it turned out it would never happen again. In a microsecond I became as clear as day in my head and without hesitating I walked brusquely up to them, pulled my jacket open, laughing and angrily slurring:

"You wanna check me out, you bastards – well go ahead then! Just search me! Come on!" Laughing cockily and making a big show standing beside Simon who just shook his head looking at the officers. They just waved me through. They didn't even waste words on drunken trash like me. My instinct had been all or nothing and, crazily, it panned out. The adrenaline kicks were always severe and this time they were unprecedented. The act of smuggling actually became a kind of drug in itself.

No matter how bad our conflicts had gotten during these "jobs" we had almost always become friends again by the time we sat in the car to begin our journey back up along the coast. But it wore me down inside and out and my stupors became worse over time. I used alcohol in a manner that I had never allowed myself to do before. We brought the exact amount of bottles that we were allowed to take across the border back into Sweden, which wasn't much in those days. The steady supply of my drug of choice and the hyper-active state of my nerves drove my consumption off the charts and way over my limits.

As a drug-addicted female I always had to violate far more taboos than a male would ever have to. This meant I had to justify my actions more, which in turn led my attitudes and behavioural patterns to become much thicker and rougher. The disease of addiction overrode all sanity.

I still had my philosophies and my God but it was all perverted now. I devised concoctions of theories suitable for my impulsive purposes but subconsciously the self-deception was always eating away at me deep inside. Many were the moments each and every day when I doubted my actions. In a spiral of repressed despair the shoving aside of any sound urges demanded more and more denial and more and more drugs. Insanity? Yes, that is the perfect definition of what I suffered – a double nature where the disease always slashed its way to victory against all that was sane and sound. In truth, I suffered all the time and it was inconceivable that I should surrender to my vulnerability, to the natural longing of my innermost but gagged being which yearned to lead a normal, healthy, liberated life. Drugs were the escape my impulses drove me to embrace – a prison cunningly disguised as freedom.

The inventiveness of this instinctive self-deceit was staggering. I put together parts from different religions and philosophies. For example I frequently used a citation from the Christian Bible that says:

"Nothing outside a person can defile them by going into them. Rather, it is what comes out of a person that defiles them." It is from a passage where Jesus was invited to eat something that was not clean according to the customs of the land he was in. The citation meant that what is impure doesn't come from what you eat but rather from who you are and what you choose to do. I plucked this from its context and applied it to using drugs, and, of course, especially alcohol.

On the other hand, the Bible talks of something that was also said in the Christian New Testament which was a warning against being like drunkards who don't get up until the middle of the day. These words rang true referring to some people not being responsible or trustworthy. I could not deny the truth of this parable but they triggered my bad conscience so this was something I never cited. Those fleeting glimpses of my double nature were painful but as long as I had drugs in my system I was locked down, unable and unwilling to act differently. A disease solely and slowly driving me to kill all that was beautiful about being me. Hurtling through life, bringing harm to others as if they weren't real. Defying all logic, defying even death.

When I woke up in the mornings, my plan was never to get plastered and insufferable. Despite this happening to me uncountable times after I had dipped into the first flask of the day, it was still never the outcome I foresaw. Figuratively throwing myself face first straight into a brick-wall, repeating this daily and always nonplussed at the result being a broken, bleeding nose.

Doing it again and again every day, it was as if I suffered from some kind of severe dementia and, undismayed, I kept on and on.

Ten

After I had been in Gothenburg for a couple of years, my mother got hold of me while I was visiting my brother. She had received a phone-call from the mother of Simon's children who had asked that Simon be told that his father had passed away. Of our parents, his father was the only one who had openly accepted us as a couple. The few times I'd met him, he had always been very nice and shown us both respect. This unwelcome news had come as a shock to his family. He had only reached 50 despite having led a very healthy lifestyle. I knew this would hit Simon hard and when I told him he suffered a terrible breakdown. It was many days before he was capable of driving us to Stockholm. I had wrapped up our ongoing business in Gothenburg and with all our money in our pockets we left for the capital. I went off my stupor and tried to be there for him, as well as I could. It was a difficult time and without second thoughts we used our funds without limits to ease the situation as far as possible. It was terrible seeing how hard it was on Simon. We stayed on for two months as roomers in the old flat of the building in which we had lived in the basement a couple of years earlier. During this time we didn't commit any crimes other than buying small amounts of pot. We tried as far as possible in an active addiction to let Simon be clearheaded so he would be able to mourn his father and be there for his kids.

As if coming out of hibernation, his mind slowly cleared and he decided to take his old job up again. He was lucky to still have his good looks despite the years of harsh abuse and was also much sought after within his trade and soon he had employment. This job was abroad and he would leave the country for several months at a time so I decided to live with my brother for the duration of this contract. We sold the car and I rode with Simon to Gothenburg in the company-car that had been assigned to him. He dropped me off at my brother's and then he drove on to the European continent. Our relationship had deepened. We had gotten to know each other in a new way with the drugs not having been the main focus during the time following his father's death. Of course the drugs had been present, as always, but using had been forced to take a back seat for a while.

Our parting was a nice one for once and I moved in with my sibling with an air of life being fresh again. I got a job immediately. It was in a lunch restaurant in the neighbourhood where I lived and only a two minute walk away. My brother didn't do narcotics so that chapter in my life simmered down a bit, but alcohol was as usual present but even this in lesser doses. I smoked some pot now and again but rarely met up with the new friends we had made in town. Instead, I bought pot expensively in parks and in lesser quantities, for my own consumption only. The amounts don't matter though – as long as I used anything at all I could never evolve as a person. It is not possible to expand and grow as a human being when you are intoxicated, however desperately I tried to tell myself otherwise. The steep dipping curve of my life only became a little less extreme.

I was very efficient at my job. My boss was a drunkard and I was soon running the place. Taking charge had never been a problem for me. His mother did all the paperwork and I managed the kitchen and delegated the chores among the staff. It was a memorable period. I didn't socialize with my colleagues after hours but at work we had a really good time. This was new to me and being a part of a team was a nice feeling. But, after a few months, my restlessness started to gnaw at me again. Through contacts I got the chance to work as a steward on a tanker and I took it.

My first port of call was Amsterdam and of course I went ashore and bought some hashish there. The quality of this smoke was top-notch. I remember coming back onboard, awfully stoned and being overwhelmed by a paranoid feeling of the bulkheads and the crew-members closing in on me. I had used pot at other workplaces but on a ship, in this super-intimate environment, the effects of the drug became ever so much more tangible.

As always, I had to use alcohol to lessen the effects of this kind of high. We made port in the Netherlands many times during this contract and my alcohol-consumption increased because of course I had to buy smoke even though I had to do thorough damage-control from the effects of it all the time. What a waste.

This was the perfect job for a person like me who enjoyed changes of scenery and if I had been a healthy person I probably would have stayed on with this ship but my drinking problems were obvious. I did my job without getting any remarks but I was constantly tipsy or worse and must have reeked of alcohol at all hours. I also made myself awkward by arguing with the cook, who was also my boss onboard. She tried to suck up to the shipping company by not putting any over-time on my work-sheets. But all in all it was a job I loved. The constant movement and all the new ports drew me in. I was also able to use alcohol during working hours. In principle I wasn't supposed to, but in those days many people did on the ships – even one of our captains had unquestionable issues with liquor. Waking up at work was also a part of this occupation that I relished, as was the fact that it was hard work. The days went by in a smoother fashion than ashore and as long as I performed my duties nobody messed with me.

I got to visit many cities in different countries in Europe during the hours when we unloaded at the docks.

France, Poland, East Germany, the Netherlands and England. I had never visited any of these countries before with the exception of France. Despite the major plusses of being a sailor, the pull of being intoxicated had more weight, of course. I signed off this ship with an unspoken certainty about this being a one-time hire. After the four-month contract I was not welcome back despite having done my job to a T.

Simon and I got together shortly after I came back home. With lots of money burning a hole in our pockets we rented a car and went on a trip with his children and his mother to Norway.

My relationship with his mother was very formal but the boys and I got along well. I had always enjoyed straightforward communication with kids, probably due to my being at a child's level in my emotional development. I also avoided communicating with them as much as possible when I was too intoxicated but during this trip that precaution wasn't necessary – I kept a low profile with my drinking. We were both on our best behaviour. Simon was driving and we both felt a huge responsibility towards his boys. When we got home and had dropped the boys off events took a U-turn though.

It had been emotionally strenuous and unnatural to be without drugs with that much money in my possession. After having been so close to people on the tanker my insides were screaming to get "a hard drug-cleansing". It was time to get back in gear. We kept the rental car and drove to my old parts of the country where I'd lived with Johan. I was still in touch with some of my old friends there. It turned into a freaked out mini-vacation with lots of drugs, me hurting myself when I was crazy drunk and having to go to hospital to get stitches in my finger and when we finally got back to Stockholm the money was almost gone. Simon got a new job and with it came a company-flat in Saltsjöbaden, one of the wealthiest parts of town, and we moved in, living together again.

I mostly drifted through the days, getting a stray job here and stealing there, but since I had money left from my wages on the ship I didn't feel any pressure to be doing anything at all. It wasn't good for me. I slipped into a state of boredom and apathy. Looking back, I think it must have been a milder form of drug-related psychosis. Simon noticed that something was amiss and began pushing me to get a job again. I went to the employment office for sailors on the Friday and on Monday I flew to Singapore, signing on as a steward on a huge cargo ship - it was at least three football fields long. The anticipation of a new adventure in life sent tingles all through my being. To be able to work like this in all the corners of the world was like a dream come true. In my mind, I imagined all the things I'd be able to do when I signed off in a few months. I would go to concerts, travel, maybe buy a new car. Who knew, I might finally get my own driver's license, even! Who knew?

I got onboard with a terrible hangover and I was also experiencing withdrawal symptoms from other drugs. I had puncture wounds on my arms from using amphetamine. When the steward who I was going to relieve showed me around the workplace and we got to the galley, I threw up into the nearest gadget which luckily turned out to be the potato-peeling machine. It might as well have been dinner, I hadn't been able to stop myself in any case. My psyche and physical state were so worn down that only one thought was echoing in my mind:

"Where can I get my hands on something to drink?"

Half an hour later, I sank my first beers and the world took on more normal proportions again.

During the first two weeks of this berth the air-conditioning was broken. We got it repaired when we docked in our first port, which was Fukuyama in Japan. The others asked me why I, despite the insufferable heat, wore long sleeves the whole time and I went on about having being raised abroad and hot weather not being an issue for me. Of course it was the markings from the syringes that I was hiding. Even to me these lies sounded thin. I couldn't make up yet another story, so keeping my back straight - and always after a few beers - I sucked up the insufferable heat, secretly dreaming of the unattainable cool water in the crew's salt-water pool on deck.

The others could think and believe whatever they pleased. I did my job taking care of the day rooms and mess halls with the adjoining companionways, keeping myself to myself all the while. In my cabin I had music, beer and books which were all I needed in the world to recuperate. The withdrawal took some time. During this whole contract, I really don't know if I actually ever got out of the mind-warp I had been in before flying off to Singapore. I had gotten on board quite confused and feeling mentally unstable and this never fully passed for the duration of the berth. Being aware of that helped a lot.

On a ship you can find all types and I played on being the eccentric and, as well as I could, blocked out the questioning glances that the others shot in my direction. Slowly I got better and started making small-talk with some of the other crew-members.

There is a word used about the mental state of becoming unstable during the course of a long period on a ship. This can happen to a person who simply doesn't have the mental strength to work in an environment as closed off from the world as a ship doing long stretches at sea. The word is "turning". In my case I can see that I had "turned lightly" even before I signed on.

We had a guy who turned during the time I worked on this ship. It was the cook who came onboard four weeks after I did. He had never been on a far-sailing ship before, only on ferries in the Baltic Sea. It showed as soon as he came on board in the way he opened up to others with no sense of integrity in this cramped environment. In a workplace such as this it is very important to keep your boundaries intact – rather more than less. In his case, he wanted to be jovial with everybody. It led to the crew either withdrawing from him or crudely playing him only to taunt him behind his back. That vibes exist between humans is very evident and tangible in such a closed milieu as this.

He also made lots of mistakes in how he performed his duties. In the evenings the cooks always prepared one platter of cold-cuts for the crew and another for the officers' mess. From day one this cook made a much more luxurious one for the officers. This made both crew and officers ridicule him even more, but no one mentioned this blunder to his face. Since this only was my second time sailing I asked why nobody confronted the guy and an old sailor answered:

"Crappy people weed themselves out automatically."

This cook also tried to get me into bed. When I refused he put me on different rough jobs that were outside my regular duties. When he refused to put this as overtime I made a huge fuss and rightly so. I even involved the captain in this feud and he approved my demands. The fact that the newbie was this incompetent, causing a problem that even became a bother for the captain, made him even more unpopular. It only proved that he wasn't the man for this job. Within two weeks he started to scream and moan in his sleep. He began moving about like a shadow against the bulkheads and reverted 180 degrees from the effusive attitude he'd had going in. I really felt bad for him but since our conflicts had been harsh I couldn't help him.

The whole situation erupted on Midsummer's Eve when an able seaman lost his temper after using too much alcohol and it was as if the whole crew's irritation with the poor man exploded, venting through this seaman's anger. The young man chased the cook with an axe. Afterwards both of them were confined to their compartments whenever off-duty and neither of them were allowed any alcohol rations. Many of the cook's chores were split among us stewards because now he was hardly speaking at all. He was in a very bad way. The event shocked us all – the evidence of three deep axe markings in the cook's door were clear tell-tale signs of workplace harassment that had gone too far. On a ship, there is no room for weaker links and people who are not cut out for this kind of living-in and working climate, and with it the relentless workload, will automatically be filtered out by keen bullying, even though the taunting may often be instinctive rather than calculated on the other crew members' part.

I was aware of the condition I was in and mobbing wouldn't have worked on me. No one even tried it. It was difficult enough to be this close to almost thirty other people and their vibes for such a long time. Keeping my blood-alcohol level balanced and steady didn't help all the way, but then it never did anymore, except for more than irregular, short moments. I managed to do my job but was very self-centred and often felt lost in muddled thoughts, worries and isolation. The "normal" people onboard noticed, but they could also see that I didn't "turn" in the true meaning of the word. Having the perspective of my condition being related to my drug abuse helped me and, as long as I did my job, the others let me be. I kept up the image/truth of being the weird one with a drink problem and still filled my space and function as one of the crew.

I often spoke to Simon over the satellite-linked telephone. He wondered if I was going to come home but I was stubborn and proud, also lured by the huge paycheck waving on the horizon. I managed to stay mentally bobbing just above the surface, so to speak. During one of these calls he suddenly proposed to me and I said yes without hesitation. In my fragile state, this turned out to be an emotional bombshell that I had difficulties handling and so I took my first hard alcohol-session on board. I was enormously happy but just couldn't cope with these strong feelings. I had been hoisting with an able seaman and one night I crashed on his sofa, totally out of it. I woke in the middle of the night to find him on top of me and I didn't dare to tell him to get off. I most certainly didn't want to have sex with him, and hadn't given him any reason to think so – we had talked a lot about our respective partners at home! But I kept quiet because I was scared. I was shocked that he would do something like this without my consent and I was also imbalanced from having done alcohol for several days. I just kept my mouth shut about it but strictly avoided the guy from then on.

We were in the middle of the Pacific Ocean on our way from Australia to Japan. The week it took for us to reach port I spent isolated in my cabin except for work hours. As soon as we were moored I went ashore and called Simon. He didn't support me in what had happened to me. Instead he began lecturing me about my alcohol abuse. I became enraged and called the engagement off immediately. Now the need to flee escalated alarmingly. I used exceedingly more alcohol for a few days and after that the rage was actually what helped me cool the dosage down. I refused to take Simon's calls and after a couple of weeks I began flirting with a guy whom I'd had my eye on since he'd signed on.

The guy who had jumped me in my sleep kept his distance to begin with and since I hadn't condoned any of what he'd done I never saw any problems with me getting into a relationship where we were both adults actually agreeing on seeing each other. But this was a mistake. Almost four weeks after we had begun to hang out the rapist knocked on my boyfriend's cabin-door when we were sitting listening to music and having some beers. We could hear that he was piss-drunk and mad. I signalled to my boyfriend that we shouldn't let him in so we just sat there silently, waiting for him to calm down and leave. Later I tried to explain what had happened. Once again I was met with disbelief.

Now the two men I had turned to and had needed support from had failed me. I knew what had happened but neither of them believed me, for them the situation had somehow been my fault because I had been as plastered as the rapist. I tried speaking to my now ex-boyfriend again but after a few failures in getting through I did my best to put it and him behind me. Now I only had five weeks left onboard and I had to suck it up. Of course, keeping steady alcohol levels which were down to my normal consumption of ten to fifteen beers from waking up until bedtime helped.

Now I felt the crews' talk building up behind my back and typically I was at home in being the alienated one. For the first time since Stockholm I actually started to grow mentally stronger. My healing-process from the confused state of mind got a kick-start. I was now on my way out of the drug-related "light" psychosis. I was in a position where I knew what had actually happened so I began following my own agenda instead of wavering on someone else's and their fictitious reality. This situation also strengthened my feelings of normalcy – I was at my safest when undisturbed in self-centredness, tipsy just under the radar and from day to day leading a secluded existence. I started to get a familiar warped control over my destiny and "well-being". Still clueless as to being under the spell of my addictive disease and actually being all but in control.

When we docked in Australia I made up an injury to be able to make an appointment to see a doctor in Wollongong. I sat in his office and he asked me if there was anything else besides the obvious lie I had come to consult him about. I didn't tell him what was going on at work but I suspect that my fragile mental state was clear to him. Very delicately he did what he could for me there and then in the medical sense, and then he started talking. He told me vivid stories of his time during the Second World War, his marriage, his children and about everyday things. He was so kind, quite the opposite to the harsh communication we used in defending our confined personal spaces onboard. He created an oasis for me there in his little office. Between the lines I understood that he could have written a certificate that would allow me to take leave of my contract, but I wasn't about to give in.

Four weeks later I signed off in Japan, stronger mentally from having stayed on. This berth had taken its dire toll though. Back in Sweden, in an apartment in Stockholm that I had been able to lease temporarily from a fellow sailor, I drugged myself senseless on booze and some, luckily, low-quality hashish for the first couple of weeks. Then Simon turned up at my doorstep and we had it out. I hadn't looked him up since I got home because I had been so trampled on and was very angry with him. Despite this he had been on my mind. We were extremely synchronised and drawn to each other in every way and he begged me to forgive him as never before, so the step to pick up where we had had left off was almost easy. We continued our flight together.

I did a couple of more contracts at sea but my days of working in a socially-accepted manner were drawing to an end. I was consumed by addiction and appreciating a life within the norms of the "co-hell-ision" of humanity was beyond my abilities. I lived following my impulses and for having time to use alcohol. Everything else was secondary.

My sailor friend returned home and I moved in with Simon at Saltsjöbaden again. When his contract ended we both had lots of money and lived at a hotel in downtown Stockholm for a while. I was now 29 years old and my addictive obsession had started to show even on the outside. I let my hair grow wild. Current fashion had never been of interest to me, my vanity lay in never wearing the latest fashion. Now I only dressed up if it suited any illegal activities I wanted to hide. I stopped eating for longer periods of time and hardly drank any water. The only thing I did that was healthy was walking days and days on end. From pub to pub, Systembolag to Systembolag (the Swedish governmental liquor-stores), from dealer to dealer or, if I was the dealer, from customer to customer.

In between I would find the most beautiful places to sit and use at. I always carried a book with me, Simon used to say he "was married to a book". I only read science-fiction because in that genre I got the best available escape from reality. Hard-core sci-fi, as I called it, was my genre. In the most complex and complicated sagas I was brought far from real time and space. Taking drugs was by now what kept me normal and reading was that special something that made my life's horizon golden in the drab routine of these waking hours. To sit and repeat the same drunken ramblings year in, year out was not an option for me anymore. The stories were the same on the benches or in the pubs as they were in the parlours. In the books I found adventure beyond this rut.

But I was bored, Simon too, and we started to get on

each other's nerves again. He got a job and after a while he managed to get me a position there too. It didn't help. I was fed up with my life being the same all the time and once again I broke off the relationship with a dramatic flare. We didn't fight with violence through the years but mainly clashed like warriors targeting each other's souls. We had shouting matches. We were renowned for our atomic-word-wars. The one just as stubborn, self-centred, witty and ungovernable as the other. Armed with the gifts of words loaded with piercing hurtfulness, we often staged huge rows.

This time I returned to Gothenburg and rented a room from one of our old customers there. I think I worked but I don't remember. I did do a lot of business though and used lots of alcohol, hashish and LSD, frequenting mad rave-parties.

It was a crazy run and when Simon called me few months later I was relieved and whatever the last fight had been about was forgotten, gone with the wind.

"Hi, it's Simon," he sounded a bit tentative, he couldn't know wether I was still savagely mad at him or not.

"Heeey! How are you doin'?!" I let him hear how happy I was that he had called me and how much I had missed him, all of this loaded in the tone of those first few words.

We knew each other and he understood, changing his approach immediately. We talked about everything as if nothing had happened. Both of us knew the madness was all about the drugs and that there was no use discussing it.

"I'm really tired of sucking up to these rich, drunken numbfucks," he said. "I'm leaving!"

He truly sounded exceptionally tired of his job.

"What do you mean 'leaving'? Where are you going to go?" I asked, almost being able to hear a sudden loud rumbling of craving in my adventurous brainstem.

"Nah, I'm just gonna rent a car and leave for Europe. I'm not doing this anymore. The continent! Here I come!!!"

Very worried that he was actually leaving the country as we spoke, it was my turn to be carefully searching:

"But, uh, are you just gonna leave, you know, just like that, all by yourself, or...?" He caught the bait at once.

"Come with, tag along, why don'tcha?! We'll do it now – just leave the idiots behind to fend for their own petty destinies. Are you game?"

I was standing with a huge, stupid grin hurting my face.

"Of course I'm in! I got a bit worried there! Thought you might be leaving me here in Idiot-Swampshire! Hehe. But I'm almost out of cash."

"Me too," he laughed, "but that never stopped us before, did it?"

"No, not that I can remember any-hoo," I replied. We hoorayed and laughed together, wildly sealing the deal.

I pitched in with a favourite citation of ours:

"On the road again!"

He replied en suite:

"This time for real, babe!"

Simon came down within the week and we bought an outfit each of presentable clothing, got our hairdos in order and went to the solarium to get a fresh but discreet tan. Within a month we had stolen a substantial amount of provisions. Tobacco, a spirit-stove, spices, coffee, long-life coffee cream, cans of tuna, pasta, books, tinned food, toiletries, sugar, salt, maps, sleeping-bags, pillows, sheets, a portable typewriter and paper along with a whole lot of other things. We were ready to go.

This was at the turn of November/December 1994. We payed a 24-hour lease on the car and by the time it ran out we were in Innsbrück, drunk as only drunkards can get, arguing in the snow on a parking lot until we passed out from sheer exhaustion in the car.

An insane and dangerous joyride had now taken me off any radar of normalcy.

I was in mind-blowing heaven, and away!

Eleven

The meaning of the word "joyride" is to drive around in a stolen vehicle solely for the purposes of pleasure. And that was our goal, but, quite honestly, it is quite impossible to be filled with pleasure when you know deep down that the ride can end at any moment, totally independent of your own will, and this most probably in a most unpleasant confrontation with the long, and at such a time not at all jolly, arm of the law. Of course I did my utmost to block out this unpleasant truth, telling myself that in the now this was the most free I had ever felt in my entire life. When we argued, as we usually did, my first impulse wasn't to run off anymore. I wanted this adventure. Praying to my God as never before using as a mantra a quote which seemed fitting for this kind of daring escapade:

"Yet not a hair on your head shall perish."

I was constantly on edge and therefore on top of the world.

When we woke up in Austria, it was in the town of Innsbruck. It was the morning after we had left Sweden and we started the day in a cold sweat, glancing around us as we started picking up all the stuff we had thrown about outside the car in our drunken outburst the night before. Thanking our lucky stars that no one had called the police, we drove off when we were done and parked anonymously elsewhere, sitting quite timidly in the front seats, planning for the next section of the journey.

We had a general picture of how we were going to pull this ride off. We didn't have that much money, so we had decided to steal the petrol we would need, but not from private cars. To do so would probably have been easier and maybe less risky, but we made this rule one of the moral codes we set up for ourselves. We agreed on stealing from gas stations by pretending to fill the car up just like any other customer and then just drive off. To steal from the petrol tycoons felt much better. I was even tickled by the idea of sticking it to the big fish: I had no perspective of it actually being the private entrepreneurs who would have to take most of the financial blows for such thefts.

Another rule was to use only alcohol and hashish.

We had set a goal when we were planning the whole thing at home which was to reach Marbella, where a close friend of my family lived. We hoped he would be able to help us find work there. I had never met him before but we needed an end goal and this was as good a plan as any. Besides that, we decided to let our intuition and resourcefulness guide us on our path. We relied on those talents because they had worked well for us in our earlier escapades into criminality.

So now, sitting in the car there and then, having made this happen "for real", we hatched a plan for how to thicken out our thin wallets - we began stealing liquor in stores. Starting right there in Innsbruck and deciding to keep on until we reached the west coast. By then, we ought to have built up a substantial loot. In port towns, restaurant owners were known to buy spirits from sailors who bought alcohol toll-free on ships, so we knew we would have a reliable set of customers. No sooner said than done – we raided several supermarkets and filled our padded ski jackets with expensive brands, smiling politely at the cashiers as we walked out, without purchasing anything. When our intuition set off warning bells in our heads after a couple of raids, we sped out of town, up into the mountains guided by an expensive and detailed map we had stolen whilst gathering provisions back home. We went on like this through town after town and our stock expanded slowly but surely. To cope with the constant high levels of tension, we also emptied a few bottles as we went, but were very careful after the scare of the first, catastrophic night's loss of control. We didn't plan to let ourselves get caught all because of a stupid stupor.

We arrived in Bad Gastein where Simon had been on a skiing trip just a couple of years earlier. We went for a beer and I marvelled at the wonderful view. We soon realised that this was not a place were we could steal as we wanted to do, so we decided to keep on driving for a bit. On the way back to the car we came across a heap of skis and ski boots left outside a hotel.

"Finders keepers," said Simon, "they'll get new ones on their travel insurance, anyway."

So we did something that we usually never did, which was to steal private property. We simply grabbed a pair of each, stuffed the gear into the car and drove off. Two sets of slalom gear "to go".

We kept on through Switzerland, quickly stopping and shoplifting in a few stores en route before we agreed on veering south into Italy. There, we met a completely different social climate. Instantly, we understood that stealing was not an option here. The watchful poses of the staff in the stores were very tangible and it didn't matter that we were well dressed and jovial, everywhere we went they were indiscriminately sceptical about everyone who entered.

We had a dream of seeing Venice and, despite the understanding that Italy would be barren to us, we went down there, ignoring the expensive parking lot and leaving the car parked on the first piazza we came to. Then followed a quicker-than-quick tour of the famous sites and the mandatory kiss on a bridge before we left, incredibly with the vehicle un-impounded, happy in many ways to have been there, but also to have been able to get away from this terribly expensive tourist trap.

Our petrol started to run low and our next fill up would have to happen in this maddeningly dangerous country. We had seen guards with guns protecting some establishments. For us, coming from Sweden, where only the police may carry guns in public, this was very disturbing. At every petrol station we had passed on the way, there seemed to be at least five grown men working at the gas pumps. In Sweden, nobody pumps the gas for you and we hadn't seen this in the countries north of Italy either. We weren't broke but we only had about 1800 Swedish Crowns, the equivalent of 180 Euros, in our pockets. The thing was that stealing petrol had now become a matter of principle. When we made up our minds to go on this joyride, we had turned our backs on the "co-hell-ision" of mankind. In our reasoning, petrol was simply too huge a factor in the mistreatment of our world to allow us to pay for it at this point. At any cost, this was a part of the plan, just as the theft of the rental car had been.

We did our reconnaissance, as usual, staking out the gas station we had picked out. It was close to a very busy motorway and the guys working there only filled the tanks for those who asked them to. We drove in and took our time with this, that and the other, washing windows, filling water, filling up with petrol and, when we were done, Simon fidgeted in his clothes as if searching for money. The guy who was standing at the pumps closest to us suddenly walked towards the station's main building and we were off in seconds. A couple of hundred metres up ahead there was a slip-road, Simon had known this beforehand and we took it, did a U-turn and in under two minutes we were passing the gas-station on the other side of the motorway. The adrenalin rush was terrible. Shaking in our seats, we went on to Genoa and drove the car straight onto the empty beach and sank lots of alcohol to deafen the serious emotional turmoil. Once again, we got too drunk but this time we didn't regress into arguing.

When we woke up we couldn't find the car keys and then the shouting started then instead. We began searching fervently and when the keys didn't show up either in our clothes or in the car, we had to start sifting through the sand with our fingers, following what routes we might have taken the night before. After a long while, we calmed down and had to admit that our trip had come to an end. Beaten, we walked towards the car when Simon suddenly stooped down on the vast beach and picked up the keys that were lying buried there. Incredible is the only word that justly describes what just happened. Very humbled, we got in, drove off and left Italy as fast as we legally could. We had the car, a full tank and the memories of a kiss on a bridge in Venice. The warped feeling of a successful trip in Italy overtook the sensation we'd had earlier about taking an extremely wrong turn south from Switzerland.

(The factors of us being thieves, driving around in a stolen car, and drug-addicts were parts of the whole "wrong-turn"-equation that we left out).

With fire chasing our scorched nerves, we stole more liquor upon getting back to the northern parts of Europe. Then we drove back through Switzerland and Germany toward our next destination, which was the Netherlands where we looked forward to smoking some hash. I longed to sit, relaxing in peace and quiet, smoking, covering up all these hyped-up emotions in a coffeeshop, a special type of café in the Netherlands where you can buy and use pot without breaking the law.

We targeted a small town in the south called Eindhoven. We judged that our stock of alcohol was nearly complete for selling and we were satisfied at having seen this first part of the project through. Now it was time for a reward. We parked in the middle of town and walked into the first coffeeshop we came across. We shopped, mixed the hash into a joint and smoked away. Soon we were sitting at the bar, stoned as quarries, drinking beer. Simon sat looking out of the window and after a while he gave me a discreet shove and whispered:

"There are police outside looking in at us. They're walking by, staring in, all the time! Look!"

Instantly, a chill went straight through me and an elaborate scenario of the car having been found, checked and found to have been reported as stolen, of witnesses having seen us enter the coffeeshop and now the police were waiting for us to approach the vehicle so that they could catch us red-handed. Simon was entirely on the same catastrophic track as I but we couldn't be sure and we definitely didn't want to have to throw away the hash we had bought for almost the last of our cash to find out. We sat there, agonizing for over an hour, smoking more and pouring beer. The police kept on patrolling the sidewalk outside the shop, staring us down. Finally it simply got too stressful to stay sitting there. We mustered all the courage we could in this stoned state and walked out. We saw a policeman further down to our right so we walked briskly in the opposite direction. There was a church a block up ahead. We looked at each other, nodded and steered towards it.

Neither of us had ever been churchgoing people but both of us had a personal spirituality of an existential nature so going into a church to say our farewells before being arrested seemed like a good idea to me in this situation. Trying to flee seemed pointless since the neighbourhood was swarming with police. Then we heard someone a bit further behind us speaking Italian. Thoughts of them having had eyes on us since Italy bolted through my brain.

We made it to the church and stumbled inside, sat down in a pew half way down the lane, hugging each other, panting from sheer anguish.

"It's been an intense trip but at least we did it!", I said and we smiled wanly at each other.

Now the church doors were pulled open and in walked five officers.

"See you later in life," I mumbled and braced myself for the arrest.

But they just walked past us. They approached some youngsters sitting in the front row and talked to them for a bit. We left immediately and decided to make for the car and check the lie of the land there. It was still in the parking space and there wasn't a uniform as far as the eye could see. We decided to drive off at once – the winner takes it all. We drove and drove, with not a clue of where we were driving to. Neither of us thought to check the map as we always used to, we only looked in the rearview mirror and soon saw an ambulance that closed in on us staying on our tail all the way out of Eindhoven and out on to the freeway. We just kept going. After a several tens of kilometres we suddenly saw a sign that said "Belgique" and when we looked behind us we saw the ambulance turn back. Without hesitation we crossed the border. Europe had recently become the EU and we expected a new surveillance tag to take up where the Dutch had left off upon entering Belgium but now all the police and strange ambulances were an absolute no-show. No one picked up our trail and after a couple of hours we stopped for the night. The whole business was a mystery. We were extremely grateful for the weird and unexpected turn of events and we talked it through several times before we fell asleep. The knowledge of hash being a potent catalyst for paranoid feelings was out of the equation since we knew we had had the ambulance trailing us all those kilometres to the border.

The next day, we drove on to Antwerp and emptied our pockets by allowing ourselves a nice breakfast at a cosy café in town. We sat there, humbly enjoying our freedom and reading the morning papers when Simon suddenly shouted:

"FOOTBALL!!!", turning every head in the crowded establishment. I jumped in my seat, still in the process of recuperating my shattered nerves from the day before.

"There was a football game in Eindhoven yesterday!"

I eyeballed him uncomprehendingly for what felt like an eternity before he continued, urging me to get his point.

"An Italian team was playing Eindhoven yesterday."

I was still in the vacuum so he spelled it out:

"Eindhoven is in a league and there was a game in town when we were there!"

Now it all fell into place. The Italians, the anti-hooligan police enforcements, the youths in the church who had been too loud for the churchgoers, the eyeing of all the coffeeshop customers - not just us...

It all became clear and we burst into uncontrollable laughter. Everything but the ambulance fell into place and that mysterious part of the puzzle we could live with. The relief was enormous. We celebrated with alcohol and joints, and finally getting to smoke without the sense of impending doom was a priceless emotional oasis. The day before, we had only had time for ten minutes of relaxation in the coffeeshop before Simon had noticed the lurking policemen. During this journey, the bodily surges of adrenalin and other things had already been numerous but the experience in Eindhoven easily took first prize.

After doing reconnaissance and asking around all day, we found our buyer that same evening. We arrived with the booze, newly showered and in fresh clothes. The owner was very happy about the expensive brands we unloaded on the table but he was a bit sceptical about the bottles being normal 75 cl size instead of the 1 litre bottles that sailors usually brought. In the end though he couldn't resist the pricey brands. We told a story of a skipper that had forgotten to put in the order for our tax-free rations and been forced to shop ashore in Africa which still made it much cheaper for him than in Europe. The story was short and we delivered it with a shrug in the way Belgians themselves like to tell stories. Smiling at him with a confidence that told him we knew we would get it sold even if not to him, the manager shrugged and made the deal. We were paid a higher price than we'd anticipated.

With our pockets filled, we happily took our wheels back up north again into the Netherlands, to another town this time, and bought more smoke for our forthcoming travels. The time had come to leave northern Europe and begin the journey through France heading toward our goal in Costa del Sol. We took a detour through Germany to raid for more provisions. We understood that the further south we got the more difficult it would be to steal. We filled our trunk with more food and coffee, soaps and deodorants and of course, most importantly, alcohol which we now stole solely for personal use.

Within ten days of leaving Gothenburg we drove into France and soon we arrived in the beautiful French capital, Paris.

Twelve

Since Simon had never been to Paris, we decided that we would go up The Eiffel Tower: but first we needed a good night's sleep. We parked on a narrow street close to Gare du Nord, a large hub in the underground Metro system of Paris, and we managed to get terribly drunk. I just needed to go to the bathroom before crashing out and so I left the car to try and find a secluded spot nearby but there were so many people around that I had to wander off for a bit. When I started back I couldn't find the car. I was overly intoxicated and staggered about for a long while without spotting it.

When I finally accepted that I wasn't able to find my way back to Simon and also after having been approached by several strange men, I decided to go in search of a place to sleep for the night. I simply went about pulling at the door handles of apartment buildings. With enormous luck I actually found one. Incredible in the middle of Paris! I started up the stairs. When I reached the top floor it turned out to be an attic where the storage areas had been turned into permanent living quarters. The hallways were used as storage space instead, and there was a urinal where I could drink water. I happened upon an abandoned thick mattress to sleep on and so this turned out to be a very comfortable place to lie down for the night. The subsiding intoxication mixed with my worrying made for a troubled sleep though.

When the tenants began stirring in the morning, moving about, emptying their chamber pots (which I learned that the French often use) I rose and left this amazing oasis that I had found in the centre of Paris. Roaming the world again I found my way back to Gare du Nord and was now keeping meticulous track of the route I took. At the station I fetched a map at the tourist information desk and carefully marked out the places I had been and where I had slept.

Many years earlier, Simon and I had agreed on meeting at the largest central station of any city if we ever got separated during our journeys. An elderly woman took pity on me and kindly let me through the turnstile into the Metro and I caught a metro to Charles de Gaulle-Étoile, which was as central a station as I could make out in Paris. I hung out there for a couple of hours but there was no sign of Simon. I finally gave up and returned to my starting-point. Again I began walking through the blocks surrounding the station, in an even more organised fashion, carefully marking my routes on the map so that I wouldn't end up retracing my steps, going round in circles. At the first pedestrian crossing opposite the station's main entrance I suddenly saw the car. But no Simon. I was so badly hung over at this point that my whole body was shaking and my soul was writhing with emotional fatigue. Since I had been in a steady drunken state for several months I was in terrible physical and mental shape when I didn't have the usual level of alcohol in my system. Waking up without any alcoholic beverage to recharge my batteries with was something I hardly ever put myself through. I tugged on all the doors of the car but they were locked. I almost threw up out of sheer exhaustion. Then it occurred to me to try the trunk. Rarely have I experienced the forcefulness of that wave of relief which coursed through me when it opened. Simon returned from Gare du Nord where he had searched and waited for me since the early morning and found me sitting in the front seat pouring whiskey as if it were water. Later, when I studied the map, I realised that I had slept in the same block as the one where the car was parked, but on the street parallel to it, on the other side of the building.

We were emotionally drained. Simon had not wanted to go on without me and I had felt the same. This was before the age of cellphones and the most plausible way we could have gotten in touch with each other again would have been by going back to Sweden. The relief was enormous and "Lady Luck" had been on our side yet again on this ride. We got our stuff together and with the map as our guide we made our way to The Eiffel Tower.

We parked directly on the street in front of the tower without any concerns regarding parking regulations and, with our last coins, we paid our way into the marvellous structure. We reckoned that this might be a once-in-a-life-time experience. Money had to be secondary to the adventures we sought. In these situations there came to mind another quote which I managed to distort into suiting my ends. It was about how the birds are fed by God and therefore we humans need not worry about being taken care of, trusting that our basic needs would be seen to.

It was actually a serious kick, getting rid of those last coins. We lived as if every moment was our last during this joyride. During this specific excursion we didn't even know if the car would still be there when we came down again. It was truly an all-or-nothing experience and we might just as well savour every single moment. Smirking triumphantly we entered the elevator. We ascended, drugged and rowdy.

At this point we weren't all that clean. We hadn't showered since the first tour to the Netherlands and all our clothes needed to be washed. We probably reeked like the filthy drunkards we were but what we lacked in hygiene we made up for in enthusiasm and nonchalant attitudes. We switched between the elevator and the stairs, laughing and swapping puns as drunk people do. We sat and smoked a joint on a ledge in a section of the staircase, just savouring the moment, all the hardships forgotten in this mental breather. Reaching the top we gaped at the view, which was formidable. We stood talking loudly, drinking the liquor we had smuggled into the tower and misbehaved as bench drunkards do in general. Suddenly a young woman next to us blurted out:

"Men Gud, så oromatiskt!" ("My God, how unromantic!") in perfect Swedish.

We turned towards her and the equally young man at her side who must have been her fiancé, and uncontrollably we both burst out laughing. A Swedish couple on an escapade of love in the most romantic city in the whole world, most probably at one of the highlights of the trip, and there we were, the addicts from the suburb back home blabbering fluent Park-bench-ish and wrecking this perfectly dreamy scenario. The contrast became too much for me. I totally lost it.

The young couple moved hastily away, looking indignant, casting nervous back-glances with a demeanour that showed that they were scared that we might pursue them like some low-lifes back home might have done. It all left me standing there laughing uncontrollably with tears pouring down my cheeks. The poor dears. My usual ability to conduct myself was too far from how I lived at this conjunction of my life. I suddenly saw clearly the unwashed, dirty and reckless unlawful person I was reflected in the eyes of these beautiful youngsters with their love and whole lives in front of them. A throb of pain manifested itself in the pit of my stomach. For a split second. The absurdness of it all deafened even that.

Simon and I were also on our dream-trip with our dream-partner but the difference between that couple and ourselves was galactic. The occasion was very uplifting for the moment but the stab of anguish was undeniably stored away and kept throbbing inside me.

After many hours we finally went down to the car which miraculously stood where we had left it. The petrol was waning again and it was time to investigate a gas station that suited our needs. After careful deliberation, we settled for a place that had several escape routes. It all seemed to go according to plan until Simon, having filled the tank, got in the car. Then a two-meter tall Frenchman came hurtling out of the cashier's office straight toward us at unbelievable speed. Simon got the car started while I instantly cut myself off from the realtime course of this terrifying reality, as if I was watching a movie. The man who closed in on us fearsomely fast, Simon's kick-starting the car and making an impossible U-turn, us bouncing off several pavements and traffic islands on our way, flying out into the dense traffic of Paris. We were both so shaken up that even though we got away and had been driving for several minutes, neither of us had thought to look at our map and neither of us remembered the escape route we had planned. Simon just drove and I just sat there and we had one common goal in mind – to get away from that crazily large, angry French person.

Somehow, after a while we wound up on the road to Versailles and I realised that we had been screaming at each other, and were still screaming, all the way. I abruptly snapped out of this chaotic shouting and tried to get Simon to calm down. It was impossible. He just kept on screaming and kept on driving at a dangerous speed. I understood that if we were to meet a police car they would arrest us with no pardon and probably a lot of beatings for reckless, dangerous and drunken driving. I screamed "Now you shut the fuck up!" and landed a right hook square on his face at 140 kilometres per hour.

Not a very bright thing to do but I was scared out of my wits. Simon lost control at this point and the car began to skid, we drove straight into the central reservation and bounced off it back into our own lane, with a flat tire as a result.

"What the fuck??!" was all he said but I could see that he was out of his panic zone.

After a few seconds, we had reviewed the situation and, quicker than quickly, we got organised to change the flat with the tiny spare tyre that was stored in the trunk, also calculating that this had to happen with great haste. If a police officer or a well-meaning private citizen stopped to give us a hand our journey would definitely end there. We were smelly, drunk and stoned. No-one in their right mind would allow us to continue driving. Simon did a record-breaking tyre switch and we managed to get back on the road again. This was yet another very, very close call. To be on a joy-ride is nowhere near as joyous as the word would have you believe. We continued with the shiny white spare in place and now our sights were set on Barcelona.

We had mentioned the idea of selling the car when we were in the planning stages of this venture but it would have to wait. We fleetingly discussed taking a detour into Andorra to find out what price we might be looking at for it but realised that we were too amateur for that. It was more likely that we would get robbed and the vehicle would get stolen. On our way down through France we stopped in a town called Mont Dore and tried to sell the skis and boots instead but the season hadn't begun yet so we held onto them. Further south we managed to sell them off on a flee market in Toulouse for a terribly low sum but we needed petrol and we had gotten very nervous about stealing gas at the stations after the episode with the giant Frenchman. We did the math and with this much money we would easily make it to Costa del Sol. We made an exception from our principles and prioritised the odds of actually getting to Marbella. No sooner said than done, we filled up and paid and then Simon drove, without stopping, straight to and through Barcelona.

Now, with the goal in our sights we actually started to believe we could make it.

On our way down the eastern coast of Spain we raided several orange farms in the Valencia province until we had half the trunk filled with oranges and tangerines. It was scary to go into these citrus fields in the middle of the night. The farmers had installed huge speaker systems that loudly warned people such as us that they patrolled the grounds with dogs and would not be responsible for the consequences if the animals caught our scent. But we had to. Both to replenish our meagre rations but also for the vitamins. We were extremely lucky and got away with even this risky criminal activity. Just three days after we had been in Paris we were in Murcia in the south-eastern part of Spain. To our great dismay we discovered that the gas wouldn't get us to our destination despite the calculations we had made and in Spain it was exactly as it had been in Italy. People were not as well-off here and it was increasingly difficult to get what we needed. We had no other option but to call my mother and ask her for some money.

Even though I had been living in the Gothenburg area recently I hadn't been in contact with my family for several years. It felt difficult to have to call her but our predicament gave us no other choice. We studied the map and decided on veering off the main road heading for a village called Águilas on the Mediterranean seafront, quite far down the Spanish east coast. There I would place the call to her and we would await the deposit. We didn't have many pesetas left but I managed to find a kind-hearted receptionist at a hotel and she placed the call for me. Mother was very happy to learn that I was alive and then she reluctantly agreed to send us the money. To celebrate this we went to a nearby mini-market and stole two flasks of strong spirits, one bottle each with very clever designs – one shaped like a Madonna and the other as a Diablo, the Devil. This cheered us up, both the symbolism and the drugs. We parked on the outskirts of the village and celebrated with the stereo blaring out Spanish pop-hits and smoking hash mixed with a lot of toasts, boasts and croaks until the early morning when we both crashed into oblivion.

I felt safe dozing off and cherished a new-felt hope for the future.

Thirteen

I woke up early and emptied my Madonna. Simon was sleeping like a log and I didn't have the heart to wake him. He had driven the car all the way across Europe and, in all, the pressure of the addictive life style had always been more difficult mentally for him than it was for me. I was tougher and firmer in my decision to lead this lifestyle. Anguish seldom took over my ability to push through another day with whatever it took to stay afloat. Another very important difference between us was that I didn't have children to make me suffer a guilty conscience for abandoning them.

I let him sleep on and snuck out of the car to have a look around the village. I found a Supermercado and went in to check out the layout of the store and get a feel of it with a thief's tentacles. I became aware of the calm and familiar way the staff welcomed me. I got the vibrations of being in northern Europe. It was strange. I managed to steal cream for our coffee and several large bottles of alcohol and put them in my roomy, expensive handbag. I paid for an onion and some potatoes, smiling amiably at the girl at the till. Then I walked happily back to the car. Simon was still fast asleep. I stood outside the car stretching for a bit, admiring the nice neighbourhood, enjoying the smell of the sea when I suddenly saw where we were parked. On the other side of the street was a huge, concrete building adorned with an enormous sign above the wide staircase leading into the complex. It said "Guardia Civil". Now, franticly scanning my surroundings, I also noticed the numerous police cars that were parked inside the low wall of the station and there was yet another one approaching as I stood frozen, staring. I smiled, feeling like a loon, tip-toed both mentally and emotionally, slipping into the passenger seat and waking Simon up more carefully than I had ever done before.

"Simon," still smiling, "for Gods' sake, you have to wake up, but don't move. Be still – we are parked outside the police station!"

He kept himself admirably cool and composed and within a minute we were driving away. I was thanking my God repeatedly and, as soon as the first shock simmered down, we shook with laughter, on the brink of crying. The line between insanity and raving lunacy is a scarily thin one at times.

"It's better to hide in plain sight," one of us managed to quote and we laughed even harder.

We thought of the car stereo that we had been playing at the highest volume half the night, the joints, the alcohol and the constant toasting. It was inconceivable that we had made it yet again.

When we'd managed to calm down, we began the search for a more suitable place to park with the help of our map - we preferably wanted to be on the other side of

Águilas. We wound up close to a park and now we made a sober and realistic plan. We knew we would have to wait at least a week for the money. We had some food. We really needed to get ourselves and our clothes washed which meant both urgent and practical chores to tend to. I told Simon about the remarkable feeling I had gotten in the village and at the store that morning. We decided to explore the surroundings when we had freshened up. There was a public toilet on the beach and after extensive lathering followed by splashing ourselves with water from the hand basin, then washing and hanging some of our clothes to dry, we walked into town.

When we had taken the turn off the motorway and on to the smaller road that led to Águilas it turned out to be bumpy and poorly maintained and we hardly met any traffic on it for quite a long way. The town was somehow isolated and remote. Well in the town centre we got hold of a local map, talked to some people and it soon became clear where we had wound up. This village was mostly a tourist village almost exclusively for richer foreign and Spanish people. There weren't that many hotels, mostly residential areas and apartment complexes owned by seasonal or timeshare visitors. The local population was quite small and since this was a town situated on a big detour from the larger highways it wasn't disturbed by riffraff. We had wound up in a paradise, given our predicament. Here they weren't accustomed to being on the constant look-out for "bandidos" because that kind of people simply didn't happen to pass by Águilas. We decided to keep as low a profile as possible. We would try to cool off and recharge our batteries after the crazy road trip, putting it mildly, that had got us down here.

It was a much needed respite and we relished it as best we could. We still "had to" get more alcohol every day but we didn't have to be on the roads remaining constantly on our toes as we'd had to the last couple of weeks.

We walked along the beach during the day and cooked food in beautiful locations in the evenings, all the while winding down with lots of rest. I had been extremely tense and worn emotionally run down. This environment helped me to get down to earth in just a few days, letting in a sensation of normality. Christmas was approaching and the Spaniards were very good at creating the idyllic mood for this holiday in the whole village. I remember allowing myself to feel melancholy seeing the small children dressed in their perfect yuletide outfits milling about in the company of parents busy shopping in the small picturesque boutiques.

Deep inside, I yearned for something else. I was preoccupied with the strong bond between Simon and me. The kicks that drugs and stealing brought with them overtook any other dreams I might have. Uncertainty and longing were continuously gnawing but my addiction was always calling louder than any other attractions. I was just so used to this behaviour of looking for a kick since childhood that I didn't really reflect on it.

Finally, the money was transferred and we could get moving. It was with a certain amount of sorrow that we left this beautiful little village, knowing that the calm relaxation would turn back into the inferno of insane unpredictability. On the other hand, the pull of having an exiting, unpredictable adventure lured us with a strong rush of anticipation. We drove off toward our goal and awe and grand dreams filled our hearts. Next stop – Marbella.

I phoned with Arne, my godfather's brother in Marbella who we were set on meeting. He told me he was just about to leave for a holiday back to Sweden but that he had been looking into possible jobs but that we would have to postpone our meeting until he got back. Simon and I had to make new plans and decided to drive on to La Linea de la Concepción, the town on the Spanish side of the border with Gibraltar.

We slept in the car one night but the feel of this town was the complete opposite of that of Águilas. This place felt vibrantly raw. As criminals we were like animals with sprouting tentacles assessing the surroundings for threats and the vibe we got here turned out to be a hundred percent correct. In the morning, we asked around and found out that La Linea was a town with a very widespread and thriving underworld so, on that very first day, we bravely drove across the border and parked in "Gib", a little way up The Rock, instead. If we were to be apprehended for car theft it felt safer to be in the hands of the British legal system than the Spanish one. That day, we also discovered the large supermarkets in Gib, which in those days were easy targets for shoplifting. This was New Year's Eve and we took the opportunity to replenish our supplies of alcohol and food among the crowds of holiday shoppers.

When the clock struck midnight Simon had fallen asleep and I stood alone outside the car listening to the ships' horns hailing in the New Year, watching the fireworks. A feeling of nostalgia crept upon me as I imagined being aboard a ship anchored in the bay below. I told myself I was free now but this surge emerged from deep down inside where I longed for the order and safety that I had felt onboard despite everything else that had occurred at sea. I actually allowed myself to go to sleep with a feeling of regret and melancholy in my chest.

The novelty and the wild-ness of being on this joyride was starting to wear off. We needed something fresh to spice up our day-to-day life. We had managed, unbelievably, to get ourselves all the way across the continent as planned and now an empty space left by that crazy feeling needed filling. On New Year's Day we talked over how we could spice things up a bit and decided to try to sell the car here. We began by getting to know people in the English community both in Gib and La Linea so as to eventually hook a buyer and we also wanted to find someone to buy hash from. Soon we found a smaller crowd of people that we began to hang out with.

With the money that my mother had sent us we began buying and then smuggling cartons of cigarettes in the tax-free zone that is Gib and take them hidden on our person across the border into Spain where we had located buyers among the tobacco stores. Our looks and our experience of smuggling made this child's play for us. We doubled our money every time we crossed and, in a short while, managed to live quite comfortably again. It was stressful having to worry about the car all the time so we parked it in a safe prepaid lot as soon as we could afford it. We borrowed a tent from one of our newfound friends and then we made camp in a park on the Spanish side. Another friend showed an interest in buying the car and we quickly made the deal. The price she paid was a measly 800 pounds. It was a terribly low price but the largest profit was the emotional freedom from the anguish of the whole thing.

We decided on taking a trip as a reward. With half the earnings we left by ferry from Tarifa, the southernmost point of Europe, sailing for Tangiers in Morocco. We were looking forward to trying the Moroccan pot which was renowned all over the world but were very clear that we wouldn't be buying hash other than for personal use. The consequences would be horrid if we got caught in the act of any major illegal activities in Morocco. We would buy smoke in smaller quantities and stay out of trouble. This journey was made to seek out adventure and kill time until my Swedish relative returned, not to end up in the Moroccan prison system.

We stood on deck watching the able seamen berth the ship to African soil. A large group of men and boys of varying age stood on the docks. We realised they were there to lure the tourists coming off the ship. I told Simon not to glance at or even speak a single word to any of them when we came ashore, but as it turned out this wasn't very easy for him. When we got down onto the quay the passengers, including Simon, with the exception of the Arab people and myself, were instantly surrounded by this crowd of tourist hunters. In the midst of a lot of lively pushing and shoving, Simon was offered every thinkable service. It was clear that I had a body language that they read instantly because not a single one of these fifty or so men bothered me once. Simon became very busy trying to communicate that he didn't need any of the offered bargains until I came and dragged him away, mumbling something polite yet curtly declining in Arabic and then we managed to get him out of the crowd.

For me it was a lovely feeling to be back in an Arab country but for Simon it was a culture shock. He was well-travelled but mostly as a tourist or in a work capacity and then always having had lots of money to spend. Now we lived a very different life. The first night we booked in at a cheap hotel in Tangiers and the next morning we bought train tickets to Casablanca. We carried what we owned and the 400 pounds we had started out with we held onto very tightly.

The hotel in "Casa" was also chosen from the size of our wallet. It was in the middle of town on a bustling street. The room was small and shabby and we shared it with cockroaches. Not that many of the little buggers really, I thought but Simon saw each and every one as an intruder. He got used to them after a couple of days though and over-all it was a friendly establishment with very welcoming staff.

Close by there was a small café which I never visited but I taught Simon some basic Arabic so that he could buy smaller amounts of hash for us. I knew that it would be best if I, as a woman, kept a very low profile. The quality of the smoke was very good and we got stuck in the hotel room for a few days before we'd gotten used to it, then we began touring the city on foot.

The culture shock for Simon was mostly based on the extreme differences between the classes in this society. Before our joyride he hadn't been this close up to everyday society in the countries he had visited. The vast gulf between the relative equality of the citizens within the safe and prosperous Swedish population and the people living here was enormous. We walked through the rich parts with high walls surrounding huge compounds with garages with room for several cars belonging to one family, and then on into the vast poor districts where people had to live on top of each other in shacks. His heart bled. I was used to seeing this from my childhood and had experience of being among the privileged, but that didn't shield me from the horrible truth of how people get put down depending on where they were born. The whys and hows of us allowing such a minuscule number of us to hoard the majority of our abundantly fruitful planet's resources were rudely awakened. Again the ways of the "co-hell-ision" fuelled my loathing and was strengthened in my justifications for being on this joyride.

We met Muhammad when we were sitting on a city bench sharing a bottle of wine. Drinking alcohol in public was not all that clever. He approached Simon and asked if he could hang out with us. Simon answered as the blue-eyed, tipsy Swede that he was and the Moroccan joined us. When we got up to leave Muhammad wouldn't listen to our good-byes but kept on, insisting that he could show us the best souk in town. Even I agreed to this and happily he led the way. I saw to it that we only walked on busy streets or else I refused to go on. When we got to the market we decided to buy just the one souvenir each and we let Muhammad choose something inexpensive for himself. After this he was impossible to shake off, of course.

We had touched on a vague idea about staying on in Morocco if an opportunity to make a living should arise. Simon asked Muhammad if he knew of any place where Westerners could get a job and our new friend became very excited. He told us of his uncle who lived in Rabat, the capital of Morocco, 90 kilometres north of Casa on the Atlantic coast. The uncle had a factory of some kind and needed workers. Being drunk and stoned I allowed myself to give some thought to this possibility, truthfully I mostly pondered over fantasies of colours and the warmth of the forthcoming springtime in this beautiful country. We agreed that he would come to our hotel five days later and then we would leave for the North together. Luckily the hotel staff got a look at Muhammad when we parted on the street outside and warned us about him. I never got a clear picture of why he was said to be dangerous but I sobered up very quickly, regaining my perspective on reality.

We stayed on for a few more days, staying clear of our newfound “friend”, and when the funds started to run low we understood that we had to go back to Spain. After two weeks in Morocco and with a few more lessons learned, we bought two bus tickets leaving on the day before we were supposed to have left for Rabat. The bus took us up to Ceuta, an autonomous Spanish city on the African Mediterranean coast where we could get the ferry back to Europe. We had literally spent our last dirham getting to the coast. We didn't have any money for the crossing. All the way from Gothenburg I had carried a small portable typewriter (without getting a single word on paper). Now we sold it, in the middle of the night, to a customer at a café right before crossing the border into Ceuta.

The few dirhams we had gotten for it would still not cover the ticket. I had to beg them to let us on board. I had brought my sailors' certificate with me and I showed it to the people in the terminal. They were truly a godsend and let us both through. Incredible! It was with enormous relief we left Africa and very gratefully we soon planted our feet on European soil again. Broke but “home” and very, very happy about it. Thoughts of Muhammad maybe having had plans to sell us, or at least me, as a slave were ghosts that had haunted my mind. I'd been in a paranoid, hash-induced state during the last few days in Casa. We thanked our lucky stars and went into a store to steal some gin bottles. Now it was time to celebrate. We found a secluded, empty beach where we set up camp and soon became piss-drunk and got into a terrible row. The regular theme of our relationship. I left, storming up into Algeciras, leaving Simon raging behind. In town I met an English woman and told my tale of being abandoned by my husband and she amazingly paid for a night at a small hotel nearby and even gave me some money. When I awoke it was early in the morning, the bed was heavenly and, as the mad rut always went in the blur of my hung-overedness, the yesterday's fight seemed absurdly insignificant. I bought some liquor and found Simon, still at the beach. We made our peace and, thanks to the lady, we could pay for the bus tickets back to La Linea. Soon we were safely back in our part of the world again.

We stayed together and struggled on, striving harder than necessary rather than being soothed due to our continuous intoxication. Looking back, not many things, if any, on this trip were romantic or cool in the actual sense. Everything was about getting away from myself as I always had. With the risky criminal acts and the ongoing alcohol abuse I was actually slowly draining myself. All the time. The highlights were artificial, always depending on the availability of more drugs and kicks. I wasn't able to admit this of course. Life seemed ordinary, the way it had been since my early teens, except with regard to the punishment I would face if caught outside Sweden which would be much more severe here. That worry always lurked in the back of my mind.

When we got back to La Linea we accepted an offer of a short-term lease on an apartment in town. I contacted Arne again hoping to find him back from his holiday but instead I found out that he had prolonged his stay in Sweden. As it happened we needed rest after the Moroccan tour. We collected the remaining 400 pounds from the car-sale at our friend's house and it burned a hole in our pockets. We started spending money way too fast.

After the lease was up we moved into an empty military barracks on the southernmost tip of the rock of Gibraltar, a typical action to help jazz up our "adventure". Always these superficial changes to spice the inane reality. I called them "God sent gifts" to frame the hardships of the mental pressure I put myself under.

Finally Arne came back to Marbella and I got on the bus to go and see him. He had his own firm offering athletic healthcare to celebrities and wealthy people on Costa del Sol and he was very prosperous. I had no experience of that kind of work but he had friends within the beauty and recreational salons and a couple of his Scandinavian friends could set me up at their successful salon in the middle of the uptown quarters. I accepted immediately and would start in two weeks' time.

Back in La Linea we kept up the smuggling and two days before we were to leave for Marbella we got caught at customs with the cigarettes. They found almost all the cartons we were carrying. Those that were left got us just enough money to buy the alcohol and food that we needed before leaving and also to buy the bus tickets. We just made it, again. Unbelievable! It was hard not to see a guardian angel mixed up in these events. Time and time again, difficult situations resolved themselves so that our journey could continue.

I started working for the two women who owned the salon. They were very happy with me and called me their sweet, pretty, nice and competent "girl" that they'd been lucky to find. What a contrast to the little bandit I actually was.

We lived in the tent and Simon found a perfect spot along the beach where we could set it up. Completely hidden behind thick shrubbery, between the beach and a fence surrounding an empty plot of land, where no one ever passed by. He would be taking care of the daily chores, finding stubs of joints until we got my first salary, washing clothes, making food and buying booze while I worked, pampering the upper class. At midday we would meet up at a supermercado to buy wine, bread and cheese, bringing this lunch down to the beach and savouring this new turn of events.

One of my employers turned out to be best friends with one of Simon's previous colleagues and soon Simon also had work. Not within his profession but as a sort of handy-man for various rich people. His first assignment was to drive a luxury car from Denmark to Marbella. He got to drive all the way through Europe again but legally this time. The wages he got from this job were enough for us to pay a first rent and deposit for a studio apartment by the sea. We had also gotten to know people who smoked hash and bought a stash of that too. Now that we were getting a steady platform for establishing a way of life on Costa del Sol I began feeling uncomfortable. Restlessness raised its ugly head. Being fenced in like this was not in my nature and I had to find an escape, an excuse – this time it was easy. Working as a kind of servant for the customers who were living the way that I had as a child felt very humiliating. This resentment started to sprout inside me.

I was attending a professional massage course paid for by my employers, I lived very comfortably and was very appreciated in the workplace but something pulled at me, as usual. One night after three-and-a-half months, the cup ran over and I provoked a major fight at home. We screamed and threw stuff inside and out of the apartment. It was a drunken brawl if there ever was one, and we were woken in the morning by the landlady pounding at our door. Simon opened and she pushed past him into the flat shouting and gesticulating in the manner only Latinos can.

"Madre mia! Escandalo! Escandalo! Porqué...? Porqué!?! Dios mio!" and so on and so forth, on the same theme.

We threw some money at her, got our tent and some clothes and left. We walked the few metres down to the beach and fell asleep again at once. I was more hung over than I had been in many years.

This was the end of what might have turned out to becoming a secure future in this Mediterranean paradise. My employers tried to get me to stay but I was done being a servile "girl" as I viewed my job. Simon really wanted to keep his job which was moving ahead with all kinds of projects but I was immoveable.

"Stay here then and grovel for these rich swines! I'm done here! See ya!" In the middle of this theatrical showdown I put my bets on the fact that he would most probably want to be with me and I was truly relieved when he called me back.

"Okay, we'll leave then."

Several days after the row I was still terribly hung over and neither alcohol nor hash cured it. I was totally out of control and lived only for using more and more trying to shut off everything inside. My thoughts lingered on all the possibilities in Marbella. All that I now had turned my back on. I was a nervous wreck.

Instead of calming down, sobering up and reevaluating my options we suddenly followed a new impulse and stole another car.

Fourteen

This car-theft was different. It was an old car that just happened to be parked with the keys in the ignition right outside the supermercado where we often bought our lunch. Another thing was that this theft affected an innocent individual. The decision was made in a split second after we spotted the keys. We jumped in and drove off, looking at each other and shaking our heads, as if shocked by this course of action. But what was done was done and we quickly picked up the tent, stuffed the essentials in a bag and left Marbella. Since the theft was local we felt under pressure to leave in a hurry. Portugal was the only possible destination. We made it to the border in exactly the time it took to drive there at the legal speed limit, only stopping once for petrol and we crossed the border without any problems. Since 1993 when many countries in Europe had gotten together to form the European Union, travelling between countries had become much less complicated. We hadn't been at a single border control since our departure from Sweden. We simply drove on into Portugal and after an hour or so we stopped in a small town looking for a store where we could steal some food.

We found a medium-sized shop and I put some bread and cheese in my purse. We were famished: even I had gotten my appetite back. We thought the staff looked at us a bit but not too much. We skipped taking any alcohol since it didn't feel completely safe. It was a long time since we'd had to shoplift anything without paying but the habit was still there, just like riding a bike. We weren't stopped on our way out but when we turned the street corner veering onto the street that ran along the back of the store we suddenly heard loud barking coming from the store's back door. Two enormous dogs, which looked more like small calves to me, ran in focused attack mode straight towards us. My legs literally buckled. Simon was used to dogs and he instinctively took on the alpha-male role. He barked/screamed, somehow using both words and growling barks at the same time as he faced them down, somehow towering over them in a most threatening manner. I couldn't believe my eyes when the dogs stopped in their tracks and started whining. It felt as if I was watching a movie in slow motion. It was surreal watching the dogs turn and trot off in the direction they had come from, their tails tucked firmly between their legs. This mad incident was a rude, although comparatively mild, awakening. We looked around us and began realising where we had wound up – in those days Portugal was the poorest country in the EU.

When we drove on, we noticed that the gardens were rigorously fenced off even if there was just one fruit tree in the yard. We looked around us and understood that it was going to be very tricky to get by in this country.

There were many Roma people who actually rode wagons drawn by scrawny horses. We noticed that people looked harried and overworked at an early age and we mostly met worn out, old vehicles on the roads.

We made our way to the tourist traps as quickly as we could. There we might get a chance to make a living if we really brainstormed. Despite this terribly precarious situation, I wouldn't let myself acknowledge any regret for having left Marbella. I don't know how Simon felt and I was careful not to ask. It had really suffocated me to be that "pretty girl" all the time. My education as a masseuse was only half finished and I told myself it was a job that I didn't want to "stoop" to practising either. I shoved down the remorse that tried to penetrate to the surface. I was still very abstinent from the last binge with the alcohol and was also in withdrawal from hash at this point.

We drove from village to village along the coast until the gas tank showed less than half full. We had luckily done a "fill-her-up'n-run" in Spain just before crossing the border and in this country it was absolutely unthinkable to even consider anything like that. Not even stealing petrol from another car was an option - we suspected that there might be a risk of severe physical danger in messing with other people's property here.

The first night, we fell asleep in a parking lot in one of the smaller tourist towns along the Algarve coast. When

I woke up there was a small trailer parked next to us and a retired couple were just leaving the van, stretching the sleep out of their bones as they smiled at me and strolled off. I could imagine them going into a cosy café to have a nice breakfast after a good night's sleep in their comfortable mobile home. Another one of those pangs of sadness and yearning to live a normal life flashed inside me. As always, such soft-hearted dreams hurt too much for me to bear. I quickly turned that beautiful thought into disgust at how exploited they must have been their whole lives, toiling at some meaningless workplace and soon the sharpened spikes of hostility gleamed in my mind.

We changed some money and bought two bottles of wine and a piece of bread that Simon ate by himself. In pressured situations I concentrated solely on the alcohol. We sat dangling our legs on a pier making plans. We came up with a vague idea of going around asking about the possibilities of getting work in the area. We found some Englishmen who owned a small hotel nearby. They informed us that it was a hard life in these parts and that they themselves had to go fishing to put food on the table during the winter months. This was discouraging news but we knew that we were usually able to make a living somehow or other and mustered all the positive spirits we were able to. But the days blended into each other and nothing new arose as far as the legal options were concerned.

We stole some books and bottles of sun cream and tried to sell some off the streets but no one bought anything from us. It started to look gloomy. I was still very shaken up since the last hard drug bash with whiskey in Marbella - it felt as if I had burned out some essential part of my usual ingenious self. I felt stunned. We had turned over every stone and began to resign ourselves to having reached a blind alley.

Our hash reserves were depleted and the consumption of alcohol lessened in proportion to our meagre funds. We didn't know what to do.We didn't dare sleep in the car anymore – we did not want to be awakened by the long arm of the law in this country. We found a park where we could sleep in the coastal village of Portimão and made a discreet camp beside an abandoned house. One morning, Simon spotted some bottles lying under the building. On closer inspection, he found out that this was a gold mine. Crawling in under the house, he found the ground littered with hundreds of bottles and all of them recyclable. We turned in several bottles a day and got money to buy bread, spread, fruit and wine. It was an oasis of light in the dark future we had begun to resign ourselves to. Strengthened by the meals and the ever-so-little positive development, and of course the alcohol helping to toughen us up too, we gained new energy and began brainstorming anew.

We were out for a drive when we happened upon a place outside the village were we camped. There were lots of people carrying boxes and stuff into a hotel resort. On a spur-of-the-moment decision we got out of the car and followed the people to see what they were up to.

Around the pool area they were preparing for a market event. We asked around for someone in charge to speak to. A woman pointed us in the direction of a large, dark man who was sitting in the shade, supervising the ongoing bustle. We asked him about the price and terms of being able to rent a stand at this event. The price was affordable and we wouldn't have to pay until the day of the market and that was three days away. We signed up on his list and got back in the car with a new spark of hope in our hearts. In two days we had to get together a tableful of attractive merchandise for tourists. We felt back on track.

We already had a small stock with the books and suntan lotion but it was only enough to cover a quarter of the tables in the stands. Now we freshened up and got into authentic tourist outfits, and we were ready. We looted wildly amongst the established tourist shops and in the evening our car was loaded to the brim with stuff: local souvenirs, sun hats, more creams and oils, books, beachwear and sandals. We had just gone with whatever the tourist boutiques supplied which made what to pinch easy to pick out but it was also very risky. By the end of the day we were both nervous wrecks and decided to go down to sit on the beach with a few bottles of wine which we had managed to get our hands on during the day. Winding down with the sound of the sea and a beautiful sunset, we were approached by two guys who started up a conversation and ended up asking if they could join us. It turned out that they had some hash and since we had wine it turned into a perfect opportunity for a spontaneous party. The evening became a huge success, the guys were very nice and in connecting with others like myself I felt an inner harmony for the first time in ages. We hadn't had any social life in the last few weeks. We talked and laughed a lot and suddenly discovered that we were freezing and that the sky had turned black. We offered the guys to sleep in the car. They gratefully accepted the offer. We drove away, parking on a flat patch a little way off on a seemingly infrequently trafficked country road. Geographically confused, at least we knew that it was close to where the market was being held the next day. We put the tent up a bit haphazardly, being intoxicated and tired. The guys asked if they shouldn't lie in the tent instead but we insisted that they get the softer bedding. They had been camping on the beach for several nights and we felt warm-hearted and dismissed their protests. Everyone fell asleep happy and satisfied. Simon and I whispered in high spirits, looking forward to the next day's possibility of being able to make a living here.

***

I awoke slowly. My dream of the ocean living on in my mind. The soothing quiet, the eternal blue that held my body in its safe embrace. The colours of light and life, the beautiful encompassing sea. I breathed in the depths, bathed in an ever-so-real serenity. Carefully, the dream let go and in crept reality. The smell I could smell I associated with snails, however they really smell. It was probably mould but the table we lay beneath at the side of the road and the tarp covering it were covered with snails. Reality hit me face-on. Since yesterday we had been on the run in Portugal. We would soon hitchhike onwards, as soon as Simon woke up, and I prayed for our protection, prayed to be allowed to get home. All hell had broken loose the night before last.

We had met the two young Portuguese guys 36 hours earlier. One of them had only just gotten out of jail after having served a several-year long sentence and the other had very recently terminated a two-year rehabilitation program. They had been sleeping on the beaches on the Algarve coast for a few days when they met us and then we'd had our wine and hash party.

"Sleep in the car, it will be much softer for you. I know how it is to sleep rough. It's no trouble for us. Nemas problemas!" I had said.

They had been so grateful and had fallen asleep among our stolen goods. A nice way to end what had been a great evening celebrating the new adventure we would be embarking on in the morning. We had grand hopes about a way out of the cornered situation we had gotten ourselves into in this difficult country. We hoped we could use the money from this first market to turn our business into a legal one.

We were rudely awakened by a confusing chaos of screams, stomping, yelling of commands followed by one or several people standing outside our tent hitting it, and thereby us, with a thick stick of some sort.

I shouted: "Una moment, por favor! Qué pasa? Tranquilo por favor! Somos turistas, una moment, una moment!"

We crawled to peer out through the opening of the tent. The guys in the car had been dragged out and lay on the ground with policemen vehemently hitting them with long batons. Everybody was screaming. There was one officer on guard near us while four or five were standing in a ring around our new friends who were curled up trying to protect themselves from the blows. I understood some of the Portuguese and the closest officer was yelling at us to hurry up.

"Una moment, por favor, passaportes, por favor", I begged and crawled back into the now all but collapsed tent. There were no passports in there but a voice inside me said. 'Buy time, buy more time'. The one guarding us flashed his lamp in our direction for shorter moments to then turn the beam towards the beating of the guys about ten metres from us seeming very eager to get over there and take part in that action. His feet seemed to drag him magnetically closer and closer to them.

"Let's take off," Simon hissed at me.

"Not yet," I hissed back and right then the policeman turned his flashlight back on us.

"Si, si, los passaportes, si, si," I said and waved my empty hands as if I had the documents right there.

"Andale, andale!" he barked and I immediately responded in a voice like an obedient child saying to the parent "I'm coming, I'm coming":

"Si, si. Nemas problemas."

Then he turned away again and I pulled at Simon, whispering "NOW!" and we ran, threw ourselves over a wall and landed on the field.

We ran. The night was charcoal black and my heart pounded so hard that my whole body throbbed. I heard the voices getting louder again and that meant they had realised that we had bolted. They shouted at each other and shortly the van was fired up and with screeching tires they stepped on the accelerator onto the country road to find us. We ran barefoot over a newly cut hay field – the shoes were left behind in the tent. Suddenly a large circle of light was lit up about 200 metres to our right. "Down!" we both hissed simultaneously, threw ourselves face down on the ground, laying flat pressing on the sharp edges of the cropped straws as the spotlights scanned the large flatland.

The only words in my head echoed "GoodGod-Good-God-GoodGod! Protect us please! Please-Please-Please!"

We had got a head start and managed to run quite far before they noticed that we had gotten away. Just far enough so that they couldn't spot us when they began their first loud, frustrated search for us.

We ran and ran, throwing ourselves on the ground when the police van's searchlights swept the landscape, ran anew and collapsed around a tree which we could curl our bodies against, desperate to catch our breath. Under cover of darkness we sneaked into a building site where we hid for the night.

If fear had overpowered the instinct to stay alive I might not be sitting here today.

Fifteen

When we woke up the morning after the raid we saw that the building we'd crawled into was a villa, or a half-built villa. We had taken refuge behind a tall heap of materials and then slept deeply, probably passing out as an aftermath of the shock. The only things we'd managed to bring with us were the clothes we had on and the passports that I'd miraculously found in the same instant the policeman had aimed his flashlight at us that final time, when I lied to him by waving my empty hands shouting,

"Si, si, los passaportes, si, si," as if I'd already found the documents. When he swept the beam away and turned back to the awful place where they were beating our friends up, I happened to catch a glimpse of the passports in a dark corner of the collapsed tent and had instantly grabbed them.

Neither of us had shoes on and my feet were throbbing and aching from the sprint across the spiky cropland.

"Dare we leave?" The question was actually more of a statement.

We had no choice but to grab the bull by the horns. I silently chanted a desperate prayer and started walking. The first lift we got was with a little, old man who, smiling broadly, pointed for us to sit on the luggage rack of his utility moped. His happy face and eagerness to help warmed me inside and we cherished getting every invaluable and bumpy kilometre between us and the scene of the nightmarishly unreal showdown. Simon and I agreed that if we made it this time it would have to be the end of this trip. If we made it to Porto without being arrested, and that was many, many kilometres away, we would go to the Swedish consulate and try to arrange for the journey back home. But I was almost too scared to even hope for such an outcome, trying my hardest not to think at all. Every second was tense. I constantly had to shut my brain off when it started wandering off, creating mind games of terrifying captures or ecstatic freedom. Mustering as much presence of mind as possible, I madly relished the moment, focusing on the view of the beautiful bright, spring-coloured landscapes on both sides of the noisy moped.

The happy old man dropped us off at a junction and there, thankfully, we immediately got another lift. This was in a car. An hour later, the driver left us at the side of the road which we ended up walking down until early evening. The mental pressure of keeping up a presence of mind and a constant radar for police vehicles was extremely consuming. When we came upon an abandoned fruit stand we crept under the filthy tarmac and fell asleep at once.

The next morning we continued to hitch-hike, picking up cigarette butts from the roadside while on foot. Later in the day we got a ride with a man who showed us great kindness. He drove to his home where we stayed in the car while his wife stuffed a bag full of food and gave it to us. Then he took us to Fatima, a village where many Catholics go as a pilgrimage. He told us we would be welcome there and probably get a bed indoors to catch up and rest. I was deeply moved by his generosity. We were dirty, barefoot and must have smelled bad but he truly went out of his way to help us. This man and his actions were a flame of warmth in the cold darkness of what had happened to us. Of course, I still couldn't face up to the fact that if I hadn't been a thieving addict this would most probably never have befallen us or our poor friends. We thanked the man from the bottom of our hearts while saying our goodbyes.

Walking aimlessly, we found a small charity and the women there gave us each a blanket. They didn't have any shoes to spare but we were glad for the warmth these blankets would give us during the chilly nights. The regular temperatures of southern Europe were late this year and the middle of April was slowly turning the days warmer but the nights were still very cold. With the blankets tucked under our arms we entered the area of the Catholic sanctuary dedicated to Our Lady of Fátima. We meant to ask if there was anywhere for us to sleep, maybe in a dormitory, or at least get somewhere to have a shower. We met a priest on a large square and when we began talking to him he interrupted and clenched his fist, waving it at our bag of food saying:

"Not blessed! Not blessed!"

Totally taken aback, neither of us could think of anything to say. The priest walked away without another glance, leaving us standing there with mouths agape. The surprise quickly turned into anger and the usual contempt and we proudly decided not to ask for anything else in this "godforsaken" place. Of course my aversion toward churches and religion was further underlined and I marched out of the pilgrimage area arrogantly citing: "Forgive them, for they know not what they do," to calm myself. We soon found a doorway where we lay down in a nook and spent the night undisturbed.

The next day, after stealing some local port wine, we gladly left the town and continued hitch-hiking north, but this day was slow. We walked for hours on end, finding lots of half-smoked cigarettes that people had generously thrown out of their car windows, listening to the birds singing and looking at the stunning landscape. Spring was evidently here with bright green fields and the impressive cork oak buds having newly burst open. The fear of being apprehended had begun to subside a little but the watchfulness was a constant companion. After finally getting a brief lift in the late afternoon, we were stranded in a small village that didn't feel at all safe to spend the night in. There was only a small number of houses, thus no doorways to sneak into, and the landscape was flat with no visible places to hide.

We sat on the side of the road contemplating the situation when two young Roma girls dressed in traditional clothing came skipping and singing, actually dancing by, where we sat. It was as if we'd wound up in a movie. Their voices were pure and the beauty in their steps was filled with joy and life. Curiosity took hold and soon we got up and followed them in the direction in which they had disappeared. Rounding a bend we spotted the camp. There were at least 40 Romani people there with lots of children playing and they were all dressed traditionally. We agreed on asking if we could sleep with them at this camp. Simon had some tinker relatives and we would use this in trying to appeal to their hospitality. This seemed like a good alternative to hiking in the dark night that was drawing near. So, barefoot and carrying our simple, worn out blankets we cautiously approached a group of women sitting at the edge of the camp and a heap of lively and inquisitive children came running, surrounding us with thousands of questions which I tried to answer in my halting Portuguese.

The women invited us to sit with them and we explained that Simon was a tinker from Sweden and that I was his wife. They asked if we had any tobacco. I brought forth the plastic bag where we had put the day's harvest of cigarette butts, after looking at the clear plastic bag thoughtfully they waved it away. I remembered two chocolate bars that we had pinched when we'd gotten the wine in Fátima and gave them to the kids. This gesture made the women melt. Two of them wandered off soon to return with two pairs of shoes, one for us each. Simon got a pair of sneakers and for me there was a pair of typical Roma women's flat shoes, black and pointy. They smiled kindly at us when we almost started to cry at receiving these unexpected gifts and we thanked them, deeply moved.

While we were putting the shoes on one of the men came up to us. He eyed us from head to toe for a few moments. I dared only give him a quick glance, he was very muscly and an all-round impressive figure. He seemed to be our age, two metres tall, not overweight but very broad. Over his white shirt he wore a black leather vest which was laden with medals. I do not know what kind of medals they were but there were a lot of them and they all but covered the whole vest. He cleared his throat while motioning for us to join him. The women had been jabbering at him the whole time while he'd studied us and now they fell silent as we followed him behind a van. I explained Simon's heritage again and asked him, as I had the women, if we possibly could sleep at their site. He seemed to be a leader or a spokesperson for the group. He nodded, very serious-looking, seeming to weigh our request and at the same time as he pulled the van's side door open. He stretched inside feeling for something and suddenly he stood there with an enormous shotgun in his fist, loaded it, pointing straight up into the air with a loud "tschuck-tschuck" and then he turned to me demanding:

"Do you wanna fuck?"

I was so surprised, at once the kind of crystal clear in my mind as usual in unexpected and threatening situations. I did the math in a micro second and laughter just tore itself loose from the deepest regions of my being. Simon had frozen, stony-faced, but when the medal-man started laughing with me, winking jovially at us, Simon smiled too. What had become clear to me in that instant was that the man would never have hurt us with all the children nearby.

I never understood why he acted that way but I had a feeling that it was some kind of test. If the reaction he had gotten had been different we probably would have been turned away. Now he pointed us to a spot on the field close by the camp but on the other side of an almost unnoticeable treaded path in the grass. He told us curtly but in a friendly tone that we could lie there and then he shook the shot-gun in the air and said in Portuguese:

"Here no police come making trouble for us!", and

then, smiling broadly he slapped Simon on the back and winked at me. Laughing heartily he went back to his people.

Beyond thankful and smiling at the medal-man's back I dragged Simon with me across the discrete border. We were still very close to the group, a few metres from the van, but it was as if a kind of marker had been drawn. We had been told to keep ourselves to ourselves and that we gladly did. The gratitude I felt at being welcomed at all and the unexpected gift of the shoes was overwhelmingly enough. I had no problems respecting this boundary which served to clarify that we were outsiders. It was evident that we weren't to socialise with the Roma.

It was still early in the evening but we were very tired. We lay one blanket on the ground and wound the other around ourselves, lying close to keep warm. It had been a long day on the roads. Also the adrenaline from the shock of the other night began wearing off. The terror of witnessing the beating of the poor guys found in "our" car, the barely escaping with our lives and also the romantic hopes with the market idea which had just been tipped down the drain. All this combined with our new situation as fugitives from the law in a rough country like this - we were absolutely drained. It was also a relief to know that we were protected and at least would have more of a chance to be warned in case the police showed up.

I drifted off listening to the people singing and dancing around a large campfire in the middle of their large gathering. It was exactly as I would have imagined a scene in a romanticised movie about how Roma people lived and I was rocked into a wholesome slumber thanking all the gods for this breather. I had almost fallen asleep when Simon shook me slightly, whispering:

"Lotten, look."

"What?" I whispered, looking around.

At our feet, eighteen pairs of eyes shone at us in the dark night. It took me a second to get the slumber out of my head and to get my sight to adapt in the darkness. Then I saw that it was the children who sat crouching, peering at us. When they saw that we were awake and that they had our attention they began asking questions in the straightforward way children do. They wanted to know where our house was, they asked about our family, our children, where we were going to go, if we had a car. I tried to answer as best I could, pasting Spanish and Portuguese words together. Watching their faces, empathetic and concerned when they understood that we didn't have any of these primary ingredients that make up a human life made me squirm on the inside. I felt more self-pity from their looks than I'd ever felt about not having that kind of life before. I was used to shutting out people's reactions to the life I lived, always shoving everyone but Simon away, but the feelings of being lost and lonely appeared vulnerable when noticed through a child's perspective. Their astonishment and grief for us rattled my defences. I couldn't shut out their heartfelt empathy regarding our rootless existence. Mercifully, they gave in at last and left us but not without comforting words, looks and pitying glances that etched into my being, never to be forgotten. Thankfully, sleep took me shortly after that, embracing me in comforting bliss.

We woke up before dawn and saw the Romani families huddling, sleeping together in five large heaps, each heap covered by an enormous patchwork of blankets. There wasn't a head or foot to be seen and they slept safely and warm in these igloos of covers. We sneaked away with more than a little envy in our hearts. On a post by the only exit from the field there hung two large blankets, much warmer and bigger than ours. We looked at each other shaking our heads - we could never steal from these hospitable people even though it was very tempting since we had been freezing the whole night under our thin crocheted worn out covers.

We understood that what they'd done for us must be very rare. It had all started out with them trying to get tobacco from us, to the two of us finally having shoes and a safe place to spend the night, feeling safer than we had since Marbella. I sent a thankful prayer in their direction and then we were "back on the road again". We were genuinely tired of roaming around and when we happened to get a lift into a small town where there was a railway station, the decision to get on a train bound for Porto was easy. We were going to go for it and chance a freeride.

At the station, a young English woman came up to me and asked if I could help her communicate with the person in the ticket booth and I translated as much as I was able to which resulted in her getting a ticket. Afterwards we chatted for a bit and I told her that we were stranded and completely broke. She suddenly just gave me 30 British pounds, which was like 40 Euros. The money was a wondrous gift, we could hardly believe it. There wasn't any time for shopping because the train pulled in and when onboard we immediately locked ourselves into a toilet, all according to plan. We were only two hours away from Porto if this panned out.

The train was packed with young men off duty from military service. They were crazily drunk and often needed to visit our hide-out. I made retching sounds for two hours. They shouted and pounded on the door the whole time. One guy even tried to climb in through the window, madly clinging on the outside of the speeding train. I taught Simon some easy phrases like:

"My wife is sick", "Sorry", "Try another toilet", and some more on the same subject. The situation with these young men was probably to our advantage since the conductor was extremely busy and worn out trying to keep these intoxicated people in a somewhat manageable order. We made it all the way. Now the journey bound for the homeland was near and it felt wonderful. Sweden hung on the horizon as one of the most human, friendly places on Earth and in Porto the closest thing to Sweden was the consulate. There, we found out that Simon couldn't get any help with the ticket home since he had used up this one-time only benefit before when he'd been stuck in Europe in his teens. It still turned out well because the money that I would get for a plane ticket would instead be used to cover the bus fare for both of us all the way to Hamburg.

The consulate was located within an old port wine factory and the Swedish staff saw to it that we were treated to sandwiches, warm cocoa and wine. That was the most luxurious meal I have ever had. Literally, ever. The money would take a couple of days to process so we used the time to explore the city. After getting cleaned up, we used some of the money we'd been given by the English woman and, after buying some alcohol, we walked until sundown. We had found an abandoned large American car in a park and returned there to sleep. It was very comfortable and probably dangerous but now we didn't bother worrying anymore. There wasn't a molecule of worry in our bodies left to spend, I guess.

It was Simon's turn to call his family to ask for money and he was able to get a loan from his sister that we would be collecting in Hamburg when we got that far. The whole trip home was turning into reality. The night before we were to leave Porto we found a bar and with our very last coins we bought five litres of wine to sustain us during the bus journey north. I used the bathroom in the bar and when I got out Simon was sitting fast asleep on the pavement minus the wine. He had been robbed without even noticing. Looking back, it was probably a blessing from above – I can just see Simon and me getting drunk on the bus, putting on a rowdy maniac show and getting thrown off on the freeway in the middle of nowhere. That exact situation had actually happened to us once before in Sweden.

That night we didn't dare sleep. The bus was scheduled to leave at 5 a.m. So instead we did Porto "by night" and got to see how people on the streets lived there. We met an eighteen-year old heroin addict, a girl who worked as a prostitute. Her story was unbearably awful. She had two children that were in the custody of the social welfare system and a husband serving a jail sentence with seven years to go. She knew she wouldn't ever see any of them again, she wouldn't live that long. I never could forget the "life" she led and her story made me hate the world even deeper. After having been invited to smoke some pot with the girl and her friends at the terminal we got onboard and the bus left Porto on time.

The first hours were spent in a cocoon-like state and, during the trip, a man showed mercy on us and invited us for a couple of beers. Probably we reeked of old drinking habits and looked pretty shaken up from not having had our regular dose that morning.

Eighteen hours later, in the middle of the night, we arrived in Hamburg, both of us pitifully sick with alcohol withdrawal. Before getting off the bus, Simon nudged me, signalling to me to wait until everyone else had left, then he had a look on the racks above the seats and amazingly he found a forgotten jacket with Deutsche Mark to the equivalent of 30 Euros in one of the pockets. We took the money, left the coat and went into the Hauptbanhof in pursuit of beer. We found an vending machine and those swallows were worth their weight in gold. We had a can each and then, with our "nerves" in better order, we fell asleep on a bench.

In the morning, we were astounded by the hordes of addicts milling around the station. I got cold feet and dragged Simon away. I didn't like the way he looked at the junkies and hippies. We got the money from the bank and bought the tickets for the last leg home. Another bus which wouldn't leave until the next morning.

I wanted to go exploring the city but Simon was obsessed with going back to the station, or truthfully, to the drug dealers there. We had a huge fight and after splitting the money, each pocketing their own tickets, we went our separate ways. I wandered off into Hamburg city, stole a dress and had an ecstatically wonderful shower at the station. Then I did downtown Hamburg. It was such a relief to be in a well-off country again. I savoured the people, stole more beer and went back to the park outside the station to see if I could find Simon. I saw him from afar sitting with a bunch of addicts and satisfied with that glimpse I continued my strolling up and down the bustling city streets.

In the late afternoon I met some "ordinary" people who invited me along on a tour of the pubs downtown. Around midnight I was dancing in a bar near the train station when I saw Simon pass by the window. He saw me too and that quick eye contact was enough for us both to know that all was well. He went on and I kept partying until it was time to get the bus for Gothenburg.

In Copenhagen, there was a stop for about 45 minutes and we invested the last money in hash which Simon ran to Christiania and back to buy. We smoked a quick joint and then we finished the last stretch of our journey.

It was the 30th of April, a big celebration day in Sweden called Valborgsmässoafton on which we light huge bonfires, or if you live in a city lots of people mainly just get awfully drunk, all to scare and burn away the winter.

We went from the Göteborgs Centralstation, crossed the street over to a couple of friends' house bringing the smoke, booze and ourselves totally high on adrenaline. I remember not being able to sleep that night, despite having been mostly awake through the past nights in both Porto and Hamburg, and I remember absolutely stuffing myself with liquid and burning drugs. Everything I used only made me even more excited. We were home and more than that - home in one piece. Not rotting, half beaten to death in some Portuguese prison. Everything we had been through seemed like a dream that had escalated into a nightmare of ghastly proportions. In the stories we told that night, to those who could be bothered to listen and those who didn't care indiscriminately, about our joyride memories we told only the "cool" and macabre tales and of course all the times we barely, but still, had gotten away with our hides.

Any substantial relief about being safely home never seemed to settle in though. Being a seasoned addict, the life I led was always a battle with the environment and my emotional disability and there was never a reprieve from having to make time and create opportunities for using my alcohol. The drug always got first priority. It always came before family, health, security and money. The fact which I closed my eyes the hardest to, was that they even came before my very life.

Now, back in the less dangerous Sweden, my addiction

leapt to unprecedented heights. Here, going berserk was child's play compared to what I'd been through, or worse, might have been through if I'd been caught on this mad European joyride.

My innards screeched for alcohol binges, my glamorised ethanol, to thoroughly cleanse all this drama away.

Sixteen

That summer was unusually cold and rainy. After living outside for a while, we rented a walk-in closet at a friends' house on the outskirts of town. My feelings of regrets for what I had forsaken when running from Marbella haunted me and I used drugs like never before. I took a huge variety - anything from LSD and Ecstasy to amphetamines and alcohol. During this madness, I got what was to be my last job. I started working at a restaurant in down-town Gothenburg. I remember biking the 40 minutes it took in the rainy weather, hating the cold. Sometimes I even allowed myself to curse the impulses I'd followed when leaving Spain, where the sun was indisputably shining right now. I had never gotten used to the cold and the winters in Sweden after growing up in Jordan. Stuck in the wettest summer in ages, I only had the mind-blowing drugs to look forward to.

That summer, we bought a new car. We lived alternately in and outside, whatever the weather allowed for, finding beautiful spots on the west coast. Sometimes, we stayed in the closet. Compared to the lovely studio we had had on Costa del Sol, living in those two, windowless square metres was almost as degrading as it had felt in the waste disposal room in Södermalm.

We decided to try to get some capital together by smuggling from Christiania again but after a few runs it just fell through. Neither one of us were in sufficiently good mental or physical shape to be able to manage getting that business on its feet again. We were burnt out after our European tour. Nothing but drugging our brains to bits was properly taken care of at this point. We also tried smuggling alcohol and hashish from Fredrikshavn in northern Denmark by taking a ferry that toured directly from Gothenburg. That plan ended in a total drunken chaos, where we woke up back home in a large park, Slottsskogen, in the middle of town with the cans of beer we had bought, which we had planned to sell on, mostly emptied by the two of us and/or thrown about during a huge row we'd had the night before. Neither of us remembered much of what had happened.

There was no end to that summer's craze. We decided to take the ferry again but not to buy any alcohol this time, only smuggling hashish instead. That venture ended in my falling asleep on the way back to Sweden, waking up, looking out of the porthole and seeing the ship moving off from the quay, leaving Gothenburg again. Simon had gotten off the boat without me after us having had yet another raging exchange of angry words on the way back from Denmark.

I had been robbed of my purse while I was asleep. The pot was still in my pocket but I had to go to the duty-free shop to steal some tobacco and liquor so that I'd survive the trip there and back. In my other pocket, I had the keys to the restaurant I worked at. The boss had the only other set, so I knew then that I had lost my job. When I ought to have been at work, opening up, I was sitting, trembling, trying to cure my hangover, on my way back to Fredrikshavn.

Again, I came to a realisation that a radical change had to be made. Still not in regard to the drug abuse but regarding income and living conditions. I spent the whole trip brainstorming. I concluded that the closet in which our 120 cm-wide mattress fit, without many centimetres to spare, was absolutely suffocating me. Moving would be number one on my list of changes. That stood out as the most urgent issue. I left the thoughts on how to make a new living to simmer.

When I returned, to Simon's and our landlord's joy, bearing pot and more spirits which I had managed to steal onboard, I told Simon my plan. He wasn't happy about moving out again but he knew that I would follow through on this, with or without him. We moved into the car and slept in it, as well as a few times at a friend's apartment in town, for the next few months.

Through the years, I had always seen to having money for my drugs without taking risks that might result in consequences threatening my "freedom" (well, except for the joyride of course). I wasn't willing to risk being sentenced to time in prison. I saw to it that the amounts of drugs or what other criminal activity I was into at the moment wouldn't be serious enough for incarceration.

When I wasn't selling those "small yet bigger" amounts of drugs I still managed to carry myself from day to day. To get 300 SEK, 30 Euros, to start the day, was easy. Then I could buy five grams of pot, sell 2/3 of that for a much more expensive price to get the start-up money back, and buy booze, maybe some food and still have some smoke for myself to last the next 24 hours. In that way, the days could go on for a while until I could get my hands on more money by, for example, stealing meat which I would then sell on to a restaurant or a private individual. Larger capital gave larger profits and I was always very inventive when it came to business ideas.

For a while, I ran a mobile pub for private parties which I named "Plenty for Twenty". Everything cost 20 SEK, 2 Euros. During another period, I sold an alcoholic beverage that had a lower alcohol content than usual in the parks. All illegal ventures of course, but I was careful. There was always money in my pocket, which meant I was always intoxicated. But this lifestyle also took its toll. It was always a hand-to-mouth existence, or can-to-mouth, so to speak. I came to a point where I had to come up with something new, something more profitable. The braincells were set to work again.

My first thought was to restart the antique books thing. There were many such stores in Gothenburg too.

We managed to get together a couple of large boxes but the buyers here weren't as eager as they had been in Stockholm. Once, when Simon was going to sell a few copies, the police were standing there waiting for him. It turned out that the antique bookstore owners, who had been competitors in Stockholm, were more a bunch of colleagues in Gothenburg and here they kept in very close contact with each other. They had all cooperated to catch us. Simon was interrogated and held for a few days and so that option became closed for us. I was fed up with all the old ways but this kind of life was all I knew. I understood that I wouldn't be able to keep any comfortable drug consumption going with the meagre funds I was scraping together. The money was burning faster and faster. We needed to make progress. So we did a few favours for our old suppliers to gather more funds to start up something new.

We knew people who knew people who were into buying and selling all kinds of goods, except drugs. It was all black market stuff and we invested more money than ever before. Meat, candy, wooden pallets, fabrics, anything that would bring in a neat profit with the least effort possible. It took the last of my energy to get this, albeit very small, business running. The pressure I put myself under was hard but I knew that if I wanted to maintain my life-style, considerable sums would need to come into play. It felt as if everything was at stake here. An all-or-nothing venture. Day and night for six months, I was busy moderating my use of alcohol, regulating its effects with other drugs, until finally the business started running itself. At the beginning of this career change, we mostly lived in hotels downtown. This became an impersonal way to live so we decided on a new goal, which was to buy a trailer. For a while, I worked completely absorbed by this dream until we could afford to buy one.

I now climbed to previously unchartered heights of addictive regularity and patterns. In tune with the profits increasing, my health was decreasing and I was in the worst rut ever. Everything revolved around the harsh reality of everyday addiction.

I acted out the pressure I put on myself by treating Simon badly and behaved with an air of superiority towards him. Everything to keep a tough and nonchalant facade. I used extreme amounts of drugs, went to parties and clubs and still lived in hotels from time to time when not in the trailer. I rarely ate and when I did it was only in restaurants and was more of a belly-fill than nourishing. The money flowed in and out and very quickly. This meant a constant hunt for new business possibilities and this just kept on winding into a very fast-spinning and never-ending spiral.

My physical and mental condition deteriorated due to this destructive way of life. We got thrown off campsite after camp-site after me losing my temper and misbehaving in a range of other unacceptable ways, mindlessly letting go of boundaries I used to be able to keep with regard to my addiction. There was only just enough energy left to keep up the polite demeanour I needed to show in contacts with the new clients. Other than that I was a complete mess. Simon started getting on at me about us having to make a change again. After the winter months, I was so worn out that I finally listened to all his "nagging". We decided to leave town and let the business rest for a bit, parking the trailer in a long-stay car park.

We left for the idyllic village of my boarding school years. Opportunities arose again. We were able to sublet a small flat in the middle of this picturesque town, with a wonderful little garden and a view over the large lake Vättern. When the money we had began to run low, we were provided for by social services, telling ourselves it would only be a very temporary solution. We would soon be on top of things again. I even surprised myself with daydreaming about a "normal" life. I realised I was extremely tired after the draining life I had led. I rested a lot but didn't get better: the habits of the last few years had taken their toll. My dreams were shattered because the strength I needed to make a change into an honest and constructive livelihood was depleted. I didn't apply for a single job.

After two months in the welfare system, we were summoned to a meeting at the social services office. In the waiting room sat my mother, sister and brother. They had reported me as a missing person with the police two years earlier and now that I was registered at a municipal organisation, the authorities had finally gotten word to them that I was alive. This was truly out of the blue and we had a long conversation during which they tried to get me to come home with them to Gothenburg. I managed to convince them that I was doing alright and averted them from going with us to our home. They reluctantly returned to Gothenburg the same afternoon without me. Simon and I left the flat the very next day. I felt hunted but, in a shady corner of my mind, I did put this occasion onto the small heap of humane experiences I was hoarding in my subconsciousness.

In truth, the possibilities for making a living in this small village were slim to nil. Nothing for a person like me who wanted to have a steady supply of whatever drug called to me at the time. The window of my family showing up became the excuse I needed to make the move to a more bandit-friendly location. The choice fell to the closest large town which was the one I had moved to with Johan and where I still knew some people. History was repeating itself, then too, the move had been to that town from this village.

This geographical change of scene didn't change anything in the end. Simon and I fought and he left for Gothenburg while I stayed on for a couple of weeks living with a guy I had known since my youth. But that quickly turned into chaos and I also made the return journey to Gothenburg, began restarting the business and Simon joined me a few weeks later. The money was better than ever and we lived alternately in the trailer which we parked mid-town, outdoors on weather-beaten cliff landscapes on the beautiful west coast, in Slottsparken, in Nordstan, a big mall downtown which was open at night in those days, and also at different hotels. This became the rut of the next three years and time just flew by. I used heroin on a regular basis for almost two of those years, only because alcohol failed me – my body couldn't keep the liquor down. Heroin never overtook my bond to the quick fix of alcohol though. The fast and destructive effects of my drug of choice were unthreatened even by this renowned destroyer, heroin.

The drugs brought one day into the next, week into the next coming week, year in and year out. Nothing new happened under the sun but in my delusion I believed it was 'grande action de luxe' and that the challenges were always "new". In reality, it was all about me getting plastered and, high as a kite, just as I had been doing since my early teens. In truth, there were no new goals attained, no evolution, nothing extraordinary at all. Two years into this, Simon began "nagging" again. He wanted to settle down, wanted us to move inside. In the year that followed, he didn't back down an inch but I refused, equally immovable:

"What do you mean? You want us to be like those sold-out run-of-the-millers now!? Why would I give up this freedom for a bunch of stuck-up neighbours, and even pay for the privilege?! Forget it! No, never ever – this is not happening!"

Simon seemed to give in then but after that he would bring it up again, time after time. Talking about kitchens, showering, washing-machines, safety, comfort, a real bed, a TV and so on and so boring. I truthfully thought it was the dumbest thing I had ever heard from him. There was not a chance in hell that I would swap this "freedom of choice" to that voluntary prison, as I regarded established society to be. It was unthinkable. Despite having had to go to hospital for alcohol detox several times in the past year, I deemed my life to be at its peak.

Without even giving his arguments and suggestions a thought I shifted into a higher gear and sped on with both the business and my addiction.

Simon's longing for more snug living quarters drove him to refurnish the trailer. He removed all the fixed fittings and bought two tiny, very nice armchairs and a small coffee table and turned one corner into a lounge area. A 120-centimetre wide mattress replaced the stiff trailer beds and he put in a thick rug and hung white curtains. It turned into a fabulous space. It felt like a new start and I hoped he would give up on his fantasising over an apartment.

Spring was in the air and warmth had begun its slow creep into Scandinavia. It was nice when we knew that the warmer seasons stood at the door. Winters in the trailer were cold sometimes since we didn't dare use the propane in case we passed out from being too intoxicated. We had disconnected the pipes as soon as we had bought the trailer, or the "Tinker-Thermos" as Simon called it. In Gothenburg, we seldom got below minus 5 Centigrade, 23 Fahrenheit, but despite our eiderdown sleeping bags, we could still get chilled to the bone.

The day he was done with the final details, we spent a night on the town to celebrate. Later in the evening, we were thoroughly partied through and both of us very much looked forward to sleeping cosily in the new, soft bed.

From a distance we could see the armchairs thrown out on the ground, among lots of other objects. The closer we got, the more we saw - it was all our stuff and it was damaged and discoloured by fire and soot. Our home was destroyed. I had left a candle burning when we had left that afternoon.

A man who lived in a house nearby came out and told us that he had been the one who had made the SOS call. The firemen had entered the trailer with smoke helmets after he had told them that there were people living inside. He had known about us for two months but had let us be since we had been on our best behaviour and kept the surrounding area clean. Many would have had us evicted despite this, since you could see what kind of people we were. That the man came out and talked to us at all helped dampen the shock a little. I was genuinely sad, at least as far as I was able to feel sadness. Simon was devastated. He had really tried to adapt to my not wanting to move inside, but now all his energy had run out. My belief in some kind of God always made it a bit easier for me to cope and find a meaning to whatever happened but now even I had to rethink the issue of our living quarters. The situation was a real knock-out. Within a month, we were subletting a one-bedroom apartment in the same part of town as where my mother lived.

I was trapped.

Seventeen

The first year, I was out of the flat 6 a.m. at the latest every day except Sundays when I put it off until it was time to walk to the pub. Sometimes, I stayed out all night and, if Simon wanted to go home, I stayed out by myself. I felt like a caged animal, escaping as soon as I could. Everything in my daily routine was animal-like, all about hunting, capturing and devouring my prey, the drugs. I kept the business afloat and decided that I wouldn't put my hard-earned money into paying rent. Instead, I registered at the local social welfare office and they put me up with rent and money for food and clothes. My disease of addiction was now evident and they didn't force me to look for a job, the money just kept coming without any demands from their part.

My craving for drugs pushed me harder than ever before and my mental health was at a new low. My faith in my God was there, as always, but now I sensed how shut-off I was from living a healthy life, though I was totally incapable of change. I almost never ate anything of substance. The only healthy things I did were walking all day long and eating fruits and drinking a lot of water. The fruit and water became a kind of mental lifeline for me since they were the only healthy things I put into my body.

Now, my mother knew where I lived and she often

came to see me. At this point, I had let go of all pretence towards her and she got to see me for who I had really become. I was so toughened in my attitudes that the pain and shame I felt when seeing her quickly passed, or rather were quickly and ferociously deafened. I often hung out in the park in the neighbourhood with my crowd of bench drunkards and she often saw me there in all different kinds of conditions. It was with other addicts that I had identified since my early teens and I didn't have the strength to beat around the bush anymore. There was also a kind of perverted pride in standing up for what I was. To live in drug addiction was my career and I had actually managed to reach a high position within this field because I had seen to always having money and therefore always having my fill.

One day, when I had been drinking beers in the park, I began to feel very strange. I left the others and walked a couple of blocks to the small pedestrian street in the middle of the borough. There I sat down on the cobblestones with my back against a shopwindow and started to cry. I was absolutely inconsolable. Many people from my circles and others who knew me through my family tried talking to me but I only screamed at them. Finally, somebody got hold of my mother, who was well-known in her part of town. She managed to get through to me. I remember it all. I felt as if all of this was happening to someone else. She walked with me to the emergency room at the large hospital close by and, there, I was put on a blood alcohol test. The meter showed a concentration of 4.7 mg/ml. For a normal person this would mean certain death. In Sweden a person's driver's license is taken away if they are caught having had 0.2 mg/ml in their blood while driving. I was admitted immediately and had to stay on the detox ward for ten days. Usually, it would have been a five-day treatment but I was so far gone they had to keep me in for twice that.

I was always very grateful for the care I got when I was treated for my alcoholism. This was my fourth detox. When I was admitted, they gave me shots of vitamin B to ensure the functioning of the nerves' synapses. I was told that it can be lethal to try to withdraw from alcohol on your own. The doctors told me that the only drug you could die detoxing from without medical care was alcohol. I had always thought it to be heroin but they just smiled wryly and told me that heroin addicts were mostly very whiny people when they detoxed and that, without competition, the most lethal drug in our society, both in the long- and short term, is the legal one - alcohol. As during the previous times, I was given Heminevrin, nicknamed "dry liquor", and it helped against the worst symptoms of the hangover. The staff came in at regular, short intervals to check my pulse 24 hours a day until the worst danger had passed. After four days I managed to eat a little.

I asked if I could get Heminevrin outside the hospital. It felt as if that could be a solution to not getting that severely drunk again. This was apparently a common request and always denied because Heminevrin was an extremely strong medication and could definitely not be used together with alcohol. I resentfully understood that yet another mind-altering substance wouldn't cure my obsession with using alcohol. I had tried changing drugs before and, up until now, nothing had helped me to calm down, to stop running or motivate me to stop, not even to lessen my consumption.

Still the fear of what might happen to me regarding my life-threatening and uncontrollable abuse made me lash out:

"So I'm supposed to drink myself to death then??!" I spat at the staff. They suggested that I take Antabuse instead.

My body struggled to repair itself. After a week on the ward I was slowly getting – marginally - better physically and mentally. The scare from having become so tremendously wrecked made me accept their "Antabuse-cure" and I began taking the pills several days before I was to be discharged.

Meanwhile, a new patient in the ward made a huge

impression on me when he told me his tale of why he had been admitted. He had been sober for nineteen years up until one month before when he'd decided to have a drink at an office party. One drink turned into several and later that evening he had lost his job. Within a week, his wife threw him out and he hadn't seen their children since. Here he was, one month later, having spent 100 000 SEK, 7700 pounds or 10,000 Euros, on booze, shaking uncontrollably and looking 20 years older than he was, sagging in the smoking area of the ward. By the looks of him, I would have guessed that he was a homeless drunkard. From his story, I vaguely sensed that I would have to have a zero-tolerance approach to alcohol if I was ever to lead a healthy life. I was definitely not in such a sacrificial mood, though. Instead, I told myself that the Antabuse would help me cut down my doses for a while and then I would learn to stay within the tipsy borders again. I might even get used to being without the drug for a few days and just go a little crazy every now and again, like 'normies' do.

I left the hospital with a prescription for Antabuse and, fifteen minutes later, I was sitting in the park with the gang, heaving beers again. All my good intentions gone with the warm breeze, sitting in the beautiful weather, savouring the luring promise of a wondrous afternoon on the bench. I recalled no different planning, there existed no other options and it was as if there had never been any. Not even the faintest echo of an option. Only bliss and thoughts of how many bottles I would need to buy to make it through the night and still have a few to carry me through before the store opened in the morning.

I used alcohol with no overly harmful effects from the Antabuse. Luckily... I had been given a large dose before I left the ward but then I hadn't taken any more. I continued as before and, after two months, I was admitted again. This time I was apprehended in the street for drunk and disorderly behaviour and, instead of taking me to a holding cell, the police dropped me off at a detox facility. The metre showed a 3,0 mg/ml blood alcohol level.

The next morning, I was back in hospital and was admitted for a five-day detox. I thought hard about this situation, about having to decimate my intake. When I got out this time, I made a deal with my mother. I let her be in charge of the money from the social welfare and only give me a small portion each day, enough to get a couple of strengthening flasks to get the day going. I saw to it that there was hashish and sometimes even amphetamines at home to break off the stupor before it got too bad and also began forcing myself to stay in the apartment more.

Now that I couldn't deafen my dysfunctional emotional state freely, the bottomless tediousness and the constant feelings of discomfort churned relentlessly inside me.

The business was slowly phased out – I could do nothing but focus on how to control my alcoholism at this point. I joined an organisation for sobriety based on seven steps. Most of the members of this small group where periodic users and, like me, most of them didn't have a desire to get to a stable state of sobriety. Despite the laid-back attitude toward sobriety, this group was too much for me. I always drank more after having been to a meeting. All the time, I longed for the calm and unity I hoped to attain with the effects of the liquor, but nowadays that effect lasted only a few minutes, if I reached it at all. Since my mid-teens I had only reached the state of mind I was chasing for short moments. Maybe an hour or, more often, less than that. The suffering, the hunt and the inner dissatisfaction had, since then, been my main steady companions - but to this fact I had turned every blind eye.

The restlessness drove me to travel again. Simon and I began visiting my siblings, who had now moved to Malmö, a town in the southern part of Sweden, and we spent weeks on end there. My criminal activities were almost down to nil, which meant that the cash flow was seriously diminishing. This resulted in my drug abuse becoming drastically decreased, whether I wanted it to or not. Time passed and I was constrained in my consumption but I still used from morning until night and every so often the binges turned sour, but not so bad as to force me to seek medical care. In my warped "reality", I had my addiction under control with the five-to-fifteen extra strong beers a day and the occasional narcotic to cool off or spice it up. But my anguish screamed out of an unquenched thirst for meaning with my life. At the beginning of 2001, I found out that we were going to have a child and, together, we decided to start a family.

"Are you sure about this?" I asked Simon. "You are more of a Joe than I've ever been. Will you be responsible and do your part as a parent, going through with this?"

He answered with overwhelming positivity that of course he would. I was scared out of my wits and couldn't in my wildest dreams fathom what parenthood meant. I thought that, with Simon sharing the responsibility and the love for our child, everything would automatically be miraculous and wondrous. Creative and enriching family life just like in the fairy tales. I really didn't have a clue.

I went to the maternity unit at the hospital for an appointment with a mid-wife there. We determined that I was pregnant and then I told her about my problems with alcohol, thinking that she already knew from my files in their on-line record system. She took this confession very calmly. After that visit, I never went back and wasn't contacted either. Admitting to my alcoholism was probably a cry for help. I told myself I had my abuse under control because I hadn't been hospitalised in almost eighteen months, but subconsciously I felt awful about the actual amount that I was using.

I began creating castles in the sky based on ideals about how my life would be with a child. This situation suddenly had me dreaming of a future which was something I had never spent any serious amounts of time doing before. These were very vague illusions of a life with a family. I painted fantasies of an existence which I wasn't anywhere near going to be able to re-enact. The reality was that I was a drug addict and that I fled into dreams about having a healthy and sound family.

I felt cornered in Gothenburg. I couldn't use the way I wanted to now that I was pregnant and also, I was a renowned addict there. I decided to ask my sister if I could move in with her and her family in Malmö while Simon would stay in Gothenburg and finish off our business and some odd jobs he had going there. My sister and her husband agreed. In April 2001, just into the fourth month of the pregnancy, I moved to Malmö.

It was nice to have a change of scene and it helped me to get a twisted kind of perspective about my addiction.

I still used but not every day and I remember noticing that I never managed to get two 33 centilitre cans down in a day during the whole term. I rationalised that having a beer or two would make me feel better and therefore the foetus wouldn't get affected by my body's own production of stressful substances from the horrible mood swings I always had when forced to be sober. Another factor in my ability to keep my blood alcohol levels down was that I had never felt better in my whole life. The utopian anticipation, or whatever it was, suited me perfectly. The worry, the chasing and always hunting pull, the emotional monsters were suddenly not as overpowering. The strain eased and I felt safer than I could ever remember feeling. I reflected about it being the hormones supplying me with some bodily chemical balance. I was also in a state of inner prayer more than any period before. During the whole pregnancy, I enjoyed living in the moment immensely. This was something I had never experienced before.

I discovered that I was very content being alone in this new city, free of Simon's and my strong but strange symbiosis. Our relationship was built on drugs and adventure and now I really needed space to take it easy and follow my own gut feeling. He came down and spent a few days with me every now and then and that was nice but it also felt good when he left.

I spent my days biking around, enjoying the beautiful summer and talking to the little life inside me and to my God. Towards the end of my second trimester, about six months in, I managed to sublet an apartment through my mother's good-will and Simon moved down permanently. In the middle of the seventh month I made the second appointment with a new mid-wife and after the check-up I was informed that everything seemed perfectly fine. Here, I made no confessions about my addiction. Everything was fine and I let it stay at that. At this point, I was still on social welfare and I have no idea how the transfer of my files from Gothenburg was done because no one ever confronted me about my addictive disease. A factor to consider in this was that I never told my social worker about me being pregnant.

The procedure that had applied to my type of "hopeless case" personality was transferred to Malmö - I never met my new social worker and probably they never realised that I was pregnant. As usual, I flew under the radar of a "normal" life and I carried on pursuing my reckless trajectory. With a growing child inside me my intake of alcohol, this potent drug, also made me a terribly ruthless person. It is frightening to think of how I was able to carry on as I did, unseen.

When we came into the eighth month, Simon was offered work on a project in another town and we agreed that he should take it. It was well-needed money. We decided that, despite the probable risk of him missing the birth of our child, this was an opportunity he shouldn't miss and off he went.

We had said that we didn't want to find out the gender of the baby, but when the birth was 10 days overdue I was feeling lonely and frightened and asked the mid-wife to tell me so as to bring renewed hope into the process. It was a little girl. I was overjoyed since this was what I'd hoped for. I was physically very worn out in the last weeks of the pregnancy and was having great difficulty moving about. Luckily, Simon got home before it was time. When we were almost three weeks overdue and a Caesarian was being planned for three days later, our daughter chose to come forth into the world the natural way. It was an enormous relief.

24 hours of labour were rough but at the same time the most wonderful blessing I had been granted in my life. I managed to pull through with only nitrous oxide and Simon's excellent words of encouragement. It was an overwhelmingly positive experience that towered over anything I had ever achieved before. I remember waking, in the middle of the night, getting up unsteadily and taking a shower. Afterwards, I stood for the longest while in silence, hovering beside the little-bitty tiny baby laying there in the plastic tub beside my bed, quietly listening to her light breaths. She was the most beautiful person I

had ever seen. She had her hands perfectly clasped as if in prayer and I was taken aback by this and had to look twice. The only honest relationship I had was with my God so her poise moved me beyond words. Even though I knew it was an unconscious act on my child's behalf, the symbolism of it brought on a force of timeless belonging and a strong urge to protect this baby, a living miracle, to the utmost of my abilities.

Reality turned out very differently and my addiction allowed neither strengthening nor protection for her.

Eighteen

Emma came in second place after the drugs. I did see to her needs to the best of my ability and of course I loved her immeasurably, but all of this through the filter of my primary priority – manipulating my unruly emotional life with alcohol. I had believed that the love and responsibility I felt for this innocent little human would overtake my destructive habits but, instead, my sense of isolation got worse. I feared that if I came out and told the truth, either my daughter or the drug, most probably both, would be taken away from me. I couldn't bear to even think about coming clean. To stop, or to restrict myself to using alcohol solely at weekends was not an option for me. The emotional turmoil was unbearable when I was sober. The impulses, sounding as if they were my own rational ideas, told me that a little, just one beer, would strengthen me and make me more able. The healthy part of me tried to counter with soft whispers about the truth of my disorder. But the loving urges were shut out by the louder voice of the egotistical justifications that were constantly hammering down on this softer voice of love. It was a very strenuous double nature, madly combatting in my brain.

Every night, I lay down to sleep choking on feelings of remorse and guilt, praying intensely for my daughter to have a good life.

Every day, I walked kilometre upon kilometre with the baby carriage packed with hot water, formula and diapers between the town's many liquor stores and parks.

My consumption was still low but I "had" to have something from waking until going back to bed. I was careful not to take too much for fear of passing out. On a couple of occasions, I smoked pot, but for the most part I was "only" tipsy: and always, never quite present with my child.

Always peering out at her through an intoxicated state.

One night when Emma was four months old, we woke to find the police standing at our bedside. We had forgotten to lock our front door and it would sometimes come open because of a draft that would blow through if the balcony door was ajar. A neighbour had called it in as a friendly gesture in case we were being burgled. When the officers sneaked in, they found us sleeping, with Emma in the crib and a bottle of wine on our nightstand. This led to a report to the social services.

I reacted calmly, since I realised deep down that I needed some kind of regulation, but at the same time it also awakened my protective instincts. The instincts to lie, manipulate and hide gained even more power and resurfaced enhanced: my most prominent characteristics. In this camouflaging game there came an adrenaline rush and my addiction flourished in this attempt at shielding us from the world. Helping Emma stay clear of the co-hell-ision became a huge concern now.

We were assigned a social worker from the "Children and Families" unit (CaF). This woman was extremely gullible. I could carry on more or less as before. An investigation was opened, which was routine in cases like this, and it would be ongoing for the next two years. During this time I could, without difficulty, keep on abusing alcohol as I had before. I left urine samples for screening for narcotics but, incredibly I didn't have to give them blood samples to check up on my alcohol consumption.

Every night, I lay beside my little girl and, in my mind, I begged her to forgive me, making plans for how the next day would be a better day. But every new day turned into the day before, with my insanity telling me that a beer this particular morning would lead to me being able to make this a better day and my raging emotions of anguish for the previous day screamed to be deafened. A never ending repetition, time and time again.

Simon's boys came to Malmö to visit their little sister. It was difficult for me to keep the facade up nowadays, despite them being there. When they had visited earlier in life I had always been the one to take it at least a bit easier on the drugs. Now that my irresponsibility had become all that much clearer to me, I used more to quiet the anguish and I felt horrible about not being able to straighten up. When they went home, I was filled with relief but also with terrifying emptiness and the realisation that the beautiful family I had fantasised about when I was pregnant was far from the reality. The repulsion for what I had become fuelled the impulse to use more and deafen everything.

To make matters worse, Simon and I were drifting quickly apart. Our stormy relationship didn't get the space it craved anymore. When Emma was six months old, we moved into a larger apartment, also with my mothers help. We hoped this would change things for the better between us but that didn't happen. I held onto the promise Simon had given me about him being there for our baby and me in this new life. A huge part of my tantrums when he didn't keep his word was about my space, my not being able to use. I wanted to have a binge at least sometimes, in the manner my dysfunction craved it, but it didn't work out that way. Simon was under the delusion that simply because I had given birth, my addictive pattern for "handling" life would suddenly disappear. I had had the same hopes for the both of us. Unfortunately, parenthood was not the cure for the disease of addiction. The norms stamped on being a woman and a mother didn't do the trick either. Just as it didn't change Simon as a result of him being a father.

My mother often came to visit us. In the end, it was she who threw Simon out. The investigation by the social services had come to an end and Emma was now two years old. I was left completely alone with sole responsibility for her, struggling with my addiction and living on social welfare. My mother still handled my money and it was deposited into her account. She portioned it out, a little every day, so that we would have food for the whole month and she also saw to it that the rent was paid. I still used part of what she distributed to buy alcohol. I hunted Simon down, obsessed with the promise he'd made, desperate for a chance to be able to flood my system with drugs but he wouldn't be persuaded to stay true to his word. I felt crazed by his betrayal, having been duped by his fine words about us being two parents sharing this responsibility.

I couldn't stand those strong emotions. I had to shut down with more drugs and, since the alcohol wouldn't be safe to use when I was "responsible" for my small child, I started dabbling in other drugs again. I found dealers who were reliable and, for a few months, I mixed alcohol, uppers and downers. Finally I was burnt out. I had never used as frantically before. The compulsion to keep myself intoxicated on a controlled level made my craze even worse. I felt hunted and imprisoned. While Simon had still been in the picture, I had been able to recuperate when the need arose but now it was all in, all the time. Keeping a steadily dazed state was a full-time job. Trying to take care of a child in this sick environment shattered me mentally at an escalating rate. Our whole situation rushed steeply downwards, bumping along in an insane race downhill.

My appearance was put to one side. Since we had closed down the business, my looks had once again slid way down the list of priorities. I had long, grey-speckled hair and wore mostly ragged, dark-coloured clothes. I looked as terribly worn out as I was. Emma didn't go to day care and the only contacts I kept up were with my mother and the deacons at the church in the borough. I was isolated, living in my safe bubble, constantly striving to keep my head above water. I didn't have the presence of mind to reflect over the terrible state our little family was actually in.

One morning in the spring of 2004, I asked my brother to come over and watch Emma for a while so that I could go outside and get a few beers in the sun. He grudgingly agreed and I got my first free time in more than six months. There, I met a very charming guy who invited me for a beer or two. I let him come home with me and there I started up a new relationship. He was very good with Emma and I got hooked on having someone to relieve me. The relationship was catastrophic though since we were both alcoholics and the only thing I truly valued was the extra time, if ever so little, I finally got.

One day when I was out with Emma, she ran straight out into the bicycle path. There wasn't a cyclist in sight but I didn't have the presence of mind to realise this and reacted instinctively, losing the straight face I rigidly put on when I was out with her. I screamed, drunkenly terrified and lost my balance for a short second. Exactly as this happened, a couple passed by. It was a couple pushing a baby carriage and the woman confronted me. I must have reeked of booze and I brushed her off with a curt remark about her being better off minding her own business. I walked away with Emma in her carriage, heading hurriedly home. I felt a nagging unease and, 20 metres from our house, a police car pulled up behind us. They got out of the vehicle and stopped me, telling me that they had gotten a phone call from a worried citizen about a small child in the care of a drunken woman. I tried to act as this was something I knew nothing about, but to no avail. My looks were easily identified. They wanted to come up and see how we lived and I cooperated without making a fuss. At home, my boyfriend was making dinner for us and was standing by the stove. The flat was neat and nicely furnished. They made the assessment that an immediate custody of Emma was unnecessary. I didn't even have to do an alcohol test but a new investigation was opened by the CaF. Now we got a new social worker and she was not as easily duped. I was also in a much more evident state of addiction this time around. The noose was tightened but again I didn't have to leave samples for alcohol abuse, only screening for narcotics. I kept using as before.

I wasn't in any shape to play the game anymore. The team from CaF were going to make a home visit early one morning. The evening and night before I just couldn't stop boozing and kept on opening beer after beer. Suddenly, it was 4 a.m. and I realised that I needed help to flee to the train station. Incredibly, I got hold of Simon over the phone. He came at six o'clock in the morning to help me with Emma and the luggage. I had decided to go to Gothenburg. We left the apartment 45 minutes before the scheduled visit so as not to run into the social workers but when we had gotten two blocks from our building they came driving towards us on a backstreet in their little municipal vehicle and braked in hard beside us. My mind cleared instantly and I pulled away from Simon to let him talk to them because I knew that I stank of booze. When they got out, they asked about our bags and we told them that Emma and I were going to friends in Småland. I made up a story about friends having invited us and even paid for the ticket and that I was not about to turn down this generous offer, such a lovely opportunity for Emma to go to the countryside. They amicably agreed and asked us to wait while they parked the car. As soon as they got in the car and drove off I hissed to Simon: "Now we run!"

We sprinted around the corner, pulling at the front doors of the apartment buildings and, unexpectedly, we actually found an open one. In a few seconds, we had dragged the carriage and ourselves into hiding. We stood there for the longest while before we called for a cab. The station in Malmö was no longer an option so we made our way to a bus stop: I got on one that took us to a smaller town nearby. We got tickets on another bus, not daring to go by train, and rode all the way up to Gothenburg on this one.

Well within the city limits, we got off a stop before the central station and took the tram to my mother's house. The police and a team of social workers had already been there and looked through her home. My mother was absolutely heartbroken by my course of action but she wanted to "protect" her grandchild and agreed to shield us until I was feeling better. The next day, I called CaF and, since we were at my mother's place, they let the whole thing be. I was given a new appointment for two week's time and was told to be back home by then. I made that meeting and continued with my alcohol abuse. CaF demanded new tests for narcotics but nothing regarding the alcohol.

After a short time back home, I was so badly drunken and burnt out that I had to leave town again. I left with Emma for the town of my birth, Borlänge, where I had family. They were shocked by my turning up without warning and by the awful condition I was in. We hadn't seen each other in more than a decade. My aunt helped us get a place to stay in a women's crisis centre in town. When explaining myself to the staff there, I put the blame on my circumstances in Malmö, on everything and everyone but myself and made up a story of feeling threatened on various fronts. Pure lies but anything went into getting a chance to recover from the terrible, constant hangover without having to go to hospital and risk Emma being taken into foster care. I used carefully-rationed amounts of spirits in the days to come, keeping my withdrawal within a humane limit. I was scared that my life would be at risk if I shocked the body too hard by quitting too fast, remembering the warning from the detox ward about alcohol withdrawal being the only deadly drug abstinence. After a little more than a week, I was well enough to travel back south to Malmö again.

After we had gotten back home, one disaster followed another in rapid succession. Simon came home to us one afternoon in August and we had a major row. We screamed and yelled at one another, which resulted in my being given an eviction notice for three months hence, on the last day of December 2004. A few days after that, the police came up to us when I was having beers with my boyfriend in a park while Emma ran around playing by herself. They dropped us off at our building and, once again, they didn't ask me to do a breath alcohol test but the social services where alerted about the incident. This happened at the beginning of October 2004. Emma had recently turned three years old and I was 38.

I really did try very hard to keep myself restrained but it was impossible. I was so caught in the impulse-driven behavioural patterns of addiction that I couldn't stand even thinking of being without the mind-altering substances flowing through my veins. To shut out such a dreadfully threatening scenario, I had to use even more to silence the panic that ensued. I was constantly governed by a roaring fear, echoing my emotional disorder.

My life was utterly unmanageable and Emma's daily routine was to be out with me on long walks during which I always had alcohol with me: at home she would watch TV and play mostly by herself. Simon had moved back to Gothenburg and wasn't interested in spending time with her, and even when he'd lived in Malmö he hadn't seen her more than a couple of times after moving out. I wasn't reachable through my tipsy state and when I was hungover I was unstable, unable to function and the filter between me and Emma was as thick as ever. Emma had me at home and I did feel a mother's love for her in my fenced-in heart but I was too far gone in my mental and emotional disability to be anything but a harmful presence to her.

There was no world in which I could function without being on alcohol. I was stuck with the image of alcohol as the reliever, clinging desperately to this delusion despite the fact that this drug hadn't had any positive effects for me in a long, long time. I followed an insane longing for the connectivity I had experienced with my drug of choice from the start, I needed that feeling to come back to me. It was hell on Earth to live like this, but I wasn't able to see that. What I did notice was that Emma suffered from the forced isolation she existed in.

Now the social services made hands-on efforts with our little family. We were soon to be homeless and they gave me two alternatives. Either we would be given a place to stay in worn-out barracks on the outskirts of town or we could go through a period of treatment at a rehab centre for mothers living in with their children out in the centre's location in the countryside.

I agreed to go to the rehab clinic for an information meeting and afterwards I weighed up the choices I had been given. Despite everything I had lived through, for the most part I had chosen the places I had lived in for myself. My isolation had been quite voluntary, even though my unhealthy emotional disposition toward alienation and the impulse-driven addiction were primary factors in those "choices". Now my hands were tied and I had only two options – and both reeked of caging me in. The barracks were terribly shabby and all sorts of people lived there. They were a last resort for the people who lived there and I could see that this place would be very harmful for us. On the other hand, going to a rehab facility was an extremely difficult alternative for me to accept. I saw the liquor store vanishing in a haze on the horizon. The decision was hard to make.

In the end, I did choose the rehab but it was not without serious qualms. The reason that weighed the heaviest though was Emma's wellbeing. I reckoned she could need a break from the city life.

Of my own accord I could never in a thousand years have come to the conclusion of a treatment centre being a solution to getting our lives in order.

Had I been on my own, I most definitely would have followed an impulse of a completely different nature.

Nineteen

We came to Malin's Minne, Malin's Memory, at the middle of December 2004. It was a Monday. The Friday before, social services had come on an unexpected visit. I was drunk and they took Emma away with them immediately. My little girl had to spend the three nights before we were due to leave at an orphanage. It was the first time we had been apart and I hardly remember that weekend. The pain of her not being there and the thoughts of her suffering were unbearable. The worst thing about it was that my mind trailed off into thoughts of her being better off without me.

I didn't have much money but what I had I poured into alcohol. The day before our departure, I was completely broke, which was something that had happened to me scarcely a handful of times through my whole addiction. My anguish set in and I hardly slept all night. The car came to fetch me early Monday morning and we went to get Emma.

She refused to look at me at first. It was horrible. I took her in my arms but couldn't find any words to console her. I had to coax her for the longest time, sitting next to her in the back seat before she at long last turned back into her usual, chatty self again. When we came to the rehab lodgings she turned silent again. She was used to it being just the two of us and must have felt my burning hostility towards being there. She refused to speak to anyone but me and for the first two weeks she only said the same two words to the other people there:

"Shove off!"

During that fortnight, she was carefully introduced to the day-care facility on the premises. She had never been to one regularly before, only to an open one that had a drop-in for kids in the company of their parents or guardians. And we had only been there a couple of times. This was an enormous change for both of us.

I was going through a horrid withdrawal. If I had told the nurse the truth about my condition she might have been able to give me something but the risk of her admitting me to a hospital was too great. I couldn't leave Emma alone in this environment. It was a dangerous detoxification: it felt as if my whole psyche was vibrating in oil and my physical health was extremely brittle. When the other clients asked me about, it I curtly answered that I had problems with my nerves. I didn't trust anybody, not even other addicts. I wasn't like them – in my way of thinking they didn't know half of what real addiction was about. None of them had lived life and tackled hardships the way I'd had to.

I just kept following the daily routines of the institution and after a week I managed to eat somewhat normally. For Emma, the food issue was a completely different matter. She had never had normal meal habits the way I'd had as a child. It became a tug of war between Emma, myself and the staff during the whole stay. At the time, I didn't realise that I had developed a severe eating disorder and that the food I had served Emma was extremely unvaried. I simply hadn't given that part of life much thought. She had gotten regular meals but mainly pasta, meatballs, fish sticks and burgers. Greens were not something I had let her get used to. Instead, I had given her lots of formula to be sure that she got enough protein, vitamins and minerals. I had no idea that formula contained as much sugar as it does.

We got through the first two weeks and Emma recovered from her environmental shock. The staff told me later that she had adapted quicker than most. I saw that she was noticeably more good-humoured every day. It was a relief but also very painful to realise how well she functioned with other people. It was too obvious that the isolation I had forced upon her was exactly the opposite of what she needed and I reflected on how she sincerely enjoyed the company of others. For my part, it was a very different story. I didn't have any issues that would have meant that I would have benefited from being in that place. I listened during the group sessions and if I spoke I said only that what was expected of me. Isolation was my only and much-relished oasis. I kept to myself as much as possible.

Many people have difficulties accepting that they suffer from an addictive disorder due to so many misconceptions about addiction. The ideas range widely from addicts not being able to hold down a job, have a family or have money, so if people have those they can't be 'real' addicts, or they haven't used large enough amounts of narcotics or alcohol to consider themselves, or be considered, to be an addict. Also, other drugs are often considered more harmful – the alcoholic points fingers at the user of narcotics, the person using narcotics is disgusted by the alcoholic, and so on. For me, and many like me, it was the other way around – I saw them all as amateurs, leisure users. I set myself apart from everyone else.

I could accept that this treatment might work for other people but not for a seasoned addict and world-despising person like me. Everything I experienced and heard at Malin's Minne was of course stored in my memory, but my days in active addiction were far from over.

This was a treatment centre that advised its clients to learn to use the twelve-step method as a means of taking care of our ongoing recovery after we went back home again. We were introduced to organisations such as Alcoholics Anonymous, AA, and Narcotics Anonymous, NA. Twice a week, we were bussed to lunch meetings to different groups at these organisations. I always felt pressure and a diffuse threat at the centre but when I sat at these meetings I experienced a sense of calm that

I couldn't explain. I thought it was the relished freedom of getting away from the suffocating environment at the institution, but in hindsight I can see that it was more than that. I related to what people there were talking about, even though it was completely on a subconscious level. My inbuilt scepticism towards organisations and non-profit gatherings couldn't find any sectarian tendencies in these groups. There, I listened to other people like never before. It was very strange.

At my second meeting a man who had been sober for 25 years looked straight at me, tilted his head a little and showing a hint of a knowing smile he said with an affectionate voice:

"There aren't any fun binges left."

I sat there and could only stare at him as if paralysed. I wanted to just run out of there but I couldn't move, so I sat there, stiff as a stick and, suddenly, the tears came. I knew what he said was true since I hadn't had a single fun spree except for a few times in my early teens and this stood out clearly in that moment. I sat there silently crying, frozen like a wounded animal and it hurt terribly. I hadn't cried from the core of my being in many years and only a handful of times in my whole life. The truth of what he'd said was unchallengeable. Even though I was well-disciplined in shutting out the unpleasant, which was an almost automatic response if something unwanted disturbed me, my defences failed to protect me against this statement. His straightforward words etched themselves onto my deepest core. It was the first thing that had rung true and irrefutable with me in a very, very long time. If ever.

Slowly, I got better physically and, without the intoxication in my life, I got more stable mentally and my days became easier to get through. My wall against the world was still there to defend me and, outwardly, I did everything that was asked of me, but inside nothing happened except that I got a lot of information about known common factors, symptoms, of the disease of addiction. That flow of information was nothing I applied to myself but I couldn't evade it. I heard about characteristics such as self-centredness, an inability to stop using drugs despite the continuous anguish and the blindness to the consequences of one's addictions and the hurt inflicted upon others. Another thing they told us was that an addictive disorder is the symptom of an emotional handicap. I heard the words but for the life of me I couldn't relate to them. As usual, I began stitching on a theory of my own instead of listening to the experience of others. I came to the conclusion that there was something physically wrong with me which meant I couldn't function without mind-altering substances in my body. I never stopped to consider the logic or the studies that had been weighed into the descriptions that these professionals had shared with us. My theory justified other aspects as well and asserted that there was something far worse wrong with me than with all the other millions upon millions of addicts in the world and I was especially unlike the ones who managed to stay clean. I would never be able to be as perceptive and honest as they were. That I fulfilled another of the characteristics, the one of irrational self-pity, never crossed my "insightful" mind...

I heard that the hell of being a slave to drugs was just as horrid regardless of amounts, living conditions, types of drug and, if you were a weekend addict, full-time or periodic user but I bucked at the thought of being like anyone else.

This characteristic of an addict's feelings of being especially different from others was one of the most common denominators. This I heard hundreds of times before but was utterly unable to see that this symptom was precisely what I was suffering from.

There were a few life stories that I happened to hear shared at meetings where the tellers had been rough enough in their addiction for me to be able to relate to them even though they weren't exactly like mine. There were also two women in the staff who had been sober for many years and I understood that they had been "professional" users in the past. These fates were stored in my memory but I continued to shut out any kind of fellowship. In that reaction, something started happening in the furthest backwaters of my consciousness, like an irritatingly gnawing itch. In retrospect, I can see that it was the first minuscule awakening of insight about my secluded personality. About my isolation, even from my own daughter. But my defences and fearful instincts still got the better of me. Sobriety loomed as a threat to my wellbeing, not as a vision of freedom.

We stayed at the treatment centre for five months. After three months, I was allowed to leave for a few days at a time at regular intervals and we went to Gothenburg where we stayed with my mother. I bought alcohol as soon as we got there. The staff understood that I had been using and tried to get me to come clean about it but I admitted nothing. They had a lot of experience with clients suffering from addiction and easily saw through me. I wasn't getting anywhere with my recovery.

Before I was discharged, we had been given a room in Malmö in a collective run by social services. I also got a prolonged treatment plan that required that Emma and I be back at the centre every third weekend. I understood that they knew I would keep on abusing alcohol and they wanted to follow up on how Emma was doing - and me too, I suppose. It was also decided that Emma would go to a daycare centre in Malmö for four hours a day, four days a week. It was a specialised place where the focus lay on both the child and the parent so I would also be present with her the whole time.

My personal space was being limited. I accepted this to a degree. Emma had blossomed and I felt better physically than I had in more than two decades. I had a notion that it could never get as bad for us as it had been before. I had taken in at least some of the information about addiction that I'd been exposed to. I believed I would be able to conduct myself better now.

When we arrived in Malmö tugging all our luggage behind us, we walked straight from the train station to Systembolaget. That was not how I had planned our arrival when I woke up that morning at the treatment centre, but the thought of a beer had grown stronger every second after we had gotten on the train and, during the 45 minute ride, the urge had overtaken any other options. Nothing else existed but getting just one sip. Emma's sad looks in my direction bit into my heart but they didn't sway me. The next day, we had planned to meet up with the rehab group to take part in an excursion in Malmö but we never got that far. I was so hungover that I had to have a "resetter" to be able to function at all.

Our hell latched on to where I had left off. I only wanted to shut out the information I had been given, I needed that wondrous binge that I had been told I never would have again and I didn't want to keep hurting Emma now that I was painfully aware that I was hurting her beyond words.

I didn't want to be who I was but I just couldn't stop myself.

Twenty

It was a Friday at the end of July and we were going out of town to spend one of our weekends at Malin's Minne. I hadn't been found out all summer and I had been doing everything according to the plans laid out for our little family. Except regarding the alcohol of course. I was in an even more isolated condition and Emma and I had not had a nice summer. Still no blood tests to determine how I used alcohol, only screenings for narcotics and alcohol breath-tests.

I woke up with anxiety over having to leave Malmö and decided that I would have two small ciders as soon as the store opened. The alcohol level would have come down to zero by the time we arrived at the rehab. No sooner said than done. Those two cans went down without a problem but then I just couldn't stop. I bought another can. I thought this was strange - I wasn't hungover and I had this very important part of the plan to fulfil. I was very strict about following through on these official commitments so as not to be questioned and having my "freedom" taken away. As always watching out for my own agenda. But not this day. There was no stopping me. I went and bought one more, then another and of course there would be no time for the body to process that much alcohol. It was as if I was looking at myself from the outside, mesmerized at what I was doing. It had happened before, innumerable times, but never as senselessly as this and was especially problematic given the danger this behaviour posed to my continued custody of Emma.

When we had gone out that morning I had brought along our weekend-luggage and we had roamed the city all day with our sights set on getting on the train. Now that I had gotten too drunk I had to tell Emma.

“Honey, we can’t go to Malin’s Minne today. I’m not feeling well.”

My little angel girl, soon to be four years old, who almost never set herself up against me, pinned me with her gaze, furrowed her brows and, furiously angry with me, hissed:

“Mother! You promised!” I could see tears burning in her eyes, the pure pain of her aching soul.

It was as if all the air went out of me and I suddenly saw clearly what I had been doing. With those three small words, she vented and expressed all the hurt, sorrow, frustration and disappointment she had been harbouring that summer. I saw how those weekends had truly been the only thing she had had to look forward to, they had been her lifeline during the months that had passed. I, who was supposed to protect her from the evils of this world, was the one inflicting this agony on her! I looked at her little face, showing such determined resolve and at the same time such bottomless despair that I could only answer her:

"Okay, honey. Of course we're going."

Come hell or worse, my heart broke for her suffering and I had to take her. I couldn't do this to her anymore.

We made the journey and, for the first time ever, the staff said that I didn't have to breathe into the alcohol meter. We could just go up to our room to unpack and dinner would be left outside our dormitory by the delivery van in a short while. I couldn't believe my ears but didn't argue.

When we were folding our things away in the closet, one of the staff members came and knocked at our door. She apologised and said that I had to perform the alcohol test anyway. One of the other clients had said that she thought I looked drunk. I blew into the gadget and literally saw how her jaw dropped.

"Lotten," she said with doubt and astonishment in her tone, "you have a 3,2 blood alcohol level!" Her eyes bulged at me like round unblinking globes. "We will bring the food upstairs for you. You are not to come into contact with the other clients!"

She shook her head as she walked off to tell the rest of the staff.

Now I understood why I hadn't felt hungover that morning - I had still been drunk.

That weekend was pure hell. I was horribly abstinent. The

social services were to be contacted on Monday and I was deliriously preparing for the worst: having Emma taken away from me. The torment crawled, pierced through my mind and body. Waking nightmares played out and scenarios spun day and night in a constant, uncontrollable, pulsating flow. It felt as if I was experiencing psychosis. I didn't know the difference between sleeping and waking. I ought to have been hospitalised. Emma was with the others and I hardly got out of bed for three days.

The decision from CaF didn't come until Wednesday. Five nights and days of nightmarish physical and mental torment. They still seem as the longest days I've ever experienced in my whole life.

There would be no emergency foster care of Emma. I was given two months at Malin's Minne as a relapse treatment period. I thanked all the Gods and all the stars and told myself that I would never, ever, put us in this position again. My parental instincts had become painfully strong these past few days and I couldn't get my head around how I could have let it get this far.

It was called a relapse treatment but for me, who had never planned to stop using, I understood that I hadn't actually relapsed. The first time at Malin's Minne I had been abstinent but not sober as in being in sobriety. I was not there with a true desire to set a new course for changing my way of life.

I didn't care what they called it, this time I was going

to learn from my mistakes and get it into my system that I could only use moderately from now on. During this treatment, I was forbidden to read books. At the first opportunity I'd had during our first stay at Malin's Minne, I got a library card in the nearest town. Now the staff explained to me that I neglected my daughter, other people and the treatment by not being present while devouring my books. This I could accept and see very clearly. Ever since I had learned to read as a little child, I had kept on reading, always and everywhere, even while bingeing on benches or in pubs and restaurants. Even though the staff told me that this was a symptom of my social inadequacy and an addictive behaviour pattern, I was blind to drawing the parallel between this obsessive behaviour and my drug abuse.

After having been in the rehab centre for three weeks, Emma and I got to go by ourselves to a nearby public bath on Sundays. These were great outings for us. During the summer that had passed, we had hardly done anything fun or sensible, since I had only been hunting for the perfect binge. One Sunday, we passed in front of Systembolaget and for the first time in Emma's entire life I told her that we would never enter such a store again. I bit my tongue the very second I uttered the words. I had a rule not to promise her anything so that I wouldn't break my promises and then hurt her even more. This promise came at a moment of weakness when we'd had a close and joyous time in the pool. I had reflected on the terrible truth of us never having enjoyed such activities together before and in an instant I suddenly had a glimpse of how our impoverished home-life was because I always put the alcohol first, at all costs. At the cost of never having fun with my baby girl.

Silently, I prayed to be freed from the guilt, it was too painful to bear. To pray to be freed from my addiction never crossed my mind.

Isolation was still my fort and I couldn't relate to people other than in the instinctive bursts of parenthood towards Emma. Everyone but my daughter were shadow figures to me. A week before we were to move back to Malmö again, I lay in bed, rummaging through my being. I searched and prayed to find something that could be at the core of my alienation. Anything, just to have something true to share in the group. I prayed to find and be able to say at least one sincere thing in all of the eight months I had been at Malin's Minne that year. I didn't know why I suddenly, in that moment, listened to that inner voice, but something subconscious, deep down inside, pounded so hard at me, incessantly urging me to rummage for something that might create a crack in the thick wall of my fort, and for once, I took heed.

The next day, I asked to be given an opportunity to

share with the group. I had to force myself to utter the words and truly didn't fully understand why this felt so important. Why did I have to put myself through this suffering and humiliation? But there was the insistent voice inside, pushing me to speak out loud.

"I have never felt as if I was a part of humanity. I have thought that if there is such a thing as reincarnation I can't have ever been born on this planet before. I don't understand how people think, how they can treat their planet and fellow humans in this awful way and I have always considered myself to be better off not taking part in the ignorance of this world!"

It felt like the most embarrassing thing I had ever told anyone. Everyone in the group remained very silent and stared at me as if I was actually an alien. Everyone but the therapist who had been sober for fifteen years. In her eyes, I saw a sparkle of recognition and a discreet expression of familiarity. There was even a hint of a smile which she tried to hold back. It was the most true thing I had ever admitted about myself. I had made the only contribution, even if it was mostly forced, to this whole stint of therapy.

After exposing myself to the group, I felt more vulnerable than any time before in my life. The others distanced themselves completely from me and I from them. For the first time, I was hurt by their shunning attitudes and that kind of emotion was new to me. I put up the steel barrier. Some fleeting thoughts of sharing my feelings of sadness with the group were quickly beheaded as soon as they dared show their vulnerability. The pain of these wanting feelings was nothing I felt I deserved.

The fact that I had opened my mouth there and then did create the tiniest crack and let the smallest trickle of truth make its way into my all-consuming fortress. It also led to the evil ruler being threatened by the army of the good. My murderous disease now stationed even more of its ruthless troops to keep the threat of healthy choices shut off. Death stood fast at my fortress' door, rising from the deepest dungeons to the highest tower. The steep road now plummeted toward the abyss.

I became more blinkered and single-minded than I had ever been. When the relapse treatment was over and we were on the 45-minute train ride back home again, I couldn't even wait until we arrived in Malmö but got off the train in Lund not fifteen minutes from home. This happened to be the town where Emma and I had gone swimming on Sundays and outside this same Systembolag was where I had recently made my promise. I resolutely entered the liquor store with all our luggage and Emma stared angrily at me, sticking her chin out and said loudly:

"Mother you promised! You said we would never go in there again!"

I cursed my weak moment. Having made that promise

was the stupidest thing I could have done and it was the absolutely worst one to break.

I had never apologised for all the times I had taken her with me into public toilets to have my pick-me-ups or because I had to refill my camouflage bottles. Every time I pushed away my anguish, reasoning that I knew I would keep doing this and that she wouldn't be helped if I pretended anything else. But now I had really done it. I felt forced to break another rule of the things I had decided not to do to her. I lied. I picked up a can of cider.

"This is not the same thing as beer. This is like fruit squash."

Quick as she is, she countered:

"Oh, but that's great, then I can have a sip too."

I felt and saw in her body language that she had seen straight through me. I remembered how sensitive I had been to grown-ups and their acting when I was a child. Despite those memories, I couldn't come clean and admit my lie and I could absolutely not walk away from the booze. I did swear that I would never put myself in this position again. Not regarding the addiction, I meant the promises...

"No, I think you would like a Coke much more," I mumbled, swearing in my mind all the way.

I broke a third rule. Never give a bribe in direct correlation to the incident I needed to cover up. I only "bribed" when I wanted her to be distracted and when I thought she wouldn't realise it was a bribe. Now it was very obvious.

An image of the horrible sinking feeling my little girl must have gotten in the pit of her stomach flashed before my eyes. I quickly shut it out. I would be drunk soon and she would be exposed to our miserable life again. A child alone and abandoned, despite being in the care of her own mother. That Coke must have come with a bitter taste. The lie had been so obvious and under the surface simmered a realisation of the amounts of alcohol I would have to use to quiet the shame and guilt. I knew she felt pain because of me double-crossing her. We both suffered immensely but her torment was by far the worst.

The pleasing, revitalising and joyous binge that I had pictured was further away than ever.

Twenty-one

Once again, a plan made for me by CaF and the treatment centre. I was to start on a project run by Malmö municipality for women with the disease of addiction. I would get a subsidised work placement and, as long as I remained sober and the employer was satisfied, I would get continuous employment after two years at the workplace. I was supposed to sign up for this soon after we had arrived back in town but it was put off. The project staff wanted me to get my everyday life sorted out first. I was told that I could start in two and a half months, in January 2006.

So, instead of working, my days consisted of leaving Emma at her new daycare centre and picking her up at the end of the day. It was a normal facility this time so I had many hours to myself. I dropped her off at 9 a.m., Monday through Friday, and picked her up at about 3 or 4 p.m. In the morning, immediately after leaving her, I went to a public toilet to pour the cans of beer, which I had hidden in my huge purse, into my camouflaged bottle. At midday, I had lunch, laid off the alcohol for a bit and rested until 3 p.m., then I went and bought whatever rations I needed for the afternoon, evening and the morning after and then I picked her up.

This was how our days went by. I felt lots of anxiety and had never been this chained to my drug abuse before.

Emma became more and more apathetic and even though I really went out of my way to try to cheer her up and get her motivated, her flame seldom ignited. Her sadness burned me in my conscience.

It happened on a Thursday afternoon in the first week of November. I was resting after lunch when the phone rang. It was the daycare centre. I wasn't supposed to fetch Emma for another three hours and I was rather intoxicated from the morning doses. Emma was sick and I had to pick her up. I stuffed as many mints as I could into my mouth and rushed over. Emma was running a high fever and was burning hot. I had to help her get dressed and then we headed home by bus. She had hardly been sick in her entire life but the few times she had she'd been very clingy. Now she barely looked at me. I tried to get her attention at least so as to be able to comfort her but she didn't want to connect with me. It hit me hard, realising that this was actually how she had been for several weeks now and I could suddenly see clearly that her distancing herself from me would only continue to get worse.

My beautiful little girl sat silently staring out of the bus window when my phone rang. The display showed that the call was coming from an unknown number. When I was drunk, I never answered if I didn't know who it was. I knew it would almost certainly be social services. Except for my mother they were the only ones in continuous and frequent contact with us.

Our lives over the past few weeks fluttered in sequence through my mind in an instant. I saw Emma's increasing and alarming suffering, my inability to shape up and, all too clearly, how the intoxication was the only agenda I had put any real effort into planning and caring about in our daily routine. I answered the call.

It was one of our social workers from CaF and she immediately heard that I was drunk. She told me that she would be coming over right away. Despite having answered the phone due to the awful realisation of how dreadful our lives had become I was now overwhelmed by the strongest urge to flee.

"I'll keep us hidden until the morning when I can give them a negative test for the alcohol."

The thoughts and emotions raged inside me but one look at Emma, who just sat there, staring blankly out the bus window, far from the happy, talkative and energetic child she had been at Malin's Minne, made me renew my resolve. There was nowhere to run anymore.

I couldn't stop using and I had proven that to myself by now. Emma deserved a fair chance in life. It took all the emotional willpower I could muster to walk us home from the bus stop, take the stairs up to the collective and stay put in our little room, waiting for them to arrive. I felt the worst pain I had ever experienced. There are no words to convey those unending minutes of incessant hurt.

Emma met the social workers at the front door and tried to act happy, instinctively charming them in an unconscious effort to distract them from my sorry state. They had forgotten the alcohol metre in their hurry to get to us but my intoxication was unquestionable, especially now that I had let go of all pretence. One of them left to get the metre anyway since they had to be able to document exactly what condition I was in.

Despair took over my struggles to remain composed and I tried to convince them to let us stay some place together. I explained that I would be able to stay sober if they locked us up somewhere. This outburst got me an empathetic hand on my shoulder and the social worker answered to my plea with sadness in her voice:

"It won't work that way this time Lotten. You have been given all the chances we can offer you at this point. You will have to make a change, but of your own volition now."

I knew that this was the way it had to be but that knowledge didn't silence the screams of anguish that sliced me raw inside. I took a moment to pull myself together and then I quietly asked to be allowed a moment alone with Emma. They nodded in agreement and I said a silent prayer to my God for guidance to be able to soothe Emma's separation anxiety.

We sat on her bed and talked for a long while. My mind was in that crystal-clear mode I got into in precarious situations, though this time I was all but emotionally shut off. We talked about the information she had gotten about addiction at the rehab centre's daycare. There they had explained to her that we were staying there because I got very sick from drinking beer. That piece of information was of great value to me at this moment.

"Emma, you know that I have been using beer ever since we got home from Malin's Minne. It is not good for you to have me around you when I'm sick like this all the time. You will be staying at a place that is a lot like our rehab. The grown-ups there are really, really nice and there will be lots of other children for you to play with too."

She hugged me and said:

"Okay. I know, mother. I know."

While we packed her bags, I told her how sad I was for not having gotten better and having caused her to wind up in this terrible situation. I couldn't show her the full extent of my screeching anguish but I did cry. Sorting through her stuff, we spoke of serious things and I also tried to focus on the positive aspects, even joking a few times between the tears. I wanted her to know, without a doubt, how bad I felt and at the same time underline that this was good for both of us. Everything to try to ease her pain as much as I could. She cried a little too and we hugged each other a lot.

"I'm coming to see you, you know. This is all my stupid

disease's fault – this whole mess is about me being very ill. You, you are the light of the world, my darling child!"

We stuffed Bear, the nicest clothes, a few books and some other items that she chosen for herself into a suitcase. It took us over an hour and then they left. I watched from the balcony as they got in the car and then they drove off to the city's orphanage with my little girl.

I sat in my room, literally howling and screaming at myself, crying out like a wounded animal. It was the worst pain I had suffered in my entire life. That little wondrous person and all the horrible hours, days and years that I had put her through. The bottomless worthlessness I felt...

I knew that Emma would suffer without me because, despite my drunkenness, we'd always had a strong bond and a child is always bound to her parent as I was to her. Despite my mistreatment of her, I loved her more than anybody, as much as it was ever possible for me to do so with my skewed emotional development. We had always done lot of talking and hugging, and had been on numerous outings but all of it was always through my filter of intoxication. Thinking of what I had done hurt too much – I blanked out the question of how the hell this could have happened. It was unimaginable.

After a while, I couldn't bare this turmoil of feelings any more. I went out and bought more alcohol and wandered aimlessly for hours. The next morning, I called the orphanage to find out when I could visit. They told me I had to wait until after the weekend and I continued binging on alcohol unrestrainedly in a manner that I had never done before. I hardly remember the next two days, all that mattered was shutting down. On the Sunday, I began cutting down and on Monday I was told that I could visit the next day.

Emma had been terribly sick over the weekend. They had taken her to the emergency room at the hospital. Her temperature had risen and she had been in a sickly delirium for three days. I felt a sort of gratitude for this. It meant that she had slowly adapted to her new environment through the veils of that feverish, dreamy state and also she had received a lot of care and sympathy in her first encounters with the staff during those first days. The feeling of being lost and her missing me had surely been present but the shock over the separation had been dampened by her having to deal with the physical ailment competing for her attention. I actually thanked our lucky stars for this.

The staff at Malin's Minne had told me that I was a very good mother as long as I was sober and also that I had given Emma some kind of solid platform despite my active addiction. This had been evident in how quickly she had adapted at the rehab centre. Now she showed her self-confidence and sense of self-worth at the orphanage as well. Despite obvious feelings of abandonment which came through, she still showed a strong sense of self and was able to play and have fun as well as cry and speak openly about what had happened.

The staff and I sat down to draw up a schedule for my visits and I suggested between 3 and 6 p.m. The children's show that she loved began at 6 so I reasoned that it would be good for her to have this distraction after my leaving. They agreed. I was allowed four weekly visits. Mondays, Wednesdays, Fridays and Sundays. I was permitted to call all other evenings to say goodnight. These calls were to be made at 5.30 p.m. On these phone-call days, I tried to keep my alcohol level as moderate as possible until that time. On the days I was visiting I had to pass by the addictive ward at the hospital and do sobriety testing first. Mostly it was breathing into the alcohol metre but sometimes they wanted to test for narcotics as well. Still no blood samples to show my actual intake of alcohol though.

Emma was allowed to go to her usual day-care centre and was picked up by cab every weekday morning. The staff at the orphanage were very sweet and competent people so Emma adapted to the routines quite quickly. Of course, she still missed me terribly and nothing could quench her longing for her mother but it was still better for her to be there. I understood this without a doubt. Finally, she had adults who primarily saw to her needs, unlike me who always had my alcohol dosage to take care of. Even when I was hungover, I was still out of balance and I never stayed sober for the three or four days it took to get well again. In the orphanage, she got to be a kid and didn't have to worry about me all the time.

I did what I could to ease her sadness and tried my utmost to give some kind of silver lining to her everyday life. We had the hours when I visited and we filled them with hugging and playing. Emma had her own room and I often brought photographs of our different family members and we put them on the walls. I brought posters from home and bought new ones and brought potted plants that she could decorate her room with. I also read to her a lot so that we could be sitting cozily together, as close as possible, for as long as possible. I was also allowed to have dinner with her. These were intense hours.

I always began the parting ritual fifteen minutes before I was supposed to leave so we didn't get more stressed out than we already were. There was a powerful mix of feelings in going through this routine. I was drained every time I left the house. It was wonderful to be near her but it was always mingled with constant sorrow and worry, shame and guilt. I longed for her even when she was in my arms.

I rode my bike straight from the visits to the liquor store and always got terribly drunk. I locked myself in the public toilet at the shopping centre and sat there, gulping down at least two large cans of the strongest beer but no relief was to be found anymore. The only effect might have been a brief distraction from my longing, replacing it with wallowing in self-pity and self-loathing until I fell asleep in my bed at night. I had 40 hours to be drunk until I had to get myself back in some kind of order and ready myself for the next visit.

I moved out from the place where we had lived together because it was a collective for single mothers who had their children with them. I got another room where only women lived and children could come to visit. I decided to tell Emma that I had moved out and that I was at the hospital ward. She had been with me to the addictive ward earlier and had met my doctor so she knew about this place. It was also at least a partial truth since I went there every time before I came to her. I tried to tell her the truth as far as possible but left out the details that might make her even sadder. I didn't want to tell her that I had a new home without her. Then she would surely want to visit and afterwards she would yearn, even more than she already did, to be allowed to move back in with me and hurting in fantasies of us living together. I was very grateful that she didn't ask me about where I slept. I had made up my mind not to lie to her again and I weighed every word in a delicate balance when we were together. I prayed for guidance to be given the right words in our conversations and to be granted the ability to ease the pain my daughter lived with. She never asked about my alcohol habits. She knew, the way children know, exactly how that wasn't working out.

The weeks dragged on with the routines of the visits and the phone calls and of course the boozing. I had called the daycare centre already on the Monday after Emma had moved and told them what had happened. I asked them to please pay attention to how Emma was doing. They called at the beginning of December and told me that she seemed to be doing fine and that she talked about what had happened, which I took as a good sign. It was a huge relief to hear that she didn't bottle it all up. The teacher asked if I would come and watch the children on the feast day of Sankta Lucia, which is on the 13th of December. This tradition, celebrating Saint Lucia with candles and singing, would be held in a shopping mall in the neighbourhood. I checked with CaF and they agreed that it would be alright for me to attend. I was always careful to ask and follow the rules regarding my seeing Emma and tried to consider what would be good for her, especially when it came to things outside of her routine.

I sat in the cafeteria when the children filed in, dressed

in the customary white robes, singing the songs celebrating light and the winter season. Several of the children, including Emma, were dressed as Saint Lucia with a crown of electric candles on their heads. I have always been one to burst into tears when children perform, feeling a mixture of joy and sentimentality, but on this occasion my tears came only from sorrow and terror as I was confronted with what my disease had driven me to lose. She was so beautiful in her innocence and her calm, composed performance. At the same time, I saw how well she fit in with her group of friends and that she actually smiled and laughed with the other children. Seeing this made me cry even harder but also gave me hope that she would make it in life, whatever happened to me. She smiled widely with pride, waving to me when she saw me sitting in the crowd. Thankfully, the lights were dimmed and she didn't see that my face was puffy from crying.

I applied for permission for us to go and see my mother over Christmas and my request was approved. We were to leave on the morning of Christmas Eve and would get to stay in Gothenburg for five days. The day before we were due to leave, I promised Emma that I would come early in the morning so that we could have breakfast together and pack her stuff without having to hurry.

"Mom, I'll keep my pyjamas on until you come and then you can dress me tomorrow!" I promised I would be there.

When I left the orphanage that evening, I took my usual route to the liquor store and this day I went directly back to my room to wrap the gifts. I wasn't used to ritual chores like this and I was bombarded with emotions which forced me to take long breaks. Thoughts of normal families and their healthy relationships had haunted me for a while and this evening it got worse, of course. I also thought of Emma's earlier Christmases and birthdays which I had hardly given any attention to. I speculated with intensified focus about whether I would ever live with her again. Subconsciously, this was a debate about whether I would be able to stop using drugs or not because that was the only way that this could ever happen. Suddenly, it was past midnight and I had one more package to wrap and one and a half beers left to finish off. I didn't think about what I was doing when I emptied the cans.

The next morning, I was making good time but when I came to the ward's emergency room where I went to do my tests at the weekend, the metre showed 0.2 blood alcohol level. I knew I wouldn't be let into the orphanage that way. I phoned and I only told the staff that I was going to be late and to Emma I said that I had to wait for the doctor before I could come to her. I lied. Again. I found a store that was open and bought two litres of Coke which I drank hastily and then filled the empty bottle with water. I peddled my bike as fast as I could to increase my metabolism and drank lots of water, hoping to help my body burn the alcohol. After two hours I returned to the hospital and the metre was clear.

When I came to Emma it was almost lunchtime and she was still in her nightgown. I could tell that she had been very worried. She was so emotionally drained when I showed up that she started blabbering questions and blurting angry accusations at the doctor for making me so late. I answered with short and indecipherable mumblings so as not to have to lie even more. I had feared that we wouldn't be able able to go as planned and was totally exhausted. But we did get to go on our trip and during the next five days I didn't have a single drop of alcohol. I had terrible troubles with my "nerves" though and had to rest a lot but it was clear that for Emma this was her Christmas in paradise. The only thing she really wanted deep down in her heart was for me to be sober and that wish had come true.

When we got back to Malmö, I was allowed to put Emma to bed in her room for the first time. It was a nice gesture from the staff now that we had been together for so many days. I left after she had fallen asleep and went directly to the pub. Thoughts of her waking and missing me and my own longing for her ached beyond ache and it was too difficult to cope with sober. I did what characters do in TV shows and the movies – I lifted the glass with the yellow liquid to "strengthen" me in this emotional chaos. Instead of living through it and growing stronger and wiser as a person, I, as always, used the opium for the masses - alcohol - to try to deafen the issue at hand. My psyche rushed down a steep and slippery slope over the next few days. My lifelong perception of the outer world being a strange place now embarked on its beginning to include my own inner world.

Social services were searching for a family for Emma. It hurt to know this but I realised that I couldn't take care of my daughter at all. I was truly grateful that these professional people had taken care of her. To me, this was a service to our family, especially to Emma. I was resigned to the fact that I put my addiction before my parenthood.

I had begun using larger amounts and if I couldn't be drunk, my thought patterns became more and more irrational and manic. I was in this state when I was finally allowed to begin at the work project in the third week of January 2006. I was expected to be sober but kept on as usual with being sober on the job and for the visits with Emma but other than that I used just as I always had. I still harboured some kind of hope that this work project might be what could save me from abusing myself to death.

The first week, we went on a trip to a large house in the country and I was horribly physically hungover and in such a terribly unstable frame of mind that I had to muster all my strength not to lose my wits entirely during the four days we were there. As soon as we got home, I got drunk and when we went on a go-cart outing the next day, I shook as much as the cart did at top speed.

I got a placement as a cleaning lady at a firm. Even though I had fantasies about this possibly being a way out of my alcoholism, I still couldn't stop. I was mentally on my knees and continued to challenge myself by getting more alcohol as soon as the thought of using arose. I had difficulties eating with Emma. If I had been on my own I would never have eaten during this period of mental disorder and alcohol frenzy.

The job worked out for two weeks before I came clean and told the staff at the project that I was still using and that I was in a very bad way. I didn't have the strength to lie and sneak around anymore. Now the last straw of getting out of this addiction was drawn and there was only the deadly path of addiction left.

I went to an appointment at my doctor's in the ward. I had been her patient since the first time we had been reported to social services when Emma had been only a few months old. This was the fourth time I had met her and I went only because I was forced to. She was usually a very temperamental person and through the years she had begged, yelled and shown fiery impatience with me but now she sounded eerily indifferent. She simply informed me that my liver was like an 80-year old active addict's, which meant that I had only months to live. What touched me most was the tone of her voice, not this prognosis – as an addict I never fully understood the finality of physical or lethal consequences. Those threats were always met with a suicidal numbness on my part. But now I actually got scared and even signed up for a few days' of group therapy session as she suggested.

The participants in this group were alcoholics who hadn't found sobriety and I got to listen to lots of facts about the effects of alcohol and the human body's reactions and counter-measures to this drug. Most of this information was a repetition of things I already knew. I was aware that this drug was lethal and a potent solvent, also that it is the most destructive substance in our society, that it was a factor in most violent crimes, and so on. But what was totally different about me attending this group was that I was actually there of my own free will this time. There was absolutely nothing to gain or to cover up for that had made me go. Nothing other than a new-found, even though I still didn't realise it, fear for my life. Every day, I sat on my chair in the conference room, awfully hungover, trembling to my very core. When the three hours were done, I went straight to Systembolaget except for the days when I was to go and see Emma. Then, as usual, I held off, but only until after my visiting hours.

The time I had spent with my daughter over Christmas, the burying of the fantasies of a job possibly being the cure for my addiction, my doctor's prognosis of my battered body and the therapy sessions – it all became too much for me. In mid-February, I started using uncontrollably which resulted in me not being able to go to my visits with Emma. I told her that I was very sick and, as always when it came to something where my addiction was the root, it was never spoken out loud, she didn't say anything and she didn't ask. She knew. Some days I couldn't even call her because I was too intoxicated.

I escalated and continued buying more booze as soon as the thought popped into my head, regardless of my being in the mood to use or not. Often, I was hardly able to go outside but I forced myself to go and get more, stumbling out the door. A few times they wouldn't let me buy any more because I was too far gone.

I had about 100 SEK every day and during this period also ruthlessly pressured my mother into giving me more money. I didn't use any money for food. Everything I got my hands on went to getting more alcohol. 100 SEK was enough to buy ten half-litre cans of the strongest beers which amounts to the equivalent of three bottles of wine and somehow I almost always managed to get my hands on double that amount. This was a large dose for me since I didn't have any nutrients in my system. I, who throughout life had kept myself mostly on the lower verges of too drunk, escalated alarmingly. I was so sick and tired of absolutely everything and I continued feeling that destructive impulse that as soon as I thought of alcohol I forced myself to get my hands on some.

Systembolaget is only open at restricted hours so I had to buy from people who sold on the black market and in a couple of stores and café's which sold liquor illegally.

My brain "worked" in high gear. It was in a constant battle between a sensation of eternal doom at the thought of never being able to get drunk again and the hovering threat of sobriety. The lie within my disorder of addiction told me that I would never lead a full life or ever have fun again if I couldn't use alcohol. One afternoon, something hit me with tremendous power – I didn't have a life here and now and definitely didn't have fun either and I hadn't for many, many years. The man from the 12-step meeting and his words came back to me. "No fun binges left". Then I bought even more, got even more drunk, all in an attempt to shut it all out.

Insanely, I thought I would maybe, hopefully, possibly tire of the whole rut if I got totally crazed by the effects of this solvent but it didn't work out - I couldn't cope with the quantities. I was too frail physically and painfully yearned to see Emma. In the middle of the second week of this deranged behaviour, I began cutting my dosage and, a few days later I could go to see her again. Emma was going to move in with a "real" and healthy family as soon as CaF could find a suitable home for her. Then I would get to roam the streets pursuing my only true purpose in life and just go and die from my sick liver. This was hell on Earth.

Over the following weeks my thought patterns became, if possible, even more irrational and I was on the brink of true insanity. I remember having a full-time problem with how other people consumed alcohol. I couldn't for the life of me understand how anybody would buy two cans of beer to last a whole weekend or one bottle of wine to share with others. What would be the point? For me these thoughts and observations were as complex as the question about the size of the universe. I could not get my mind around it and stared, scrutinising people's shopping carts and investigating their choices at the shelves. Somewhere deep inside, I sensed that this was a crazy person's behaviour and dilemma but that dim realisation didn't stop me from brooding about it all my waking hours. It was as if I existed in a nightmare and the thinking never stopped. It didn't matter how little I had used or if I was at alcohol level zero – the craze never let up. I suffered terribly from the disease of addiction and the lies that constantly consumed my sanity.

One afternoon, when I was walking through a park near my building, I saw a group of Arab women. Lots of children belonging to this picnicking group were playing around them. The grown-ups were singing and dancing. The scene collided in my mind - the laughter and the dancing, the food and the healthy companionship. I knew they didn't use alcohol. I knew it. The reality of this crept into the fringes of my confused state and became a beacon toward seeing that some people lived full lives without intoxication.

I lived very close to an AA meeting which I had visited when I was in rehab. I often walked past it when I was on my way home. I remembered the warmth between the people in there, the spark in their eyes and the hope in the message of freedom from the obsession that they had conveyed. I brooded about being one of the few who would never be able to get sober, never be able to be true enough with myself. Despite my convincing arguments towards failing in that department I at least left the questions of "what if?" and "what if not?" open in my mind. I sneaked by the address, my soul tip-toeing past the windows, silently suppressing the longing for the fellowship, continuing walking onward, horrifically absorbed by the suffering I was trapped in. Constantly haunted by the suffering Emma was trapped in...

Comparing my situation with the self-love and mutual respect I had seen among some of the people in those rooms made my sickness all the more defined and I begged for the memories of that companionship to be erased. A friend of mine had brought me to a meeting once when I was drunk but I had never gone back of my own free will. I felt too dirty and dishonest. I had no desire to stop using.

Emma had built relationships with the people at the orphanage and I resigned myself further to the fact that I would never have the possibility to give her the quality of life she deserved. I went to the ward to get an Antabuse cure only to carry me through for Emma's sake until CaF found a family for her to move in with. That process was really taking a long time. The social secretary had told me that they were very careful because they wanted to find the right people to match Emma's needs and that it was better to let it take time than to rush into something that might not work out. Now my child had been away from me for four months.

It was a Wednesday when I took the first Antabuse pill. It didn't help, I still heaved my beers. On the Friday I got piss-drunk and woke up in an awful state at 6:45 a.m. the next morning and there wasn't a single pick-me-up flask anywhere to be found. I put on my rain clothes right on top of my pyjamas, went down to the yard and got my bike out. The café where I usually bought my strong beers under the counter opened at 7 and I stood in the pouring rain on the sidewalk with my hands on the handlebars when my whole world suddenly collapsed. The sorrow and despair that instantly filled me was all-consuming. All the distorted thoughts from the past few weeks, or even years, forcefully hit me at once. A question arose from the depths of my being and suddenly I scrutinised my whole outlook:

"Is this all I'm going to do with my life?"

My surroundings faded and I felt myself standing in a corner. All I could see around me were bottles of liquor that beckoned, closing in on me, their demands for my attention relentlessly suffocating my spirit. It was as if they had their own life and I was only a lifeless puppet bound to comply with their urging invitations to pick them up. I felt the strength of their calling and my own powerlessness over the overwhelming temptation. It was as if I had awoken from a long, all-encompassing nightmare and now, all of a sudden, I saw myself as I truly was – in the grip of a drug that only wanted to consume me and never ever gave anything back. Out of the depths of my being, I felt a sensation of being nauseatingly full, addiction seeping through every single cell of me, filling every corner of my body, atoning with every vibration of my emotions. On the inside, a cry of sheer existential anguish arose from the insight into what I had become.

Desperately, I prayed, deeply and honestly. For the first time in my life, I sincerely asked for guidance. I was ready to do anything and everything. I remember the exact words:

"God. Please! I'm going to let you help me now. Show me what to do!"

This cry sprang from an explosion of love for my life. I put my powerlessness in the care of the loving power that I had always believed in but had never turned to as wholeheartedly as now. The words came from a desire to find a way to be freed of my active addiction. I felt truthful, fit for the fight, not at all weakened by showing myself unable. From the belief that it was my destiny to use alcohol until I died because I couldn't get my act together, I realised, then and there, that I needed help and was willing to accept it and take responsibility to do whatever it took. Evidently, it was a journey that I would need to hear about from others who were already on it. On my own, I would surely be wiped off the Earth by the alcohol luring me again. Out of the blue I somehow recalled a meeting schedule from one of the 12-step fellowships.

"There is a meeting at 9 a.m.!"

I went.

The desperation that had filled me seconds earlier was exchanged for the hope that arose out of thinking about what the 12-step method had meant for so many others.

People from all walks of life. That trusting vision carried me to that meeting. This was the first meeting I ever attended that sprang from my own desire to stop using.

Afterwards, I asked myself how I would be able to make it until the next one and the answer came at once:

"Go home, rest, try to eat something, go for a ride on your bicycle, take a shower and then it will be time to go again."

I didn't even reflect over that voice being the insanity I had feared the last few months and that had now fully bloomed. Thankfully, the underlying sensation of being loved and safe made room for neither doubt nor fear. The trust that coursed through me was so tangible. I was invaded by gratefulness and decisiveness.

The thought of alcohol made me feel physically ill. The always urging impulse to use was gone. I searched through myself and couldn't find it. It was incredible. I, who had been possessed by the craving to change my moods for the last 25 years couldn't detect an inkling of that needy, constantly-gnawing feeling anymore. The only want I felt was to make it to the next meeting and that want wasn't spiced with the familiar, drenching craving. I was terribly hung over but this was a purely physical ailment, the mental discomfort was gone. The incessant primal hunter-gatherer yearnings to chase after alcohol and fill the constantly whining hole had always conquered my attention before. Now there was peace.

It was 10.30 a.m. on the 11th of March 2006 and, amazingly, all was well.

Twenty-two

It was a beautiful morning. I had been clean for six days and still hadn't had the slightest urge to get drunk. To be untouched by any mind-altering substances was, to say the least, an existential shock. It was as if a new world was making itself known to me. I stood on the balcony, looking out at the traffic, the small park across the street and the morning bustle of people below, taking in, as much as I was able to, the idea that I actually belonged to this world. I couldn't claim to be rejoining the world since I couldn't remember ever feeling this way before. It was a sense of freedom that is impossible to know if you haven't been through living with such a deranged and distorted mindlessness. To be able to just be, without the persistent compulsion to silence that insatiable, nagging yearning, was a miracle. I was so nauseatingly full up of the rut of doing alcohol. It was amazing that it had dawned on me at last.

I let all my thoughts go and savoured the pulse of the city. I needed to be a part of it and got dressed, obeying the call of my bicycle. I cycled tens of kilometres every day. It helped me steer the focus away from my ghastly physical shape and untangle all the confused threads sprouting in my mind. These troubles were replaced by physical activity and keeping my eye on the wild traffic in Malmö. At the same time, I was filled with the joy of my world swishing by.

This day was my visiting day at the orphanage. I had been there every time I was supposed to, even though my health had been very strained, but this day I was much better at last and felt a tingling expectation vibrating inside me. Emma was, as always, overjoyed to see me and we read books, talked and played until it was dinnertime. I managed to eat better than I had since I'd sunk my last beer. Improving in these elementary things were huge steps for me. After dinner, we went to her room and I sat down on the bed. I was quite tired. Emma came and stood right in front of me. She took my hands in hers and looked deeply into my eyes, then she said, pensively, in a calm but confident tone of voice:

"Mother, you have got well. Now I can move back home!"

Speechless, I looked at her. She, who had hardly ever mentioned my disease throughout all these years, now hit the nail square on the head. There and then, reassurance sank in about this happening for real. I had been in a frenzy of activity during the last six days. Everything in a preventive manner, doing everything to keep the drugs at bay. I had put huge amounts of effort into physical, mental and spiritual exercises. That I actually hadn't used any beer or wine at all these days apparently hadn't truly sunk in. But now, with Emma's serene, matter-of-fact face peering up at me with her clear, wise look, a reassuring understanding sank in. A belief that this could actually be real – that I could really be able to live like this! It was an exhilarating sensation of truth that continued to fill me – I knew I was going to take my deadly disease seriously and always be responsible for recovering from it. Pulling Emma towards me, I hugged her tightly. There was an aching lump pounding in my throat and I sat her down on the bed next to me. I had to explain some important things so her hope and trust would continue to grow. The process would be very long before I gained the trust of the social services, and not only them – I myself needed to be confident that I had gained the stability and, also, the ability to take care of my child. This wasn't all that evident to my child who only wanted to come live with me now. Her whole posture showed it.

"That is true, my darling. I have stopped using beer. Do you remember what they told you when we were at Malin's Minne? That I was ill because I get very sick from those drugs?" She nodded slowly in serious thought.

"Good," I said," and now I have stopped." I weighed every word. "But it is going to be quite a while before I have recovered enough from this disease to be able to be a good mother to you. I have to get better so that I can take care of you from morning until night and right now I'm in a phase of healing my mind and body. I have to be at the hospital every day and go to meetings - you remember the kind of meetings we went to from the rehab centre? Yes, that kind. I'm doing lots of things and everything is going to get better in a wholesome way."

I studied her carefully to see that she was connecting the dots and she was.

"I've been so sick, honey. I am so sorry for everything I have put you through. For it all to have come to this for you!" Now the tears came, the overwhelming pain of all that my wondrous little girl had been forced to live with, how she had suffered. In the depths of this sorrow, the smallest beginning of an understanding of my condition emerged – I had truly been insane. Only a deranged person would have a drug's pull overtake the instinct of parenthood. Sitting there, looking into my daughter's eyes, her innocence and my love for her showed me how sick I had been to have mistreated her in that horrible way. No sane person would ever do what I had done!

I hugged her again, sobbing:

"You really are the best ever, sweetie. I am so grateful to have you in my life! We will always have each other, you and I. It's only going to get better from here on in. Together, we will see this through."

She stroked my back, comforting me and said soothingly:

"It's okay, mommy. Everything's okay."

I looked into her eyes and smiled through the veil of tears.

“We will manage this with splendour, honey. The strength of the love we have for each other will carry us through the tough times ahead. That is my absolute conviction!” I kissed her forehead and she smiled back.

“Me too, mommy. Me too!” Her little face, smiling with complete trust was the highest-quality spiritual candy my battered soul could hope for. I felt a joy rise within and began joking with her using a 1950’s anchorwoman voice, hovering tickling fingers closer:

“The two members of the superhero Säfström family pointed their magic flying noses to the sky and flew to the fringes of the atmosphere – UP, UP,UP, and awaaay, to save a swirling tickle-belly from soaring off into space! TICKLE ATTAAACK!!!”

Emma faked defending herself, screaming with laughter and squeaking:

“Stop... mother – pleeease!” We rolled on the floor, slowing down. We lay on our backs, looking at each other, her love shone towards me as she smiled.

All the hurt and all the terrible things dissolved into the here and now, as we both got an oasis of emotional breath in the midst of these huge and strenuous happenings.

My gratefulness felt no boundaries. This was for real.

“You are the most courageous girl I have ever known. And also the loveliest!” Panting happily, we both got up and sat still on her bed for a bit and I could see how she was storing up my words with pride and love.

"I will be doing everything to get better now and, in the meantime, I want you to have as much fun as you ever can. Okay?"

She gave me that wise little smile and threw in a couple of blinks for good measure. When it was time for me to leave she hugged me, hardly wanting to let go. We had to talk for a longer time than usual. While we talked about things to help her appreciate the life she had now, at the same time, I told her of how I longed for the day when we would live together again. It was a difficult and delicate balance. I prayed silently for guidance to be able to say the right things to ease her pain. I don't know how spirituality works, I only know that it does. The words came and I left a reliant child waving in the doorway, suddenly turning, running back into the house shouting something about the TV-show that had already started. Our longing for each other was natural and never shunned. I believe this infused hope and showed Emma my love in abundance. To accept that we missed each other and talk openly about it gave my little girl some of the strength she needed.

Those moments just before I left her at the orphanage, looked very different now. Before, I could only see the alcohol's illusory relief hanging on the horizon and then I had truthfully seen mostly to my own pain. Now I still had to make our goodbyes brief but most of the focus lay on making Emma's suffering bearable, for her own sake.

That day, I had to stand beside my bicycle for a while when I got outside. I couldn't stop crying for quite some time. The penny that Emma had caused to drop through her clear-sightedness into the muddy well of my emotions had moved me beyond words – the insight of my actually being freed from the use of drugs stood out as an immovable, clean pillar inside. Her sharp mind pushed my own foggy and confused state into diffuse beginnings of a realisation of how much I missed her. There I stood, holding onto my bike for dear life, drenched in a terrible throbbing shame about what I had done and, especially, what I had not done for her when I had been drunk. Finally, I had to calm myself down and used the same method I had used to comfort Emma. I found a calm place inside, rummaged around looking for love for life, summoned my gratitude and brought forth how amazing and wonderful it was that I had found a way out of the sickly phase of my disease. Now I "only" had to keep on doing what I had been doing until now and I got on my bike to go to a meeting - my new routine after our hours together. What these meetings gave me was like night and day compared to the alcohol routine before.

During that last week, I had been to the ward at the hospital and given them a proposal for how my contact with them might proceed.

"I would like to come here every day of the week to use the breathalyser. Including Saturday and Sunday. I want to maintain my sobriety at all costs and I don't trust myself. I would also like you to do "happy surprise testing" for other drugs and also test my blood to determine if I have used alcohol – it is too easy to get drunk and then come here when the breathalyser doesn't register the alcohol anymore. Would that be possible?"

The staff member I talked to had seen me as a human wreck for the last couple of years and answered without hesitation that it would be fine for me to come and do the breath tests every day of the week. They would have to check about the other testing because it depended on who would be picking up the bills. I suggested that they get in touch with CaF within the social services and after two days they had gotten the green light from them to go ahead with my suggestions.

My desire to stay clean was the positive force that fuelled my every waking moment. I would have done anything to keep the freedom I had found. But I had fooled others, as well as myself, before. I couldn't fully comprehend that this liberated state really could be my new existence so I was very strict about keeping to my new routines and the meetings.

I was in terrible physical health. I shook all over, had

muscle cramps and my emotions were unnervingly all over the place as if thrown about in a briny, stormy sea. When I caught myself spinning away in treacherous and slippery thought patterns, I had to calm down as best I could, find the serene place inside me and let that new remarkable inner peace take over.

In the daytime, I was busy with just being and doing basic things like eating properly as far as I was able, keeping myself clean and tidy, going to meetings at my self-help group and maintaining my schedule with Emma. Thankfully, I was able to sleep and through getting this well-needed rest, I healed much better. I hadn't slept much in the past decades, since an intoxicated body only passes out, never getting the wholesome recuperation of true sleep. The bodily functions had instead been very busy breaking down the poisonous particles of the alcohol and narcotics. Now I could doze off out of normal tiredness and with the relaxing knowledge of a day well spent. I was living in a new world.

A veil had slightly been drawn aside, letting in light that shone like a nourishing river, ever-so carefully starting to clear up the muddle in my mind.

Twenty-three

During the second week, I booked a dentist's appointment, which was something I had always put off before, except when the pain had been unbearable. I also called Malin's Minne and asked to be let back onto their after-care program. They agreed and I felt safer knowing that I would be seeing my therapist again, along with other mothers, for these weekly sessions. There, I would be able to talk about the many new situations that often seemed very scary to me. I also contacted Anna at CaF and told her that I had become clean. She compassionately asked me:

"You know that we have to keep looking for a foster care placement for Emma, right?"

For the first time, I was able to hear the caring tone in her voice. She had probably always been empathetic about our situation but I hadn't been capable of listening back then. She had been in our lives since I had been reported for being drunk with Emma in town. She was also behind getting us into a treatment facility, but it was only now that I could appreciate everything she had done for us, seeing her for the professional care-giver she was. I realised that my whole world-view was undergoing serious editing.

"I do understand that," I managed to reply, with my suffering throbbing in my throat,"but I just thought that now, since I have found my way out of my active addiction, it could be better for Emma to stay at the orphanage until I've come a little further on in my recovery. Instead of her having to be moved about and getting to know even more people that she will have to be separated from when she's moving back in with me again."

I was so sure of having found my way out of my insanity but was also very naïve. In this department of social services, they had a lot of experience with families with similarly problematic backgrounds to us and Anna knew how slim the chances were that an addict with my long and serious history of addiction would actually make it in the long run. It would be much, much worse for Emma to move home with me if I then went and started using again.

"We will be following through with the plans we have made for Emma and, if everything works out, she will absolutely be moving back with you again. Right now though, the most important thing is that you take care of yourself. I will give you the next appointment with us as soon as possible. Keep doing what you're doing with the meetings and visits with Emma and you'll see that it will all turn out for the best for the both of you."

It was awfully painful to have to hear this but afterwards the logic of what she meant sank in. Emma would be much better off in a cosier environment than at the institution. This was a thought I had touched on even while I was using alcohol but it still hurt a lot. The idea of foster care was tainted with a lot of fear. All the stories I had read about where children got treated very badly when in the care of strangers. Fears about paedophiles, psychological and physical terror, fears that the people involved would only be after the money they would get from the municipality for taking her under their roof and the idea that Emma's emotional growth would be neglected were thoughts, among many others, that whirled about in my head, causing strenuous emotional turbulence. There was also a deeply-buried dread of this family being much better for Emma than I could ever be.

I had to be vigilant in monitoring my emotional state and talking about these catastrophic visions to avoid them dragging me down. I had heard that 90 percent of all our fears are of things that will actually never happen. This abnormal waste of energy was something I couldn't afford right now. I shared with my therapist and at the self-help meetings about my methods of keeping these nightmarish thoughts at bay and during the days, when I became worried, I prayed and listened to my gut feelings. Also listening to others, letting other people in between my ears while hearing them talk about their paths in life, helped me keep this mental tornado at a bearable distance. I was still anxious but managed to calm myself to a more sound parental concern, even if I had to do it 50 times a day.

My days weaved into one another with the daily visits to the hospital, maintaining a healthy diet and resting, going to my self-help group, sometimes two or even three times a day. I also took moderate exercise and then I had the visits with Emma. At the collective, there were four women, including me, and two of them were active in their addiction – one with narcotics and the other using alcohol. It didn't bother me at all. I kept myself to myself and only used the communal areas for cooking and the bathroom. Going into my third week of recovery, I wrote in my diary:

"I have to get my act together and go out and meet people. It's not healthy for me to be by myself so much!"

HALT* is a term used in connection with recovery processes. It stands for Hungry, Angry, Lonely and Tired. I learned that these four states are important to look out for as a recovering addict - throughout my entire life. At the beginning, it sounded trivial to me but as early as in my third week I became aware of the importance of these basic life supporting cornerstones. If any of these states were to affect my well-being, the risk of me losing ground was too big. I realised that maintaining a healthy diet (HUNGRY) and isolation (LONELY) were my biggest Achilles heels. These things did not come naturally to me but I had already begun to give huge focus to the preparing and eating of meals. After the first weeks my ability to eat got better but I still forgot to do it and had

*These four states are actually cornerstones in any form of recuperation.

got into the habit of reminding myself daily. Isolation was immensely more difficult – this appeared to be a case of moving mountains. This state had been "of my own volition" (if I could actually call any of the impulses I had followed since childhood 'choices'. The word choice suggests that sound deliberation has been made before acting on the decision).

I didn't know how to relate to others in the ordinary sense. I made up my mind to visit an organisation for former addicts and criminals who had turned their lives around and were drug-free and were focused on being law-abiding.

It was difficult for me to pull myself together to go there. I felt tiny and dirty, worried about being regarded with distaste, and a whole hoard of other, illogical fears. I had to pep myself with facts: that the people there were just like me, that I would get a chance to get to know others who had made the same changes I had and that it was more than necessary for me to have something to do in the daytime. Everything to keep my new lifestyle going. Two days after I had made my decision, I pulled myself together and went. None of the scenarios which I had drawn up came to pass. Rather, as in any café, most people there were friendly and welcoming. I was deeply moved. Here, I got to sit down by a computer and I created an e-mail account. For the first time in my life, I surfed the internet. This had an incredible WOW-factor for me.

I was like a dried-out sponge and a girl who was working there helped me a lot. Every bit of information about using the internet was absorbed down to a T.

My inner and outer journey was boosted by my breaking the isolation this early. Now I met others even though I was far from letting anyone into my personal space yet. Daring to go there at all gave me a true sense of self-worth, something I never truly had as an arrogant and nonchalant ruffian.

I had begun my social development and it was an enormous step for me. It wasn't as if I walked in there and chatted with my fellow humans from the start but for me to summon the courage to go at all, saying "Hi" and then buying a cup of coffee was like standing on the stage of the Metropolitan doing a live broadcast in front of the whole world! I swelled with pride and filled up with new courage and resolve every time I got on my bike to go there. These baby steps filled my being with sound content. I was carefully building the human that is me. My gratitude at being free grew stronger with every passing day, just as my trust in being able to continue living like this grew as long as I took care of my disease.

In the difficult moments, those two emotions were what carried me - gratitude and trust. The experiences I'd had from day one showed me that the difficult moments were always outweighed by the good times I experienced. Small dishes of life in this new reality came to me. It was slow but it was true and I savoured every second of it. At the beginning of May I had to apply the strength I had found from this love for my new way of living to its fullest.

I got the phone call I had been dreading – CaF had found a family for Emma.

Twenty-four

My insides writhed. It felt as if I had a cramp in my soul. I had to try hard to get a grip so as to be able to maintain my emotional and spiritual balance. CaF had told me that finding a family had taken such a long time because they wanted a good fit for Emma and me and I did believe them, even though that fact didn't extinguish my feelings of helplessness and worry. I had been able to handle these churning emotions until now but this time they resurfaced with force. The spectre of the atrocities that could befall my daughter haunted me every waking hour and, at night, the nightmares followed. I cried from the worry and for all the terrible things I had put her through. I cried for the decades of addiction, for having been so egoistical and self-centred, for the impulsive pursuit of insane trains of thought that had led me on all those years when the effects of alcohol and other drugs had ruled my mind.

It was devastating to realise that I'd lived in the grip of such mindless lies for so long. Only an insane parent would put their child through such a traumatic ordeal. Had I been sane, this would never have become her reality. The difference between then and now was startlingly apparent. I wept for the pain Emma would have to suffer even now that I had become sober. When life was beginning for me it must have seemed to be ending for her.

How could my addiction have made me that person? In those days, and that was not all that many days ago, I had actually believed that alcohol would strengthen me...

Louise from CaF and I went to meet the family, Mona and Ulf, a couple in their fifties, in the middle of May. I was beside myself, both in a positive sense and with the effort of struggling to keep my scepticism at bay. I tried to get into the frame of mind to be able to give these people an honest chance. When social services were taking care of Emma, I had signed a form giving my consent, which meant that I wanted to have a great deal to say about what happened in her life. I truly hoped that these people would be a good match for us and I didn't want to come across as a narrow-minded or aggressive person, especially if this was to be the start of a long-term relationship. At the same time, I had to be honest with them about my qualms and make them understand that Emma and I had a very close-knit bond so they would know that we talked a lot. This might minimise the risk of them acting up if they were bullies or worse. I was terrified that Emma should be put in harm's way more than she already had been in her life.

They greeted us outside their house and welcomed us with open arms, and with what felt like real warmth. Rather quickly, the chemistry between us felt good. They invited us in for lunch, which was a delicious casserole. We talked openly about my nightmares but also about the hopeful possibilities I envisaged and they told me about their thoughts on the situation and what plans they had made. What they said sounded rational and kind-hearted - it seemed as if they were set on the four of us having a strong relationship with each other. They also told me that they had just bought a new house and would be moving into it around the same time as Emma was coming to live with them. This sounded very good, since it meant that Emma would be a part of making this her new home in more ways than one. They also told me that they had been a half-way house until now and that Emma would be their first full-time boarding child. I was very clear when I pointed out that Emma would be moving back home as soon as I was more stable and, since none of us knew when that would be, it came across more as a statement and clarification on my part. I needed to hear myself say it as much as I needed them to know, I think. We also talked freely about an introduction phase that would lead up to Emma moving in. I would be the one to inform her that we had found a family that seemed nice.

Before we left, I asked for a photo of the two of them together which I could show Emma when I was going to tell her about the unfolding of these upcoming events. Having a picture of Mona and Ulf would help me help her to accept this move. I would be able to tell her that I "knew" them and that they seemed to be very nice people. The meeting had gone so well that, before we got into the car to leave, we actually gave each other a hug and my smile toward them felt sincere.

My concern for Emma when I wasn't with her came from the normal and healthy "burden" of being a parent but my thoughts around catastrophic outcomes were probably more linked to the self-centred part of my disease. I reflected on this as we drove back home and also gratefully savoured the relief of finally having met the people Emma was going to be living with, which lessened the uncertainty factor considerably.

This was an inevitable stage and I thanked Louise for having been thorough in searching for a good family. She answered that it was unusual for a parent to handle this kind of situation with the child's best interests in the foreground. I took this compliment on board because it was a very difficult inside job working on my acceptance of the whole situation. I had begun to realise that I was a lioness of a mother with a fierce protective instinct. My spontaneous impulse told me to grab my child and flee to the jungles of the Amazon. If they'd had Swedish standards and as many self-help organisations there, who knows...!

A sound instinct of protection toward myself also soothed the pain I experienced about all of this. I truly understood the importance of getting a sturdy platform in my recovery before Emma could live with me again and, during this time, she needed a stable daily life with normal routines. I made a new plan with CaF about when I should tell Emma about the new phase of her life, so that the people at the orphanage and pre-school would be prepared for any reaction this information might trigger in her. The staff at the orphanage had been through many situations like this and knew that it was a good idea to keep an extra eye on the child throughout such a process. All children reacted strongly but the ways in which they showed it could vary from brooding to aggression. I prayed for the ability to tell Emma this news with sincere love, honesty and enthusiasm in my heart to give her the possibility of developing a feeling of adventure and a positive attitude towards moving. In only two short weeks she, would be embarking on the stages of the adjustment process in her new home. I prayed for all the love in the world and then it was time to tell her this important news.

We had been given access to a private room in the orphanage where we could talk in peace. I had mentioned that this move was coming throughout her whole stay here, even when I was still using alcohol, so she knew the day was coming. I brought it up simply and candidly, like pointing out a positive fact of life. I trusted this to be a good development which I was glad of because, as children who grow up with parents with emotional diseases always are, Emma was a genius at reading my emotions.

I showed her the photograph of Mona and Ulf while telling her how nice they were and that we had become good friends.

"We hugged the last time we met and they are really looking forward to meeting you! Guess what?! They have a pool! I have told them that you are going to have swimming lessons this summer and I'll be visiting as often as I can. I think it's going to be great. They seem to be kind people. You an I will of course talk on the phone and see each other and then you can tell me what you think of them."

Emma scanned me, peering silently for what felt like an eternity and what she recorded could only have been my love and calm attitude toward this situation because suddenly she tilted her head and her face burst out into a big smile and she simply concluded:

"Okay mom. We'll try them out!"

I had succeeded and the conversation that followed was about all the adventures she would be having and a lot about the pool. She also asked me about my recovery process, as if she wanted to reassure herself that she was really coming home for real one day. I could honestly tell her how I was getting better every day but that I had been so seriously ill for such a long time, it would be a little while yet before I was well enough to be able to take care of her again.

"It's perfect that you can live in with Mona and Ulf for the time being but I will miss you all the time! I have lots to do at the hospital to get better and in the meantime you'll be living in the countryside where you can relax and play while I work at recovering back here in the city."

She nodded in solemn thought and I could almost see her brain working over these facts.

This talk went better than I had expected in my warped catastrophic fantasies. I seemed to have managed to inspire her into looking forward to moving and, most importantly, that it was okay for her to feel that way about it. We put the photograph of Mona and Ulf on the wall of her room next to the ones of our family. Then a pang of grief struck me and I grabbed her and we hugged for a long while.

"I am going to miss you all the time, just so you know!" I gave her a sad smile and I noticed that this had a comforting effect on her. She knew that I loved her always.

When I left that day, I was completely exhausted. I cried and felt gratitude all at the same time. Later that evening, I called the staff at the orphanage to ask what had happened after I'd left and they said that Emma had expressed curiosity and that she seemed to be looking forward to meeting Mona and Ulf two days later. They complimented me because it was clear that she experienced this as something positive, even though she was nervous about it. I was proud of Emma and myself, even if this feeling was tinged with some small worry about having done this too well. An almost apocalyptic sensation lingered, one of her ending up liking it better with them than me, but this uneasiness passed. I would always be her mother and she would love me more than anyone in the world. There was no such thing as "too well" in this process. The only right thing to do was to continue showering her with love and enthusiasm throughout this journey. My gut-feeling was that I was going to make it, which meant that Emma would definitely be moving back with me one day.

I tried to persuade CaF to let me be there when Mona and Ulf were to meet Emma for the first time but they wouldn't budge on that one. Their experience in this field told them it could be too strenuous for the child, who could easily feel a conflict of interests. I could see the logic behind their reasoning and that they were keeping Emma's best interests at heart but at the time it was terribly difficult - I wanted to be a part of everything in my daughter's life now. I was sure my presence would have had the opposite effect by letting Emma see how much I liked Mona and Ulf and thus strengthening their bond. Today, I understand that CaF's assessment might have been correct. It would have been too difficult for us and it was probably best for her to have an undisturbed focus on Mona and Ulf. The only consolation was that I was on the right track and my resolve to keep on doing the right thing was strengthened even further. My patience was being brutally tried but I was clear-minded and reluctantly saw both sides of the argument.

The last day of Emma's stay at the orphanage, I was allowed to come and visit, bringing ice-cream for all the kids, and, after the farewell-party, we packed all her stuff into a bag. Then, suddenly, she was 60 kilometres away. The first two weeks, I wasn't allowed to call or see her. This was all in accordance with the standard planning for a child's integration into a new home but, luckily for me, an exception was made, probably because I was drug-free, and I got to come visit with Louise on the first Monday of the second week. I was careful to show just enough of having missed her and just enough enthusiasm and I hugged and talked earnestly with Mona and Ulf. I focused on making this visit turn out as well as possibly possible so that Emma would see that we all liked each other. We didn't have to playact either because we really did get along wonderfully. Emma visibly watched us all but after a while she relaxed, clearly content that we were all friends. Then she showed me her room, happily chattering, and then the house and the large garden. She was very comfortable and I gave myself a mental pat on the back. This was going to work out fine. Of course, she embraced me for the longest time when we were about to leave and I had to make great use of the routines and tricks we had developed at the orphanage. Emma had her ways of managing these difficult good-byes and we managed to pull through this time too. We had discussed what the telephone schedule would be like and now I could tell Emma when we would be speaking next. I could also tell her when I was coming to see her and she calmed down. As always, I told her that I missed her and she beamed with love, smiling and winking back at me. I could tell that she knew my heart belonged only to her now and it was wonderful!

When we left, a new kind of peace moved into my heart. I had gotten to see the results of my hard work at making this situation as painless and positive as possible for Emma and it had really panned out well. I had given this my full attention. Now I could redirect a lot of this focus back towards my recovery where it was dearly needed, both mentally and physically. I was very grateful for CaF's cooperation and, when needed, their direction. I did need a lot of time to recuperate without rushing and taking on too much responsibility too soon.

The fact that I'd had my recovery to concentrate on in addition to everything else was a godsent. At the meetings and in my sessions with my therapist, I could share my hope, my sorrow and my possibilities in everything that went on around me. I listened to other people all the more and took in what they expressed from their experiences and love of life. I was smitten with this clean and fresh way of living.

Outside the meetings, I did my spiritual work-outs, strengthening my gratitude and trust as the platforms to keep my longing, my despair and especially, my impatience to get Emma home, bearable. I noticed that my faith in finding solutions was more cemented than ever and I relied on finding ways, if I just took the time to look for them. I rested in the safety of this newfound way of handling life. I knew that, after the darkness of my yearning, there would come the light of encompassing rays of belonging. I prayed for my life, because I realised that if I let my catastrophic thoughts of what might befall Emma take over my positive attitude, my sobriety could be endangered. I had to take care of my life and give myself love. I was reminded of my anguish when I was in the active phase of addiction and this suffering was now indisputably smaller in every way.

I went to my self-help group, took responsibility for maintaining my emotional balance, did my little spiritual work-outs and watched out for HALT as well as I could. If I skipped any of these "medicines", I understood that my disposition to flee might take over and most probably the lie of drugs bringing some form of relief would appear as the miraculous alternative. If that lie overtook my sanity, I would surely die. That much was clear.

No drug had been invented that would deafen or minimize the guilt and shame I would feel and I wouldn't, couldn't and didn't want to go there again.

Twenty-five

It might appear as though my social skills were healing very quickly, if you look at how I managed my communication with CaF, but this was definitely not the case. My love for Emma and my concern for her well-being ruled my actions in these conversations. When it came to Emma, I listened a lot to my intuition, my gut-feeling, and, socially, I was at my most relaxed with her. She knew, whatever I said, in the simple straightforward way that children do, who I was and how I felt so, with her, I could be completely at ease. With CaF, I focused on being 100% honest and very matter-of-fact. It was easy now that I didn't have anything to hide. In all other social contexts, I was extremely inhibited and inexperienced. I remember feeling as I had when I was a child, back inside the bubble of my isolation, observing the world around me, not participating. The difference now was that I finally had found a way to practice how to be a part of humanity and I began to pray for the courage to further develop in this ability.

I began to reflect on how I had been arriving at the meetings just minutes before they were to begin and then slipping off as soon as they had finished, before anyone had the chance to strike up a conversation with me. It resembled how I acted when I went to the organisation for ex-offenders where I, unfortunately, hadn't found very much guidance in helping me learn how to interact on a more intimate level.

I longed for the communication that I saw the others engaging in in the recovery rooms but I didn't dare stay on and linger. I decided to begin doing practical things in the group. I had heard from others that doing something for someone else would strengthen my ability to relate and nurture a sense of belonging. I could see the logic in that. Through giving a small amount of my time, I would be getting an enormous amount of personal growth by interacting with others. There was no hesitating. I needed to have been sober for 90 days to be allowed the responsibility to keep a key for the facilities, coming before the others to make the coffee and put the meeting format in order. I hadn't been without drugs long enough yet but I was desperate to join, so I asked the person who opened the 7 p.m. meeting on Sundays if I could come and just be there and help him until I had scraped together my first 90 days. He said that I was more than welcome to perform this service alongside him. This was a 25-year-old man who had become sober when he was 21. He was a great source of inspiration for me. The amazement of being able to relate to people of all ages and from every thinkable walk of life was wonderful.

I continued to sneak in and out of all the other meetings for a long time to come but at this one, I had to start greeting people when they arrived. I even chatted from time to time, but to begin with I only spoke when spoken to. In this service position, we had to stay afterwards to clean up and now and again I got to answer when people called their "Bye-byes". It took a while but slowly I became more courageous. I began saying "Hi" sometimes, when someone I had seen before showed up, and finally I even added a careful "See you" after a "Bye-bye". At first, these words of greeting where tainted with an illogical sensation of rejection. It was as if I expected the other members not to ever want to lay their eyes on me again.

A lot of inner work was put into investigating this lie and the delusions my imagination blew up about how the others were supposed to be judging me. It was amazing that this tiny service, a couple of hours per week, could be such a powerful tool for punching a hole in my sense of being an outsider. The words "hello", "goodbye" and "see you" had of course passed through my lips countless times during my life but rarely, if ever, had they been loaded with their true meaning of welcoming another person into my sphere or wishing to have them there again. This was an extremely clever way of laying a foundation for how I could reverse the thoughts and feelings that were instinctively pulling at me to continue living my life in isolation, which was at the core of my dysfunction. Crushing the lie of being apart even in a room filled with people...

I slowly learned to use these tried and tested actions in the moment on a daily basis. I greeted neighbours, I held up doors for people with a smile and even making small talk, I helped out with little things in all kinds of random places if I could. The feeling of being an actual part of this world gained space and a wondrous sense of belonging grew in my heart.

At Malin's Minne, a woman who had been going through recovery for eighteen years had held a lecture on the importance of having a twelve-step sponsor. It was about asking someone, preferably of the same gender, within the twelve step program of your choosing, and that you would feel comfortable turning to in a more personal manner, to be your sponsor. At the meetings, one listened and shared without interrupting and never commenting on other people's shares. Now I felt the need for someone to contact in a more informal way. I summoned the courage and asked around. The woman that became my sponsor was perfect for me at that time. She told me about many experiences, both unexpected and other very similar ones, from her years in addiction and she also helped me by telling me about her day-to-day joys and challenges. I told her about my journey and it suddenly hit me that she was the first healthy adult person I had ever been completely honest with. This brought an enormous sense of relief. There were so many things

I could never share at a meeting out of concern for my personal integrity but with her I didn't have to hold anything back. I hadn't had the slightest idea that this was what was going to happen when I asked around for a sponsor. I was embarking on my first deep and honest relationship with another human being. When I came to her with questions or told her how I viewed things, I knew she would never judge me. It was a huge step in breaking down the wall I had kept impenetrable for as long as I could remember.

The twelve-step program became a deeper emotional and practical part of my recovery. I understood that I was the problem – not the drugs. To be able to recover, I had to be in a life-long process of change on all frontiers of existence. I felt like I could rely on this method because working with it had brought aid to innumerable other addicts who had managed to create a life in sobriety with quality experiences, personal growth and harmony. The way the steps were developed, I could see that working with this program would help me get to know myself and thereby gain the ability to know other people. I wanted to live my life in a way that would reflect my new-found honouring of life. I had already experienced much happiness and growth, these priceless virtues which had begun to stir inside me, and I wanted more of this. The logic of the steps and the order in which they were listed spoke to me and, even for a scrutinizing critic like myself, the results only showed positive effects among those who worked with this method on a regular basis. I wanted a meaningful life. My instincts told me that if I didn't learn to live with my tendencies for escapism and my emotional disorder, the risk of me turning into a bitter sober alcoholic were more probable than not. Then sobriety couldn't matter less. I asked my sponsor to help me work through the steps, she agreed and then I got started.

I'm very glad that I had already understood when I was in rehab that the mentioning of God in the twelve-step organisations isn't linked to any specific belief or religion. In these meetings, society as a whole is represented as a miniature spectrum and anyone is welcome. Atheists sit beside believers and are as common or uncommon as at any workplace or on any sidewalk in the world. The head-banger with the square dancer, the banker with the schoolteacher – everyone is an equal and sitting there for the same reason. The organisations were spread world-wide, which also told me that this method is only targeting the common denominators within people having the same difficulties, not the differences.

I heard many ways to befriend the use of the word 'God' – Good Orderly Direction and Getting Off Drugs, being two of them. Another way of defining a higher power could be thinking of the group as a whole as being the unconditional loving platform, Group Of Drunks – GOD. I, as everyone else, had my own personal way of relating to this spiritual part of recovery and, thankfully, it was no one's business but my own.

If this method had been designed with a certain type of idea about God or no God at all in mind, I could never have been a member of it and it seemed to be that way for everyone in these rooms. The freedom of belief was a cornerstone of these fellowships and this made it possible to apply the method to combating this terrible disease all around the world.

I was amazed at there being organisations that allowed such freedom for the individual. No fees, no leaders. I never felt cornered. Rather, my sense of being free to explore the reality around me expanded every day. This freedom also helped me learn to show care and affection for myself. In order to know what it was like to appreciate my humanity, I needed to nurture my ability for self-love and respect - being in that development, knowing the beauty of being a person, I was suddenly able to give the same love and respect to Emma and other people.

Everything about living a day-to-day life was new to me. The closed-minded and cut-off life I had led before now made even tying my shoelaces a revolutionary practice. Before, when I was heading out the door, it was always to get the hurdles out of the way so I could continue my constant, downward-spiralling hunt. Everything with the goal of having personal space on the horizon to achieve mind- and mood-alteration through drugs. Now, when I tied my shoes, it was with a sense of safe trepidation that fresh, healthy and rewarding experiences were on hand. Moments of true joy constantly burst inside me in both small and big things. I even felt gratitude for the difficult times because what I felt now was real and it could never be worse than before.

My whole world was steadily renewing itself and my thankfulness grew at a steady pace. Life was not the same old treadmill that had only gotten all the more rickety and life-threateningly worn down by the second, as it was before.

Now I was sane enough to make choices about how to handle things and was no longer caught in the lie of being a victim.

Twenty-six

Now the beautiful weather came to Malmö. It was June of 2006 and a heatwave pushed in from the south westerly coast. This warmth reminded me of Jordan, where I'd had my best memories, before my disease exploded and the early years of drug abuse set in. The heat also brought emotional memories from those most harmonious days of my life. Since I wasn't going to get to see Emma as often as I had when she'd lived at the orphanage, I came to the decision that I would enjoy this summer as much as possible. If everything worked out well for me, CaF said that Emma would be moving back with me in November and then our lives would be filled with a normal daily routine. I told myself that I would try to make this summer an utopian one.

I didn't act my age and I was aware of that. I had missed out on living through so many stages of life and had so much to learn and catch up on. This summer I would re-enact the stage of how a sun-worshipping, healthy teen-age Lotten would have spent lazy days on the beach. I bought colourful dresses, tops and shorts and a portable radio with headphones. Then I cycled with a big smile on my face and loud music blaring out on kilometre-after-kilometre long excursions around the town and along the beaches. Sometimes, I noticed people turning their heads when I came flying by. This only made me smile even more and a happy thought soared through my being:

"If you only knew how I have spent my life, walking through pure hell on Earth, despising all living things, and compared that to what I have found today, you would be smiling too!"

I must have looked a bit loony and I probably was. Happy, in a mild state of existential shock and therefore on the bright side of loony. And I was happy to be – as long as I was clean, any state of mind was good.

I knew I had to pamper myself to help me let go of my focus on Emma, but it wasn't easy. Now I got to see her once every week and twice every other week. We went on outings to Helsingborg, the town closest to where she lived. We went to the beach and sometimes we took the ferry across to Denmark where we often went swimming in a beautiful cove near a real-life castle, which was magical for a little four-year-old. I was still going to the addiction ward every day as usual, both for alcohol and narcotics testing, so these outings meant that CaF trusted me to do things that many others might not have been given permission to do. I handled this with exemplary punctuality and always communicated everything that went on.

My sound parental urges were getting stronger every day and this in the middle of the whirlwinds of emotions, personal growth and all-round impressions. I sought lots of guidance in the parenting field, at the after-care, from CaF and in meditation. I also asked other sober parents and my sponsor, who was also a mother, and so I got a lot of input on how people handled parenting. As the weeks went by, the longing for my daughter to be by my side became both harder and easier. The insight of still being too sick to take care of us both became more evident at this stage and us living apart seemed quite sensible for the time being. I had to perform inside exercises to accept that it was alright for me to recuperate alone and that this new way of life would sink in better at a gentle pace.

Simon was no longer in our lives. He had moved back to Gothenburg the summer of the year that we had separated and since then he hadn't contacted us. My mother ran into him sometimes and I reasoned that if he wanted to hear how Emma was doing he could always ask her. Thoughts of contacting him came and went away again just as quickly. I knew now that healthy parenting had been distant from my own reality only a few weeks earlier. The realisation of how mentally ill I had been helped me bury the hatchet. No one had been able to persuade me that there was a better life without drugs. Not until I had found my own desire to do anything and everything not to pick up the bottle again. Of course, the person who had reported me to the social services had saved our lives in a way but the actions to keep my sobriety in the long run had to be my own. With a huge sense of sorrow for Simon, Emma and myself, I had to let go of him and keep on healing.

Luckily, I only seemed to get as much as I could handle during those first stumbling weeks – thankfully I never understood how mentally worn down I actually was. All the happiness and gratitude protected me from seeing my true condition. Somehow, I came to see what I needed to do when a situation arose and somehow there was always enough energy to follow through.

I really had found a way out – I wasn't going to have to die in degradation as a tormented wreck. Finally, I was going to exist in the real world and be part of an evolution. Since I had spent most of my life in a grave sickly state, I now found thankfulness in almost everything. Following the advice of my sponsor and also having heard many people share about this in the meetings, I began writing a gratitude-list in the evenings.

Writing things down helped me enormously. I had so much constantly swirling in my mind, a relentless buzzing of both positive and negative things. Writing down the positive things made me cement the nurturing aspects, which was the more preferable platform for me to build on.

A typical list could look like this:

I am grateful because -

I am clean

I am able to recover

I am able to evolve

I am honest

I can ask for help

I have a place to live

I have my self-help group

I have a bicycle

I go to the dentist

I dare to share at the meetings

I was reported and was offered help which I accepted

I trust that there is a power greater than myself which only wants what is good for me

I am alive

I have the world's most wonderful daughter

Emma is doing well

Emma is living with a good family

I am a good parent today

I thank God for my life.

Goodnight, sleep tight, World.

My beautiful little Emma, you are so wondrous and brave. I love you and I love me.

I wrote many and long lists like this one and could go to bed with strengthened feelings of hope and comfort.

It was a powerful tool. Medicine for my torn soul. Medicine to help me bear living with all the harm I had caused. Medicine to let me see the light in the moment and be allowed the energy to go on.

Putting Emma towards the end of the list was a conscious decision on my part. The newly-awakened parental instinct urged me to put all my focus on her instead of on my vitally essential recovery. Learning this new way of life had to come first and this was one way to underline the importance of this to myself. If I didn't learn how to thoroughly care for my inner self, my dysfunctional emotions and the unreal thought patterns would regain ground and then I wouldn't get to be a parent at all. Indisputably, I saw how quickly that would lead me back into isolation, the maddening loneliness: deafening this pain with the drugs would inevitably lead to my death. I felt a responsibility towards my existence and it was to take my self-help methods most seriously and take the routine of them to heart.

I didn't have a clear picture of what defined the disease of addiction but every day brought me more experience of the fact that it was the inside as well as the outside that helped me puncture the unhealthy mind-games that sneaked up on me. I hadn't been haunted by cravings for alcohol yet and was extremely grateful for this. I had heard of many addicts who had to fight for their abstinence. My "rock bottom" had been so hard and had sunk in so deep that the only thing that happened when

I thought of booze, or being drunk, was that I felt an instant mental nausea combined with a sensation of feeling stuffed. This actually affected me physically. This might seem to have been the end of my need for recovery but, after two months of sobriety, something happened that made me realise just how watchful I needed to be.

I was sitting in my room reading some literature from my self-help organisation. Heeding the advice of my sponsor, I used to sit and read for about ten minutes every day. The words that morning described the way I had felt for so many years. It was almost uncanny how similar the thought patterns described on that particular page were to my own experience. It was as if I was reading about the outlook I'd had on life while I was abusing alcohol. The isolation and delusions. Also, the inability to control how little or how much I was going to consume, which might work out one day but get totally out of control the next.

I had understood that the literature of the twelve-step fellowships went through rigorous processes before it was approved for publishing. The texts were up-dated, read and re-read by numerous members before they were voted and re-voted on. All to get the message through with common denominators, searching out a solution, a path for recovery, that would best speak to as many as possible suffering from this disorder.

Sitting there reading, I was filled with thankfulness when my heart filled up with the sensation that I wasn't alone and that there were others all around the globe who had experienced the same affliction. It was a tremendous relief - I would be able to make it without having to use again just like the millions of people using this method to recover. I sat, pondering this beautiful feeling, really snuggling into it, with joy and security filling me up. This was the strongest experience of love and trust I'd had up until now. After a little while, I kept on reading. When I came half-way down on the next page, I read a passage about alcoholics in the workplace and suddenly a thought pierced my brain:

"Oh! So I probably don't have any problems with alcohol, after all!"

I was astonished and stopped reading out of pure shock. It was as if I was having an out of body experience. I had gone from having felt such belonging and recognition only seconds earlier, to this! Sitting there by myself, I suddenly started laughing, totally perplexed. The difference between the safe, loving feeling from the previous page, to this absurd brain-ghost that so coldly and wisely stated this "fact". Such an obvious lie - what fiendish drivel. The laughter just tore itself from my deepest insides. The difference between the two states was too vast and contradictory for my mind to manage. It was like a sick joke. Of course it also scared the sh*t out of me. That my sobriety hung by such a thin thread was all too evident in that moment. Such a striking distortion of reality gave me a clearer picture of what my disease actually looked like. The voice in my head had sounded like my own thinking! This disease was truly a deceiver of life. The delusion of alcohol not being harmful was not even me deluding me - it was a disease of the mind trying to kill me and get me to hurt the people around me. This was an alarm-bell that I gratefully took on board and integrated into the core of my being.

I shared about this at the meetings and saw other members relate to having had this happen to them too. I saw recognition in their small smiles, head-shakes and nods. The creepy and fearful emotions were soothed by seeing that I wasn't alone in having had this happen to me. I understood how people could believe that this was their own "logical conclusion" and follow this heartless impulse to use - a behaviour that baffles non-addicts all over the world – the alcoholic who relapses despite innumerable and agonising consequences.

Instead of being overwhelmed by fear of how my affliction was a mental disease with a death-defying nature, I turned it into hope. Like so many others, I could learn to live with having such bizarre ideas without having to fall for them. I reconciled more and more with this being a life-long process of recovery and in this, paradoxically, a spirit of serenity and safety seeped into me. The fight was over – I had found a sustainable way out. I was extremely thankful for having been born in a time when successful self-help methods for addicts were spreading throughout humanity.

As always, my critical nature toward coalitions was alert, though. From day one, my desire to remain sober had been stronger than my impulse to isolate myself. Now that my body and mind had gone through the first stages of acute healing, I noticed things more clearly about the self-help organisation that I had joined. There was absolutely no one who led these groups or who tried to lead me. The members coming there were going of their own free will and most of their personalities showed some kind of contentment and they seemed to have functional lives, so this method must be generating a positive result or else they wouldn't be coming back. There was no peer pressure. The careful steps I took were the paths I needed.

The cornerstones of the twelve-step method - meetings, step-work, being of service in the maintenance of the non-profit organisation and sponsorship – were things I was going to keep working at and even this was something I completely chose for myself . Not a single member told me that I had to do anything. The proof was the quality of my everyday life which was getting better and I could only guess that it was the same for the others.

I reflected on the fact that I couldn't see much likeness with how twelve-step meetings were often portrayed in movies and TV series. The fatalism that the role-model showed in these screen adaptations was seldom what went on in real life. I would never have come back to such a gathering had there been anywhere close to as much low-key drama, with constant and unproductive brooding over the shame and guilt of the addictive years. Also, overly-resigned characters with extremely low self-esteem would have repelled me at once. I needed inspiration to turn my behavioural patterns around and, in real life, this was what I got at these meetings.

Of course, some of those low-key emotions and self-images came up in me due to the hurt I had caused the people around me and to myself. But if I was to find a way of life that inspired me to stay sober in a positive trajectory and to make amends, I needed to share about how to turn my thoughts around from these shameful and destructive patterns. This was vital for me. I rather remember hearing people share about hope, courage, honesty and strength – even in difficult and sad stages of lives. This was the spirit these gatherings spread inside my being. A message that told me that sobriety would always bring out the best in me, whatever happened.

After a meeting, I would be filled with a fresh outlook, an inspiration to take on new challenges, new visions and often with renewed joy and a strengthened resolve to search out the possibilities in my daily life. If I had shared about or listened to hardships this would also deepen my trust and respect for continuing to live sober

– the possibilities to find ways to manage the most difficult challenges were apparently endless.

I began walking with a straightened back, dressing better and when I looked people in the eye I could see the other person's gaze teeming with life. Extraordinary revelations on a daily basis.

At the ward, a nurse said something that rooted itself in my heart:

"It is usual for people who have managed to break off their addiction to start viewing life as people do who, in other situations, have cheated death."

The understanding of how important it was for me to take responsibility for my recovery deepened from this viewpoint. Not as a reluctant must-do chore, but as a loving commitment to myself, Emma and the vibrant humanity our little family was finally a part of.

I had now been clean for almost three months and had gotten braver when it came to talking to others after the meetings. One Friday evening, one of the girls asked me if I wanted to come with her and three others to a dance club down-town. I hesitated because I was still uncomfortable hanging around with others for longer periods of time. But I knew I had to make changes to this behaviour so I took a quick moment to assess my instinctive reaction to decline.

In this situation it wasn't only the company I was

holding back from, it was also, of course, the club environment. I had never been out dancing without being under the influence before, at least not since I had left my parents' home. With this afterthought, I realised that this occasion would be the best opportunity to get some practice in for going against both of these huge fears.

One - I would be with others who abstained from drugs so if I got an impulse to buy a beer it was out of the question anyway.

Two - being in a club where it would be more about mingling and looking at people rather than sitting in a quiet restaurant to chat for hours made this more of a socially "light" practice-run for me.

I decided to go with them on, what I filed under 'a study visit on the town'.

We entered the three-storey, heaving nightclub. I bought a soda at the bar, which brought on a very strange, out of place feeling. I didn't feel as alien as I had imagined I would, though. I remembered that, back in the day, I had cared little of what other people in such places were up to and now that I was sober I could see that everyone was satisfied to be taking care of their own business.

I tried my wings on the dance floor but discovered that I couldn't relax. It was more uncomfortable than fun so I stood, happily savouring my soda and looking at the people enjoying the club. That was more than interesting and I had several insights during this night out. The first one being how "normies" used alcohol. I got the impression that many just did it to be able to loosen up a bit and dare to clown around more than they would have done if they were sober. Some people could go out, have a few drinks, dance, act a little whimsically and socialize without the buzz being the primary focus. This was a completely new revelation for me. This brought on the other insight which was that this type of party-goer had never been and would never, ever, be me. I stood and studied a part of humanity that I had never known existed. I felt a pang of sorrow for what my club years had been like. The entertainment was primarily being buzzed. If that was fulfilled then I could hopefully enjoy myself for a little while but only until the buzz needed refilling. Now that I felt this sorrow, I noticed that it was also tinged with remarkable joy and consolation. The sorrow was bound to the hollow life I had led. The joy and the consolation lay in the complete acceptance that I did not want to have that drugged state of existence back in my life and I didn't have to. I wanted to party but I wanted to learn how to party for real.

The fact that I couldn't relax enough to enjoy some moves on the dance floor that night was something I had almost counted on. It was too early for me. My desire to experience partying for real was born that night though. I dearly looked forward to going out, dancing, whimsically wild, partying with my new circles of friends.

I felt completely confident that this dancing dream would come true one magical evening in my disco-lit future.

Twenty-seven

One day, when I had been sober for almost three months, I suddenly started to feel very dizzy. I had to break off from my usual routine and, after having been to the ward, I went straight home. I had done some laundry in the morning and now I took a bath towel that was still wet, lay down on the bed and put it on top of me. My head was spinning with several of the slogans that were used in the twelve step method:

"Easy does it", "First things first", "Slowly but surely", "One day at a time"...

I wondered if I was going crazy, feeling the world slip out from underneath me, then I called my sponsor. She listened to me without interrupting as I described the loony dizziness I felt and then she put the inevitable question to me:

"But, Lotten, what have you been eating lately?"

My mind fell instantly silent and after some thought I replied:

"Yoghurt and bananas. It's summer!"

Her simple question helped me realise the problem. I had been eating a solid breakfast but had skipped wholesome lunches and dinners completely. The matter of taking care of my eating habits was truly like a whole new world to me. I had lots of delusions about what healthy diets could be for me, despite having some knowledge of nutrition. This was because I applied what I knew to what might sustain a healthy person. For me, who had been subconsciously anorexic amidst all the drug-using and the constant stress I had put myself through, to have only a light lunch or to go on a diet wasn't even worth considering at this stage. My sponsor had experience of some similar difficulties with getting food issues in place and her insights helped me a lot. It suddenly dawned on me that my recovery, and therefore my life, could actually depend on this "side-issue". I was amazed that taking care of this part of the important watchlist within HALT had completely slipped my mind.

It took me several days to recover from this crash. I truly had everything to learn about the basics of living and now the top issue was putting together a healthy diet that suited a recovering addict. I had gained 25 kilograms since the first time around at the treatment centre. I had over-indulged in candy, sodas, jams and, at every meal, lots of food. Now I felt very uncomfortable in my body and evidently couldn't go on a diet so I had to decide on a long-term plan instead. It would be impossible to rid myself of all these kilos through sheer exercise so I was radically going to be careful about what I put into my body. My new health plan included always riding my bicycle or walking to get wherever I was going and in whatever the weather and also, most importantly, learning to eat regular, nutritious and tasty food. The first few months, I made shrimp sandwiches on whole grain bread with plenty of vegetables almost every day. I also ate tons of fruit salad with unsweetened cream. These were my two favourite dishes in the whole wide world and I used them as 'carrots' during this initial change of habits. To keep my motivation for learning a new way of eating, I created an enjoyable diet that I could look forward to.

Through having such positive changes to weave into my everyday life, a sense of a wholesome purpose ever-so slowly but surely began to take root in my every-day existence. When the difficult waves of sorrow and pain for all the awful things I had done swept through me and the agony of missing Emma ached inside, these loving things I had started to do for myself carried me, strengthening my resolve, sometimes one minute at a time. I would do anything to keep taking responsibility for my recovery, working with determination at being a better person.

Midsummer's Eve came and went. Since I couldn't be with Emma, I had gone on a camping trip with a non-profit sobriety organisation. CaF had explained the importance of Emma having this holiday to bond with her "new family". They used those exact words and I was devastated. I remembered the promise they had given me about her getting to move back in with me in November and I had hung on to that, but now I got an uneasy feeling in my gut. When I got back to town I contacted CaF to book a new appointment so as to get a clearer picture of their planning for Emma's and my reunion. This meeting was scheduled for after all the vacations and the summer went on with my routines of biking and taking care of how I ate, sunbathing between the meetings, my dental appointments and the wondrous, heavenly visits with Emma. I worked hard at building a new platform for my life and used the time well but always in the company of sore longing. At last, the day of the meeting with the social workers at CaF arrived.

It was early August when I sat down with Anna and Louise. I told them what I had understood of the time schedule they had given me, the promise of Emma's moving back home in November. Their response was a tough blow to my spirit.

"Since Emma came into custodial care in November last year and these cases are re-evaluated every six months that re-evaluation is what is going to happen in November. May is the earliest date for her moving back that we can give you."

Another six months! I felt my emotions go into distressing cramps and I sat as if frozen, unable to speak while the tears started streaming down my cheeks. I had really believed that Emma would be moving back with me and I had even talked to her about it. Now that I looked back I saw that the date which I had pried out of Anna and Louise in the spring may have been vague, even though I had really pressed them hard to get a straight answer. I had asked them about it repeatedly and now I was confused about what question they had actually answered. I hadn't gotten their reply concerning November in writing either.

Several other things occurred to me during this meeting. The room that Mona and Ulf had decorated for Emma had been costly, meticulously prepared for a little girl. The Midsummer's celebration that I had been excluded from. The glances Mona and Ulf had exchanged when I had talked to them about November. CaFs' vague answers that I now began to presume had only been to keep my hopes up rather than any actual planning on their part. I suddenly saw that they might have had an entirely different agenda all along. An agenda based on me probably not making it and therefore they were, from their perspective, seeing to Emma's well-being and safety by readying her for a long-term placement with her "new family".

I expressed my views on all this from what I experienced as a very undermined position. It took all my energy to describe how sure I was about my resolve to stay in recovery. I told them that not even this upsetting news made me want alcohol again – which, in truth, surprised even me. I also described Emma's situation at Mona and Ulf's home. She was behaving as a child would who was visiting her grandparents during the holidays. I had noticed that she manipulated them into getting what she wanted in a manner that I would never have accepted. She wasn't getting the guidance I would be giving her. I told them of how I'd had to stop Mona and Ulf giving Emma any more gifts, since the amount of presents she received, several times a week, was in conflict with how I viewed a child's upbringing and also it was a standard I wouldn't be able to keep up when Emma moved back with me. Mona and Ulf were truly lovely but they didn't know her as I instinctively did.

I was not going to accept anything less than written notice of their decision this time. I told them that I would keep on going to the hospital even after Emma had moved back home – I was doing this because I wanted a life for myself. That Emma was a part of my life was indisputable but my sobriety was not something that I relished solely because of my parenthood. Everything I told Anna and Louise was sincere and especially on the issue of my continuous recovery. It wasn't fathomable that I could go back to leading the life of the sickly, arrogant and ruthless person I would become again if went back to using drugs. Regardless of what would happen in this or other matters in my life, I would do everything I could to stay on this path.

As humbly as I could, I stood fast. I clarified that Emma had been placed under their care on my own volition and that I wanted a written copy of this meeting so that I could take this matter further up their ladder. In my gut, I knew irrefutably what would be best for Emma. I wouldn't back down. I couldn't do more than this but I was determined to keep my word to my little girl and I would fight with all I had to get her home as soon as possible. Her separation from me had begun as soon as she had come into this world. Now that I finally had something to give her, there had to be an end to this detachment. Together, we could begin our individual healing processes in earnest and I would have the greatest chance to amend the harm I had caused her.

I had been very grateful for her placement when I had believed that I was going to die of my active addiction to alcohol and this evolution into a responsible parent was, mildly put, bewildering at times. It was an unbelievable journey and this insight made me realise that it must have been even more surreal for Anna and Louise. When I had talked about what our lives had actually been like before my sobriety in earlier conversations with Anna, she had expressed feelings of having been deceived by my expert manipulations of her and her team. All the lies I had fed them when I was still using had been so well-oiled that not even she had doubted me, despite her many years of working in this field. When I had told her what the summer between my two treatments had actually been like for us, she exclaimed:

"But Lotten, how then can we know that you are really truthful now when you have been so cunning in misleading us before?"

I could only reply with the only test I wouldn't be able to pass if push came to shove:

"If I stop going to the ward to volunteer drug tests or if I stop following up on my contact with you, then you will know. The only assurance I can give you are these things – whatever I say is irrelevant. That is how an addict works. The physical proof I give you is the only way you will be able to know what I am actually doing. I can tell you from the bottom of my heart that I will always keep taking care of my disease – to be in the sick phase of addiction is not an option for either Emma or me. But words are, as you say, easily stitched together. Keep tabs on me – for both Emma's and my sake. The law allows you to look out for Emma and you'll do that by checking up on what I'm doing, not by listening to what I'm saying."

They wanted the process with Emma's move to drag on longer but I stood my ground. I was sure that Emma would be better off with me by her side. She would develop and strengthen unwanted behavioural patterns all the more as time went by. I could see clearly how she had become more and more obstinate toward Mona and Ulf every time I visited. For a child, one month is like six months for an adult. This meant that her little world, in which she had been confined since she was born, would strengthen its hold on her by the minute as long as she was away from me.

I was very clear at this meeting that I wanted more frequent contact with CaF from now on, several times a week, and that I was going to do everything to enable the reunion with my daughter as soon as possible. All according to the plan as I had understood it from the beginning. This would not drag on longer than necessary. I parted with them, telling them that I expected the written decision within the next couple of days so as to be able to lodge an appeal against it.

After this meeting I was ridden with emotional pain and completely drained physically. I was fuelled only by a fighting spirit which burned on the inside. I would give this my all. The chance to get to live sober was one I would savour and take responsibility for, whatever they believed. I would never even have considered bringing Emma to live with me if I hadn't been 100% sure of my commitment and resolve towards staying in recovery. During the rest of my life, I would pray that I would be allowed to remember my gratitude toward having found a way to cheat the lethal affliction that I bore.

That same afternoon, I called CaF and got the number to contact the head of their department and for the next few days I put pressure on the staff there. My emotional state was very burdened and I would never have made it without my self-help group and I was also carried by the spiritual methods I had developed. The sensation of my everyday existence verging on the unmanageable was very tangible. Never in my life had I been so close to the pure vibrations of my emotions. Illusions of having been tough and street-smart in my past were now laughable. I had never known challenge until now! I felt as if I was being thrown about in a dinghy, harassed by a raging ocean of raving emotions. I sought lee where I was used to doing so by creating an escape route, but this time not with my liquid drug. Re-channelling this inner storm onto something outside myself was this time focused on an obsession that was also dangerously mind-blowing – I became infatuated with a man...

He was a recovering addict too and I had felt a strong attraction to him for a while. Now this pull suddenly reformed itself into what I labelled as "being in love". When I thought of him at the start of this infatuation, I was possessed by an adventurous sensation that would momentarily overlap with the anguish of missing my child. But soon the whole emotional carousel became a centrifugal plague. I couldn't bare keeping this whirlwind of feelings bottled up so I decided to tell him how I felt. I simply called him and forced the words out:

"Hello! I need to tell you that I love you."

He was silent for several seconds and then stammered:

"Well, er, Lotten, I, er, think this lies entirely within you."

In my brain the whole thing wasn't over just because of his response. I was used to always getting my way since I had been in my active addiction and even earlier than that as well. As this was a highly addictive situation, a 'no' on his part did not end my obsession. Rather, my daydreams of us as a couple became even more vivid. I lived with this impulse surging through my system for another couple of weeks, but without involving him again.

The turning point came during one of my trips to visit Emma. Suddenly, and with distinct clarity, I could see my focus being on this castle in the sky instead of being in my usual meditation on how the upcoming day with Emma could turn out into the best visit for us. This was the beginning of the end. I was suddenly able to see that the impulse that soared within was disturbingly similar to the urge I'd been driven by when putting my well-being in the illusory cradle of intoxication. It became evident that I needed to make a change in my approach and for the upcoming hours with Emma I summoned all my strength to redirect my energy back to the reality of what was truly important in my life.

My desperation to be freed from the plague that these feelings of infatuation had become made me turn to prayer. With something resembling the same fervour I had felt on that distant morning in March when the drugs' mastery over my sanity had become clear to me, I begged to be freed of this obsession. I had tried to get rid of the hurt from this infatuation in other ways than prayer but to no avail. It felt silly that such a worldly matter should have drawn me this far off-balance. This yearning, eating up all my waking hours, had sneaked up on me as a sweet longing but had now turned into a terribly destructive pattern. When I now fell into prayer I prayed earnestly, all the way up from the tips of my toes.

I woke up the next morning and was taken aback at finding a serenity harbouring inside. I hadn't felt this calm in weeks. I searched inside but couldn't find a trace of the obsessive rut. The silence and ease felt as it does when a storm has blown over. An actual physical sensation of relief had anchored itself in the depths of my being. I still carried the illusion of being in love in my thoughts but the emotional anguish was gone. Over the next three or four days the last remnants of my airy fantasy slowly dissipated and the infatuation finally lifted and I was able to see the real world again. This was a remarkable experience. A focused inner effort had resulted in freedom from a destructive cycle that had kept me in its lying grasp of escapism.

I was baffled at prayer having had such an impact on this infatuation's obsessive kidnapping of my mind. To use prayer in this situation was a result of a despair so strong, that this rock-bottom had driven me to my knees (literally). I was not active in any type of spiritual gatherings or other rituals, but I believed that the freedom I now experienced was a result of me sincerely realising that I needed help – that I had been on a very dangerous path. My relationship with my God was strengthened and I continued to pray for guidance despite the overall scientific outlook I had on the mysteries of life.

I realised that I had been walking on very thin ice and got yet another thing to be very grateful for – I had taken care of myself without having to take "refuge" from this obsession by relapsing into drug abuse. I spoke to the guy and told him that I had regained my sanity. I explained that I had confused the very nice person he was with being in love.

I was back in the real world and my actions were once again focused on my recovery and Emma's homecoming.

Twenty-eight

When summer meets up with autumn, Emma has her birthday. This year, she turned five and the whole family, her brothers and their mother, her grandparents and my siblings, my cousins and their children and even a few friends of the family had sent money so that I could buy gifts from them to bring her. I asked Mona and Ulf if I could come very early that morning so I would be the one to wake her and they agreed. Filled with a tingly, twirly feeling, I left home at 4 a.m., overloaded with packages. The wonder of being able to celebrate this birthday in recovery! I had experienced her third birthday sober when we were at the treatment centre but then I had only been abstinent. There is a huge difference between being in the process of recovery and being in forced abstinence from intoxication. I sat on the bus and reflected on the difference between how much better I could take in the outside world now in comparison with my stunted spirit back then. It was as if the simple things I did today for my well-being were absolute mind-openers. I was often amazed these days at how the world had opened up to me since I'd realised that I had an emotional disease. I smiled to myself, thinking:

"Talk about a paradox." Thankfulness spread throughout my being at the chance I had been given. The warmth of this love for life throbbed joyously inside and my smile grew wider as the bus drove me nearer my beautiful and loveable little birthday girl.

That day was a milestone for our little family. Before the treatment centre, I was indifferent to all celebrations and holidays. I hadn't celebrated Emma's first birthday because I "reasoned" that she was too small to remember it anyway and the money, however little, could be put towards "strengthening" me instead. Now that I actually had a drug-free brain and was healing, my thought-patterns were as different as night and day compared to how they had been then. It was vastly important to show her how valuable her life was to me and to everyone else who loved her. I had even put Simon's name on a parcel even though we hadn't been in touch for a long time. It was crucial that Emma get into her system that she belonged and was loved. I knew that the gifts weren't of primary importance to her. The only thing she wanted deep down was to have a parent who was sober all the time. But the symbolic celebration and the attention she would be getting from her extended family and friends was something that I knew would make her very happy and this day would contribute to her recovery process.

I sang the birthday song silently, she opened her eyes slowly, saw the candle sitting on top of the ice-cream cone and her shout of happiness echoed her genuine surprise. Her beautiful little face outshone the candle flame. Her joy moved me to tears. We spent the whole day together. We swam in the pool in the garden, watched her favourite shows on TV, had sausages and in the afternoon we went for a walk into the village to buy more ice-cream. I was completely unprepared when she abruptly stopped, looked angrily up at me, knotted her small fists, shoving them into her sides, and said:

"Mother! You knew that this would happen if you kept on using alcohol! How could you let this happen to me?!"

This was the first time she had shown her feelings about this situation in such a straightforward manner, and she did so with startling focus and force. It took a moment for me to regain my composure following this sudden contrast from the happiness I had felt about the successful celebration and our, or rather my, invigorating walk in the sun on this joyous day. I had to take a micro-second to turn inward for guidance to be able to give her a truthful and sincere response.

"I was so sick in my thoughts, my darling. I didn't understand what I was doing. You remember when I used beer, right?"

She nodded, with eyebrows contorted and her mouth pursed white. I could see that she was on the verge of tears but too angry to be able to cry. I continued, with desperate fervour: I had to get through to her.

"Do you remember what they said to you at Malin's Minne about why we were there at the treatment centre? That thing about me getting very, very ill from using the beers and wine?"

She nodded to these questions but I saw that she wanted more from me, a real answer. Not just a repetition. Silently, I begged my God: 'Please, please, please. Let me tell her a truth that soothes her pain. Please!' The words came to me:

"I couldn't stop. I didn't believe I could live or be a good person without those drugs. I couldn't cook or clean without them. I was so stuck in the habit of heaving those cans and bottles that I even imagined that I could never be a good mother without their content inside me."

Now she finally answered. She blurted out, sounding completely baffled:

"What? Did you really believe that?!"

She peered silently at me for a couple of seconds, with the utmost expression of surprise on her face and then she started laughing. It was a laugh that tore itself from the deepest part of her and she was almost bent double. The look she gave me when she could speak again was glistening with a new spark.

"Mother, then you truly were very sick, because you were an awful mom!" The laughter possessed her again, the giggles bubbling forth.

I was a little shocked at first, but suddenly the absurdity of the lies of the addictive mind hit me with full force and, unexpectedly, I joined in the laughter. I had truly felt that I wouldn't be able to function as a human being without modifying my moods. When the truth was brought into this new light, seeing how the reality of that mood-altering had really turned out, it made me laugh myself to tears.

It was an amazing liberation to see Emma react in this beautiful, clear-eyed manner. I trusted that whatever happened with the process of her moving home she still had a flame burning inside her and this new understanding would help her get through whatever hardships might befall us for a while yet.

When the worst giggle-attack had subsided, I described how I was working hard toward getting better and that she would be able to come home as soon as CaF and I could see that I was well enough.

"I miss you so much, all the time. Even now, you know," I gave her a lopsided smile and tousled her hair. She laughed at this old joke but I could still see that she acknowledged that I was also in pain. I hoped she took in how seriously I was working toward us living together.

"Anna and those people know how it is for mothers and fathers who have the same disease as I do and I trust their opinions as well as my own. Just so you know that I am working very hard all the time because I want you back home with me as soon as I feel strong enough. I listen to both Anna and my doctor and, of course, I go to the meetings every day – I never want to get that sick again. Ever!"

She let this sink in for little while and then she tilted her head, squinting with one eye, and said:

"Okay mother, I understand now. You really were a terrible mommy back then!" And then she laughed even more.

Her remembering, in the simple way she put it, moved me deeply. I felt a profound gratitude that we could both see my disease in this simple fashion. The disease of addiction is so easily identified by the comparison of how I reacted to impulses back then with how I was learning to act in a responsible way now in recovery. I had not been sane. Emma began trotting along, heading purposefully towards the ice-cream stand and I watched after her for a moment. Looking inside, I was surprised to find that I wasn't feeling guilty or shameful in this instant. This kind of liberation usually presented itself when I was seeing the true nature of my disorder. Comparing the difference of how my body, mind and emotional state were now to how they had been then was of vital importance to me. What I did feel was a tremendous sorrow at having this terrible affliction and that no one during the whole course of my life had known how to react to the fact that I had suffered from the disorder of addiction - a deadly and harmful disease that caused so much suffering, and not only to me. The horrid insights about the terrible things I had done to others and also knowing that it had been by a hair's breadth that I had survived. Emma had nearly lost me! These thoughts throbbed in my mind but now they didn't bring forth the usual self-reproaching emotions, rather I felt gratitude soaring within. Jogging up along-side Emma, walking in the sun, holding hands with my miraculous little girl and soon deep in conversation about love of life and trust. Knowing that as long as I lived, I would be responsible, every day, for recovering from this gruesome disease, taking measures so as not to become that terrible person again. Safeguarding the freedom from drugs by letting it be my primary purpose in life. Then I would be free to experience wondrous days like this one countless times in the future.

Life was truly rich and I was going to keep it that way!

This birthday was, thanks to this conversation, the best day I had ever had (with exceptions made for the day I had come into recovery, of course). This was also the best conversation Emma and I had ever had. Leaving her that evening was tinged with a heavy sense of loss but at the same time the assuredness of the day when we would live together as a family coming closer had grown much stronger. That platform, which we both sorely needed, was much more tangible now. Our talk had anchored the certainty that my sobriety was for real even more steadily in my heart, and in the midst of loss and longing, my gratitude for being alive soared.

My delusion about the "co-hell-ision" was being remodelled, my destructive rantings replaced by the wonderful possibilities I could see for being a part of the coalition, being a human among humans. As it did daily, the wonder of how my views on life and living had changed filled me with warmth and love. The next step in my integration into the world was just around the corner and, at the beginning of September, I began my rehabilitation into becoming a working member of society.

The project had been started by two women with around twenty years of sobriety each and was aimed at women who had been living outside the norms of society and who were recovering from an active addiction. We participants were a very varied little crowd of people, ranging from housewives with a wine problem to a person like me who had been homeless and had led a life of crime. There were yet others who had become addicts through the healthcare system giving them prescription drugs and then a few other girls and ladies in between.

I was given the opportunity to approach a "normal" routine in life, at a pace that was adapted to my individual needs. I wouldn't get grades that I could use in a formal way but to begin this procedure of entering into society, taking baby steps, was a brilliant method to get people like me started. I chose to take Swedish, Maths and English and to learn more about using computers. I also applied for a program where I was introduced to activities such as going to the gym, visiting theatres and going to the opera. I attended a crash course in healthy eating. We also went out into the town to visit different municipal offices and we took tours of the parks and learned more about our town. I even got the opportunity to visit a beauty parlour. There was so much I hadn't done and it was the same for the others. I had always read books but there were women at this project who were in their forties and had never been to a library!

It was a weird feeling to get insights into what "ordinary" people filled their lives with. The questions I had battled with during those last awful weeks of my alcohol abuse, about what people did or didn't do, how much they used alcohol or didn't, and how they could possibly be leading fulfilling lives without getting intoxicated at every turn – all these mind-blowing mysteries were now getting their answers. This new part of the puzzle was a veritable smorgasbord for finding out how I wanted to enrich my life and what I wanted to fill it with.

There were many other things woven into this project. One was for me to learn to keep my appointments and stick to a schedule. Another was that I had one of the project managers as my mentor. This was very important since they had had the same disorder as me. They had an eternity of experience at living sober and the one I was paired with was using a different method to recover with than I was. I found it very useful to be able to listen to tips and tricks from both of them and when I needed more personal guidance I could speak privately to my mentor. I got to know yet another "grown-up" more closely.

Maybe the most important conversations we had were the spontaneous ones about everyday things, since I was completely inexperienced at taking part in casual conversations. Now I was to let others into my sphere and also maintain ongoing, professional relationships. The other participants were at varying stages in developing these skills and people are of course different, but it was comforting to know that we all had difficulties regarding our social development – I wasn't alone. I think knowing that we all came from the same background of an addictive disorder made me dare to do more. Energy-wise, I was depleted after the three or four hours I spent there, four days a week. I got a deeper understanding of how mental and emotional strain was physically draining to me and the others: even the managers told of experiencing the same fatigue, even after decades in recovery. Once again I got a clue about the nature of the social, emotional, impairment which I had suffered all my life.

I was very glad to sit in a classroom again. I absorbed as much information as I could. I began writing again, which was a dream I'd had since I was a very little girl.

Throughout my years in active addiction I had felt too dirty and shut off to value or save anything I wrote. Deep down I had known that I wasn't myself. It all went into the trash. Here, I was encouraged by the teacher I had for both Swedish and English:

"I am not your friend and it would be a cheap trick to play on you if what I'm about to tell you weren't true." She eyed me to see that I was following. "You are a very good writer. You should pursue this and enrol on any course that would help you develop this talent."

Oh dear! That was very difficult to take in. I suddenly had great difficulty writing and had to stop because of the tornadoes of emotions that were building up me. I couldn't grasp why her praise would hurt so much. Of course I was very happy, but the teacher and I had to lay out a plan for writing exercises. This helped and the knot loosened after a few weeks. My creative writing picked up where I had left off in senior high school. It felt wondrous!

It was also a huge relief to have something sensible to do in the daytime. My troubles concerning Emma's situation were momentarily dispelled and came down to a more manageable level. I also got to discuss my thoughts and concerns with the other parents, plus the two project leaders were single mothers whose children had been small when they had come into the recovery process.

I still hadn't made any close friends so this was a step toward learning to be around other people. I got to take part in others' accomplishments and share my own with them. We talked about our hopes and fears. For me, who had always been under the illusion of understanding everything with my myriads of theories, it was as if a burden had started to be lifted from my soul and I began learning something of humility when I took account of others' views on the world and their approaches to problem-solving. Carefully, I began letting other people into my life. I had Emma there, of course, but other people had started to become actual existing beings to me. In my addiction, which had been so terribly strong in its pull, I had only used other people as a means to furthering my ends. What happened to me now was enriching in a way I could never have imagined.

The journey of letting others into my life had begun at the twelve-step meetings where I had understood that I had to take account of the experience of others to save my life. Now this process continued with me carefully letting cooperation, communication and coexisting with others become cornerstones of my daily life. I was a baby in the arena of being a human among humans and, thankfully, I could accept that this would take time. Even if this were to be a daily process taking the rest of my life to get used to, I felt assured that I would be able to manage my relationships better with time and patience.

When I got into this project, I had finally come to the top of another waiting list. I had been waiting since my first week in recovery to get therapy sessions at the hospital's addiction ward. I wanted to do everything in my power to heal and now I was able to start upon yet another path. The therapy began with six sessions in which I was to answer questions and tell the therapist about my whole life. When they were done, I was told that we would now focus the therapy on my emotions. I remember my reaction to this being that it sounded quite vague and even a bit dopey. My days were filled to the brim with emotional storms and therefore, I reasoned, there couldn't be any problems with me feeling feelings and I told my therapist so. She replied by stating that I understood a lot on a theoretical level but often seemed out of sync with my emotional response. After a moment of reflection on what she had said, I still couldn't grasp anything at all from her point of view and said so:

"I have to believe what you are telling me but I really can't see what you mean."

However, the reliance on getting exactly what I needed and as much as I could handle worked for me now and I could go along with her judgement and was able to let it go.

Now I had four wholesome courses of action, all aimed at creating a manageable life: my commitment to the twelve-step method: my weekly attendance at the treatment centre's aftercare: the project which was like a school for learning how to become a functioning member of society and a professional healthcare procedure with conventional medical practitioners. All to safeguard my sobriety, strengthening and filling my new life with quality and growth. Everything to make my new life desirable to me. Every day, I experienced my faith being as strong as I believed it could ever get, only to find that the next day it had grown even deeper, warmer and more stable. It was a fresh and wonderful way to lead life.

Carried by this trust and my constant gratitude at being liberated from intoxication, I lived each day savouring this miracle.

Twenty-nine

I didn't tell Emma about the move back with me being postponed. I wasn't going to make this worse than it already was. I waited for written confirmation of what had been said to me at the last meeting. I would speak to Emma about it again when I had a date confirmed in writing. The question of how in the world I could have misunderstood their answers to my insistent demands that they tell me when she would be allowed to live with me again was a puzzle that haunted me daily. I knew that I had asked them many times and in overly clear terms, just to be sure to rule out any misunderstandings. Everything so as not to be giving Emma false hopes and, all the same, I had gotten it wrong. I couldn't know if this was actually a misunderstanding or if they had given me false hopes just to calm me down. I had tried to be as perceptive and foresighted as possible about this important issue. Emma's peace of mind and well-being depended on me not causing her more distress than she felt already. Remembering how confused I had been in those earliest days, I had to consider the possibility that I had interpreted what I wanted to hear from their vague answers, or maybe they had just wanted me out of their hair. And so the possible explanations went on in my head, day after day, over and over. Several times each day, I had to slow down my racing brain and breathe, redirecting my focus to ward off this analysing, this brooding obsession.

I had kept the pressure on the staff at CaF by talking regularly to them and leaving a lot of messages. This was a period of emotional stress like I had never experienced before. My disorder was still present and my self-confidence was frail this early on in my recovery. I really don't know how I managed to pull through.

One morning in October, I got hold of Anna and, once again, I began underlining the importance of getting the written documentation as soon as possible. Eight weeks had gone by since they informed me of the possibility of May next year being Emma's homecoming date. I was getting extremely frustrated at living with this uncertainty hovering over my every waking hour. Thankfully, I was determined to keep myself in recovery. This prolonged wait was enough to break anyone! My hands were tied as long as I didn't have a transcript of their plans for my daughter. Angrily, I continued talking and blurted out whatever I had to ventilate:

"I thank my lucky stars that she still doesn't understand that November is next month!"

Anna broke off my tirade with six simple words:

"We have come to a decision."

"What?" My speech was lost and my entire being became completely silent in an instant, listening for what was to come. Anna continued:

"I want to begin by saying that this is against Louise's and my advice, but you do have the law on your side."

She didn't sound happy. The whole world disappeared around me. All that existed was to hear what was coming next.

"There is a date set for Emma moving back with you full-time on the 2nd of January 2007 and we need to set up a meeting to schedule the routines for her to get the reintegration process back into her daycare group off to a good start and for her to get used to living with you again."

Anna spoke very curtly and I wasn't going to rub salt into her wounds of irritation by cheering wildly - as I was on the inside - but only said:

"Give me an appointment and I'll be there!"

A warm sensation was spreading inside me and I added a solemn:

"Thank you," which Anna answered with a muffled:

"Mm."

I restrained myself, wrote down the time of the meeting, hurried through our goodbyes and when I had hung up, my legs buckled beneath me. I couldn't fathom that this was actually happening. I shouted "Weeehoooo" or the like, sitting on my knees, and began laughing like crazy. I realised that, inside, I had been preparing myself to settle for May. I also realised that this catastrophic spiral had escalated so badly because I had subconsciously been fearing that it might not ever happen... Weeehoooing some more and much louder, I then called my sponsor. Even positive thoughts were to be treated with care and best shared with someone.

CaF and I worked out a good schedule for Emma's reintegration, setting an easy pace. As part of the plan, we were to spend Christmas together with my mother in Gothenburg. New Year she would celebrate with Mona and Ulf and this was something I wouldn't be arguing with. They were important people in our lives. I took care of the schedule with the daycare centre and when all this practical stuff was in place the time had finally come to tell Emma.

She didn't have the months clear in her head yet, or at least she hadn't mentioned the diversion from the original plan. Now I told her that the move home had been put back ever-so slightly by CaF, but only by a few days. Then I moved the conversation onto telling her the exciting news of her already spending her first weekend with me already from the following Friday to Sunday and that I would pick her up at preschool on Friday. I also told her that she would soon be going to her old daycare centre for a few days at a time until it was time to come and live with me for real again. This changing of the subject to the positive events to come proved to be a good tactic because she forgot all about the postponement and became wild with joy about sleeping over at my house so soon. The joy and relief I saw in her eyes was heart-breaking. It showed how she had kept her head above water all this time. For her, it had been the longest year since she had been moved to the orphanage. I don't know if I could have coped with the true burden of what Emma had been through if I had realised her struggle earlier on in my healing process.

I knew that being a full-time, single mother was going to be hard and that this would be the first time I was actually able to be a parent at all. It was hard on many single parents living in the isolation of modern society. For my child to be with me was unquestionably the best for her though and, as long as I continued to take care of my recovery, everything would work out for the best.

A big difference would be that I would have to lessen my going to the self-help meetings. During the eight months that I had been sober, I had been able to go to at least one but often as many as three meetings a day and I knew in my heart that I had laid a solid foundation for this new development in our lives. I knew that I would be able to make at least five meetings per week even after our daily routines set in. It had also been approved that Emma would go to Mona and Ulf's every other weekend so I could get a chance to recuperate, recover and work on my social life. I looked with confidence to the future.

There was one snag though and it was a rather huge one.

Where were we to live? In the collective, there were two women who were in a bad way in their addiction. Someone had reported this to social services only a couple of weeks earlier. One of the women was moving out while the other had a calmer period and was giving drug tests. I would be able to have Emma with me at the collective during the shorter stays that we had planned but we couldn't live there when she moved back permanently. I discovered something very strange in this situation – I was completely unable to look for an apartment. As soon as I searched through the ads or when I was about to make phone calls to different landlords, I became agitated and got completely stressed out, my brain shut down and I went emotionally numb. Totally cut off.

All through my homeless years I had been a wizard at fixing places to stay, shaky living situations that had always worked out, and now I was suddenly paralysed in anything that had to do with this. I was bludgeoned into an even worse inaction by a suffocating sensation of irresponsibility. I tried to see that finding us a home was the loving course of action to take for our little family but to no avail. Whichever way I tried to turn or not to turn this matter, the result remained the same. I could not do a thing! Social services had promised us an apartment in the area where Emma had her preschool and that was comforting but I really didn't want to live in a place where the neighbours would know that we were social welfare "cases". None of these motivational facts changed the pulsating resistance that overwhelmed me at the thought of looking around. I guessed it must have to do with my years as a homeless person and probably so far back as to all the moving about since I was four months old. I remembered how I had used, manipulated and let down so many people in my subletting and squatting years. Finally, the pain of trying became too strong. I had to pray to my God for relief from this excruciating and unmanageable task.

"I know that this has to be as it is meant to be. I can't do anything about this. Please give me the serenity to accept that this task is over my head! I'm letting this go and asking to be able to experience trust that Emma's and my needs will be seen to."

The sorrow was fresh again, remembering how I had driven myself to scraping rock bottom but, thankfully, within a few days my worries subsided. Of course there was the lurking feeling of me being an utterly irresponsible head of the family, but then having only fleeting thoughts about buying the paper to look at ads made my head instantly feel as if it was filling up with rocks from the wolfs' belly in Little Red Riding Hood and I couldn't change it. Instead, I had to put extra effort into doing good things for myself on a daily basis. Anything to keep my mindful self-love and respect on an acceptable level. It was hard work but it paid off and I could rest, having mustered the feeling of trust that I had prayed for.

That first weekend we got to spend together was like heaven on Earth. We talked all the time, went for long walks and watched the children's channel together, and then came the wonderful moment of beddy-byes when I got to read to my little angel. These evening rituals had been founded at Malin's Minne and I had actually kept them alive since then. I had missed these moments immensely. After reading, I sang quiet lullabies until I could hear her breathing carrying her into the realms of sleep and I dozed off beside her. I awoke in the middle of the night and relished the joy at having her there, lying awake for a long time, thanking my God and snuggling in her soft hair. The emotions were so strong that they verged on being surreal. I had to get up to write a gratitude list to come down to Earth again and then I was able to get back to sleep.

In the morning I woke her up by lightly rubbing her back, whispering:

"Little-cotton-ball, it's morning. Time to wakey-wakey." I kissed her lightly on the cheek and then, the most beautiful sight of all, she woke up, blinking slowly, giving me a satisfied, sleepy smile as she mumbled:

"Mother!" She stretched out her arms with a dreamy happy-face, locked her little arms around my neck and kissed me back.

What an indescribably wondrous reality. I had to hold on to the moment, treasure the now, because it felt as if my emotions would carry me off, twirling in this whirlwind of happiness and then my sanity would be taken along for the ride. The wonder of us finally getting to have a life together. A real life! A sane life. Our awful existence polluted by my addiction was over.

It was such a gift that the truth of it was difficult to grasp. Emma's reaction to moving back in with me seemed more self-evident to her than to me. To her, it was just how it was supposed to be. I tried to let her outlook influence me because I was totally overwhelmed. Suddenly, I could get small notions of what my therapist had meant by me having to learn to get to know and learn to handle my emotions. That Sunday, dropping Emma off at Mona and Ulf's was easier than any time we had parted since November of the year before. I think I smiled all the way back to Malmö.

Now my days were spent taking care of all the irons in the fire and I continued letting go of the question of our living quarters as soon as the issue arose, several times a day, in my head. It was hard but all the practical chores helped me live in the here and now and the sensations of gratitude and trust carried me as I weathered the storms.

One evening, a friend who had brought me to a meeting

while I was still using alcohol called me out of the blue. She said that her mother had been visiting and when she had been taking the elevator up to my friend's floor she had spoken to a man who lived in the building. He had told her that he was moving out because he had bought a house. He happily told her that he was going to call the landlord to terminate his lease as soon as he got through the door of his flat. My friend thought of me at once when her mother told her the neighbour's story. She called me straight away to encourage me to contact the landlord the next morning. Suddenly, I felt my blockage come undone. It was as if a physical clasp had been unfastened! I rang them first thing in the morning. The office told me that I could view the apartment and gave me the number of the current tenant. I called him and we decided on 7 p.m. that same evening. I felt very satisfied with having done something to secure our living situation but understood that my chances of getting this apartment were minuscule. I had debts and wasn't employed.

I pressed the buzzer of the apartment and the man let me into the high rise in the centre of town and I took the elevator up to the ninth floor. The flat had the same layout as the one my friend lived in a couple of floors directly beneath this one in the complex. I had been so happy for her and also a bit jealous when she had gotten her lease there. The layout was very well-thought out and it was roomy. Also, the address would be perfect for us. Emma's daycare centre was on the next block and my home group in the twelve-step fellowship was only three blocks away. I tried to tell myself that, however this turned out, I would have gotten to see the most remarkable view of my city, but deep down I fell in love with the place instantly.

The next morning, I called the landlord and told the woman who managed the building that the apartment was a hundred-percent match for what Emma and I needed. I told her that we had lived in this part of town almost all the time since my daughter had been born. I was honest and told her about my debts and that I was studying at the moment, but of my past life I kept my integrity intact. I didn't lie, I just didn't tell her everything. My mother and her husband had agreed to be guarantors on the lease if I didn't pass their qualifications process. The woman I spoke to promised to get back to me as soon as she could.

Two days passed and when she hadn't called I rang her. She informed me that they couldn't accept guarantors and that I couldn't get the lease because of my financial situation. I hung up but was fired up with an illogical urge to keep fighting for this apartment. I sat down, turned my focus inward and asked:

"How can I proceed?"

Within a minute, an idea came to me and I called social services. They informed me that if the landlord agreed to have the municipality as a tenant, they would sign the lease for me because I had a child. I called the office again and told her of the offer I had been given and gave her all the contact information. Again I stressed that this flat would be the perfect home for us and that I would soon be in a job. She said that they would look into it. I had done all I could and prayed for serenity and kept the fire burning, fuelling my hope.

The days went by. With a phone call, I ensured that all parties were in contact with each other but other than that, the whole matter was out of my control now. I realised that it would be a miracle if we got the apartment. The neighbourhood was very attractive and despite its' Soho-like resemblance, our block was rather quiet for being in such a creative and lively part of Malmö. The building was right next to Folkets Park, the People's Park, a big, green space for leisure and activities with great significance in both the town's and our little family's history. The complex also had a huge yard in which Emma could play unsupervised because it was situated one floor above street level and was not accessible to anyone other than the tenants.

I rode my bike past the block every day, looking up at the windows of the apartment, dreaming. All my waking hours were spent in reflection and meditation to try to keep calm. Trust weighed down my prayers in between futile attempts, aware of the impossibility of doing so, but still nagging and only half-joking, at 'manipulating' my God:

"Hey, you know how great this would be for us, right? Think of Emma! Yeah, yeah, "Thy will be done", of course, and all that... but still!" At the same time I was smiling, hoping and wailing like a small child inside.

I had to nourish acceptance to be able to handle it if we didn't get it. In the midst of this craziness, I managed to maintain some sort of serenity and took extra-special care to manage my emotional health. I could feel how applying recovery methods made my life better with every passing minute and this kept my gratitude quite stable and always in focus. I was also careful to allow myself to feel hopeful. To hope was a much more comfortable feeling than preparing for the worst.

When the call from social services came, two weeks had gone by since I had been to view the apartment. With a concerted effort I stilled myself inside, ready to meet whatever the outcome.

"I have just hung up the phone from talking to the landlord and everything is ready." The words came like an echo from a distant universe.

What had she said? Ready? Everything is ready?? Everything? What does that mean? It must mean... We had gotten it?! Had we gotten it? I couldn't believe it:

"What? Is it true? Are we going to get to move in?!"

Ulla had been involved since the first collective

between the two rehabs where we had lived when CaF had come to take Emma to the orphanage. She had actually been there accompanying CaF on that very day. Now she laughed.

"Oh yes, Lotten. It's true. You will be moving in January 2nd."

"But that's when Emma's moving back with me! Then we'll be able to move in together. This is incredible! How?! What happens now? When do we sign the contract? How will this work?"

Ulla kept on laughing and I interrupted myself to join her. I experienced the now familiar surreal sensation again but underneath that swirl there simmered another, very uncomfortable feeling. I fell silent and Ulla continued:

"Come up to my office on Monday and then we will sign a lease that will be between you and us. We will be signing with the landlord tomorrow and then you will sublet from us for the time being. Eventually, you will be able to take over the contract. Take it easy and I'll see you soon." I could hear her smiling but I was unable to speak now. She said softly:

"You are worthy of this, Lotten. What a great job you are doing for your sobriety and for your daughter. It is pure joy to follow you on your journey. And hey - congratulations! Nicely done finding this apartment on your own!"

I thanked her, hearing my voice coming from some distant part of me and then we said good-bye. I was at the project and sat in a private room and I had to stay there for a while. Ulla had pinpointed the awkwardness I was feeling. Did I really deserve this? The uneasiness was related to how I had lived my life. The manipulative, ruthless and nonchalant Lotten who always stepped on people to reach her own ends. At this moment, the knowledge of me having been insane at the time due to my addiction, which I claimed to have internalised, was far from me. That awful person did not deserve this privilege! I had to start repeating Ulla's words to myself - I was worthy of this. The responsibility I took for staying sober was something I had accepted to be doing daily for the rest of my life. I wasn't going to become that terrible person again. Ever. Whatever happened in my life, I would put my recovery first. The awkwardness lingered and I kept affirming the me of today into my system, clearing away the self-loathing memories to be able to view the image of who I was now. I stilled my inner being and brought forth thankfulness for what we had been given and for having found the desire to take on this second chance in life. To make things right to the best of my ability. Gratitude was always the sure card to play in any situation – good or bad.

Anyone would have been overwhelmed by such an

opportunity and I had to put that factor into the equation. Finally, I pulled myself together so I could at least leave the room to join the others. I was met by hugs and congratulations when I told them. It felt better but I still couldn't grasp it. I suspected that that would be a long process. It had too large an impact on Emma's and my situation to be able to digest. At least not yet. So many things whirled about in my head. That we had gotten our home in the exact place that I had wanted with the perfect date to move in on, which made it possible for us to do the housewarming together. The perfect layout of the flat, the incredible view and the large bathroom that even had a bidet which I remember us having in our house when I was a child... There were so many things about it that made the apartment so right - and most important of all was the wonder of us getting a home. I couldn't fathom how this had happened.

I still had gnawing mind-ghosts that whispered that other people who had lived responsible and honourable lives would have a true right to this flat. This revealed to me that I was very tainted by the all too common view of people with the disease of addiction being unworthy and incorrigible people. Despite having gotten a somewhat better awareness about my drug addiction having been a desperate kind of self-medication - a mad, ruthless chasing for a better life.

Apparently I still fought the old windmills.

Since it seemed that I was unable to get past the disturbing feeling in my gut, I made a complete turn-around in my thought patterns instead. I started to think of Emma. She was absolutely deserving of a beautiful home. A perfect home where she would get the chance to heal and grow up in a safe and pure environment. As all methods are good except for the bad ones, this became the method I used as a starting point for letting joy seep into my heart for having found a home for us. Again and again, I would turn my thoughts around, back to my innocent little girl and her well-being, savouring her rights to this home. Then I could feel unspoiled gratitude.

To see myself as a worthy recipient of anything as wonderful as this fresh start sat much, much further in, but I trusted that, in time, an appreciation of self would come to me too.

Thirty

All through November and at the beginning of December, time seemed to stand still. Luckily, I had a lot to do. I was preoccupied with picking Emma up and dropping her off again at Mona and Ulf's. It was great to be able to take her to her old preschool again. I had told the teachers something of how life had been for us before she was sent to live at the orphanage and they said they couldn't believe it. Remembering how mentally unstable I was due to the alcohol abuse and how worn out I had been, I was probably even more surprised by the fact that they hadn't noticed. How could it not have shown? I couldn't get my head around how they hadn't seen the terrible shape I was in. My acting talents and evasive manoeuvres must have been very elaborate. I got tired just thinking of the energy I had put into misleading everyone in the circles I moved in. There was material to fill volumes with all that I was relieved at not having to be hiding and lying about these days.

One Friday morning in early December, I left home at 4.30 a.m. to pick Emma up so that I could drop her off at the daycare facility at 9.30. She would be staying with me until Monday afternoon after spending the whole day at preschool. When I had left her with the teachers on Friday, I went straight to the ward for my daily visit there. I was waiting in line for my Antabuse when one of the nurses came and said that they wanted me to provide both blood- and urine-samples for analysis. I was always happy to do this because this reminded me of the freedom I had found in not having to manipulate my surroundings anymore. I was never afraid of what the test results would be because I was clean and had nothing to hide. It was a mental pat on the back for me for all my successful efforts, so to speak. Ever since Emma had come into this world, I had had many unpleasant experiences at this ward over the years. Now it was the other way around and every visit was worth its weight in gold. I was thankful for having these people by my side on this journey. I brought Emma with me there every day of that weekend. It was good for her to see that I took care of myself and to get an idea of the easy relationship I had with the people on the staff. They all doted on her and I could see that she felt safe and proud to be allowed to take part in such an important and regular routine in my daily life.

We had a lovely weekend, and when Monday came round I dropped her off at 8 a.m. Then I rode my bike to the project, filled with the anticipation of this being just the way it would be when she moved in with me. I arrived, poured myself a cup of coffee and sat down by the computer to practice expressing some of the joyous emotions I was experiencing in a writing exercise. My phone rang and it was Anna from CaF. Bursting with enthusiasm, I told her how I had taken Emma to preschool that morning and about of the wonderful weekend we'd had. She listened to my ramblings and then I asked what she had wanted.

"Well, I got a call from Mona and Ulf this morning. They said that you had smelled of alcohol on Friday when you picked Emma up."

The world faded and all I heard was the dead silence on the other end of the phone. In a second, ranges of emotions rushed through me – shock, surprise, terror and finally an encompassing fear of how I was to prove my innocence of this. I exploded:

"No, no, no! That is not what happened! I went to the hospital right after I left Emma at daycare on Friday and there they asked me to give them both blood and urine samples for testing. That was only three hours after I had been to pick Emma up. The results will show that I have not been using alcohol or any other substance at all. What they suspected did not happen!"

Within a couple of seconds following this outburst I continued furiously:

"Do you mean to say that they let Emma leave with me even though they thought that I was drunk!? That they let her stay with me the whole weekend without contacting you or the emergency service within your department?!"

A tsunami of rage welled up inside me.

"That would have been severe child abuse! And severe negligence on their part! Think of what it would have been like for Emma to have to be with me if I had actually been drunk!"

Anna seemed taken aback by my outbursts because she didn't say anything, or maybe she never got the chance to. She must have heard that I meant every word. It would have been emotional torture for Emma to be wrenched away from all the love and hope she now harboured. To be forced back into the isolation with her sickly, intoxicated parent whom she put her trust in and loved more than anyone in the whole world. I was severely pissed off!

"They are supposed to put her safety before everything else. That is their responsibility! You will have to clarify this with them so that no other child is ever put at such a risk. What if it had been true?!"

I was close to tears from despair. Anger and memories of how it had been before tumbled in my mind, blending with a fear of what would happen now.

Finally, Anna spoke but what she said made me even more mad.

"Well, they just didn't know what to do."

I exploded again.

"That is not an excuse! They had one obligation toward my daughter, for goodness' sake, and that was to see to her being safe and to let her start her healing process from the hell she grew up in! How can letting her back into that inferno of mental abuse be something they could even so much as hesitate about stopping? Alright if they didn't want to confront me thinking that I was under the influence of alcohol – the risk of violence is imminent with people who are drunk - but they still should have called you as soon as we had left the house. At once! Everything to get Emma out of harm's way... No, Anna, you have to talk to them about this. I am so angry right now. I am so angry I can't even think about what torture it would have been for Emma if it were true. I will drop her off this afternoon as planned and we will stick to the schedule we drew up. You will have to speak to the staff at the hospital. I was there on Saturday and Sunday. Get them to give you the test results as soon as they can. This will not disrupt our plans and Emma will not be worried because of this. She already knows when I am supposed to pick her up for her next stay in Malmö. There have been enough disappointments in her life!"

Now I was almost crying but my sense of dread was stronger. Within me, scenarios of how Emma had been put in harm's way since her birth flowed forth, replaying in my head. This terror was mixed in with images of how it could have been for her during these last few days if I had actually been drunk as they feared. If it had been as they suspected, it would not have been acceptable for them to have had any kind of misplaced empathy or the slightest hesitation at taking protective measures.

We ended the conversation with Anna saying that she would get back to me within the hour. I sat down in an empty classroom and my whole body shook. I thanked all the gods and their entourage of protective angels for having been asked to give specifically those really thorough drug tests on Friday morning. Those tests were sure to trace alcohol usage as far back as three to four weeks. Since I knew what I had and hadn't done, I wasn't worried about the results. My anguish sprung from all the memories that resurfaced and also the worry that this turn of events could, in any way, cause Emma's moving home to be postponed. What if CaF decided that they wanted to see the test results before we could continue the planned schedule? What if I wouldn't get to see her again for in weeks?

I didn't get anything out of this winding spiral of thoughts other than the same worried questions coming back, over and over again. I went to one of the project leaders and asked to talk to her. I had to get out of my own head and share this with someone else. When I was in this turbulent emotional state, my emotions became too much for me to handle on my own. I needed someone else to help me distance myself and concretise exactly what had happened. We sat down in a private discussion room and, after talking and listening for a while, I managed to calm down a bit.

The situation was out of my hands now and I waited for the call from Anna. It was a rough hour to kill before the phone rang and Anna told me that she had gathered as much information as she could from all parties involved. The test results would be ready within a week but, she said, in the meantime we would stick to the plan. She agreed with me that it would be hurtful for Emma if we disturbed the schedule she was set on. I underlined yet again the importance of Anna talking to Mona and Ulf about them having a responsibility to act without hesitation on such suspicions. Thanking Anna for working this out, I hung up.

I couldn't go to the Swedish class I was supposed to attend but I remained at the project. I had to have people around me while I tried to sort out the thoughts raging in my head and, more importantly, the emotions that whirled inside me. I couldn't sort through them all. My feet steered me to the empty room again and I sat down, closed my eyes and prayed for serenity. There wasn't anything more I could do about this mess but there was a lot to take care of inside. What had this awoken in me?

Instinctively, I understood that it was important to let my emotional storm blow over before I left the offices. I couldn't risk these feelings getting the upper hand on me. This was by far the worst emotional craze I had experienced since I had gotten clean. If, in my mind, the world turned into an unmanageable place, I knew that the risk of turning to the old method, alcohol, as an emotional crutch, was a part of my disorder. As far as I could, I invited silence into my being and turned to a loving presence. Anger and fear were human feelings and perfectly healthy reactions to this situation, but for me they also represented danger. It was essential that I look at myself experiencing them so that I could move on into safer emotions such as understanding and empathy. It was also essential to clarify sound boundaries for what was okay in circumstances such as these and what wasn't.

Images of my relationship with Mona and Ulf came to me. Ours had evolved into a very honest and easy relationship during the months that had passed, which might be one reason why they had hesitated and gotten their loyalties mixed up. The way they had chosen to, or actually not to, go about this was still terribly wrong toward Emma but I had to try to understand how it could have happened at all. I also had to take into consideration that "ordinary" people probably didn't understand the extent of the helplessness and suffering children with parents with excessive alcohol habits experience. Alcohol is constantly profiled as a harmless beverage, and is seldom set in the context of it triggering as much violence and harm as it does. We seldom talk about how alcohol passes on hereditary emotional inadequacy - it is the drug many people use instead of maturing emotionally: "handling" feelings by using alcohol in situations when the need arises to face hardship, happiness or sheer boredom.

There are so many proverbs and excuses for drunk people's deranged behaviour which are constantly used to minimise the damaging effects this legal drug has on our society's social and mental health problems. Many of us have had our own experiences of black-outs, temper tantrums and following impulses while dangerously lacking in judgement. The amount of people who have witnessed the effects of alcohol in their close vicinity are many, many more than the number of actual addicts and they also display erratic and harmful reactions to alcohol and its consequences. We are raised listening to and repeating these excuses and downplaying the dangerous psychological effects. We learn to turn a blind eye, to "forgive" or dote on drunk people and, as the years go by, this becomes a deeply-rooted reaction for most of us and it sets in almost instantly at the sight of intoxicated people.

The harm that Emma would have come to if I had been drunk that previous weekend was evidently not as obvious to Mona and Ulf as it was to me. If they had been able to see the trauma that that weekend would have been for Emma they would never have let her be exposed to me.

The happy la-la-land of the alcohol commercials where no one becomes deranged, violent or changed in their personalities by using this drug must have been their subconscious reference when they assessed the situation and let Emma stay with me. That was an absolute and definite opposite of what her reality during those three days would have been.

These thoughts came to me and were woven into the agitated state I was in. As strange as it may sound, this understanding was what finally helped me calm down. A serenity spread through my being. I wanted to keep up a good relationship with Mona and Ulf for both Emma's and my sake. They were caring and jovial people and had become good friends of mine. The gratitude toward the unknown person who had called the police in the late summer of 2004 now arose within me, as it often did, and I kept it in my focus until I felt empathic love being the emotion that dominated my spirit. Then I dared to leave the offices and went straight to a self-help meeting. Remembering to take care of myself was going to be more important than usual in the upcoming hours. I knew that if I kept to doing what I had learned to do to keep myself in recovery, I would get through this crisis as well.

When I picked Emma up from daycare I was quite composed again and when I dropped her off I could talk to Mona and Ulf about what had transpired on Friday without getting angry. I told them matter-of-factly that I hadn't relapsed and that I had, incredibly enough, been asked to give samples for long-term drug use testing which would show that I had been sober. I couldn't help but clarify my standpoint though:

"If you ever suspect anything like this again, don't hesitate to call social services immediately. I don't plan on ever using again but if I were to do so and had gotten as sick as to drag Emma into that insanity, she would have to be protected from me at all costs!"

I think they took it well. It can't have been easy for them to be put to this criticism. Even though I tried to explain this to them calmly, they must have understood how I felt. I hoped they had heard from CaF too. They didn't say much - what could they say? - but our relationship continued to work well. They meant a tremendous lot to both Emma and me.

Sitting on the bus during my journey back to Malmö, I thought about what I had done to take care of my health this wild day. My goal to turn the fear and anger into feelings that instead would nurture my ongoing recovery had yielded positive results. I tried to imagine what could have been the outcome if I hadn't been so thorough in my efforts of reflecting, going to a meeting and asking for help. Probably, I would have escalated into hatred and created a superior attitude because, as far back as I could remember, that was the instinctive way for me to react.

I had been able to take other people's advice and taken time out to pray and meditate, or as I like to call it, time to reflect and search inward for answers. This had helped me get another angle on the situation, which I had been able to lean on the whole day. Reflecting on the day showed me how much I had learned about actually using the methods I had heard about to take care of my psychological disease. I was still confused and in emotional turmoil but I had managed to make this day manageable, even fruitful. I had heard, over and over, from others with the same disease that this affliction readily drives the recovering addict to confuse reality with mind-ghosts. This was why it was so incredibly important for me to use these methods – not just know of them. 'Easy does it, talk to someone and work for your recovery' had literally saved the day. The results of my actions had steered me toward reality rather than being caught in ideas that weren't real. Serenity settled in where distressing worry would otherwise have reigned.

A very positive outcome of these events was that I carefully made a solid plan for our trip to Gothenburg that Christmas. I asked my therapist to help me get in contact with an addiction ward in Gothenburg so that I could go there for my sobriety tests while we were at my mother's and also to take my daily dose of Antabuse. There was a clinic in central Gothenburg where I could go. I then showed this plan to CaF. Now I was leaving nothing to chance. The feeling of there being wildfire at large still chased me after that crazy Monday.

Another insight I got was to keep on taking my Antabuse. I had been thinking about stopping ever since I had been sober for about a month. I had been so sure that I had finally found a way that freed me from the obsession to use drugs, but now I felt that for the sake of CaF and also for my own safety, I would continue taking the pills for a while longer. At least until Emma had lived with me for six months. Then I would take the question into consideration again. When I compared the nine months I had been sober with the 25 years of active addiction, I saw that accepting these extra six months with Antabuse as a safeguard was only being logically careful.

In mid-December, I was informed that we would get the keys to the apartment a few days earlier than planned. Emma and I were getting back from my mother's on the 27th and we would be getting the keys that same day. I booked a moving company for the 28th so Emma would be part of the whole moving in process. She wouldn't be leaving until the 29th. It was amazing that we would be doing this together! Filling our home with furniture and deciding/arguing about where everything should be. I looked forward to this with eternal thankfulness. It just stunned me how life's small and huge parts had fallen into place in this miraculous fashion.

Before we left for the Christmas celebrations, I arranged to show Emma our soon-to-be home. Emma stood nailed to the floor by the window in what was to be her room, looking hypnotised out at the beautiful view over the town of her birth. I almost had to tear her away and that was the best motherly thing I'd had to do in my whole life up until then.

The apartment felt very large. I only owned a bunk bed, a sofa-bed, a coffee table, a small bookshelf and a desk, but I wasn't worried. I was going to receive some financial aid from social services - 5000 SEK to spend on furniture and kitchen appliances and I was comfortable with shopping second hand. It was going to be absolutely fabulous! I had a small TV-set, a VHS and I was on the lookout for a cheap DVD player to make our home feel complete. We high-fived in the elevator on the way down and were in complete agreement about how perfect our new home was going to be.

A few days before leaving for Gothenburg, I saw an ad for a much-discounted recordable DVD player and called my mother to ask if I could get a loan that I would pay back over four months. She reacted with silence and when she finally spoke I heard the fear in her voice. The memories struck me of how I had called her over the years about money and all the terrible lies I had invented to get her to "lend" it to me. The hesitation and anxiety I heard coming from deep inside her now made me see, with unwelcome clarity, how I had used and hurt her and how this had been horribly abusive behaviour on my part. It was disturbingly harsh to realise this when I was in recovery, suddenly able to take in what I had so ruthlessly ignored over the years. The pain she had felt through watching her child in that slow, protracted, suicidal pattern. I had been forcing her, dragging her into it, with no empathy at all. Only listening to what I wanted, when I wanted it and treating her as if she owed me something.

It was a rude but welcome reminder of what I had done and where I had come from. Also of who I would become if I relapsed. I had lived in a bubble of joy for a while now and had almost started to take this new way of life for granted. My mother's reaction to such a small request, and it was a small sum of money really, put my being an addict for life in a more understandable perspective. I couldn't afford to forget. Neither could I expect that my loved ones would be able to recover quickly from their decades of hurt from my sickly actions. I could only hope that my mothers hurt would be soothed with time and my patience. I would be lucky to gain her trust in time.

She lent me the money but in this situation it wasn't the DVD player that was the prize but the insight that I would have to be much more careful with my family and loved ones. My helplessness at not being able to take away the pain she had suffered hardened my resolve at being resolute in taking care of my recovery. For the rest of my days.

Soon I was going to see my mother for the first time since I had begun to recover and I hoped that this meeting would give her something to strengthen her in her healing process.

Thirty-one

Emma had Christmas gifts lavished on her, from everyone, near and far. It was almost too much for her. I made a note to self for the next celebration, which would be her sixth birthday, to keep the amount of gifts to a more reasonable level.

My mother kept telling me how happy she was for all our sakes. I remember taking the tram daily to go to the ward in Gothenburg and timed these visits with going to a twelve-step meeting. I thanked my lucky stars that I could care for my recovery even while travelling. I had heard that it was possible to go to meetings in many other countries. I looked forward to travelling abroad and meeting other recovering people in exotic places around the world.

I was bombarded by a turmoil of feelings with all that was going on at the time and noticed that I was often distracted from being in the here and now. I fought to stay in the present and was successful to a varying extent, grateful that I knew how to watch out for myself. The days dragged themselves forward at this point. I was unable to digest the upcoming move at the same time all the aspects of this Christmas. My need for escape pulled my attention towards the 28th and, at the same time, the joy in my little girl's eyes and smiles, plus my mother's unusually quiet and reflective manner washed through me, making this Christmas the best ever, on any scale. The gratitude I felt was natural and the longing for our own home was too, but my affliction making the pull toward something other than the here and now made these feelings disproportionately strong. I did my inner spiritual workouts to try to calm down. I managed to have moments where I was able to enjoy the adventures of the here and now while experiencing a joyous and sound anticipation about soon moving into our dream home.

My memories of that Christmas are dim. Managing such emotions was very strenuous this early on in my recovery. My body was probably overdosing on natural, bodily substances from the kicks that all these emotions triggered in me. I slept and rested a lot. When I felt bad about being so drained, I had to turn to my deepest self, that silent inner room, and remind myself that everything was better now than it had ever been in my entire life. So, as usual, I had to actively do things to recall the reality of how my life looked today. In this case, I turned my guilty conscience around to thankfulness for being sober and the fact that Emma and my mother hadn't been this happy for ages and that wouldn't change just because I rested a lot. When the truth of those things sunk in, a harmonious sensation would soar through me and a smile would spread over my face. I could fall asleep or rest in front of the TV without putting myself down.

The 27th did arrive at long last and we left for our home town. I got the keys to the flat and the next morning the movers came. The previous evening, Emma and I had walked back and forth, carrying lots of stuff through the park that lay between the collective and our new home. I was in constant prayer and meditation and, to my surprise, I actually managed to fall asleep beside Emma in the bunk bed that evening. Probably, all this turmoil had cost me what energy I had left after the long days of waiting and longing. I literally slept like a log.

The next day, everything flowed just as it was supposed to with the movers. Of course, with the typical commotion caused by tenants moving in and out from both addresses and the fact that a few of our things were too large to fit inside the elevator. I was extremely unsynchronised with the perfectly wondrous reality and my thoughts and emotions. In my head, I knew that we had a home now and that this was miraculously wonderful. I had an expectation that I ought to cry out of pure joy but was very subdued instead. Now and again, these emotions did swell and escaped me in unexpected outbursts, as surprising to me as my surroundings. A yippeee-ing here and a woohooo-ing there combined with a jump for joy. I even hugged one of the movers, to our mutual astonishment and confusion.

As always, I found comfort from having heard about these kinds of clueless and uncontrollable emotional experiences from others recovering from mood-altering substances. I just had to chill and calm myself down, actively drawing forth acceptance of having an emotional disorder and keep on carrying stuff. I relied on getting more able to handle spontaneous and bombastic behaviour with time.

I managed to laugh about it and overall the whole day was as if it had been taken out of a happy-happy-ending scene from a Hollywood film.

Emma was like a fish in the ocean, adapting matter-of-factly to this being our home and her way of accepting this as a natural development in life with the naturalness and simplicity she beamed out made me catch on too. The happiness and trust in her words and body language gave me a sense of security.

After a long day, we were finally able to sleep in our new home for the first time.

I took Emma out to Mona and Ulf's on the 29th and returned to a quiet and messy flat. I used the silence to try to get a grip. I sat down with some take-away food on the built-in breadboard on the kitchen counter and tried to get my head around how this chain of events had played out. My conclusion was that it was anything but strange that I had a hard time digesting this reality. From my friend's mother being in the elevator with the previous tenant and the fact that they had spoken to each other, to us now having a unimaginably fresh start at beginning to build our little family's new life was truly like some fantastic saga. I thanked my God and let my steady companions, Gratitude and Trust, take over the controls. This was the only way for me to go about handling this, otherwise I would most probably burst with the happiness that bubbled within me.

I put myself to work assembling Emma's bunk bed and then I tried to start unpacking some of the bags and boxes. I noticed that I was beginning to rush, unpacking at a faster and faster pace and so I broke off to go to a meeting instead. Sitting and listening to others and their joys and obstacles dissolved my racing mind. Nine-and-a-half months with this new way of living felt like an eternity and at the same time it was the short time it was for learning a new way of being. I was like a baby who had just learned to crawl and was very inexperienced in communicating and sorting through what I was experiencing. "Easy does it" was one of the most useful mottoes of the twelve-step organisations, I felt, and I really tried to put it to good use on a daily basis.

New Year was closing in and I had volunteered to help with the party that was going to be held in our twelve-step group's meeting room. I had been on the planning committee and was one of three who had done the shopping and were responsible for the food, desserts and drinks. On New Year's Eve, we met at my place to chop the fruit for the fruit salad and then we were going to bring the bowls, bottles and snacks over. Suddenly, I had to do something that surprised me. I had to back down. I had worked in the restaurant business and had experience of and competence at organising much more complicated events but, suddenly, I was completely unable to even lift a finger. It felt as if I was letting everybody down. The others came over because we had everything stored at my place since I lived so close by. I told them I would be sitting down and letting them do all the work. The reaction I got to this was a compliment:

"It's not easy to take a step back. That is a sign of knowing yourself and respecting your limitations."

They both nodded and the guy who had said it smiled and joined me and there we sat, looking at the third one of us who happily chopped away at the oranges and bananas. She told me not to worry since there really wasn't that much left to do. We talked about the device of "Easy does it". To me, this had firstly meant that I was abstaining from the use of alcohol and my criminal activities. Now it started to sink in deeper. As an addictive personality, I had to apply this motto to my daily life in ways that I hadn't had a clue about before. I had to spread out my energy during the day. If I got too drained, the risks of me fuelling up with alcohol or some other drug would be imminent. The fact that I had instinctively withdrawn from this party-fixing was probably a sign that I was alarmingly drained of strength. When they left, I stayed at home, promising to come over for a little while later on.

I was very glad at having had these other two over. Having friends who so easily understood what I was going through was a priceless gift in my life today. I realised that this feeling of belonging was something I would have to nurture all my life. The effort I had put into my social training really proved itself as being worth every second. Finally, I had other people in my life. My heart filled with love. I was also very thankful that I had done such a caring thing for myself, even if it was as simple as standing up for feeling the need to rest.

Later that evening, I went over to the party and when people asked me how I was, I felt the urge to put on a mask and say that I was all better now. But, instead of pulling the "never-better"-story out of the bag, I said that I was quite tired and drained by all that was going on in my life at the moment. Several people comforted me by telling me about their own recollections of similar experiences and I was met with a positivity that rubbed off on me.

During the evening, I got a little better and it started to feel perfectly alright to be me. I mingled, ate from the delicious plates and bowls, had several exotic drinks and looked at the crazy people flocking on the dance floor, ecstatically raving and disco-dancing to old and new hits. I wasn't there yet but knew that soon it would be me bouncing off the dance floor. Lately, the twinges of a dance-mood had started to sprout inside.

I stayed on until just after the New Year's toast when the town was reverberating with church bells ringing and the sounds of fireworks going off shaking my neighbourhood, Möllevången. On the way home, strengthened by many hugs and mutual well-wishes of new possibilities for the 365 days to come, I felt myself thawing inside and was flooded with a sense of self-respect and compassion. It was okay to take a step back as I had done that evening and it was more than okay to have achieved what I had done in these last few months. I could fall asleep with a deeply-rooted feeling of love and trust. I was comforting myself in a way I had never done before.

My thoughts moved through the events of this past year, these short, eternal months. I cried for a little while. For whom and for what I didn't know, and in that moment it didn't matter. I let the confusion be what it was, loving it unconditionally too and it was wonderfully liberating to ease off the pressure, letting it out with the tears.

This was the best ever kick-off to a new year. I was emotionally richer than ever before and I had my daughter, people and love in my life. What more could I ask for? I would keep on being responsible for my recovery, Emma was on her way home and these swirling emotions and whirling thoughts could not kill me, even if it seemed as if they would from time to time.

Our little family, a new home and a new life stood at my doorstep.

Love filled my heart to the brim and rocked me soothingly into the realm of dreams.

*

I had blown up balloons until my head was swimming. I hung them among twirly ribbons in crazy colours and I had written a large "WELCOME HOME" sign which I had taped to the front door, of course with more balloons.

We were going to eat our favourite food – pizza. For dessert, we were having a humongous ice-cream cake - we would be cake-ing until we could cake no more.

The 2nd of January was going to be a family celebration day for ever and ever more. We were finally going to start the creation of our little family together. The joy I felt was all-encompassing.

Emma was on her way up in the elevator and the world was no longer a strange place to be.

Epilogue

Dance of life

The music filled me.

There was only room for the hypnotic tones of The Jungle Book

- its captivating rhythms, the masterful lyrics.

The laughter rose unrestrained, hearing Baloo get tickled.

The tears flowed freely when The Girl sang her melancholy song,

appealing to the lost, little Mowgli.

The little boy so unaware of his longing to belong.

*

Cat Stevens, Bob Marley, Pink Floyd

- wide awake I let them play on the strings that were my feelings.

In the evening, verging between the lands of dreams and reality, I dozed off

- hearing new, uncaught compositions which carefully crept forward, forming untamed and quieting lullabies.

*

I danced, whirling.

Led Zeppelin – The Crunge.

Donna Summer – Love to Love You Baby,

I swirled to the queens and kings of jazz.

Always when no one saw. When everyone was sleeping.

From pure joy, in an unrestrained expression.

Until, one day, someone told me of the strangeness of my swirls,

and others stared, laughing along.

*

I flayed in angry thrashes. Drunken, maddened and resentful.

Ever thirsty, I sucked the music dry through filters of chemicals.

My freedom in the tones,

in the winding embrace of the timeless waltz,

was dead.

*

Listening carefully.

Pedalling, with a warm summer breeze stroking my skin.

The music stirred me in my awakening.

Impregnating my being, so amazingly freed.
I smiled, I sang and my heart rejoiced.
Finally. Hearing music.
Is this the first time? It sounds so ever-new...

*

I watched others dance.

I tried but the rhythm limped in my healing soul.

I grieved, longed to heal even more.

To get to enjoy playing on the floor,

moving in the tones once more.

"It will come. It will," the whisper soared assuredly through me.

"Be gladdened. It will come."

*

The room throbbed with music.

The love, the pure, the ancient pounding of rhythm.

The notes playfully leaping, reaching within.

Reverberations at the core of my being.

Suddenly, worried, I glanced around me.

Was anyone laughing? Are they seeing that I'm not okay?

STOP IT!

I am beautiful! I am more than okay!
I am like them, and they are like me!

I invited in the love for life, and, as if not to scare me,
it carefully snuck up on me,
seeping forward from the innermost corner of the deepest space within,
and I danced!
The music breathed through me,
weaving a flowing carpet, thick with happiness and sorrows.
Weaved on a loom of purest gratitude.

*

I swirled, from the tingling tips of my toes.
Finally I danced!
I whirled with joy, again!

There is Strength in Asking for Help

There is help to be found.

For the addict as well as for other people who are harmfully affected by addiction.

There is love, courage and strength in asking for help and advice.

The organisations dealing with these issues are many and can be found all over the world.

Addiction is something that takes no heed of factors such as gender, faith, a persons' role in society or their financial stature.

Unfortunately, substance abuse is a worldwide affliction.

Contact a healthcare centre for more information.

You can always be anonymous when asking. If you live in a small town, there is always the possibility to call another town.

Maybe you can ask someone you trust to look for the answers you seek.

One powerful tool is to search the internet for people or organisations to contact.

When you embark on the quest for finding a solution, you will have taken the first step toward doing something.

However small a step it might seem to you, in reality it is a huge hurdle to overcome -

actually it is a giant leap as you are boosting your willingness to work toward change.

This is true whether you are an addict, a co-dependent or are victimized in any way by this gruesome disorder - and also if you are a professional care-giver.

Remember that taking action towards finding a successful path to recovery is a journey you embark upon out of great love for yourself and those around you.

You are also welcome to send an e-mail with questions and reflections to our Publishing Company.

We will try our best to be of assistance.

Together we are strong!

info@saltodevita.com

Conformément aux statuts de la Société des Textes Français Modernes, ce volume a été soumis à l'approbation du Comité de lecture, qui a chargé M. François Moureau d'en surveiller la correction en collaboration avec M. John Dunkley.

ISBN 0768-0821
ISBN 2-86503-248-5

Quatre comédies (1701-1707):

Les Trois Gascons
Le Bal d'Auteuil
Le Port de mer
Le Petit-maître de robe

Edition établie et annotée
par John Dunkley

Nicolas Boindin

Quatre Comédies

texte établi, présenté
et annoté par John Dunkley
Paris, Société des Textes Français Modernes 1997

REMERCIEMENTS

Je tiens à remercier le Carnegie Trust de la subvention qui m'a permis de poursuivre les recherches nécessaires à ce travail, ainsi que l'Université d'Aberdeen qui m'a accordé un congé de recherche pour le mettre au point. J'ai le plaisir aussi d'exprimer ma gratitude à l'égard de Monsieur François Moureau, pour les précieux conseils qu'il m'a donnés, à Madame Jacqueline Razgonnikoff, qui a si souvent mis à ma disposition son expertise sur la Comédie-Française, et à ma collègue, Madame Danièle Smith, qui a eu l'amabilité de relire mon texte. Je ne saurais trop exprimer ma reconnaissance envers les nombreux conservateurs de bibliothèques de province qui ont répondu à mes demandes de précisions bibliographiques avec une obligeance à toute épreuve.

INTRODUCTION

Boindin, un des derniers libertins érudits.

Deux ans après la mort de Nicolas Boindin, survenue à Paris le 30 novembre 1751 à la suite d'une intervention chirurgicale, François Parfaict, qui hérita des papiers littéraires de l'écrivain, publia chez Prault une édition de ses œuvres en deux volumes [1]. Parmi ces papiers figurait un document autobiographique, que Parfaict publia en préface à son édition. Au contraire de ce qu'il affirmait, Parfaict supprima un petit nombre de phrases et de paragraphes qu'il jugeait peu judicieux de rendre publics. Le texte de ces suppressions figure dans le manuscrit français 22158 de la Bibliothèque Nationale de France et fut publié en 1975 par Jean Balcou dans son *Dossier Fréron* [2]. Ces deux sources nous fournissent les renseignements les plus amples que nous ayons sur la vie de l'auteur, qu'il convient de compléter par l'apport d'un document jusqu'ici négligé et par les nombreuses allusions qu'en font Grimm et Voltaire.

Né à Paris le 29 mai 1676, Nicolas Boindin, aîné de deux frères, n'était pas robuste, et ce fut, dit-il, sa faible

1. Voir la liste des éditions de Boindin à la fin de cette Préface.

2. La bibliographie donne la description précise des ouvrages cités dans notre texte. Les pages du *Dossier Fréron* consacrées à Boindin vont de 110 à 112. Elles m'ont été signalées par F. Moureau.

santé qui le porta à la lecture et fit de lui un 'philosophe avant l'âge de raison'. Lorsqu'il parle de ses lectures de jeunesse, ce sont toujours les auteurs latins et grecs qu'il cite, goût qui n'avait rien d'exclusif, mais qui s'affirma avec les années. Ses préférences allaient à la comédie davantage qu'à la tragédie ou à l'épopée, et il appréciait particulièrement Plaute, Térence et Aristophane. Il lisait plus volontiers Lucien, Tacite et Horace que Virgile et Homère et appréciait surtout ceux qu'il désigne par la phrase 'les autres Anciens qui pensent à la moderne'. Les études philosophiques qu'il fit au collège lui déplaisaient, dispensées comme elles étaient par 'un professeur entêté des principes de l'Ecole', tandis que Boindin recherchait de préférence ce qu'il appelle des 'choses et des idées claires'[3]. Autrement dit, notre auteur s'avérait résolument moderne et cartésien à une époque où censures et interdictions pleuvaient sur l'œuvre de Descartes et où sa popularité ne cessait de grandir dans les cercles intellectuels[4]. Ces exigences intellectuelles de l'élève allaient se manifester plus tard dans les travaux qu'il fournit à l'Académie des Inscriptions et Belles-Lettres.

L'apport biographique du *Dossier Fréron* est du plus haut intérêt précisément parce que Parfaict supprima dans son édition des œuvres de Boindin tout ce qui touchait de trop près à son athéisme de même qu'une référence au frère ennemi de l'auteur, convulsionnaire qui l'avait ruiné,

3. 'Mémoire sur la vie et les ouvrages de M. Boindin, donné par lui-même', in *Œuvres*, 1753, I, p. vi-xxiii; p. viii, ix .

4. Georges Minois consacre des pages lumineuses à la censure de l'œuvre de Descartes, qui était 'rejeté en bloc, mais utilisé par morceaux', et souligne à juste titre que le danger qu'il représentait était dans son esprit beaucoup plus que dans ses écrits. Il ajoute pertinemment que 'la censure ne peut rien contre un état d'esprit' (*Censure et culture sous l'Ancien Régime*, p. 124-129). Voir aussi A. Kors, *Atheism in France, 1650-1729*, p. 271-279.

dit-il, en procès poursuivis depuis trente ans [5]. Athée, il le fut depuis sa plus tendre jeunesse, car, prétend-il, il s'imaginait que ses leçons de catéchisme n'étaient réellement qu''un piège qu'on lui tendait pour mettre sa patience à l'épreuve'[6]. Parmi les philosophes qu'il étudia avec passion plus tard, et dont Parfaict ne transmet pas les noms, figuraient Sextus Empiricus [7], Charron, La Mothe le Vayer et, surtout, Descartes, Bayle et Fontenelle. Le premier était le pyrrhonien qui écrivait contre les sciences de son temps; Charron, penseur orthodoxe et ami de Montaigne, fut taxé de libertinage au dix-septième siècle, et La Mothe le Vayer, associé de Gassendi, de Naudé et de Patin, était, même dans les périodes de sa vie où il fut le client de Richelieu ou le précepteur de Louis XIV, un sceptique notoire. Boindin témoignait aussi une grande admiration pour Fontenelle. Il ne lui manquait que la discrétion de ses modèles. Dans un passage qui résume parfaitement les caractéristiques majeurs de sa pensée, il avoue ne pas s'être suffisamment surveillé dans ses discours et s'être trop abandonné à son penchant pour le pyrrhonisme. Il exprime son incertitude sur la valeur de l'apport des sens, ses doutes sur la lumière de la raison, sur l'immortalité de l'âme et sur le libre-arbitre; il embrassait le relativisme moral, et suspendait son jugement sur tout ce qui était inapte à la démonstration - position évidemment lourde de conséquences.

Afin de pouvoir succéder à son père au poste de Trésorier de France au bureau des Finances[8], Boindin fit

5. *Dossier Fréron*, p.112. Dans son *Journal*, Barbier évoque l'arrestation du frère de Boindin, embastillé à la suite d'une réunion de convulsionnaires tenu chez Madame de Vieux-Pont, en décembre 1737 (*Journal historique et anecdotique*, II, p. 182-183).

6. *Dossier Fréron*, p.110.

7. *Ibid.* Sextus Empiricus vécut à la fin du deuxième siècle de notre ère.

8. Mouhy le désigne comme 'Procureur du Roi [...] ' (*Tablettes dramatiques*, p. 35), et le *Dictionnaire de biographie française*

des études de droit, rapidement et sans enthousiasme. Il s'essaya au métier des armes en 1696, mais sa faible santé lui ferma cette carrière[9] . Il se consacra désormais à une vie d'érudit. Dès 1698, il fréquentait le café Laurent, 'pépinière de toutes les académies', et ce fut là qu'il lia connaissance avec La Motte, Jean-Baptiste Rousseau, Saurin, Fontenelle, Roy, Danchet, Crébillon et les frères La Faye .

1701 vit la première création dramatique de Boindin, *Les Trois Gascons.* Composée en collaboration avec La Motte, cette pièce subit les feux de la rampe à la Comédie-Française le 4 juin. La curiosité qu'avaient exprimée leurs amis de savoir la part de chaque auteur dans la composition de la pièce les encouragea à écrire séparément une deuxième comédie. Celle de Boindin, *Le Bal d'Auteuil*, connut sa première à la Comédie-Française le 22 août 1702, et celle de La Motte, *La Matrone d'Ephèse*, le 23 septembre. Cette dernière disparut de l'affiche après la neuvième représentation. Boindin reconnut que *La Matrone d'Ephèse* était 'plus délicate et infiniment mieux écrite' que sa propre comédie, 'dont le sujet [...] était plus riant et l'intrigue plus piquante', et il estima que son sort avait été moins brillant parce que le sujet en était 'triste et lugubre'. Si l'histoire a retenu le titre du *Bal d'Auteuil*, c'est moins en raison de ses qualités comiques, pourtant indéniables, qu'à sa réputation d'avoir déclenché la censure dramatique systématique [10]. Dès le 24 juillet 1702,

---

attribue effectivement ce titre à son père (VI, p. 800). Voltaire précise 'Trésorier de France et procureur du Roi de sa compagnie' ('Catalogue de la plupart des écrivains ...', in *Le Siècle de Louis XIV*, *loc. cit.*, p. 1 140: 'Boindin').

9. Il nous apprend que sa santé s'améliora avec les années, mais qu'il souffrit régulièrement de migraines jusqu'à l'âge de cinquante ans (*Œuvres*,1753, I, xxiii).

10. Notoriété imméritée voir notre article 'Theatrical Censorship and Nicolas Boindin's *Le Bal d'Auteuil* (1702)'. Le nom de François Parfaict, et non celui de La Porte, devrait figurer à la note 11 (p. 189).

l'assemblée des Comédiens avait émis quelques réserves prudentes sur l'œuvre soumise à son jugement: 'La Compagnie a accepté la pièce à condition d'en retrancher quelques mots un peu trop libres et quelques scènes un peu trop longues, et qu'elle sera approuvée par M. d'Argenson' [11]. Deux séries de représentations, qui indiquent le bon accueil fait à la pièce, eurent lieu à la Comédie-Française au cours de l'été et de l'automne; elles furent suivies par une présentation à Versailles le 2 janvier 1703, qui déplut à Madame Palatine, dont les plaintes entraînèrent l'interdiction de l'œuvre.

Ce fut en 1703-1704 que Boindin composa une troisième comédie, *Le Port de mer.* Revue en collaboration avec La Motte, la pièce connut sa première à la Comédie-Française le 27 mai 1704. Elle constitue le succès le plus durable de Boindin. Fort appréciée par le public tout au long du siècle, elle s'attira les éloges des professionnels de la critique, tels que Mouhy et Voltaire. Cet accueil venait peut-être, au moins en partie, de son actualité qui, par hasard, ne se démentit pas avec le temps. Boindin élabora une quatrième comédie, *Le Petit-maître de robe*, qui date de 1707, dans l'intention de la soumettre à la Comédie-Française, mais les registres d'assemblée des comédiens n'en portent aucune trace. Cette pièce ne fut jamais, au contraire des trois autres, imprimée du vivant de l'auteur. Sur sa qualité, les avis sont partagés. Les éditeurs des œuvres de Boindin parues en 1787 constatent sans nuances que 'cette pièce est assez faible' [12]. En revanche, Parfaict explique qu'elle fut gardée en portefeuille parce que 'l'auteur n'y avait pas mis la dernière main', mais il affirme que 'le sujet de cette pièce est simple et peut-être un peu trop, mais elle est dialoguée dans le goût du vrai comique, vif et

11. Archives de la Comédie-Française, 'Feuilles d'assemblée' du 24 juillet 1702. Voir aussi J.-P. Vittu, 'Public et folies dramatiques', p. 94 (ci-après : 'La Comédie-Française 1680-1716').

12. P. 22.

naturel' [13] . Selon Henri Lagrave, la pièce fut interdite [14]. Boindin venait, en 1706, d'être nommé censeur royal... [15]

L'amitié de Boindin et de La Motte se refroidit, sans qu'on puisse savoir le moment exact de leur rupture. Les deux auteurs se disputèrent (d'après l'autobiographie de Boindin) parce que les comédies de celui-ci avaient été publiées, sans que leur collaboration fût signalée, dans un recueil ayant pour titre *Théâtre de M. Boindin.* C'est celui d'un recueil factice paru chez Ribou en 1714. Mais un recueil constitué des mêmes comédies avait paru déjà en 1705 sous le titre: *Les Œuvres de Mr. Boindin.* Dans l'intervalle avait surgie l'affaire de couplets (de 1710), et, selon la notice qui figure en tête de l'édition des *Œuvres* de Boindin publiée chez Prault en 1746, ce fut à l'occasion de cet indigne épisode que leur rupture fut consommée. On ne peut savoir si cette querelle eut lieu dès 1705 ou en 1714, à une époque où l'amitié des deux auteurs était refroidie au point de leur permettre de se disputer sur une erreur dont ils semblaient n'avoir cure en 1705. On comprend d'ailleurs mal pourquoi La Motte se serait alors fâché sur ce point, puisque les deux recueils attribuent sans sourciller à Boindin *La Matrone d'Ephèse*, comédie que La Motte composa seul. On se demande aussi pourquoi La Motte n'intervint pas auprès du libraire Ribou dès 1705 pour qu'il corrigeât les éditions ultérieures[16] .

En 1706 aussi, l'Académie des Inscriptions et Belles-Lettres ouvrit ses portes à Boindin, qui y entra en qualité

---

13. 'Avertissement', p. ii.

14. *Le Théâtre et le public à Paris de 1715 à 1750* , p. 62.

15. Ce qui prouve que l'affaire du *Bal d'Auteuil* n'était pas d'une ampleur à lui porter préjudice.

16. Selon les frères Parfaict, La Motte publia seulement en 1730 la pièce sous son nom (*Histoire du théâtre français*, XIV, p. 266; réimp. : III, p. 466).

d'associé. A sa fondation en 1663, la 'petite Académie' était une commission de quatre membres qui avait pour mission de proposer des sujets pour les tapisseries royales, de choisir tableaux et statues, de dessiner des médailles et de suggérer des inscriptions pour les monuments royaux. Le roi accepta le projet de réforme de l'abbé Bignon qui entra en vigueur le 16 juillet 1701 et qui avait pour effet d'orienter les travaux de l'Académie vers l'érudition classique et historique [17]. Ses quarante membres étaient répartis en quatre classes: les honoraires, les pensionnaires, les associés et les élèves. Choisis pour 'leur érudition dans les belles-lettres et leur intelligence en fait de monuments', les membres de l'Académie, qui se réunissaient les mardis et les vendredis de quinze à dix-sept heures, devaient fournir, à tour de rôle, un mémoire. Conséquence imprévue sans doute, l'accent mis sur des études fondamentalement profanes favorisa le recrutement de membres agnostiques ou athées. Comme le remarque très justement l'historien Maury, certaines communications lues aux séances de l'Académie auraient été mises à l'*Index* si l'Eglise s'en était préoccupée[8].

Par sa formation et la pente naturelle de son esprit, il n'est guère étonnant que Boindin fût athée déclaré, sinon discret. Maury écrit à son sujet que '[sa] curiosité et [son] esprit d'examen ne s'arrêtaient pas devant les décisions des conciles' [19], mais d'autres témoignages, dont il sera question plus loin, prouvent qu'il soutenait son incrédulité d'une manière singulièrement retentissante pour l'époque. Il désignait, par exemple, publiquement Dieu et l'Eglise par les sobriquets de Monsieur de l'Être et de Jacotte [20].

17. Rozière et Chatel, *Table général et méthodique*, p. vii-viii, et Isambert *et al., Recueil général des anciennes lois françaises*, XX, p. 386-392 et XVIII, p. 584-585.

18. *Les Académies d'autrefois*, 2e partie, p. 52 et suiv.

19. *Ibid*., p. 55.

20. G. Minois, *Censure et culture sous l'Ancien Régime*, p. 191-192.

Toutefois, Maury rappelle qu'aux alentours de 1710 il était plus dangereux d'être janséniste qu'athée.

Boindin lut devant les académiciens ses dissertations sur les tribus romaines, sur les noms des Romains, sur la forme et la construction du théâtre des Anciens et sur les masques et habits du théâtre ancien[21] . Cependant, il parut vite trouver impossible de concilier les responsabilités de ses fonctions de trésorier - d'ailleurs une sinécure - avec la présence exigée aux séances de l'Académie. Il fallait excuser toute absence de plus de deux mois, et on examinait de près, sous menace d'exclusion, les raisons de ceux dont l'assiduité était prise en défaut. Si Boindin assista peu aux séances, on ne songea pas à l'exclure[22] et il sollicita sa vétérance en 1714. Une lettre du chancelier de Pontchartrain datée du 19 mars 1714 informa l'abbé Bignon que le roi acceptait que Boindin fût déclaré vétéran et que l'élection d'un nouvel associé se tînt le vendredi suivant[23] .

Plus souvent que l'Académie, Boindin fréquentait le café de la veuve Laurent, et ce fut parmi les habitués de ce café que survint, en 1710, l'affaire à laquelle son nom reste attaché : celle des 'couplets'. J.-B. Rousseau, auteur de trois comédies agréables mais éphémères, et d'une œuvre lyrique considérable, était d'un tempérament peu avenant. A l'occasion de la première de sa comédie du *Flatteur*, qui eut lieu à la Comédie-Française le 24 novembre 1696, l'auteur aurait fui son père, venu assister au triomphe de son fils, parce que sa profession de cordonnier lui faisait honte[24]. Boindin reprocha cette dureté à Rousseau qui

---

21. Rozière et Chatel, *op. cit.,* aux numéros 634, 978, 1 008 et 2 359.

22. L'abbé Boutard, trop peu assidu aux séances, fut déclaré vétéran en 1708 (Maury, *op. cit.*, p. 35, n. 2).

23. Archives de l'Institut, Z. 201, f. 214-215.

24. Voir Voltaire, *Œuvres complètes*, XXII (*Mélanges*, I), p. 331-332, et F. Gacon, *L'Anti-Rousseau* , p. x et 222; l'ouvrage

inséra des vers contre son censeur dans son *Epître à Marot.* Rousseau était aussi en délicatesse avec La Motte et son ami Danchet, auteur de l'opéra d'*Hésione*, joué avec succès à l'Académie royale de musique au moment-même où son propre *Capricieux* était en représentation à la Comédie-Française[25]. Imaginant que La Motte, Saurin et Crébillon étaient les auteurs d'une cabale contre *Le Capricieux*, Rousseau composa des couplets qui parodiaient *Hésione*, vers qu'il récita à son ami Duché en plein café[26]. Ce fut Saurin qui, par la suite, obtint de la veuve Laurent son expulsion du café.

Des copies manuscrites des couplets qui provoquèrent 'l'affaire' furent déposées à la porte de divers habitués du café Laurent le 2 et le 3 février 1710, peu de temps avant l'élection de La Motte à l'Académie française. Parmi les

---

fait de nombreuses références au mépris de Rousseau pour son père, y compris dans une 'Histoire véritable et remarquable, arrivée à l'endroit d'un nommé Roux, fils d'un cordonnier, lequel ayant renié son père, le diable en prit possession', attribuée à Autreau. Certains exemplaires contiennent cette satire en deux versions, dont une sous la forme d'une feuille dépliante entre les pages 222 et 223. Notons que deux éditions distinctes de cet ouvrage sortirent des presses de Fritsch et Böhm en 1712, comportant respectivement 512 et 534 pages, et qu'il constitue aussi le troisième volume des *Œuvres de Rousseau*, publiées la même année par la même maison. Toutes nos références se rapportent à l'édition en 534 pages.

25. La pièce de Rousseau eut dix représentations entre le 17 décembre 1700 et le 5 janvier 1701. Le nombre d'entrées baissa de 1309, à la première, à 294 à la dixième représentation. La première d'*Hésione* eut lieu à l'Opéra le 21 décembre. La musique d'*Hésione* était d'André Campra (Parfaict, *Histoire du théâtre français*, XIV, p. 187 et n. (b), réimp. III, p. 446) .

26. Cependant, Rousseau les désavoua dans une lettre adressée à Duché (Parfaict, *op. cit.*, p. 186-189; réimp. : III, p. 446-447). Pour le texte et les circonstances de ces couplets, et leurs suites, voir Parfaict, *ibid.*, p. 192-215 (réimp. : III, p. 447-453), et A. van Bever, *Contes et conteurs gaillards*, p. 13-14.

personnes visées par ces couplets venimeux, se trouvait La Faye l'aîné, qui, par la suite, agressa Rousseau devant l'Opéra. Celui-ci porta plainte et fut lui-même attaqué en dénonciation calomnieuse, plainte qui fut renvoyée par le président de Lamoignon. Les vers qui visaient Boindin étaient les suivants :

C'est par lui [Saurin] que s'est égaré
L'impie au visage effaré
Condamné par nous à la roue ;
Dinboin, athée déclaré
Que l'hypocrite désavoue[27].

François Gacon, le 'poète sans fard', consacra deux ouvrages à ruiner la réputation de Rousseau et il y reproduisit les couplets en question, les mémoires et les plaintes lancés de part et d'autre.

Un acte du Parlement daté du 7 avril 1712, rendu par contumace, déclara que Rousseau 'a été déclaré dûment atteint et convaincu d'avoir composé & distribué *les Vers [impies]*[28] *, satiriques et diffamatoires*, qui sont au *Procès*, et fait de *mauvaises Pratiques* pour faire réussir l'*Accusation Calomnieuse*, qu'il a intentée contre Joseph Saurin, de l'Académie des Sciences, pour raison *de l'envoi* desdits Vers diffamatoires au *Café de la Veuve Laurent*, pour Réparation de quoi ledit Rousseau est *banni à perpétuité du Roiaume*'[29]. Les termes de l'acte couvraient, aussi bien les couplets que d'autres vers de Rousseau qui avaient déplu aux dévots, ce qui explique peut-être la sévérité de la

27. Cité par F. Gacon, *Histoire satirique*, p. 18.

28. L'édition en 534 pages porte la leçon 'impurs'; nous adoptons celle de l'édition en 512 pages.

29. Cité par Gacon, *L'Anti-Rousseau,* p. 530-531. Cet ouvrage de Gacon reproduit tous les documents se rapportant à l'affaire: p. 395-525. Ils sont publiés aussi dans les *Œuvres de Rousseau,* nouvelle édition, Londres, 1753, 5 vol. Un recueil composé des feuilles volantes originales se trouve au Département des Manuscrits de la BNF, sous la cote: nouv. acq. fr. 24444.

sentence. Par la suite, Rouseau fut rayé des membres de l'Académie des Inscriptions[30].

Alexis Piron a laissé quelques remarques sur Rousseau, peu flatteuses mais d'un ton plutôt résigné qu'hostile, et qui datent de l'époque où ils se séjournaient tous deux à Bruxelles:

> Rousseau est devenu mon vieillard de la mer [...]. Son assiduité me sert à me le développer, et je vous avoue qu'il n'est pas trop bon. C'est un consommé de Panurge et de la Rancune. Il ne dit bien de personne, et je ne l'échapperai pas plus qu'un autre, quelque attention que j'aie à lui complaire, et quelque goût qu'il paraisse prendre à moi.Tout autre qui le connaîtrait moins se flatterait qu'il aurait quelque pudeur et qu'il n'oserait médire de quelqu'un qu'il loue à toute outrance; mais je vois que ces sortes de contradictions ne l'embarrassent point du tout. Il pousse même les choses à une grande imprudence pour un homme d'esprit; et quand on le connaît, on ne peut plus s'étonner de ses malheurs[31].

Le plus curieux est que Boindin laissa, à sa mort, un *Mémoire pour servir à l'histoire des couplets de 1710* où il tâchait de justifier ce paria. Il y accusait Malafer, Saurin et La Motte qui, détestant Rousseau, auraient cherché à ruiner sa réputation en ajoutant des couplets scandaleux à ceux qu'on savait que leurs ennemis avaient déjà composés. Au moment de la publication du *Mémoire* de Boindin, Rousseau était mort depuis dix ans et La Motte depuis vingt. On trouva curieux qu'il ait attendu, avant de le publier, un moment où cela ne pouvait plus avoir d'effet. Selon les *Anecdotes littéraires, 1750-1762*[32], Boindin

30. L'abbé Bignon et Gros de Boze, Secrétaire perpétuel de l'Académie, écrivirent à Pontchartrain le 12 avril 1712 pour connaître les ordres du roi à la suite du bannissement de Rousseau. Pontchartrain répondit le 22 avril que le roi ordonnait son exclusion; voir le *Registre journal des assemblées*, année 1712, 1ère partie, f. 280-281 et 412-414.

31. Lettre à Mlle de Bar, *Œuvres inédites* de Piron, p. 10-11.

32. BNF, ms. fr. Smith-Lesouef 105, f. 107. La mention est datée du 6 janvier 1752. Information fournie par F. Moureau.

n'avait pas voulu publier l'histoire du procès de Saurin et de Rousseau de son vivant 'par respect pour M. D'Aguesseau et pour la maison de Noailles'.

Voltaire réagit dès que Pierre Robert Le Cornier lui apprit, par une lettre datée du 24 mars 1752, la nouvelle de la publication du *Mémoire* de Boindin[33] et il inséra sa réfutation dans son 'Catalogue de la plupart des écrivains français', une annexe du *Siècle de Louis XIV*, alors sous presse[34]. L'argumentation du philosophe, qui avait quinze ans et deux mois en février 1710 et qui fut ensuite un ennemi féroce de Jean-Baptiste Rousseau, est très éloquente, mais on ne peut lire sans sourire une lettre qu'il adressa le 26 août au Président Hénault, où il révèle un aspect inattendu de sa méthode d'historien: 'Je suis persuadé qu'il est impossible que La Motte, Saurin et Malafaire [*sic*] aient comploté la conjuration des couplets. Je suis très au fait de cette affaire. La mère du garçon que Rousseau fit suborner servait chez mon père'[35].

Dans les années qui suivirent sa retraite de l'Académie, Boindin occupa ses loisirs par de nouvelles

33. Voltaire, *Correspondence* XII, Best. D 4848. La note 5 de la page 462 affirme que le *Mémoire* de Boindin était le résultat d'une haine qu'il entretenait depuis quarante ans contre La Motte: Boindin, homme de peu de talent et de moins de caractère, aurait détesté La Motte, qui aurait eu trop de bienveillance pour laisser sentir sa supériorité naturelle : ces hypothèses paraissent tout à fait déplacées. La lettre Best. D 14283, expédiée de Ferney, nous apprend que Voltaire commanda au libraire parisien Jacques Lacombe un exemplaire des *Œuvres* (1753) de Boindin le 17 juillet 1767: ces deux volumes se trouvent aujourd'hui à Saint-Pétersbourg dans la bibliothèque de Voltaire (n° 442). On y relève aussi un exemplaire du *Port de mer* (Paris, Ribou, 1713) (n° 443) (sans doute le **P 2** de notre bibliographie), œuvre que Voltaire cite avec faveur dans le 'Catalogue' du *Siècle de Louis XIV*.

34. Sa réfutation est incorporée aux articles sur La Motte et Saurin (Joseph).

35. Best D. 4997.

études. Il avait présenté quatre dissertations devant l'Académie et en gardait d'autres en portefeuille que Parfaict publia après sa mort[36]. Son 'Mémoire sur les sons de la langue' présente un certain intérêt[37] . Boindin voit dans l'alphabet français à la fois 'disette et superflu': disette en ce que bien des sons n'y sont pas représentés par des lettres; superflu parce que les groupes (i et y), et (c, k et q) ne représentent chacun qu'un seul son. Boindin préconise l'usage des accents pour marquer la différence entre les nombreuses voyelles qu'il distingue, et celui de signes spéciaux pour distinguer les caractères muets. S'il refuse de proposer par là un projet de réforme de l'orthographe, il prétend se fonder sur son évolution rationnelle. Il accepte, d'autre part, les différentes prononciations régionales, malgré une nette tendance à privilégier l'accentuation de la capitale. Ces réformes pourraient aider les enfants, les provinciaux et les étrangers. La dissertation se conclut par des réflexions sur d'autres grammairiens du temps: Maupertuis, Buffier, Olivet, Dangeau et l'abbé G[irard], par exemple.

En 1719, Boindin publia des comptes rendus sur le théâtre parisien contemporain, où il s'amusa à adopter une approche toute contraire à celle qui avait marqué ses dissertations pour l'Académie. Lorsqu'il se mit à rédiger ses 'Lettres historiques sur tous les spectacles de Paris', il décida de s'intéresser à la période moderne, car, expliquait-il à son destinataire anonyme : '[...] je n'aurais jamais eu

---

36. In *Œuvres* II (1753).

37. Il jugeait que la linguistique était plutôt du ressort de l'Académie française que de celui de l'Académie des Inscriptions, aussi se contenta-t-il de montrer son mémoire à quelques amis, car 'il ne voulut point [le] faire imprimer, de peur de paraître reprocher à cette illustre Compagnie de négliger les choses dont elle devrait faire son principal objet' (*Œuvres* (1753), I, p. xviii). Certains ouvrages récents que commente Boindin dans sa dissertation font pencher pour une rédaction tardive.

assez de courage et de patience pour lire un tas de bouquins, qui en m'instruisant de plusieurs choses nécessaires, m'auraient en même temps fort ennuyé; et comme il arrive presque toujours que les ennuyés sont ennuyeux, je n'aurais eu pour tout fruit de mes peines que le chagrin de vous avoir fait bailler '[38].

Ces «lettres» sont au nombre de quatre et se rapportent à la Comédie-Française, à l'Opéra, au Théâtre-Italien et à la Foire. Boindin y donne de précieux renseignements sur l'organisation de la Comédie-Française - l'effectif de l'orchestre, sa rémunération, les assemblées des comédiens, le processus pour arrêter le choix des pièces, les parts d'auteur et les conditions qui font qu'une pièce 'tombe dans les règles'. Il note aussi le préjudice porté à la Comédie-Française par la concurrence de la Foire[39]. Mais l'essentiel de ses lettres est occupée par des commentaires un peu fades sur les ouvrages nouveaux. Les goûts personnels de Boindin y affleurent peu. Il déplore comme 'préjugés de l'enfance' le peu d'estime accordé aux acteurs[40], loue le *Crispin rival de son maître* de Lesage, et admire Dancourt en tant qu'acteur seulement, de même qu'il admire le jeu de Guérin, de Beaubour et de Mademoiselle Desbrosses. A Mademoiselle Beaubour, il réserve un mépris total[41]. Mais le lecteur qui chercherait dans ces *Lettres* l'esthétique de Boindin dramaturge resterait sur sa faim.

Son rang respectable, ses quelques essais dramatiques, son érudition auraient suffi pour lui ouvrir les portes de l'Académie française. Son autobiographie nous apprend[42]

38. 'Première Lettre historique sur la Comédie-Française', in *Lettres historiques sur tous les spectacles de Paris*, seconde partie, p. 4-5.

39. P. 10-17 et 35-38.

40. P. 39-40.

41. P. 41-48.

42. Voir surtout les pages xx-xxii.

que, face à l'opposition de La Motte, devenu son ennemi, Boindin avait espéré faire appuyer sa candidature par de puissants amis, tels le duc de Bourgogne et Fontenelle. Mais le duc mourut en 1712, et la voix de Fontenelle alla à La Motte. Une quinzaine d'années plus tard, ce fut sur d'Ombreval[43], son cousin, et le comte de Morville[44], 'dont il avait l'honneur d'être allié', que Boindin fonda ses espoirs, mais en vain. Les portes de l'Académie devaient lui rester toujours fermées, car le cardinal de Fleury s'opposa alors à sa candidature en raison de son athéisme devenu notoire[45].

Il semble qu'il ait passé les trente dernières années de sa vie moins à écrire qu'à parler, car, s'il se fit une réputation d'athée, ce ne fut pas le résultat de ses publications, qui sont rares. On cite parfois une parodie intitulée *Polichinelle sur le Parnasse*, que Boindin aurait composée et lue dans un café en 1733 en réaction contre les lignes peu amènes que Voltaire lui consacra dans son *Temple du goût* :

---

43. Jean-Baptiste-Nicolas Ravot, seigneur d'Ombreval, était 'Avocat Général en la Cour des Aides de Paris en 1705, Maître des Requêtes ordinaires de l'Hôtel de Roi en 1722, Lieutenant Général de la Police de la Ville de Paris en 1724, Intendant de Tours en 1725 et Conseiller d'honneur en ladite Cour des Aides' (La Chesnaye-Desbois et Badier, *Dictionnaire de la noblesse*, vol. XVI, p. 806B-807A).

44. 'Charles-Jean-Baptiste Fleuriau, comte de Morville, Homme d'état, membre de l'Académie Française (1723), né le 20 octobre 1686 à Paris, mort à Versailles le 2 février 1732. Il fut successivement Procureur Général du Grand Conseil, ambassadeur en Hollande (1718), ministre de la Marine en remplacement de son père (9 avril 1722), puis des Affaires étrangères (10 août 1723). Il fut disgracié le 19 août 1727' (L. Lalanne, *Dictionnaire historique de la France*, p. 766B).

45. Voir M. Prévost et R. d'Amat, *Dictionnaire de biographie française*, p. 800B-801A.

> Un raisonneur avec un fausset aigre
> Criait : 'Messieurs, je suis ce juge intègre
> Qui toujours parle, argüe et contredit ;
> Je viens siffler tout ce qu'on applaudit.'
> Lors la Critique apparut, et lui dit :
> 'Ami Bardou, vous êtes un grand maître,
> Mais n'entrerez en cet aimable lieu ;
> Vous y venez pour fronder notre dieu :
> Contentez-vous de ne le pas connaître.

> M. Bardou se mit alors à crier : 'Tout le monde est trompé et le sera ; il n'y a point de dieu du Goût, et voici comme je le prouve.' Alors il proposa, il divisa, il subdivisa, il distingua, il résuma ; personne ne l'écouta, et l'on s'empressait à la porte plus que jamais [46].

Moland affirme que Boindin lut *Polichinelle sur le Parnasse* en plein café et qu'il voulait aussi faire graver un dessin satirique [47]. Mais, si elle a jamais existé, cette parodie, qui figure dans la liste de Brenner [48] , s'avère aujourd'hui introuvable.

En revanche, nous avons retrouvé une pièce volante intitulée: 'Harangue de M. Boindin à sa rentrée au café Procope le 12 janvier 1744' [49]. Avec un certain humour,

---

46. *Le Temple du Goût*, in *Œuvres complètes* , éd. L. Moland (1877), VIII, p. 563-564. Dans une note qui se rapporte à la lettre de Voltaire à Cideville en date du 2 août 1733 (Best. D. 642), on lit: 'in addition to the play by Nivault and Romagnesi [...], there was a one-act parody by Nicolas Boindin under the title of *Polichinelle sur le Parnasse* (Brenner 2848 [*sic*])' .

47. *Œuvres complètes de Voltaire*, VIII, p. 550, n. vi (p. 549-550; voir aussi G. Desnoiresterres, *Voltaire au château de Cirey*, p. 15-18.

48. *A Bibliographical List of Plays* [...] *1700-1789*, n° 3848. E. Carcassonne n'y fait aucune allusion dans son édition du *Temple du Goût* (Genève, Droz et Lille, Giard, 2e édition, 1953), mais en revanche il parle des parodies de d'Allainval et de Romagnesi.

49. Bibliothèque Historique de la Ville de Paris, cote 103 833 (s.l.n.d.).

Boindin - ou celui qui parle pour lui - y infirme le bruit qui courait, lors de sa récente maladie, d'un ébranlement de son indifférence religieuse, quoiqu'il ne nie pas avoir fait 'quelques démarches', sans doute auprès des autorités ecclésiastiques. Dans cette harangue burlesque, il fait allusion à ses 'premiers sentiments' et à son 'système si judicieux sur la nature de l'âme et sur son existence', sans développer ses idées, sans doute bien connues de ses lecteurs... Vers la fin de son discours, il fait même allusion à un vague prosélytisme auprès de jeunes auteurs qui fréquentent le café :

> Aux raisonnements que font la plupart, on connaît que leur esprit n'est point encore dégagé des préjugés de l'enfance. Quoi de plus utile pour la République des Lettres que d'en faire secouer le joug à ceux qui en doivent être un jour les plus illustres membres? Sans cela, quel désordre n'y apporteraient-ils pas? Leurs ouvrages seraient remplis partout de faux principes. Je puis me flatter d'avoir rendu plus d'une fois à la Société ce service important: j'ai fait tous mes efforts pour leur donner des idées justes et pour leur désiller les yeux sur mille erreurs, fruit des impressions reçues dans le bas âge. J'ai tâché aussi de leur faire comprendre ces maximes si vraies : que nous sommes nés pour le plaisir, et que nous devons, autant qu'il est en nous, contribuer à notre bien-être. J'ai eu la consolation de voir mes leçons profiter, et plus d'un prosélyte sortir convaincu de la solidité de ma doctrine, et n'attendre que l'occasion pour la mettre en pratique (p. 4).

Le baron Grimm note que Boindin était 'un des hommes de ce pays qui avait le plus d'esprit et de connaissances, et l'incrédule le plus ferme et le plus scandaleux qu'il y ait jamais eu' [50]. Ailleurs, il écrit : 'Cet écrivain était connu par quelques dissertations et quelques pièces de théâtre, mais beaucoup plus par une incrédulité publique, raisonnée, audacieuse et scandaleuse' [51]. Voltaire note, de son

50. *Correspondance littéraire*, II, p. 127.

51. *Ibid.*, p. 118.

côté, dans son 'Catalogue de la plupart des écrivains', que Boindin était 'un critique dur', constatation étayée aussi par les vers que La Faye lui consacra après leur rupture :

> Oui, Vadius, on connaît votre esprit.
> Savoir s'y joint, et quand le cas arrive
> Qu'œuvre paraît par quelque coin fautive,
> Qui d'Hélicon blesse le moindre rit,
> Plus aigrement qui jamais la reprit?
> Mais on ne voit qu'en vous aussi se montre
> Goût de louer le beau qui s'y rencontre,
> Dont cependant maints beaux esprits font cas.
> De vos pareils que voulez-vous qu'on pense,
> Eh quoi, qu'ils sont connaisseurs délicats?
> Je n'en voudrais tirer la conséquence
> Mais bien qu'ils sont gens à fuir de cent pas.[52]

Voltaire affirme aussi que le mauvais caractère de Boindin était connu, et La Porte et Clément évoquent aussi son 'humeur bizarre et [son] caractère insociable'. Une nouvelle à la main, datée du 2 décembre 1740, apporte un complément d'information sur la perception générale du caractère de Boindin. Un certain M. Rochart, avocat, puis acteur chez les Italiens, était un personnage bizarre, connu pour ses plaisanteries. L'auteur de la nouvelle, qui rapporte que Rochart avait demeuré trois ans dans la maison de Boindin, rue Garancière, sans payer de loyer, note que 'c'est tout dire qu'il a attrapé M. Boindin'[53] . Par ailleurs, Voltaire reconnaît son érudition en évoquant ses 'excellentes recherches sur les théâtres anciens' et sa 'jolie comédie du *Port de mer*', de même que les bonnes moeurs de cet 'homme respectable'[54] . La Porte et Clément évoquent

52. Voltaire, *Notebooks*, I, p. 275 (*Complete Works* , vol. 81, 1968).

53. Arsenal, ms. 11463, f. 136. Information fournie par F. Moureau.

54. 'Catalogue de la plupart des écrivains ...', *loc. cit.*, p. 1140-1141 (*Œuvres complètes de Voltaire*, XVIII, p. 353).

aussi ses moeurs 'aussi pures que peuvent être celles d'un athée' et continuent:

> [...] son coeur était généreux ; mais il joignit à ces vertus la présomption et l'opiniâtreté [...] Cependant il se plaisait à donner de bons avis aux jeunes auteurs, les aidait à mettre leurs ouvrages en état de paraître, leur gardait le secret, et les dispensait de la reconnaissance, liberté dont plusieurs profitaient volontiers. On peut se rappeler de l'avoir vu, durant bien des années, fréquenter journellement certain café très connu. Son goût, son érudition, lorsqu'il parlait littérature ou science, se faisaient aisément remarquer[55] .

Voltaire s'indigne surtout du procédé de Jean-Pierre de Bougainville, le frère aîné de l'illustre navigateur et secrétaire perpétuel de l'Académie des Inscriptions, qui, au moment de la mort de Boindin, lui refusa l'éloge d'usage: 'c'était lui qui avait accusé Boindin d'athéisme, et qui l'avait persécuté même après sa mort. [...] [il] priva Boindin de l'éloge funèbre qu'il lui devait'[56] . Victoire à la Pyrrhus, car, en mai 1754, le marquis d'Argenson pouvait déjà noter:

> J'observe, dans l'Académie des Belles-Lettres, dont je suis membre, qu'il commence à y avoir une fermentation décidée contre les prêtres. Cela a commencé à paraître à l'occasion de la mort de *Boindin*, à qui nos dévots refusèrent

---

55. *Anecdotes dramatiques* , III, p. 53-54.

56. Best. D 11667. Né à Paris le 1er décembre 1722, Bougainville fut admis à l'Académie des Inscriptions à 23 ans. Il laissa des traductions et des ouvrages sur la Grèce antique. Candidat du parti religieux de la reine à l'Académie française à 32 ans, il ne fut élu qu'en 1754 en remplacement de La Chaussée, avec la protection de Madame de Pompadour. A l'occasion de sa mort, survenue le 22 juin 1763, Bachaumont écrivit que 'cette perte peu importante [serait] facilement réparée'; voir Emile Gassier, *Les Cinq Cents Immortels*, p. 293. Pour le détail de ses œuvres, voir G. Grente et F. Moureau, *Dictionnaire des lettres françaises. Le Dix-huitième siècle*, 1995, p. 216.

service à l'Oratoire et éloge public. Nos philosophes déistes en furent choqués, et, d'après cela, à chaque élection, on se met en garde contre les prêtres et les dévots. Nulle part cette division n'est si marquée, si nette, et elle commence à rendre des fruits [57] .

L'auteur dramatique.

Boindin entama sa brève carrière dramatique dans une période généralement regardée comme particulièrement terne pour la Comédie-Française, marquée par les difficultés et les déceptions. Pour décrire la période de la fin du règne de Louis XIV, la critique emploie volontiers la métaphore du soleil couchant (Lancaster, Blanc), et on note que la tradition des deux troupes parisiennes, la Comédie-Française et l'Opéra était 'volontiers sommeillante'[58] . On constate 'un climat de gêne et de rigidité [...] sous le triste règne de la veuve Scarron'[59]. On discerne, à la Comédie-Française, plusieurs facteurs qui se combinaient pour entraver (mais non pas pour arrêter) le progrès vers un renouveau théâtral : 'Des privilèges, la tyrannie de quelques comédiens l'enfermaient dans un rôle de théâtre officiel que la direction des Premiers gentilshommes de la Chambre ne contribuaient pas peu à consolider'[60] .

C'était l'heure des tragédies-formule de Campistron et de Lagrange-Chancel. Baron prit sa retraite, pour la première fois, en 1691. En 1694, on entra dans une nouvelle phase de la Querelle du Théâtre avec la publication de la 'Lettre d'un théologien' du Père Caffaro, suivie de la réponse de Bossuet, les *Maximes et réflexions sur la comédie*. Le parti dévot, groupé autour de Madame de

57. *Mémoires et journal inédit*, IV, p. 181.

58. Henri Lagrave, *Le Théâtre et le public*, p. 7.

59. Martine de Rougemont, *La Vie théâtrale*, p. 214.

60. François Moureau, *Dufresny*, p. 255.

Maintenon, avait réussi à détourner le roi du spectacle et cherchait depuis une dizaine d'années à instaurer la censure théâtrale, tentative qui allait aboutir en 1706. La fermeture du Théâtre-Italien, le 14 mai 1697, marqua la réussite du parti dévot et contribua à l'appauvrissement de la vie culturelle parisienne.

De son coté, la Comédie-Française, elle-même surveillée, profitait de son monopole pour faire adopter des mesures vexatoires contre les théâtres de la Foire. Le 10 février 1690, elle obtint une sentence contre Alexandre Bertrand, qui avait fait construire un théâtre dans le Préau de la Foire Saint-Germain. Il fut démoli le jour même. Après mai 1697, les Forains se précipitèrent sur les dépouilles du répertoire des Italiens, qui, bien avant leur départ, s'orientaient vers la farce, les *lazzi* et l'acrobatie qui faisaient la fortune des théâtres de la Foire. En 1703, le Parlement harcela ceux-ci en interdisant les *pièces*, pour ne permettre que des 'scènes détachées'; au spectateur revint alors le plaisir de discerner leur liaison cachée... En 1706, ce fut le *dialogue* qu'un arrêt de la Cour interdit. On contourna le nouveau règlement par l'usage du monologue et du mime. Faute de pouvoir démolir les théâtres de la Foire en 1707, les autorités leur interdirent l'usage de la *parole* en 1709, et les acteurs recoururent aux pancartes et recherchèrent la faveur de l'Académie Royale de Musique. Boindin lui-même nota que la somme de 35 000 livres que les Forains versaient à l'Opéra pour user du privilège de chanter était excessive par rapport à leur bénéfice annuel de sept à huit mille livres et avait entraîné leur banqueroute avant 1718 [61].

---

61. *Lettres historiques* ['Sur le Théâtre de la Foire'] , p. 1-2. C'était en raison de ce privilège que l'entreprise foraine s'intitulait officiellement l'Opéra-Comique; le public en parlait cependant toujours comme des 'danseurs de corde' .

Ces années difficiles pour la Comédie-Française furent cependant marquées par certains noms que la critique a retenus: Regnard, Dufresny, Destouches, Dancourt, Crébillon. Certes, leurs travaux atteignent rarement le grand public actuel, qui, quitte à s'intéresser de temps en temps à la reprise d'une 'curiosité théâtrale', ne retient du siècle entier que les noms de Marivaux et de Beaumarchais. Le répertoire du début du dix-huitième siècle fut dominé par les œuvres de Corneille, de Molière et de Dancourt, ce qui en dit long sur la position délicate où se trouvait la compagnie [62]. Ainsi que le suggéra Brillon, si les spectateurs admiraient Molière; ils ne s'enthousiasmaient pas forcément pour d'éternelles reprises [63]. Cependant, la mission de la compagnie était, en partie, de préserver le patrimoine culturel accumulé depuis le temps de Richelieu. L'admiration que le public vouait aux œuvres de Molière le rendait difficile sur les tentatives de ses successeurs qui ne faisaient pas faute de déplorer cette concurrence d'outre-tombe. 'Plût au ciel qu'il ne fût venu qu'après moi', lamente le Poète du Prologue du *Négligent* (1692) de Dufresny [64]. En 1705, Regnard constate avec une tristesse de circonstance que depuis la mort du maître, 'La comédie en pleurs, et la scène déserte, / Ont perdu presque tout leur prix'[65]. Même chanson, même refrain de la part de Destouches dans l'Epître liminaire du *Médisant* (1715): 'Molière en mourant a brisé son pinceau', et Destouches le suit 'de loin, et toujours chancelant'.

62. Pour une analyse détaillée des programmes, on consultera H. Lagrave, *Le Théâtre et le public*, 3ème Partie, Chapitre 2, p. 309 et suiv.

63. 'Qui oserait soutenir qu'on admirât aujourd'hui Molière?', voir *Le Théophraste moderne* (1699), cité par F. Moureau, *Dufresny*, p. 417.

64. Sc. 3.

65. *Les Ménechmes*, Prologue, scène première.

J.-P. Vittu a constaté la faiblesse de l'assistance à la Comédie-Française dans la période de 1689 à 1712. Le nombre maximum d'entrées est enregistré dans la saison 1689-1699 : 193 000, et le minimum, de 107 000, dans celle de 1711-1712. La médiane pour l'ensemble de la période 1680-1716 est de 136 000[66]. Afin de lutter contre la désaffection du public et la concurrence de la Foire, les Comédiens-Français trouvèrent deux expédients: diminuer le nombre relatif de représentations de tragédies et jouer fréquemment les petites pièces en un acte sorties de la plume d'acteurs tels Legrand et, surtout, Dancourt[67]. Le moment était donc favorable pour les compositions de Boindin.

La collaboration avec La Motte et *Les Trois Gascons.*

La collaboration dramatique ou littéraire laisse presque inévitablement dans le vague la contribution de chacun des collaborateurs. On ne résoudra sans doute jamais la question de savoir qui, de Dufresny ou de Regnard, eut le premier l'idée de faire d'un joueur le protagoniste d'une comédie. Dans les cas où la collaboration s'avère fructueuse, le problème se complique, car les collaborateurs s'effacent derrière leur création, et la tentative de préciser l'origine des éléments particuliers échoue devant la réussite même de l'entreprise commune.

---

66. 'La Comédie-Française (1680-1716)' , p. 98-99 et graphiques 2, p. 134. Cf. F. Moureau, *Dufresny*, section III, Première Partie, Chapitre premier, p. 255 et suiv.

67. Les choses en étaient au point que, le 27 octobre 1712, les Comédiens reçurent l'ordre suivant : 'Sa Majesté étant informée que les Comédiens jouent le moins possible de tragédies, ce qui est contraire à l'usage et au plaisir du public, ordre leur est donné de jouer alternativement une pièce sérieuse et une pièce comique, à peine de 300 liv. d'amende payable par la troupe en général, à moins que nous n'ordonnions autrement'; cité par J. Bonnassies, *La Comédie-Française, histoire administrative*, p. 134.

A notre sens, la collaboration de Boindin et La Motte ne pose pas vraiment de problème. Cependant, on a émis des suppositions qui méritent d'être examinées. Selon le 'Mémoire sur la vie et les ouvrages de Boindin' (1753), les deux auteurs collaborèrent, on l'a dit, pour *Les Trois Gascons*. Leurs confrères et les spectateurs désirant peut-être savoir la part de chacun des auteurs dans cette comédie, ils composèrent seuls deux nouvelles comédies: Boindin, *Le Bal d'Auteuil* et La Motte, *La Matrone d'Ephèse* . Ils reprirent ensuite leur travail en commun, dont le résultat fut *Le Port de mer*, de 1704, composé par Boindin et revu par La Motte[68]. Par la suite, leur collaboration s'interrompit, et Boindin composa seul *Le Petit-maître de robe* en 1707, mais cette dernière pièce ne vit jamais les feux de la rampe.

Déjà en 1746, les *Œuvres de théâtre de Monsieur Boindin* affirmaient dans la Préface, que *La Matrone d'Ephèse* était entièrement de La Motte, *Le Bal d'Auteuil*, totalement de Boindin, et les deux autres pièces représentées, des deux auteurs en collaboration. L'éditeur affirmait la bonne foi de Boindin: 'Bien loin de vouloir s'attribuer la part que Monsieur de La Motte peut avoir dans ces deux pièces, Monsieur Boindin serait ravi que celle qu'il y a lui-même pût être attribuée à Monsieur de La Motte: et c'est moins pour s'en assurer la possession que pour se faire honneur d'avoir été en société d'ouvrages avec Monsieur de La Motte qu'il fait cet aveu'. Cependant, si la collaboration des deux auteurs était connue dès l'origine, et l'incorporation de *La Matrone* dans les éditions des œuvres de Boindin de 1705 et de 1714 considérée depuis longtemps comme une fantaisie de libraire, pourquoi fallut-il le rappeler, avec toutes les précisions et à deux reprises, en 1746 et encore en 1753? La réponse est peut-être dans les *Anecdotes dramatiques* de La Porte et Clément, où on

68. *Œuvres* (1753), I, p. xiii.

trouve l'affirmation sans doute courante et ancienne, que La Motte était le véritable auteur des *Trois Gascons*: 'On prétend que cette comédie est de La Motte seul. Il l'avait composée, dit-on, pour avoir son entrée à la Comédie. Se trouvant indisposé, il pria Boindin d'aller la présenter aux Comédiens. Ceux-ci en entendirent la lecture avec de si grands applaudissements que Boindin, séduit par leurs éloges, la laissa inscrire sous son nom, et profita des entrées'[69] . La circonstance semble fort douteuse, et nous sommes enclin à attribuer l'origine de cette histoire à la mesquinerie de certains habitués du café Laurent, très conscients du contraste qu'il y avait entre les personnalités des deux écrivains et peut-être aigris par l'affaire des couplets. Il est loisible de remarquer : 1°, que Boindin était amateur de comédies, tandis que les dons de La Motte se manifestaient beaucoup plus dans les domaines de l'opéra et de la tragédie, malgré sa tentative italienne des *Originaux* (représentée en 1692) et quelques comédies fournies à la Comédie-Française [70] ; 2°, que La Motte ambitionnait une carrière dramatique, tandis que, après 1707, Boindin délaissa le théâtre, sauf, peut-être, pour écrire *Polichinelle sur le Parnasse*; 3°, qu'une telle supercherie l'eût couvert de ridicule et d'opprobre; 4°, que Voltaire, très informé de l'histoire littéraire et des bruits qui couraient, en aurait presque certainement parlé si l'histoire avait été généralement prise au sérieux au moment de la mort de Boindin. Il nous semble donc qu'elle peut être écartée.

Au contraire de Dancourt et de Legrand, Boindin ne transforma pas un événement d'actualité en petite comédie de mœurs. Le projet qu'il élabora avec La Motte consista à

---

69. II, p. 246. Les éditeurs de la *Petite Bibliothèque des théâtres* (XII, 1787, p. iii-vi) contredisent La Porte et Clément, mais sur l'affirmation de Boindin-Parfaict de 1753.

70. Voir Joannidès, *La Comédie-Française de 1680 à 1920. Tableau des représentations par auteurs et par pièces*, p. 57B-58A.

utiliser une autre possibilité offerte à qui voulait fournir une de ces petites comédies dont le Théâtre-Français avait besoin aux alentours de 1700: la refonte d'une comédie oubliée. Ils choisirent *Les Trois Orontes* de Boisrobert[71], comédie qu'ils avaient, selon toute probabilité, lue, car seuls deux ouvrages de Boisrobert avaient été représentées à la Comédie-Française : *La Jalouse d'elle-même* , qui eut dix représentations en 1681-1683, et *La Vraie Didon*, qui en connut une seule en 1683. *Les Trois Orontes*, comédie créée en 1652, fut imprimée par Augustin Courbé l'année suivante. La pièce elle-même était inspirée par un conte du même auteur, intitulé *Les Trois Racan*, qu'il disait fondé sur un événement véritable. Selon les éditeurs de la *Petite Bibliothèque des théâtres*, le marquis de Racan, devant se présenter un jour devant Mademoiselle de Gournay, qui ne le connaissait pas, se fit précéder par deux de ses amis qui se servirent de son nom. 'Lorsqu'il se présenta lui-même en troisième lieu, écrit-on, elle le prit pour un imposteur et, quoique, sur sa réputation, elle eut beaucoup d'envie de le voir, elle le chassa de chez elle, à grands coups de pantoufle'[72].

Le schéma de la pièce de Boindin et La Motte suit le modèle de Boisrobert, qui est en cinq actes et en vers. Cependant l'intrigue de leur comédie est sensiblement différente de la sienne. Dans la pièce originale, Oronte, le héros bordelais, a quitté son amante Cassandre, bordelaise

---

71. Voir la *Petite Bibliothèque des Théâtres* (XII, p.iv-v). François Le Métel, sieur de Boisrobert (1589-1662), poète, romancier, dramaturge, est l'auteur de dix-huit pièces. Ses nombreuses comédies des années 1650 exploitent la popularité de la *comedia* espagnole.

72. *Ibid.*, Mademoiselle de Gournay était la fameuse Marie le Jars, la «fille d'alliance» de Montaigne. Le texte ajoute: 'L'anecdote des trois prétendus Racan est très vraie. Le marquis de Racan en convenait lui-même, à ce que dit le troisième volume du *Ménagiana*'.

aussi et toujours amoureuse, pour obéir aux ordres de son père et épouser Caliste, fille du riche Amidor, habitant de Paris. Don Fernand, le père d'Oronte, avait donné à son fils une lettre d'introduction à Amidor, qu'Oronte avait confiée à Cassandre comme gage de son amour et comme preuve que, sous le prétexte de se rendre à Paris, il allait s'absenter de Bordeaux et se cacher 'en quelque lieu' . Mais il se rend à Paris malgré sa promesse. Cléante, qui aime Caliste, se met d'accord avec la mère de celle-ci, Fénice, pour se présenter à Amidor sous le nom d'Oronte, muni d'une fausse lettre de Don Fernand, préparée par le louche Monsieur Yves. Celui-ci est le frère de Lizette, la servante de Caliste, et remplit les fonctions de Secrétaire de Saint-Innocent et de Procureur fiscal de la Pissotte. Dans la rue, Oronte aperçoit Cassandre, qui s'est déguisée en homme pour le suivre à Paris, et il est clair qu'ils s'aiment toujours. Cassandre s'étant introduite chez Caliste sous le nom d'Oronte, a su lui plaire, et Cléante le provoque en duel pour l'avoir supplanté dans le cœur de sa maîtresse. Cassandre lui explique alors son identité véritable, et ils unissent leurs intérêts. Amidor congédie le véritable Oronte, le troisième de ce nom à se présenter, mais Gyron, un banquier de Bordeaux fixé à Paris, révèle à Amidor la vérité, qu'il sait parce qu'Oronte s'était arrêté chez lui en arrivant de Bordeaux pour changer de vêtements et toucher des lettres de change que Don Fernand avait envoyées au banquier. Philippin, le valet d'Oronte qui sert Cassandre de bon cœur (mais qui accepte très volontiers un pot de vin de la part de chacun des intéressés), va annoncer à Oronte qu'il vient d'apprendre par lettre que Cassandre est morte d'amour pour lui, afin d'apprendre ensuite à celle-ci la réaction de son infidèle amant. Amoureuse de Cléante, Caliste essaie pour sa part de dégoûter Oronte en le traitant avec froideur et en jouant la timide. Oronte est réduit au désespoir par le rapport de la mort de Cassandre, puis, quand la nouvelle se révèle fausse, on lui raconte, pour raffiner sur ses tourments, que, imitant son inconstance, elle a trouvé un mari dans Cléante. De leur côté, Lizette et

Monsieur Yves déclarent à Amidor qu'Oronte est réellement un acteur, déjà marié, qu'ils ont vu dans les rôles de marchand d'orviétan, de magicien, etc. Amidor s'avoue incapable de comprendre la situation : 'Que diable est-ce ceci donc? Je ne sais qu'en juger' (IV, 6). Mais par la suite, il oblige Lizette à lui apprendre la vérité en la torturant physiquement avec des coins de fortune! Finalement, tout s'explique, et la pièce se termine sur les trois mariages 'corrects' de Cléante avec Caliste, d'Oronte avec Cassandre et de Philippin avec Lizette.

De l'imbroglio romanesque, Boindin retient un certain nombre d'éléments tels que la situation initiale, le voyage de Bordeaux à Paris, la Gasconne déguisée et la menace d'un duel. Mais il transforme les personnages (Cassandre et Philippin, par exemple) et accentue la caricature. Le rôle du père, puisé dans le répertoire des vieillards bernés, est conforme aux normes de la farce et de la parade ; il prête sa fille aux volontés d'un frère qui désire que sa nièce soit alliée à 'une des meilleures maisons de Gascogne' (scène 3). Ce type de vieillard estime que l'argent et le rang doivent constituer des 'raisons sans réplique' et réduire à la soumission une jeunesse retorse qui a la fâcheuse insolence de 'se mêler de vouloir' . Comme l'Amidor des *Trois Orontes*, Monsieur Oronte est le barbon victime des stratagèmes des jeunes amants et de leurs adjuvants. Boindin retient de son modèle l'incompréhension du père devant une situation qu'il ne peut donc maîtriser, et qui sombre enfin dans la mièvrerie d'un attendrissement ridicule (scène 5). C'est moins le spectacle du père qui choisit l'époux de sa fille qui est censé faire impression à cette époque que ses préoccupations roturières (l'acquisition d'une fortune et la promotion sociale) et la tyrannie avec laquelle il compte imposer ses volontés. C'est la volonté poussée au paroxysme, mêlée à la faiblesse émotionnelle, qui se fond en caricature de la paternité. Conformément à la fantaisie de libération qui règle le mouvement de la farce, la fille, qui n'oppose que des protestations respectueuses à la brutalité du discours paternel, recourt facilement aux stratagèmes proposés par les adjuvants, stratagèmes justifiés par la logique de la farce qui empêche aussi le vieillard de les comprendre, donc de les déjouer.

Les sentiments amoureux des adjuvants, de même que ceux des protagonistes, ne se développent pas, mais, chez ces personnages à connotations populaires, ils s'annoncent sans ambages dès la première scène. Les serviteurs sont des plus conventionnels, réclamant des gages (naturellement) impayés et vivant à l'affût des pots-de-vin. Le valet est, comme d'habitude, victime des chantages de la servante qui lui promet le mariage si l'intrigue tourne bien, ce qui est toujours le cas. A l'inverse des normes sociales telles que les imposaient les maîtres de l'époque, les valets et servantes de comédie ignorent jusqu'au mot de fidélité, qu'on prisait alors davantage que les compétences spécifiques. Cependant, les serviteurs de Boindin ne cherchent pas à sortir de leur condition, comme le feront ceux de Lesage, mais se contentent de montrer un certain cynisme allègre dans leurs relations avec la classe des maîtres.

Le peu de fidélité du serviteur Frontin (justifié à ses yeux par les coups qui lui ont tenu lieu de gages) est doublé d'une certaine lâcheté calculée, de convention elle aussi[73]. Mais Boindin construit autour de ce trait conventionnel une scène géniale qui rappelle les *lazzi* des Italiens, où le valet est tiraillé par ses deux maîtres, qui le terrorisent avec leurs épées dégainées (scène 8). Comme dans *Le Bal d'Auteuil*, Boindin laisse aux acteurs une large part dans l'interprétation des rôles. Même en ces circonstances,

73. Voir Jean Emelina, *Les Valets et les servantes*, p. 226-227, 289 et 309-313.

Frontin se permet ces jeux de mots dont son créateur se montre assez friand[74] .

Boindin pousse la satire du Gascon beaucoup plus loin que ne l'avait fait Boisrobert. Grâce à l'inventaire du personnage dressé par Charles Mazouer, nous sommes à même d'apprécier le nombre de comédies où il figure - une quarantaine entre 1660 et 1720 - et ses caractéristiques [75]. Dans la majorité des pièces, il joue le rôle de l'amant rejeté et se retrouve souvent dans les épisodes où s'impose le déguisement, qui, sous bien des formes, est un composant particulièrement manifeste de la dramaturgie de Boindin. Selon Charles Mazouer, l'histoire littéraire du Gascon se confond, au seizième siècle, avec celle du *miles gloriosus*[76], et André Tissier affirme que le personnage était l'héritier de trois types de fanfarons du répertoire de la comédie : le *miles gloriosus* (d'origine latine), du matamore (du théâtre espagnol) et du capitan (du théâtre italien)[77]. Ce fut Saint-Evremond qui le premier créa un Gascon de comédie, Matamore adouci, dans le personnage superficiel et vaniteux du marquis de Bousignac, qui figure dans *Sir Politick Would-be*, composé entre 1662 et 1665. Le succès du personnage proviendrait, selon Ch. Mazouer, du centralisme louis-quatorzien qui encoura-

74. Sur les sens de *devoir* .

75. Voir 'Le Gascon dans le théâtre comique sous Louis XIV', in *L'Image littéraire du Gascon. IIe colloque de littérature régionale*, publié par 'Les Cahiers de l'Université de Pau et des pays de l'Adour', n° 21 (1984), p. 85-108. Le Gascon apparaît aussi dans les arts plastiques de l'époque; nous avons de Nicolas Lancret (1690-1743) un 'Gascon puni', d'après lequel Nicolas de Larmessin (1684-1755) exécuta une gravure en taille douce qui porte le même titre.

76. Ch. Mazouer cite particulièrement le Chapitre 42 du *Tiers Livre*, et *Le Baron de Faeneste* de d'Aubigné.

77. Voir *M. de Crac*, p. 17. Pour une indication de la fréquence du type au dix-huitième siècle, voir, *ibid*., p. 18-19, n. 6.

geait les Parisiens à nourrir un sentiment de supériorité vis-à-vis des provinciaux: 'les provinciaux, et singulièrement ceux qui viennent des terres d'oc, font rire la noblesse versaillaise et les honnêtes gens de Paris, sûrs de la supériorité de leurs usages, de leurs mœurs, de leurs modes, de leur goût et de leur langue; pour ce public, la province est un monde autre, lieu de tous les ridicules'[78]. Voilà qui explique peut-être l'évolution du personnage au cours du siècle, qui finit par sombrer dans la pure caricature. Selon A. Tissier, 'les Gascons [...] perdirent leur physionomie réelle; désormais il faut amuser à leurs dépens; seule compte la caricature : on simplifie, on exagère, on tombe dans la loufoquerie, on tourne les qualités en ridicules et les travers en défauts; les Gascons authentiques, les vrais Cadets de Gascogne, ne devaient guère se retrouver dans ces charges'[79].

Certes, on rencontre aussi, par exemple, des Normands ridicules - on pense à Madame Turcaret, avec ses modes et ses cercles bourgeois -, mais le Gascon avait ceci de particulier que sa prononciation était très sensiblement différente de la norme de la «Ville»[80] . Ces deux origines provinciales se trouvent satirisées dans les personnages de Mathieu Crochet et de Fijac (déguisé en baron d'Aubignac) du *Bal* de Regnard (1696). Les vantardises de d'Aubignac ressemblent d'assez près à celles de Spadagnac dans *Les Trois Gascons* :

> Vous ne connaissez plus le baron d'Aubignac,
> Vicomte de Dougnac, Croupignic, Foulignac,
> Gentilhomme gascon, plus noble que personne,
> D'une race ancienne autant que la Garonne? (scène 12)

78. 'Le Gascon dans le théâtre comique sous Louis XIV', p. 87.

79. *Op. cit.*, p. 21.

80. Ch. Mazouer cite, statistiquement les plus nombreux, les personnages originaires des provinces du sud-ouest: Limoges, Angoulême, la Gascogne, le Pays Basque, le Languedoc; *op. cit.*, p. 91 et les notes 23-26.

La prononciation provinciale, indiquée de manière phonétique dans notre texte, pouvait être signalée de trois façons différentes dans les textes de l'époque. Les auteurs pouvaient, comme ici, inscrire les particularités de la prononciation gasconne (conventionnelle) dans leur texte; ou ils pouvaient indiquer dans une didascalie que le rôle, rédigé en un français normal, devait se prononcer 'en gascon', ou encore, ils pouvaient faire suivre la première apparition du personnage par la mention 'parlant gascon'. De là, le critique peut conclure qu'on laissait les acteurs eux-mêmes libres de constituer leur 'style gascon', langue théâtrale de convention, signe du 'fait gascon' plutôt que reflet d'une réalité linguistique[81] .

Le déguisement d'une femme en Gasconne paraît au théâtre avant 1701 dans *Monsieur de Pourceaugnac* (1669)[82] et dans *Colombine, avocat pour et contre* de Fatouville (1685). La Julie de Boindin est bel et bien gasconne, mais c'est son sexe qu'elle déguise. Les caractéristiques 'gasconnes' incorporées à son portrait (scène 2) facilitaient ce genre de déguisement, précisément parce qu'elles se constituaient la contrepartie des bienséances internes de l'esthétique classique, qui demandaient qu'une femme montrât les qualités jugées appropriées, telles que la modestie, la retenue et la douceur.

Les auteurs avaient le droit de distribuer les rôles aux comédiens pour la première série de représentations d'une pièce nouvelle. Aussi peut-on présumer que Boindin en choisit les meilleurs pour la création des siennes. Cette supposition n'est pas sans importance pour les conjectures qu'on peut émettre sur la distribution probable des *Trois*

81. Voir Ch. Mazouer, *loc. cit.*, p. 93-94.

82. II, 7. Lucette est languedocienne ou gasconne; 'on n'y regarde pas de si près'. Voir Molière, *Œuvres complètes*, II, p. 1 408, [p. 623], n. 1 .

Gascons au moment de sa création. Conjectures, puisque ce ne fut qu'en 1765, deux ans après l'arrivée en fonctions du secrétaire-souffleur de la compagnie, La Porte (dit Delaporte), que les Registres de la Comédie commencèrent à indiquer la distribution des rôles.

La première série de représentations fut au nombre de huit. Globalement, ces huit occasions réunirent vingt-trois acteurs, treize hommes et dix femmes, mais ils ne participèrent pas tous chaque soir au spectacle. Les noms de trois d'entre les hommes paraissent huit fois dans les Registres: La Thorillière, Lavoy et (Etienne) Baron. Deux autres furent présents en sept occasions: Guérin et Beaubour. On peut écarter le nom de Beaubour, car, malgré son interprétation supérieure de Valère dans *Le Joueur*, il jouait plutôt dans les tragédies[83]. En restent quatre, qui semblent tous convenir parfaitement à un rôle dans notre pièce. Isaac-François Guérin, sieur d'Estriché (1636-1728) était fils de comédien et épousa en secondes noces Armande Béjart, veuve de Molière. Il avait, selon Lyonnet, 'un naturel parfait et une diction juste et sage' et remplissait les rôles de premier confident dans la tragédie et les rôles à manteau (c'est-à-dire les hommes d'un certain âge) dans la comédie. Vu son âge à l'époque de la création des *Trois Gascons*, le rôle de Monsieur Oronte lui aurait convenu. Etienne Baron (1676-1711), fils du célèbre Michel Baron, fut reçu à la Comédie en 1695. Il incarnait les jeunes premiers, malgré son jeu apparemment un peu froid, et il est loisible de conjecturer que le rôle d'Eraste lui fut attribué. La spécialité de Lavoy (v. 1661-1726) était les rôles à manteau, les

83. Tous les renseignements biographiques que nous donnerons ci-après sont puisés dans le *Dictionnaire des comédiens* d'Henry Lyonnet; on y renvoie le lecteur pour de plus amples précisions. L'absence de Guérin le 26 juin n'aurait pas fait de problème, car, en raison des voyages à la Cour, la majorité des emplois était doublée; voir H. Lagrave, *Le Théâtre et le public*, p. 292.

paysans, les valets et les grands confidents. Du fait qu'il incarnait les paysans, on peut supposer qu'il aurait bien pu débiter du gascon de théâtre et, par conséquent, prendre le rôle de Monsieur de Spadagnac. Pierre Le Noir, sieur de La Thorillière (1659-1731), remplissait surtout les rôles à manteau, les valets brillants, les petits-maîtres et les ivrognes. Selon les sources, il était beau, avait une voix pleine et sonore et un jeu rempli d'action. Il incarnait Hector du *Joueur,* Carlin du *Distrait*, Strabon de *Démocrite*, etc., et occupa ce type d'emploi jusqu'à un âge très avancé. La Thorillière aurait probablement joué Frontin, dont le rôle très actif aurait convenu à son jeu, que Lyonnet évoque comme étant 'rempli d'action'.

Le cas des actrices est plus compliqué car, sur les dix femmes qui étaient présentes en huit occasions, *Les Trois Gascons* ne pouvait en inclure que trois. Sur les dix actrices en question (Mesdemoiselles Desmares, Champvallon, Beauval, Godefroy, Grandval, Dufey, Clavel, Des Brosses, Duclos et Beaubour), nous retenons les noms de la Desmares, de la Beauval, et de la Grandval, pour leur attribuer respectivement les rôles de Lucile, de Marton et de Julie[84]. Mademoiselle Desmares (1682-1753) était la fille de l'acteur Nicolas Desmares. Elle débuta dans les rôles d'enfant en 1690, fut reçue en 1699 et se retira en 1721. Le début de sa carrière fut caractérisé par la création des rôles d'amoureuses: Rhodope dans *Esope à la Cour* (1701) et Thérèse dans *Le Double Veuvage* (1702). Elle semble avoir été particulièrement talentueuse, puisque, selon Lyonnet, elle incarnait les premiers rôles tragiques et qu'elle déployait une verve folle dans les soubrettes du répertoire. En ce début du dix-huitième siècle, Mademoiselle Beauval incarnait toujours les grandes sou-

84. Nous nous dispenserons d'exposer les raisons qui nous ont amené à écarter les sept autres noms de notre liste, et de préciser leur biographie et leurs spécialités .

brettes. Elle naquit vers 1648-1649 et fut abandonnée sur le parvis d'une église. Une blanchisseuse la recueillit et l'éleva jusqu'à l'âge de dix ans, lorsqu'elle fut prise en charge par un comédien du nom de Filandre, avec qui elle débuta dans la carrière dramatique. Elle incarna le rôle de Nicole dans *Le Bourgeois Gentilhomme*, où Molière avait exploité son tic qui était de rire presque continuellement en parlant. Elle était, selon Lyonnet, 'le type de la servante à la gaieté communicative'. Elle créa Marton dans *L'Homme à bonne fortune*, Marton dans *La Coquette*, Catau dans *Le Grondeur*, Nérine dans *Le Joueur*, Lisette dans *Le Distrait*, et bien d'autres. La liste est longue, et Lyonnet de conclure qu'elle 'fut la soubrette idéale de Molière, de Regnard, de Brueys, de Baron, de Palaprat!'[85]. L'ordre du Dauphin selon lequel Mademoiselle Desmares devait la doubler provoqua sa retraite le 8 mars 1704. Mademoiselle Beauval, actrice très exacte, était d'un caractère acariâtre et eut au moins dix enfants. Elle disparut en 1720. Mademoiselle Dangeville (dite la Grandval, 1676-1769) avait débuté à la Comédie-Française en 1700 et s'était spécialisé dans les rôles d'amoureuses et de princesses tragiques. 'Plus belle qu'intelligente, nonchalante, distinguée, elle avait pour elle le charme de l'organe', écrit Lyonnet. La participation des acteurs que nous avons nommés dans une représentation à la Cour aurait pu appuyer nos conjectures, mais *Les Trois Gascons* n'y furent jamais joués.

Le Registre porte une note des frais d'établissement de la pièce, qui consistèrent en 72 livres pour la musique et 44 livres pour le ballet. Ces frais représentent des sommes déboursées une fois pour toutes dès la première. Les frais journaliers, qui y sont notés aussi, comprenaient trois habits de femme à 13 livres et quatre habits de danseurs à

---

85. Jal lui consacre un long article biographique (*Dictionnaire critique de biographie et d'histoire*, p. 155A-159A).

12 livres. Ces habits auraient donc été loués pour chaque représentation. Le plus grand nombre d'entrées se monta à 930 le soir de la première, le 14 juin 1701, lorsque la pièce accompagna *Cinna*. Ensuite les entrées varient entre 410 et 588, puis commencent à baisser sensiblement le 28, avec 294 entrées. La première série de représentations valut à Boindin 181 livres 10 $^1/_2$ sols.

La critique de l'époque accueillit favorablement *Les Trois Gascons*. Les frères Parfaict, qui notent la ressemblance entre notre pièce et *Les Trois Orontes*, estiment qu'ayant resserré l'action, Boindin a 'jeté une grande gaieté dans la pièce'[86] . Les remarques du marquis d'Argenson sont particulièrement intéressantes:

> Le déguisement d'une jolie actrice en homme plaît toujours au public; mais si cela est beau, cela n'est plus nouveau présentement. Tout ceci fait une assez jolie intrigue de farce ou de comédie italienne. Paraître sous le nom de son rival pour en dégoûter ou en ragoûter, cela devrait être abandonné aux Italiens; mais nos auteurs en prennent où ils peuvent. Ces pièces-là se jouent bien et plus vivement que de bonnes pièces de caractère[87].

Le travesti masculin d'une femme possédait des résonances sexuelles auxquelles un parterre aurait sans doute été très sensible - le marquis aussi, semble-t-il -, et sa réflexion explique peut-être aussi la présence du même déguisement dans *Le Bal d'Auteuil*, où il revêt des allures encore plus suggestives. Si d'Argenson trouve que *Les Trois Gascons* sont une pièce 'assez jolie', il la trouve assez peu conforme à la dignité qu'il associe à l'image de la Comédie-Française; mais, en 1701, comme nous l'avons vu, nécessité faisait loi. La dernière réflexion du marquis

---

86. *Histoire du théâtre français*, XIV, 1748, p. 219 (réimp., III, p. 454).

87. *Notices*, I, p. 107.

laisse affleurer le désir généralisé de trouver autre chose que les comédies de caractère dans la lignée de Molière et préfigure l'évolution que le genre allait connaître entre les mains de Regnard, de Dufresny et de Destouches. Le seul critique moderne à s'occuper de la pièce, Lancaster, apprécie la rapidité de l'action et la vivacité du dialogue[88].

Les huit représentations que la pièce connut dans sa nouveauté, entre le 4 et le 30 janvier 1701, furent interrompues par la fermeture du théâtre entre le 9 et le 21, à l'occasion de la mort de Monsieur. Une reprise eut lieu en mai 1730, mais elle n'alla pas au-delà de quatre représentations. On remarque que le début de la saison 1730-1731 vit également la reprise des *Trois Cousines* de Dancourt (1700) et des *Trois Frères rivaux* de La Font (1713). On pourrait donc conclure que le même sens de l'humour qui programma *Atrée et Thyeste* avec *Le Souper mal apprêté* (le 15 juin 1726) motivait l'élaboration de ce 'Festival des Trois'. Trois nouvelles représentations eurent lieu les 7, 9 et 12 décembre 1750. Une série intermittente de représentations du *Port de mer* se fit entre août et novembre, et on le redonna à la fin de janvier 1751. La reprise des *Trois Gascons*, à titre expérimental sans doute, attira en trois soirées 651, 679 et 690 entrées, ce qui est légèrement en-dessous de la moyenne pour le mois. La pièce principale était à chaque occasion la *Cénie* de Madame de Graffigny, créée le 25 juin 1750.

Le Bal d'Auteuil.

Boindin composa seul cette comédie, et elle eut la première de ses dix représentations à la Comédie-Française le 22 août 1702, et sa dernière le 30 décembre. Elle jouit depuis cette époque de la réputation d'avoir déclenché la censure de Madame Palatine qui, choquée lors de la repré-

88. *Sunset*, p. 267.

sentation qui eut lieu à Versailles le 2 janvier 1703, communiqua ses sentiments au roi, qui fit désormais interdire toute représentation de la pièce[89].

La princesse n'était pas de la coterie de Madame de Maintenon, loin de là, et elle portait un vif intérêt au théâtre et témoignait beaucoup de sympathie pour les comédiens. Elle avait averti les Italiens des risques auxquels leurs imprudences les exposaient et regrettait leur exil. Elle regrettait également le conservatisme croissant de la Cour depuis la désaffection du roi pour les représentations théâtrales. Elle avait pleinement conscience des difficultés qu'il y avait à écrire pour la scène comique, mais reconnaissait également que les bonnes intentions ne justifiaient pas les mauvaises réalisations[90]. Somme toute, elle était amateur éclairé de théâtre et nullement prude[91]. Cependant, elle était homophobe, et les objections qu'elle souleva contre la représentation du *Bal d'Auteuil* sont sans doute à mettre sur le compte de cette attitude et de son idée du bon goût .

La censure des pièces de théâtre existait sous diverses formes depuis le seizième siècle au moins. Il était interdit

---

89. Voir notre article, 'Theatrical censorship and Nicolas Boindin's *Le Bal d'Auteuil* (1702)'. Mouhy écrit: 'Il vint un ordre d'en suspendre les représentations après la dixième, et c'est depuis ce temps que toutes les pièces de théâtre ont été soumises à un censeur' (*Tablettes dramatiques*, p. 31). Cette affirmation est une simplification grossière.

90. Voir ses réflexions sur la difficulté de composer des comédies autres que celles qui étaient centrées sur la satire personnelle: *Correspondance* (éd. E. Jaeglé), I, p. 274 , lettre du 14 septembre 1702. Elle trouvait *La Matrone d'Ephèse* et *L'Opérateur Barry* 'détestables'; *ibid.*, p. 278. *L'Opérateur Barry* fut représenté le 11 octobre 1702.

91. F. Moureau, 'Du côté Cour, la Princesse Palatine et le théâtre', *Revue d'Histoire du théâtre*, 1983, 3, p. 275-286.

de mettre en cause la monarchie (1516), de jurer et de blasphémer (1536 et 1553). Il était toutefois permis aux Enfants de la Basoche de monter des satires, à condition que le spectacle fût préalablement soumis à l'approbation du Parlement (1594). Des dispositions analogues furent prises en 1609 qui stipulaient que le texte de toute comédie ou farce devait être communiqué au Procureur du roi qui, s'il en approuvait la représentation, devait signer le rôle ou le registre des comédiens. En 1641, une déclaration de Louis XIII défendit les gestes et les paroles obscènes. Mais l'application de ces règlements s'avérait généralement impossible.

La surveillance des représentations théâtrales par le parti dévot dans la décennie 1690 et ses efforts pour faire introduire des mesures coercitives efficaces n'aboutirent qu'en 1706, trois ans après l'interdiction du *Bal d'Auteuil.* La réfutation du *Nouveau Testament de notre Seigneur Jésus-Christ* de Richard Simon que Bossuet se proposait de publier avait, en 1702 précisément, provoqué un débat qui touchait le droit que réclamaient les évêques de publier des ouvrages théologiques sans solliciter le visa des autorités temporelles. Elle opposait Pontchartrain à Bossuet et à Noailles et occupait le chancelier (qui y perdait le soutien des dévots) plus que les problèmes suscités par le théâtre, sans doute jugés d'importance mineure. Quand *Le Bal d'Auteuil* fut interdit, les équivoques obscènes présentes dans certaines scènes étaient précisément ce qui préoccupait le parti dévot depuis une dizaine d'années, mais si la pièce favorisa la mise en place de la censure, elle ne la déclencha pas .

Pas plus que pour *Les Trois Gascons*, nous ne savons au juste quelle était la distribution lors de la seule série de représentations que connut la pièce. Cependant, il est possible d'envisager un certain nombre d'hypothèses. La pièce eut dix représentations à Paris et une à Versailles. Celles de Paris eurent lieu les 22, 24, 26 et 28 août, les 3, 5, 7 et

9 novembre, et les 28 et 30 décembre 1702. La représentation à Versailles se fit le 2 janvier 1703. Or, les Registres de la Comédie portent les noms des acteurs et actrices qui jouèrent à ces dates et signalent les grandes pièces qui constituèrent le spectacle principal : *Andronic, Nicomède, Rodogune, Manlius, Les Femmes savantes, Le Menteur, Dom Bertrand, L'Homme à bonne fortune, Dom Japhet* (deux fois) et *Géta*. Etant donné que l'élément constant du spectacle est *Le Bal d'Auteuil*, il s'agit d'isoler les cinq acteurs et les cinq actrices qui correspondraient aux rôles masculins et féminins de la pièce (on peut exclure du calcul le personnage muet du Tabellion) en relevant les noms de ceux qui jouaient chaque soir ou presque[92]. La totalité des acteurs présents à une soirée quelconque de la série (ne fût-ce qu'une seule fois) se monte à dix-huit et, celle des actrices, à douze. Parmi les hommes, quatre participèrent à la série entière, soit onze fois : Guérin, Ponteuil, Desmares et La Thorillière. Compte tenu de la pièce principale et de la spécialité des acteurs - parfois peu concluante puisqu'un acteur pouvait très bien jouer les rois dans les tragédies et les paysans de comédie -, il est possible de suggérer qu'Etienne Baron joua du 22 août jusqu'au 5 novembre 1702 inclus et le 2 janvier 1703, et qu'il fut remplacé par Du Boccage le 7 et le 9 novembre et le 28 et le 30 décembre. Du Boccage avait déjà joué une autre fois seulement dans la série, le 3 novembre, et il est possible qu'il prît alors un des rôles mineurs dans *Les Femmes savantes* (L'Epine, Julien ou le Notaire?).

Le cas des douze actrices qui participèrent à la série de représentations est plus clair. Trois actrices jouèrent à onze

---

92. Selon Beauchamps, le Prologue ne fut jamais joué (*Recherches sur les théâtres de France*, II, p. 299). Certes, le nombre des acteurs présents à toutes les représentations (parfois en se doublant) équivaut aux rôles masculins dans la pièce elle-même, mais il n'est pas exclu qu'un acteur ait tenu un rôle dans le Prologue et un autre dans la pièce.

représentations, deux autres à dix, et une à neuf. Les six autres actrices atteignirent des totaux nettement plus réduits, entre une et sept présences. Celles qui étaient présentes à onze reprises furent Mesdemoiselles Beauval, Grandval et Thérèse Dancourt, à dix, Mimi Dancourt et Mademoiselle Dufey, et à neuf, Mademoiselle Desmares[93]. Il est possible qu'elles furent suppléées par Mesdemoiselles Fonpré et Champvallon ou, pour une fois, par Mademoiselle Desbrosses. Parmi les actrices qui assurèrent entre neuf et onze présences, seule Mademoiselle Dufey ne participa pas à la représentation de la Cour, mais Mademoiselle Duclos, qui n'apparaît nulle part dans la série, était là. Remplaça-t-elle la Dufey? On ne peut l'affirmer. Puisque seuls les meilleurs acteurs y étaient convoqués et qu'il aurait été raisonnable d'y envoyer ceux qui savaient le mieux leur rôle, il est tout aussi probable, mais non certain, que Mademoiselle Dufey joua en fait des rôles mineurs dans les spectacles principaux que *Le Bal d'Auteuil* accompagnait.

Ayant isolé les acteurs qui participèrent peut-être aux représentations, nous proposons la distribution conjecturale suivante : Monsieur Vulpin - Guérin ; Monsieur Cidaris - Ponteuil ; Eraste - Etienne Baron, puis Du Boccage ; Frontin - La Thorillière ; Lucas - Desmares ; Madame Cidaris - Thérèse Dancourt ; Hortence - Mademoiselle Dangeville (dite la Grandval); Menine et Lucinde - l'une, Mademoiselle Desmares, l'autre, Mimi Dancourt; Marton - Mademoiselle Beauval. Cette distribution s'étaie sur les spécialités des acteurs telles que les indique Henry Lyonnet dans son *Dictionnaire des Comédiens Français* . Certains acteurs, qui n'auraient pu participer aux représentations des

93. Mademoiselle Grandval épousa son camarade Charles Claude Botot, dit Dangeville, le 9 septembre 1702 et figure, après cette date, dans les Registres sous le nom de Mademoiselle Dangeville.

Trois Gascons, paraissent dans les Registres sous la rubrique du *Bal d'Auteuil* . Nicolas Etienne Le Franc de Ponteuil était le fils d'un riche notaire qui 'ne rêva que théâtre dès sa plus tendre jeunesse'. Né en 1673, il fut reçu à la Comédie-Française en 1701 et se spécialisa dans les rôles de rois et de paysans. Sa diction naturelle fut fort apprécié par Lesage, quoiqu'il n'acquît jamais une grande réputation. Ni Guérin ni Ponteuil ne nous semblent parfaits pour jouer ces rôles. Nous les proposons pour remplir les rôles de Monsieur Vulpin et de Monsieur Cidaris, surtout parce que, selon toute vraisemblance, La Thorillière et Desmares jouaient Frontin et Lucas. Né vers 1645, Nicolas Desmares, frère cadet de la Champmeslé, excellait dans les rôles de paysans, et ce fut pour lui que Dancourt imagina nombre de ceux qui figurent dans ses pièces. Il créa les rôles de Martin dans *L'Homme à bonne fortune*, de Simon dans *Le Muet*, d'Ambroise dans *Le Flatteur* et de Toutabas dans *Le Joueur*. Quant à Eraste, il nous semble possible que le personnage fut incarné d'abord par Etienne Baron, ensuite par Du Boccage. Le premier créa le rôle de Damon dans *Le Flatteur*, du Chevalier dans *Le Distrait*, d'Agélas dans *Démocrite* et de Dorante dans *Le Double Veuvage*. Antoine Chantrelle, dit Du Boccage (1674-1757), débuta à la Comédie-Française le 29 mai 1702 et tenait habituellement l'emploi des confidents tragiques et des utilités dans la comédie.

Les rôles de Madame Cidaris et d'Hortence sont plutôt effacés. Pour le premier, nous proposerions volontiers Thérèse Dancourt (1663-1725). Epouse de l'acteur-auteur Dancourt et fille de La Thorillière, elle se spécialisait dans les rôles d'amoureuses et, d'après ce que nous apprend Lyonnet, elle avait un charme que la présence de ses filles sur le théâtre n'éclipsa pas. Le rôle d'Hortence, qui conviendrait, semble-t-il, à une débutante, fut dévolu, pour cette raison peut-être, à Mademoiselle Dangeville. Les rôles de Menine et de Lucinde auraient pu être confiés à Mademoiselle Desmares et à Mimi Dancourt. Notons que le talent qu'avait la Desmares de 'déployer une verve folle dans les soubrettes du répertoire' conviendrait aussi au rôle de Marton. Mimi Dancourt (1685-1780), fille de l'auteur dramatique et de Thérèse Dancourt, resta au théâtre après le départ de sa soeur, Manon, en mars 1702. Elle était douée d'une voix remarquable et remplissait les rôles d'amoureuses comiques et des soubrettes; ces derniers firent sa réputation. Or, si elles ne prenaient pas les rôles de Menine et de Lucinde, l'une ou l'autre aurait pu incarner Marton. Sinon, il est vraisemblable que ce fut Mademoiselle Beauval qui le fit. Si le groupe de comédiens que nous avons cités créa *Le Bal d'Auteuil*, il est certain que la représentation réunit quelques-uns des plus grands talents de l'époque. On remarque que Lyonnet signale le jeu *naturel* de certains, ce qui permet de supposer une souplesse très bien assortie à un texte qui imite, non sans une certaine subtilité, le style des théâtres plus populaires.

Parmi les 'feuilles d'assemblée' conservées aux Archives de la Comédie-Française, celle du 24 juillet 1702 signale la présentation du *Bal d'Auteuil* aux Comédiens :

> Mr Boindin a lu à l'assemblée une comédie en un acte qui a pour titre Le Bal d'Auteuil. L'auteur s'étant retiré la Compagnie a accepté la pièce à condition qu'on en retranchera quelques mots un peu trop libres et quelques scènes un peu trop longues et qu'elle sera approuvée par Mr D'Argenson [94] .

Selon Beauchamps, ce fut pour l'impression seulement que la pièce se vit divisée et élargie en trois actes avec un Prologue[95]. Il affirme aussi que le prologue ne fut jamais

94. J.-P. Vittu cite, par erreur, la date du 24 *janvier*. La Comédie-Française 1680-1716, p. 94.

95. Beauchamps, *Recherches sur les théâtres de France*, II, p. 299-300 et Parfaict, *Histoire du théâtre français*, XIV, p. 265 (réimp., III, p. 466). L'impression dut suivre de près la première représentation, car le permis de d'Argenson est daté du 31 août 1702.

représenté, et que la version en un acte n'était pas très différente de celle que nous possédons[96] . Il signale les changements selon un exemplaire de sa collection personnelle, aujourd'hui introuvable[97]:

Edition originale, scène		**Antérieurement, scène**
Acte I		
	1	5
	2	6
	3	1
	4 - ajoutée	
	5	7
	6	8
	7	9
Acte II		
	1 - ajoutée	
	2	2
	3	7
	4	4
	5 (avec additions)	10
	6	18
	7	11
	8	12
Acte III		
	1, 2, 3 - ajoutées	
	4	13
	5	14
	6	15
	7	16
	8	17
	9	19
	dernière	20

---

96. Sans être strictement nécessaire, le prologue est intéressant pour la dimension supplémentaire qu'il offre de la mise en abîme qui est caractéristique de la pièce (voir *infra*).

97. Il écrit: 'J'ai un exemplaire de cette pièce, où tous ces changements sont marqués': *Recherches sur les théâtres de France*, II, p. 300. A la mort de Beauchamps, sa bibliothèque fut acquise en bloc par Madame de Pompadour.

Il ajoute que le Divertissement n'avait subi aucun changement[98]. Selon Beauchamps aussi, ce fut la version en un acte qu'on joua. La version imprimée, parue au cours des représentations, n'a donc *jamais* vu les feux de la rampe.

Les dix représentations de la pièce rapportèrent à Boindin la somme très modeste de 243 livres, 7 sols. La part d'auteur la plus importante fut de 42 livres, 2 sols, le 24 août, et la plus basse de ... rien, le mardi 7 novembre, lorsque le nombre d'entrées fut de 207 et la recette totale, de 240 livres, 12 sols. Les entrées les plus importantes furent celles du jeudi 28 décembre (969) et du jeudi 24 août (785). La moyenne des entrées pour les trois mois est respectivement de 516 $^3/_4$, de 535 $^1/_2$ et de 724 $^1/_2$: la pièce fut désavantagée par le fait d'être lancée dans la saison creuse et peut-être parce que le spectacle principal était chaque fois une tragédie en août et une comédie en novembre et en décembre. H. Lagrave indique que, dès le début du dix-huitième siècle, les mardis et les jeudis étaient de 'mauvais' jours pour la Comédie-Française en raison de la concurrence de l'Opéra. Il est loisible d'interpréter les 785 entrées à la seconde représentation comme le signe d'un intérêt déclenché par la première qui avait eu lieu deux jours plus tôt. Il ne semble pas que les tragédies du 22 et du 24 août fussent pour quelque chose dans la différence du nombre des entrées, car on note qu'en 1702 *Andronic* connut quatre représentations contre les trois de *Nicomède*, proportions gardées dans l'ensemble de la décennie 1701-1710, où *Andronic* eut 37 représentations et *Nicomède*, 28.

Si certains éléments des *Trois Gascons* étaient conventionnels (les Gascons, le lieu de la scène), *Le Bal d'Auteuil*

98. Il ne mentionne pas de scène 3 originale. La musique du ballet figure dans le *Recueil d'airs sérieux et à boire de différents auteurs, pour l'année 1702* . Le texte seul du ballet fut imprimé avec la pièce.

montre plus d'invention. L'action est encadrée par un Prologue et un ballet. Le Prologue présente *Le Bal d'Auteuil* précisément comme une comédie où les aventures des personnages du Prologue sont la cible de la satire. Si le thème du mariage contrarié est très conventionnel, Boindin injecte dans ce cadre des personnages à résonances nettement plus louches que ceux qui s'y trouvent normalement. De surcroît, il situe son action ailleurs que dans le Paris traditionnel, dans la banlieue Auteuil[99].

L'ancien village d'Auteuil, qui a suscité une abondante littérature historique, offrait un intérêt particulier à l'époque de Boindin. Village pittoresque orné de prairies et de vignes, Auteuil était une des vingt-quatre communes limitrophes de Paris[100]. Plus 'campagnard' que Passy, Auteuil attirait le beau monde de Paris qui 's'y mettait au vert' dans ses maisons de campagne dès le début de l'été. Certains grands noms de la littérature classique - Molière, Racine, Boileau - y demeurèrent, par exemple. C'est précisément cette ambiance de vacances et de détente galante, dans un contexte rustique, que l'on retrouve dans *Le Bal d'Auteuil*. Le jardinier, Lucas, est à la fois un paysan traditionnel de comédie et la caricature d'un villageois des environs de Paris tel que le métropolitain pouvait les rencontrer[101]. Boindin donne à son jardinier la déformation

---

99. Malgré son titre, *L'Ambigu d'Auteuil* (Paris, Veuve Combe, 1709) de l'abbé mondain Laurent Bordelon est un roman-nouvelle qui se passe à Paris dans les lieux à la mode et chez une certaine Madame d'Auteuil pouvant cacher un personnage réel (Mme d'Aulnoy? Mme d'Auneuil?).

100. Hubert d'Orgemont y avait découvert en 1628 des eaux 'ferrugineuses' que Louis XV allait particulièrement apprécier. Dans la seconde moitié du dix-septième siècle, le village couvrait 350 hectares et comptait 70 feux.

101. Lancaster suggère que le personnage est calqué sur son homonyme de *L'Esprit de contradiction* de Dufresny (1700) (*Sunset*, p. 269). Si tel est le cas, Boindin eut le bon goût de choisir pour modèle une des petites comédies les plus appréciées du siècle.

professionnelle d'envisager les contacts humains sous un jour botanique et lui attribue aussi des allusions sexuelles aptes à renforcer son caractère de personnage théâtral 'populaire'. La nature métaphorique et allusive de son langage se présente comme le reflet comique des travaux linguistiques de son créateur.

Comme dans de nombreuses œuvres de l'époque, la tournure que donne l'auteur à la formule du mariage contrarié (presque le seul thème que la comédie connaît) est d'ordre cynique: toutes les femmes sont légères et infidèles, le mariage dégoûte les partenaires, qui ne cherchent qu'à s'humilier mutuellement et ne sert qu'à favoriser et à justifier l'adultère. L'inconstance est naturelle dans les deux sexes, et hésiter devant la perspective d'une aventure est signe de timidité, de pruderie ou de mœurs à l'ancienne - 'un bel habit qui n'est plus à la mode' [102] . Dans ce domaine, *Le Bal d'Auteuil* n'offre rien d'exceptionnel, et la comédie ne fait que remplir la fonction de travestir et de traiter des expériences vécues en faisant abstraction de ce qu'elles pouvaient comporter de pénible.

Cependant Boindin innove lorsqu'il joue avec la vieille dialectique de l'être et du paraître sous la forme comique du caché et du révélé. Frontin, de valet infidèle qu'il était, devient Lolive le valet-espion qui se démasque devant sa victime de manière à ne pas être reconnu (I, 2 et 5) et qui se dit 'jamais mieux masqué que lorsqu'il se montre tel qu'il est'. De même, Madame Cidaris décrit à son mari leur propre histoire; pour sa part, il compatit, se dénigre inconsciemment et l'encourage à une vengeance impossible (II,

---

102. Destouches, *L'Irrésolu*, V, 1. Si Lancaster a quelque raison de conjecturer que Lucinde et Menine sont 'des femmes de réputation douteuse, probablement des courtisanes', leur présence illustre - de même, paraît-il, que leurs gestes équivoques sur scène - le fait que la Maison de Molière se laissait aller à une tolérance croissante; voir *ibid.*, p. 268-269, n. 8.

6). Dans l'intrigue en miroir, Frontin dévalorise Marton qu'il ne reconnaît pas sous son déguisement, et, en tant que dame de condition, elle avale sa fureur, quitte à l'assouvir sur son infidèle partenaire, une fois leur identité éventée, par un de ces actes d'agression physique dont le valet est typiquement victime. Le jeu particulier du valet et de l'épouse délaissée fait partie du grand jeu de déguisement qui constitue la force motrice de la pièce et reste un des éléments du répertoire comique traditionnel que Boindin exploite le plus .

Chez Vulpin, le célibat meublé d'aventures et le mariage blanc représentent un jeu où le signifié de l'un revêt le signifiant de l'autre. Menine et Lucinde, travestis en homme, se font des avances: déguisement d'identité sexuelle qui permet d'élaborer des scènes lesbiennes sous les apparences de l'homosexualité masculine - trompe-l'œil démenti par des paroles à double sens[103] , donc déguisées: '[...] les femmes ne m'ont jamais tentée / Oh! ce n'a jamais été mon faible non plus' (II, 4).

Le déguisement de la personne facilite celui de sa présence. Madame Cidaris feint d'être partie pour Paris, et revient sous un déguisement à Auteuil. Son mari, la croyant en ville, reste à Auteuil, après avoir déclaré son intention de partir pour ... Versailles. D'une façon générale, déguisés ou masqués, les personnages cherchent à percer le mystère de l'autre tout en gardant le leur. Si Lucinde et Menine sont toutes deux déguisées, chacune se trompe alors sur l'identité de l'autre et révèle en même temps sa véritable identité à l'autre. Madame Cidaris est déguisée, mais son époux ne peut l'être. Marton maintient son dégui-

---

103. Même procédé que dans la déclaration de Lolive, *supra* . Le jeu du travestissement et des malentendus qu'il peut provoquer n'avait rien de neuf; cf. Benserade, *Iphis et Iante*, représenté (probablement) pour la première fois à l'Hôtel de Bourgogne en 1634, et imprimé en 1636 (avec une page de titre de l'année suivante).

sement, tandis que celui de Frontin est percé à jour tout de suite. L'avantage du déguisement va donc systématiquement aux personnages féminins. L'aveuglement de commande qui permet le déguisement du corps de fonctionner en tant que ressource dramatique est nécessairement doublé d'une surdité sporadique qui accepte le déguisement de la voix ou qui n'intercepte pas les apartés. Les multiples feintes arrivent à former jusqu'à sept représentations emboîtées: Frontin, sous l'identité de Lolive, porte le masque et joue le petit-maître devant Marton déguisée en dame de condition, dans la pièce en trois actes que le Prologue présente comme la représentation des mésaventures des habitants fictifs d'Auteuil, eux-mêmes représentés par des acteurs.

Le Bal d'Auteuil est la plus longue et la plus complexe des comédies de Boindin, comme l'atteste le jeu que nous venons d'évoquer. C'est une œuvre éminément théâtrale qui, sans l'interdiction royale, aurait peut-être eu une longue carrière. Le cas du *Port de mer* est différent, car cette comédie, plus courte et moins subtile, fut de loin la plus populaire de toutes.

Le Port de mer

Entre la première, qui eut lieu le 27 mai 1704, et le 2 juillet suivant, *Le Port de mer* eut vingt représentations, chiffre qui indique un très appréciable succès. Les dates des représentations furent le 27, le 29 et le 30 mai, les 2, 4, 6, 8, 10, 12, 14, 16, 18, 20, 22, 24, 25, 26, 28 et 30 juin et le 2 juillet. Le nombre d'entrées le plus important fut enregistré le 29 mai et se monta à 1 066, plus du double de la première, à 511. La pièce principale fut *Bérénice* le 27 mai et *Ariane* le 29. La moyenne des entrées durant cette première série de représentations fut de 440. La baisse saisonnière de l'assistance allait se manifester plus particulièrement à partir de juillet. Toutefois, certains soirs de juin virent une assistance très clairsemée: on compta 81 entrées le 9 juin, par exemple, lorsque le spectacle réunissait *Les Femmes savantes* et *Le Souper mal apprêté*[104], et 115 le 11, lorsqu'on produisit *L'Ecole des femmes* et *Les Plaideurs*. D'une façon générale, ces chiffres tendent à confirmer la constatation de J.-P. Vittu que le public le plus aisé s'intéressait surtout aux nouveautés[105]. La totalité des parts d'auteur que reçut Boindin fut de 386 livres. La pièce fut jouée vingt-et-une fois à la Cour entre décembre 1704 et février 1788[106], et cette circonstance amena, selon toute probabilité, l'impression d'une des éditions dont il sera question plus loin.

Les Archives de la Comédie-Française contiennent une série de volumes manuscrits qui portent le titre de *Chronologie des pièces restées au théâtre et des acteurs d'original*[107]. Aucune distribution n'y est notée pour *Les Trois Gascons*, et la seule mention du *Bal d'Auteuil* concerne sa suppression. En revanche, sous la rubrique du *Port de mer*, est consignée la distribution suivante.

M. Sabatin	Guérin
Benjamine	La Dancourt[108]
Marine	La Demarre [*sic*]
Mr Doutremer	Sallé[109]

---

104. Encore une combinaison qui a peu de chances d'être fortuite.

105. Voir *op. cit.*, p. 98-105, surtout p.104 .

106. Toutes les représentations eurent lieu à Versailles, sauf une à Fontainebleau, le 10 novembre 1772.

107. Volumes de petit format, reliés en cuir, datés de 1775, sans cote. Madame Sylvie Chevalley les a recopiés soigneusement dans des inventaires intitulés *Distribution de la création des pièces du répertoire*. Les deux documents portent la même erreur sur la date de la première : le 29, au lieu du 27 mai 1704.

108. Mimi Dancourt.

109. Jean-Baptiste-Louis-Nicolas Salley, dit Sallé, naquit vers 1671 et mourut en 1706. Après avoir été capucin, il devint professeur de musique, et débuta à la Comédie-Française en 1701. Il se spécialisait dans les rôles de Gascons, d'ivrognes et de petits-maîtres.

Léandre	Baron
La Saline	Lavoy
Aly [*sic*]	Dangeville[110]
Brigantin	La Thorillière

La *Chronologie*, établie soixante-et-onze ans après la première de la pièce d'après des documents inconnus[111], comporte, semble-t-il, des erreurs. Nous avons adopté pour *Le Port de mer* le même dispositif que pour les deux autres pièces et noté la présence ou l'absence de chaque acteur pour chaque spectacle, grande et petite pièce, pendant la totalité de la première série de représentations, soit vingt soirées[112]. Les acteurs et actrices présents en vingt occasions furent Messieurs Sallé, Dangeville, Dufey, Desmares, La Thorillière, Poisson, Lavoy, Fonpré et Legrand, et Mesdemoiselles Desmares, Mimi Dancourt, Dangeville et Dufey. L'acteur Duboccage fut présent en dix-huit occasions, à partir de la troisième représentation, mais la liste que nous avons établie n'offre le nom d'aucun remplaçant évident. La distribution compte dix hommes, huit femmes et un singe, et les rôles principaux demandent six acteurs et deux actrices.

Nous n'avons aucune raison d'écarter de la liste de 1775 les noms des acteurs et des actrices qui participèrent vingt fois au spectacle. En revanche, il nous semble impos-

110. Charles Claude Botot, dit Dangeville naquit en 1665 ou en 1669 et mourut en 1743. Reçu sociétaire en 1697, il ne se retira qu'en 1740. Il était le mari de la Grandval et jouait les rôles de niais à la perfection. Il prit les rôles de Thomas Diafoirus dans *Le Malade imaginaire*, de Chicaneau dans *Les Plaideurs*, et du Maître de philosophie dans *Le Bourgeois gentilhomme.*

111. Il faut postuler soit des documents inconnus soit des traditions conservées au Français, puisque les Registres ne portaient pas en 1704 le détail des distributions.

112. Nous renvoyons le lecteur à l'ouvrage de H. C. Lancaster, *The Comédie-Française, 1701-1774*, pour les titres des grandes pièces.

sible que Guérin et Etienne Baron aient rempli des rôles principaux dans la pièce, car ils ne furent présents que deux et neuf fois respectivement durant cette série de représentations. Par contre, Poisson et Legrand, qui étaient tous deux présents en vingt occasions, ne participèrent vraisemblablement à aucune des onze tragédies qui composèrent treize parmi les vingt spectacles. Paul Poisson (1658-1735), qui bredouillait, se rendit cher au public par les rôles du Marquis dans *Le Joueur*, et de Crispin dans *Le Légataire, Les Folies amoureuses* et *Le Roi de Cocagne* de Legrand (1718). Marc-Antoine Legrand (1673-1718) monta sur les planches de la Comédie-Française pour la première fois en 1695, puis, après un séjour en Pologne, y apparut de nouveau le 21 mars 1702. Il remplissait des rôles comiques, et composa plusieurs petites comédies en un acte du type de celles que fournissaient aussi Dancourt et Boindin. La Comédie-Française possède un fichier en cours d'élaboration qui regroupe les rôles auxquels allusion fut faite dans les revues contemporaines, notes personnelles, etc., afin de combler les lacunes que laissent les insuffisances des *Registres* antérieurs à 1765. Le dépouillement de ce fichier nous apprend que Poisson joua Brigantin en 1724 [*sic*], et Lavoy, Sabatin en 1708[113]. L'ensemble de ces informations nous incline à suggérer la présence d'une quatrième erreur dans la *Chronologie* de 1775 par laquelle le rôle de La Saline fut attribué à Lavoy, et de proposer Lavoy pour Monsieur Sabatin, La Thorillière pour Léandre, Poisson pour Brigantin et Legrand pour La Saline.

On pourrait alléguer plusieurs raisons pour expliquer la réussite soutenue de cette comédie qu'on représentait en moyenne environ vingt-quatre fois par décennie jusqu'à la

---

113. Cependant, ni les *Registres* de Lancaster ni le fichier des Archives de la Comédie-Française, où sont notés les voyages des Comédiens à la Cour, n'évoquent de représentation en 1724. Il est possible que le fichier porte 1724 au lieu de 1704.

Révolution: l'intérêt du sujet et des personnages très pittoresques, la rapidité de l'action, les jeux verbaux, etc. Beaumarchais peut s'être inspiré des scènes 2 et 14 dans son *Barbier de Séville*[114].

Les allusions à l'actualité de 1704 sont nombreuses. Le lieu de la scène est Livourne, l'un des grands ports de commerce de l'époque dans le grand duché de Toscane, qui possédait un marché d'esclaves[115]. La pièce évoque sur un ton badin l'actualité de l'esclavage et de la piraterie de même que le contexte général de l'équipage des galères, mais *Le Port de mer* n'étant pas un drame comme le sera plusieurs décennies plus tard *L'Honnête criminel* de Fenouillot de Falbaire, les évocations de certains aspects rudes de la vie contemporaine sont dénuées de tout jugement moral. Jean-Baptiste Colbert et ses successeurs avaient eu pour ambition de rassembler le nombre de rameurs nécessaire pour les galères, en achetant des esclaves, en faisant condamner un nombre maximum de criminels à la peine des galères et, solution de fortune, en engageant des 'bonnevoglies', un personnel rémunéré et libre, mais qui avait la fâcheuse habitude de déserter[116]. La

114. De même que la scène 2 du *Port de mer* rappelle (de bien loin) *Andromaque* I, 1, elle ressemble par certains de ses aspects à la rencontre de Figaro et d'Almaviva dans *Le Barbier de Séville*, I, 2. Si, à la scène 14 de notre pièce, Sabatin ne permet à Benjamine de prendre l'air qu'à travers ses jalousies, Rosine se trouve dans le même cas dans *Le Barbier*, I, 3. Brigantin tâche d'empêcher Sabatin de voir l'entretien entre Léandre et Benjamine, de même que Figaro dans *Le Barbier*, III, 12.

115. Voir M. Vigié, *Les Galériens du roi, 1661-1715*, p. 68-69.

116. *Ibid.*, p. 63-64. Dès 1670, les 'bonnevoglies' pouvaient refuser d'être mis à la chaîne, à condition de perdre la moitié de leur solde, mais la mise en place de l'inscription maritime en 1672 permit de les remplacer par des 'mariniers de rames', qui étaient des conscrits, et on note la disparition des 'bonnevoglies' après 1676.

composition des équipages est clairement reflétée dans les personnages de la pièce. Certes, nombre de spectateurs avaient pu voir les condamnés aux galères lors de leur départ pour Marseille, puisque Paris était l'une des trois villes où ils étaient rassemblés[117]. Les vols de Brigantin offrent un écho comique à des problèmes contemporains touchant l'ordre public, et les rapports de police de d'Argenson évoquent entre autres de nombreux rixes, vols et duels survenus aux environs des théâtres[118]. Doutremer-Salomin, le pirate, est, lui aussi, un reflet de l'actualité. Les lecteurs de romans avaient rencontré des pirates dans le *Polexandre* de Gomberville (1629), et Regnard, Lesage et Prévost, pour n'en nommer que les plus connus, allaient continuer à alimenter cette veine littéraire, teinte aussi de l'exotisme des récits de voyages, très goûtés au dix-huitième siècle, et des contes de fées transmis par Perrault et ses successeurs. L'historien Gérard Jaëger décrit ainsi la période 1685-1725: 'Ce début du XVIIIe siècle marque l'avènement de l'âge d'or de la piraterie, pour des raisons d'économie et de politique européennes favorables à son immense expansion'[119]. Les causes économiques et politiques qui favorisaient l'essor de la piraterie en tant que réalité et que thème littéraire se trouvaient doublées peut-

117. A partir de 1670, les trois grandes chaînes qui traversaient régulièrement le pays partaient de Paris, de Rennes et de Bordeaux (*ibid.*, p. 136).

118. *Rapports* , p. 84 et 227, et *Notes* , p. 19-20, 41-43, 54, 62-63. Paul Cottin explique la police des théâtres dans son Introduction aux *Rapports,* p. cxxxii-cxxxv, de même que J. Bonnassies, *La Comédie-Française, histoire administrative*, p. 329-330 et p. 331, n. 1. H. Lagrave cite deux autres allusions au problème des vols au théâtre, l'une de Barbier (1721) et l'autre du lieutenant de police Marville, qui date de 1742. Les montres et les tabatières étaient des objets de choix pour les voleurs (H. Lagrave, *Le Théâtre et le public*, p. 57, n. 97).

119. Voir *L'Aventure maritime*, p. 27, 28. Les flibustiers furent dispersés en 1697 après la dernière expédition de Carthagène; aussi beaucoup se tournèrent-ils à la piraterie.

être par le fantasme des spectateurs d'échapper pour un temps par la magie du théâtre au 'dirigisme politique et moral rigoureux' qui marquait les premières années du dix-huitième siècle[120]. Ainsi Doutremer est-il une figure mythique autant que la caricature du marin accoutumé à vivre dans une micro-société aux manières rudes, parfumées de l'odeur du tabac (sc. 6), habitude fréquemment représentée aussi dans les scènes de genre hollandaises de la fin du dix-septième siècle comme le symbole d'une existence de plaisirs intimes[121].

Le 'barbon' de la pièce, Salomin, est juif, et Boindin confie à Brigantin la tâche de le présenter. Il fait son portrait 'trait pour trait'[122] : 'l'usure, la dureté, la défiance, la fraude, & le parjure, avec quelques régles d'arithmétique' (sc. 2). Bien que la description que Figaro fait de Bartholo soit d'une tout autre envergure, on retrouve dans les deux cas la même juxtaposition ludique de qualités disparates[123]. Marchand d'esclaves, usurier et homme d'affaires en train de méditer une banqueroute frauduleuse, Sabatin constitue une caricature de Juif tel que la mentalité populaire se le représentait alors.

---

120. *Pirates, flibustiers et corsaires*, p.20; voir aussi les lumineux chapitres que G. Jaëger consacre à la littérature des XVIIe et XVIIIe siècles, p. 177 et suiv. Cf. aussi *Dix-huitième Siècle*, 22, 1990, n° spécial: *L'Œil expert.Voyager, explorer* (sous la direction de F. Moureau).

121. Par exemple, Adriaen van Ostade, 'Zwei Rauchende Baueren' (1664), Dresde, Zwinger, n° 1399; David Teniers le jeune, 'Grosse Dorfkirmes mit tanzendem Paar' (vers 1662), *ibid.*, n° 1083; Adriaen van Ostade, 'Im der Dorfschenke' (vers 1660), *ibid.*, n° 1396; et David Teniers le jeune, 'Intérieur de cabaret avec fumeurs', Louvre, RF 1961-79 .

122. Chez Boindin, ce jeu de mots ne peut être l'effet du hasard.

123. *Le Barbier de Séville*, I, 4. La plaisanterie sur le nom du barbon est aussi commune aux deux pièces: Almaviva estropie celui de Bartholo (II, 12), tandis que La Saline fait du nom de Sabatin une cacophonie hébraïsante digne d'une parade (sc. 2).

'L'idée que le 'Français moyen' se fait du Juif au XVIIIe siècle', note Pierre Pluchon,

> porte encore la marque du Moyen Age. On n'aime pas, on suspecte le fils d'Israël, parce qu'il descend de la race traîtresse qui a tué le Christ, parce qu'il pratique une religion particulière, mêlée, dit-on, de superstition, dans des établissements réservés, parce qu'il prête à un taux usuraire, parce qu'il concurrence les indigènes dans leurs activités, parce qu'il appartient à une sorte d'association internationale secrète où il trouve relations et moyens. Bref, l'opinion populaire, par une espèce de croyance héritée en bloc des siècles passés et abritée de tout examen rationnel, accuse l'Israëlite d'exercer de 'cruelles exactions', de pratiquer de 'pernicieuses usures', de faire 'outrage aux saintes hosties', ou d'avoir crucifié des enfants le Vendredi saint, ou d'avoir 'maltraité l'image de notre Seigneur'. Et, quand dans la rue on échange injures, on se traite tout à la fois, de voleur, d'excommunié ou de Juif'[124] .

Boindin ne s'occupe nullement de la religion de Sabatin, sans doute parce qu'il regardait du même œil le judaïsme et le christianisme. C'est uniquement l'inhumanité du personnage et la malhonnêteté de ses affaires commerciales qu'il évoque. Quoi qu'en dise Marine à la scène 11, son indifférence sentimentale n'a rien de spécifiquement juif; la majorité des pères-'obstacles' des comédies lui ressemblent assez. Boindin rejoint la tendance qui imprègne la pensée de la classe dirigeante de l'époque et caractérisait sa politique. A partir de la première moitié du dix-huitième siècle, on n'évoquait plus 'le risque que pouvaient courir les âmes des fidèles au contact de ces mécréants' que 'par pure tradition, et pour mémoire', à tel point que le Conseil du Roi prit, en 1741, la décision d'ouvrir les marchés français aux Juifs sans daigner consulter

---

124. *Nègres et Juifs au XVIIIe siècle*, p. 64.

les évêques[125]. La pensée de Boindin va dans le même sens, tandis que la perception populaire reste marquée des a-prioris religieux.

En revanche, si le rôle d'Hali est le reflet d'une vague d'orientalisme qui marqua la fin du dix-septième siècle, le jargon qu'il parle fait partie d'une tradition nettement populaire. On connaissait bien la virtuosité des Forains dans le maniement du jargon et la fréquence des prétendues langues qu'ils employaient - le grec, le turc, l'indien et ... l'ogre. Avec Hali, Boindin ne fait qu'adopter une formule dont le succès avait été éprouvé ailleurs. La 'piraterie' des styles dramatiques devint d'ailleurs le sujet d'un prologue intitulé *Les Comédiens corsaires* de Lesage, joué à la Foire Saint-Laurent en 1726[126].

On a pu identifier le changement comme un élément central de l'art rococo et du carnavalesque[127]. En ce sens les trois pièces que nous venons d'examiner rentreraient dans les deux catégories esthétiques. Les fréquents déguisements, l'ambiguité des identités sexuelles, les alliances qui se forment et se dissolvent, les intrigues que dénouent non pas des solutions mais des chansons en sont la preuve. Dans une certaine mesure, *Le Port de mer* renchérit sur les deux autres pièces en ce sens que l'ensemble des personnages réunis par l'intrigue est à la fois plus disparate et,

---

125. René Moulinas, 'Le Conseil du roi et le commerce des Juifs d'Avignon en France', *loc. cit.*, p. 178-179.

126. Dominique Lurcel, *Le Théâtre de la Foire au XVIIIe siècle*, p. 13, 16-18 et p. 33, n. 10.

127. 'Change is central to the rococo, and to the carnivalesque. It is figured in the comic theatre of the rococo in various ways. One is disguise. The device is traditional. But in the theatre of around 1700 it is pushed to bravura extremes' (R. Howells, 'Rococo and carnival', *loc. cit.*, p. 215). Les deux articles de R. Howells signalés dans notre bibliographie apportent de précieux renseignements et avancent des arguments particulièrement suggestifs.

tout comme le cadre, plus exotique. La vague du rococo ne cessa de déferler qu'avec le milieu du siècle, ce qui permet de souligner encore une fois l'opportunité de la pièce. Ce fut précisément au milieu du siècle aussi que Préville commença à prendre le rôle de Brigantin, ce qui contribua certainement à maintenir l'intérêt qu'y portait le public.

Dans son étude, *Style rococo, style des Lumières*, Roger Laufer parle de 'ce style du sourire, de la désinvolture [...] ou plus précisément de la distanciation ironique. Le lecteur se trouve renvoyé en arrière, à distance de ce spectacle mouvant. Ainsi est opérée la mise en question caractéristique du rococo'[128] . C'est précisément cette distanciation, ce refus de l'affectif que requiert la farce, mais là où *Le Port de mer* s'avère dans le droit fil du rococo, c'est dans la mise en question ironique de la probité. On parle de l'esclavage comme d'une pratique parfaitement acceptable. Voler des tabatières et des épées serait préserver la tranquillité des spectacles. La banqueroute frauduleuse serait le plus ordinaire et le plus sage moyen d'assurer l'avenir de sa famille. La piraterie serait un art. L'utilité de l'arithmétique consisterait à faciliter la tromperie. Et tout cela sur le ton le plus enjoué. L'honnêteté est une commodité rare, joyeusement dévalorisée, et la malhonnêteté passe pour le plus véniel des péchés dans ce monde renversé.

Par ailleurs, les jeux avec la langue, qu'on peut discerner dans les autres pièces (les métaphores de Lucas dans *Le Bal d'Auteuil*, par exemple), foisonnent dans celle-ci. Rien que dans les deux premières scènes, par exemple, on joue sur le sens des mots : la justice ne *va* pas en mer mais elle y *envoie* ; on joue sur l'euphémisme: l'habillement très reconnaissable du galérien Brigantin serait 'un petit désha-

---

128. Paris, 1963; cité par R. Howells, 'The rise of the rococo', *loc. cit.*, p. 95-96.

billé de mer'; un bagnard parodie les grands classiques, citant Racine pour se comparer à Oreste, et La Saline à Pylade; cynique, La Saline pastiche le style de la religiosité populaire: 'l'amitié s'altère-t-elle, quand la vertu en est le fondement?' On attribue à Sabatin une série grotesque de prénoms; on s'envoie des portraits antithétiques d'autrui comme on se renverrait une balle, et ainsi de suite tout au long de la pièce. L'esprit, le déploiement ludique de toutes les ressources de l'humour verbal sont précisément taillés à la mesure d'une farce légère. Qui plus est, cet 'esprit', cette façon d'incorporer à tout prix des bons mots au dialogue dramatique, firent fureur dans le théâtre comique de la première moitié du siècle, comme en fait foi la critique qu'en fait régulièrement le théâtre de Destouches.

Le Petit-maître de robe.

La dernière comédie de Boindin diffère sensiblement des trois autres, à commencer par un certain manque de verve dans le dialogue. D'ailleurs, l'évolution des situations comporte trop peu de surprises. C'est peut-être la conjonction de ces deux défauts qui porte préjudice à la pièce.

Le Petit-maître de robe ne fut pas imprimé du vivant de l'auteur et parut pour la première fois dans l'édition de François Parfaict en 1753. Selon Henri Lagrave, 'la pièce ne fut pas permise par le lieutenant général de police'[129], et il cite d'autres comédies, interdites de la même manière (*Le Faux Savant, Le Dissipateur, L'Enfant prodigue, L'Amour musicien*), parce que leur satire visait les représentants des corps constitués, notamment les magistrats[130]. Certes, la notice que lui consacre d'Argenson porte à croire

129. *Notices*, I, p. 106, n. 7.

130. *Le Théâtre et le public*, p. 62. Notons aussi en passant que la satire des petits-maîtres assis sur la scène (sc. 10) ne semblait guère pouvoir plaire à cette partie de l'assistance.

que l'interdiction découla du mécontentement qu'aurait témoigné la noblesse de robe[131]. L'interdiction arrêta net la carrière de cette pièce avant même que les comédiens n'en fissent la lecture. Selon l'Avertissement de Parfaict[132], elle n'avait jamais paru au théâtre ni connu l'impression, seulement parce que 'l'auteur n'y avait pas mis la dernière main', mais nous sommes enclin à discerner là un prétexte.

Le sujet de la pièce - les vices supposés de la magistrature -, est loin d'être neuf[133]. Il suffit d'ouvrir le troisième chapitre de *L'Envers du Grand Siècle* de Gaiffe pour y voir réunies les censures morales inscrites tant de la comédie (*Les Plaideurs, Le Misanthrope*), que chez les moralistes. Bodin, Pasquier et Montaigne critiquent la vénalité des charges. Primi Visconti note l'ignorance et, partant, les 'décisions stupides' des 'fils de bouchers' nantis, devenus juges. Le père Lejeune, dans son sermon contre 'Les Péchés qui se commettent au Palais', évoque la préparation dérisoire à laquelle ces magistrats doivent leurs grades et la damnation qu'encourent le magistrat lui-même, ses examinateurs, le père qui lui a acheté sa charge et le confesseur qui l'absout. Le père La Rue fustige leur frivolité: seuls les occupent le divertissement, la conversation mondaine, les jeux de hasard et les tricheries, les spectacles, les lectures amusantes ou pernicieuses. Mais ils ignorent tout de leurs

---

131. *Notices*, I, p. 105-106. D'Argenson possédait un exemplaire des *Œuvres* de Boindin (1753), conservé à la Bibliothèque de l'Arsenal sous la cote 8° BL. 13125. Cet exemplaire porte sur la feuille de garde des notes manuscrites de Soyer, secrétaire-bibliothécaire du marquis. La majorité des notices furent rédigées entre 1748 et 1756 (*Notices*, Introduction, I, p. 27). D'ailleurs, il n'est pas exclu que d'Argenson ait eu communication d'un manuscrit par la voie de la censure; voir *Notices*, I, p. 31, n. 47.

132. P. ii.

133. F. Moureau, 'Le petit-maître intrigué: espace du libertinage au théâtre jusqu'à la Régence», *Eros philosophe. Discours libertins des Lumières*, F. Moureau et A.-M. Rieu éd., Paris, Champion, 1984, p. 119-135.

obligations. Gaiffe cite la lettre du Président du Parlement de Guyenne qui prouve que, moyennant finance, on attribuait des charges à des novices incompétents[134], et il évoque les célèbres pages de La Bruyère où le moraliste évoque la vanité, la mollesse, l'intempérance et le libertinage des jeunes magistrats qui imitent les mœurs des petits maîtres[135]. Gaiffe cite aussi la vie scandaleuse du conseiller au Parlement Le Maye, qui tenait une académie de jeu particulièrement louche, affaire qu'on retrouve aussi dans les *Rapports de police* de d'Argenson[136].

Le Petit-maître de robe est la seule des comédies de Boindin à être fondée sur un fait de mœurs contemporaines. Ses deux premières pièces relevaient de la fantaisie pure, et *Le Port de mer*, tout en faisant allusion à des questions d'actualité, possédait des qualités purement dramatiques indéniables, et le siècle ne s'y trompait pas. On ne pourrait pas en dire autant du *Petit-maître de robe*. D'Argenson jugeait que 'le sujet [de cette comédie] aurait bien rempli cinq actes'[137]. Nous croyons au contraire que, vu les tendances générales du théâtre comique de l'époque, et en reprenant l'opinion du critique lui-même, à propos des *Trois Gascons*, selon laquelle 'ces pièces-là se jouent bien et plus vivement que de bonnes pièces de caractère' ,

134. *Op. cit.*, p. 140-141.

135. *Les Caractères, ou les mœurs de ce siècle*, Ch. 7, 'De la ville', voir *loc. cit.*, p. 280 et 511-512 ('Clefs et commentaires') où le portrait que fournit La Bruyère est identifié comme étant probablement celui de Jean-Antoine de Mesmes. Gaiffe cite aussi des cas précis d'incompétence, de vices de caractère, etc., évoqués dans la correspondance secrète entre Colbert et les intendants de province (*op. cit.*, p. 142-147).

136. Gaiffe, *op. cit.*, p. 151-153, et *Rapports inédits du lieutenant de police René d'Argenson (1697-1715)*, p. cvi-cvii, 165, 168, 177, 233 et 240. L'affaire Le Maye, évoquée pour la première fois le 22 février 1705, allait toujours bon train en avril 1708.

137. *Notices*, I, p. 105.

Boindin eût mieux fait, au lieu d'évoquer un *état* de mœurs, de transformer un *trait* de mœurs en 'boindinade'.

Si Boindin n'avait pas à chercher bien loin le nom de Fatenville, il exploite bien la ressource de l'hôtel garni pour réunir les personnages principaux. L'hôtel garni comportait deux avantages en tant que localisation dramatique: celui d'être 'inclassable', car il en existait de très luxueux aussi bien que de très modestes [138], et celui de respecter l'unité de lieu, comme dans *Le Joueur* de Regnard et *L'Irrésolu* de Destouches, par exemple. D'ailleurs, le nombre d'hôtels garnis dans la capitale, surtout dans le faubourg Saint-Germain, connut un remarquable essor à la fin du dix-septième siècle [139]. Un autre trait de mœurs qui relève de l'actualité est le duel dont Fatenville menace Eraste (sc. 3). Le duel, pratique qui, depuis la Renaissance, décimait la noblesse française, fut à maintes reprises défendu sous Louis XIII et sous Louis XIV. La médaille de 1679: 'Le Duel aboli', frappée à l'occasion de la promulgation de l''Edit du roi portant règlement général sur les duels' de la même année, était le reflet de la volonté royale mais non de sa réalisation politique[140]. Plus d'un demi-siècle allait encore s'écouler avant que la pratique ne commençât à tomber graduellement en désuétude - et cela pour des raisons qui ne devaient rien à la législation. Mais au temps où Boindin écrivait, on se souvenait sans doute très bien des pièces de Molière où se déployait la propagande contre le duel. Micheline Cuénin y consacre des pages éclairantes dans son étude du problème[141]. Elle y cite le bon sens et le peu d'empressement à s'offenser du héros épo-

---

138. Voir A. du Pradel (Nicolas de Blégny), *Le Livre commode des adresses de Paris pour 1692*, I, p. 316-321.

139. *Ibid.*, I, p. 317, n. 1.

140. L'Edit fut publié au mois d'août et enregistré au Parlement dès le 1er septembre.

141. *Le Duel sous l'Ancien Régime*, p. 195-196.

nyme dans *Sganarelle, ou le Cocu imaginaire*[142]; le Sganarelle du *Mariage forcé* qui subit 'les violences d'un irresponsable qui n'a gardé de son éducation noble que des automatismes aveugles'; et le bretteur empanaché des *Fourberies de Scapin* - 'un maniaque, un fou dangereux'. Mais celui qu'elle considère comme le personnage de référence en ce qui touche le point d'honneur reste l'Eraste des *Fâcheux*: quoique brave, il refuse, par respect pour les interdictions royales, de se laisser entraîner dans une rencontre avec Alcandre[143] . En revanche, la promptitude de Fatenville à provoquer Eraste en duel, puis à reculer, était la marque à la fois du criminel d'Etat et du lâche. Le duel étant une manière noble de vider des différends, on constate que la poltronnerie s'identifie avec la robe, donc, avec un état qui ne se distinguait pas toujours à cette époque d'avec la roture.

Toutes les occupations de Fatenville se rapportent au paraître: son habit (que, suivant une habitude aristocratique, il oublie de payer), son goût de la bonne chère, sa recherche du plaisir (la danse, la bonne compagnie, etc.). Comme dans *Le Bal d'Auteuil*, le protagoniste fréquente des actrices, dont la réputation hasardée indique assez quel est son mode de vie. Le portrait satirique comprend donc des éléments d'animalisation (la nourriture, la sexualité), de réification (le personnage devient 'une machine à plaisir' au fonctionnement stéréotypé) et de diminution (la composante intellectuelle est réduite à l'égoïsme). Avec cela, le personnage fait parade d'une désinvolture méprisante à l'égard des femmes (sc. 15), déjà réifiées par le

---

142. Elle parle du 'succès extraordinaire' de cette comédie, et les chiffres de Joannidès confirment sa popularité. Dans la décennie 1701-1710, on la joua 80 fois à la Comédie-Française (*La Comédie-Française de 1680 à 1920*, p. 74).

143. *Les Fâcheux* , I, 6. A l'époque, les duels impliquaient parfois jusqu'à une douzaine d'adversaires.

mariage arrangé, ce qui dénote une mentalité profondément anti-sociale. Il n'y a rien dans la composition de Fatenville qui ne soit monnaie courante dans les comédies de l'époque. Il en est de même pour le rustique Lucas, le Président guindé et la Comtesse procédurière[144]. Il serait difficile de trouver quelque chose dans des scènes tournant autour d'erreurs d'identité (sc. 11), de la franchise désastreuse d'un paysan (sc. 12) ou d'un dialogue de sourds (sc. 13) qui compensât la présence de personnages platement conventionnels.

Manuscrits et éditions.

Les Trois Gascons

Le permis d'imprimer de ce texte, signé Le Voyer d'Argenson, porte la date du 31 août 1702 (la même que celui du *Bal d'Auteuil*) et se place donc quatorze mois après la première série de représentations. L'édition originale, qui comporte 47 pages de texte, parut d'abord en brochure chez Pierre Ribou. L'édition devait s'écouler très lentement, car on la trouve incorporée aux recueils factices des pièces de Boindin que Ribou diffusa en 1705 et en 1714. Une seconde édition du texte parut chez Prault, dans les *Œuvres de théâtre de Monsieur Boindin* (p.[1]-56) en 1746, et une troisième, dans le premier volume des *Œuvres de Monsieur Boindin* que Prault publia en 1753 (I, p. [1] - 56)[145]. Nous reproduisons le texte de l'éditon originale d'après l'exemplaire de la Bibiliothèque Nationale de France : 8° Yth 17638 .

144. Le Lucas de cette pièce est totalement dépourvu de la parole ingénieusement métaphorique de son homologue du *Bal d'Auteuil*.

145. Il était normal qu'un imprimeur cherchât à reproduire le plus exactement possible la pagination d'une édition antérieure afin d'économiser le papier.

Les Archives de la Comédie-Française détiennent un manuscrit de souffleur des *Trois Gascons* (ms. 52). Il est de la main du souffleur-copiste Lapierre, ancien copiste de l'Hôtel Guénégaud, qui passa à la Comédie-Française au moment de sa fondation et y travailla jusqu'en 1705. La plus significative des variantes est l'omission dans le manuscrit du 'divertissement coupé de danses et de chansons' qui fait suite à la dernière scène du texte imprimé. Il est peu vraisemblable que le manuscrit représente un texte revu par l'auteur. On pense plutôt que Boindin aurait porté chez les Comédiens un manuscrit (pour les besoins de la lecture préalable) dont le ms. 52 serait la copie légèrement modifiée pour la représentation (changements de mots et de didascalies), qu'il aurait récupéré pour le communiquer ensuite aux services du lieutenant de police (pour la censure) et finalement à l'imprimeur. En revanche, il est très probable que le texte tel que le transmet le manuscrit fut celui de la représentation, étant donné qu'il n'existait encore aucun texte imprimé en 1701 et que l'omission du divertissement final se justifiait tant par le nombre d'acteurs et l'entraînement chorégraphique qu'il exigeait que par sa conception peu conforme aux normes de la maison[146].

Le Bal d'Auteuil

Ainsi que nous l'avons indiqué plus haut, Beauchamps affirme que l'unique série de représentations à la Comédie-Française se faisait sur un texte différent de celui de l'édition originale : 'elle [la pièce] n'a jamais paru au théâtre comme elle est imprimée' [147]. Puisque l'exemplaire sur lequel il fonde son observation semble perdu et qu'aucun manuscrit de la pièce ne nous est parvenu, nous nous trou-

146. Pour des précisions sur les danses qui terminent les pièces, on consultera Anne L. Witherell, *Louis Pécour's 1700 Recueil de dances* et son ample bibliographie.

147. *Recherches sur les théâtres de France*, II, p. 299.

vons dans l'impossibilité de nous prononcer à ce sujet. Beauchamps note que 'le divertissement était le même' dans la version primitive et dans l'imprimé, ce qui incline à supposer qu'il fut effectivement représenté.

Nous reproduisons ici le texte de l'édition originale d'après l'exemplaire conservé à la Bibliothèque Nationale de France sous la cote: 8° Yth 1639. De même que l'édition originale des *Trois Gascons*, celle-ci fut par la suite incorporée aux recueils factices que Ribou composa en 1705 et en 1714. Une deuxième et une troisième éditions parurent dans les *Œuvres de théâtre* (1746) et les *Œuvres* (1753). Les paroles du divertissement final furent données avec le texte, mais la musique fut publiée par Ballard, dans le *Recueil d'airs sérieux et à boire de différents auteurs, pour l'année 1702.*

Le Port de mer

La popularité de cette pièce lui valut trois éditions séparées et deux en recueil[148]. L'édition originale porte la permission de d'Argenson datée du 29 février 1704, et nous la reproduisons d'après l'exemplaire: 8° Yth 14467 de la Bibliothèque Nationale de France. Cette édition se trouva incorporée aux *Œuvres de Mr. Boindin* composées chez Ribou en 1705. Le recueil factice de 1705 dut entraîner l'épuisement de l'édition originale, car nous n'en avons trouvé aucun exemplaire incorporé au recueil intitulé le *Théâtre de M. Boindin*, que Ribou publia en 1714. En revanche, ce fut une seconde édition qui y figura, mais elle fut certainement envisagée, mais non lancée sur le marché, environ quatre ans plus tôt. Elle présente un certain intérêt

148. Nous tenons normalement compte des seules éditions parues du vivant de l'auteur ou ayant son autorité, mais, comme nous l'expliquerons plus loin, nous faisons ici exception d'une édition isolée du *Port de mer* dont la parution ne peut être datée avec certitude.

car elle porte une approbation, datée du 1er novembre 1704, pour 'les Pieces qui doivent composer le Théâtre François'. Ribou ne publia par la suite aucun recueil sous ce titre, et on présume que son projet dut être remis, car le privilège (signé Delaunay), imprimé à la suite du texte de cette seconde édition, est daté du 11 juillet 1710. Il est donc loisible de conjecturer l'existence d'une certaine demande commerciale pour *Le Port de mer* seul qui se soutenait assez bien pour encourager Ribou à le réimprimer, puis à utiliser cette nouvelle édition en recueil, sans doute pour écouler des invendus des *Trois Gascons* et du *Bal d'Auteuil.* (Rappelons que certains exemplaires du recueil de 1714 incorporent aussi *La Matrone d'Ephèse*). C'est sans doute parce qu'elle était à l'origine destinée à faire partie d'une collection qu'on n'y trouve jamais de page de titre, mais seulement un faux titre sans indication de date.

Il existe une troisième édition séparée de ce texte à laquelle fait aussi défaut la page de titre. Imprimée en beaux caractères, elle comporte 72 pages et présente un texte plus aéré que les éditions que nous avons déjà évoquées. Elle est extrêmement rare, car nous ne l'avions répertoriée que trois fois. Le filigrane ne nous apprend rien sur la date de cette édition mais, à en juger par les variantes et par les leçons rejetées, elle se situe après 1753. Or, il nous semble *possible*, vu la rareté et la localisation des exemplaires - un des trois appartenait à la bibliothèque de Marie-Antoinette - , qu'il s'agisse d'une édition à petit tirage, préparée pour les représentations qui eurent lieu à la Comédie-Française et à la Cour après la mort de l'auteur. Cependant, la page [1], signée A, porte la mention 'Tome I', que nous ne saurions expliquer qu'en invoquant, soit un projet de reçueil qui n'aboutit pas -, car il n'existe aucun recueil (ni de demande de permis d'imprimer) dont *Le Port de mer* soit la première pièce, position qu'imposerait la pagination du texte - soit une simple erreur de prote, explication très peu satisfaisante. L'exemplaire détenu aux Archives de la Comédie-Française (sous la cote 1 POR

Boi) constitue un 'manuscrit de théâtre', en ce sens que La Porte y apporta des modifications au texte et surtout aux didascalies pour les besoins de la représentation[149]. Deux autres couches de notes manuscrites désignent, aux pages [70] à 72, les acteurs qui prononcèrent les vers de la 'Fête Marine'. Le nom de Pin (orthographié *Pain*) et le fait que les notes soient de la main de La Porte permettent de conclure que cet exemplaire existait déjà dans la décennie 1760[150]. Mais la date de son impression reste mystérieuse. Il semble *possible* que ce texte fût tiré à la seule intention de la Compagnie, comme s'il n'existait plus suffisamment d'exemplaires du texte isolé pour permettre l'établissement du spectacle après la parution de deux recueils des *Œuvres* (en 1746 et en 1753), puisque la publication des recueils autres que factices marquait normalement la fin de celle des brochures. On pourrait cependant alléguer contre cela l'habitude de faire recopier des rôles, qui devait revenir moins cher à la Compagnie. En revanche, la présence d'un exemplaire dans la bibliothèque de la reine Marie-Antoinette à Trianon nous amène à nous demander si l'impression se fit pour une des représentations à la Cour dont les Menus Plaisirs couvrirent les frais[151]. Quoique cette édition nous semble dépourvue d'autorité, nous en relevons les variantes (à l'exception de celles qui ne portent que sur le découpage, et donc sur la seule numérotation des scènes) pour fournir une idée des modifications que subit le texte au moment de la représentation. Nous désignons ce manuscrit de souffleur par le sigle CF.

149. Cet exemplaire est relié en velin, et les initiales de La Porte figurent, avec le titre et l'auteur de l'ouvrage, sur la reliure.

150. Pin laissa peu de traces, car Lyonnet note simplement que Pin était le nom d'un acteur qui débuta à la Comédie-Française en 1766.

151. Seule une recherche approfondie dans les Archives de la Maison du Roi (Archives Nationales, série O) serait capable de confirmer nos conjectures sur la production d'éditions limitées et tardives.

Une copie incomplète du rôle de Doutremer, qui ne porte pas d'indication de date, mais qui est certainement du dix-huitième siècle, se trouve reliée dans le manuscrit 3113 (t. 2) de la Bibliothèque de l'Arsenal. Nous relevons la seule variante qu'elle comporte par rapport à notre texte de base en lui attribuant le sigle D.

Le Petit-maître de robe

Ainsi que nous l'avons déjà indiqué, nous ne trouvons aucune trace de cette comédie avant la publication des *Œuvres* en 1753. Les frères Parfaict n'en disent mot dans leur *Histoire du théâtre français*, et la notice que lui consacre d'Argenson se rapporte au seul texte que nous connaissions[152]. Nous reproduisons le texte de l'exemplaire : Z. 27525 de la Bibiliothèque Nationale de France.

Les *Œuvres*, 1746 et 1753

Il est très vraisemblable que les deux éditions collectives, les *Œuvres de théâtre* de 1746 et les *Œuvres* de 1753, reflètent la volonté de l'auteur, et nous en tenons compte dans notre relevé des variantes. Celle de 1746 est très rare (quatre localisations), tandis que nos recherches ont localisé vingt-quatre exemplaires de celle de 1753. Il est loisible de penser que les pièces de théâtre déjà connues - sauf une - intéressèrent moins le public que les dissertations inédites de l'auteur.

Principes de l'édition.

Nous avons respecté l'orthographe des éditions de base, de même que la ponctuation, sauf dans les cas où celle-ci présentait des erreurs manifestes (affirmations suivies d'un point d'interrogation, etc.). Dans ces cas, nous

---

152. *Notices*, I, p. 105-106.

avons corrigé notre texte d'après la leçon de la première des éditions postérieures à faire autorité. Nous avons corrigé de même des coquilles évidentes et nous les consignons sous leur forme originale dans notre liste de leçons rejetées. Sauf dans le cas où une orthographe s'avère infirmée par les pratiques normales du temps («vaten»), nous ne rangeons pas parmi les leçons rejetées les graphies qui n'altèrent pas la prononciation («gratieusement», «tu ès», «crain»). Nous y rangeons cependant les orthographes qui passent à l'oral mais qui, à l'écrit, entraînent une erreur grammaticale («au genoux», «elle à raison»).

Leçons rejetées

Les Trois Gascons

Scène
1 veux-tu des airhes?
2 FRONTIN lc quittant brusquement.
2 mais anssi furieuse à proportion
2 tu sçais qu'on lui envoyât le portrait
2 plus d'amoitié son gendre
7 SCENE VIII
7 tu sortiras mort au vif !
[11] vous aurez à faire à moi

Le Bal d'Auteuil

Prologue: il me semble pourtant que je sommes tous deux de grands sots

Acte I
Scène
3 une fille [...] qui a toujours êté tenuë fort serré !
7 je ne sçais encore pour où m'y prendre

Acte II
2 on vout prendroit, morgué,
2 Madames de Paris
3 Eh oüi, vrament : c'est un Marquis

3 à vous d'être bon amis
4 pour qui vous ttahiroit-elle !
6 Mad. CIDARISE. Ainsi, Monsieur, si j'avois le malheur
6 Mad. CIDARISE. Non, ce seroit vous tromper
7 n'osent plns se montrer que sous le masque
7 un poing formé qui vous décèle !
8 LUCAS *trouvant Frontin au pieds de Marton.*

Acte III
Scène
7 qu'a vous donc fait de Monsieur le Chevalier?
9 Mad. CIDARIS. Oh pour cela, non, je l'en dispence
[10] Oüi, je suis toujours là même
[10] FRONTIN *se jettant au genoux de Marton.*
[divertissement] dancer en écho une frelane

Le Port de mer

Scène
2 que veux donc dire cet équipage ?
2 quelque autre petite chose quelle interpretta
3 Je ne sçay qui me tient
3 il n'i a que six mois
3 Tantpis, c'est un agrément
3 Mais à quelle diable de manoeure
4 Va-ten donc m'atendre
4 Pour toi vaten sur le Port
4 Comment donc, qu'elle dificulté
5 M. Doutremer à ma parolle
6 Elle à raison
8 M. SABATIN. *luy dondant sa main toute gantée*
11 vous allez dabord aux invectives !
11 Il n'en démorderoit pas
12 je mourrois d'impatience
12 Jusqu'à la derniere syllable.
12 On a aimé quelque fois !
12 ils semblent qu'ils nous fassent exprès là
15 vous m'aviez autre fois-parlé pour ma fille ?

16 que veut donc dire dire tout ceci ?
16 Trève d'éclaicissement.
16 Qu'elle est vôtre résolution ?
17 M. DOUTREMER *lui arrchant des mains les Pierreries.*
17 A la forza, justititia, justitia !
Feste marine LE CHOEUR Jeunes coeur, venez aprendre
Feste marine L'autre AUSTRALIENNE *continüe*
Nôtre bauté, toujours nouvelle,

Le Petit-maître de robe

scène
1 Oui, vraiement, nous sommes devenues
2 les a-ton amenés ?
6 vous ne faite point d'attention
10 je ne sçais qui me tient
11 LE PRESIDENR. Quelle extravagance
11 le plaisant *qui proquo* !
12 Que vous a-til donc fait
12 je les ferai morgué haper
12 vos réprimandes & vous, tiren ttoutes deux à leur fin
12 & renméne tes chiens
13 Fh, quel miracle de vous voir
15 Ce maraut de Bourguignon est lontems
15 Mon portrait est de bon goû au moins
15 je veux que vous voyez cette tête-là
15 Tu ne les trouve pas !
17 A tu vû Eraste ?
19 *Vous belles, qui pour prix*
[20] encore un jugement prononncez
[20] *D'un fils donc Frontin soit le pere*

Editions autorisées parues du vivant de l'auteur[153]

Nous attribuons à chaque édition un sigle (imprimé en caractères gras) sans faire de différence entre les textes publiés en brochure et les textes incorporés à des recueils. Nous employons les abréviations suivantes pour désigner les localisations des exemplaires : Arsenal - Bibliothèque de l'Arsenal (dont BNF, Arts du Spectacle); B - Bibliothèque de; BHVP - Bibliothèque Historique de la Ville de Paris; BM - Bibliothèque municipale de; BNF - Bibliothèque Nationale de France; BNU - Bibliothèque Nationale et Universitaire; CF - Bibliothèque-Musée de la Comédie-Française; M - Médiathèque de ; (rf) - recueil factice.

T1

LES / TROIS GASCONS , / ***COMEDIE*** **. /** De Monsieur B*** . / [fleuron - panier contenant cinq fleurs sur socle semi-circulaire] / A PARIS , / Chez PIERRE RIBOU, proche les / Augustins, à la descente du Pont-neuf, / à l'Image S. Louis . / [trait] / M. DCCII . / AVEC PERMISSION

A-D6 : p. [1]-47: texte. P. [48]: permis d'imprimer daté du 31 août 1702, signé M. Le Voyer d'Argenson.

p. [1] - page de titre ; p. [2] - personnages; p. 3 - page de départ du texte, avec bandeau (vase avec rose, plus deux fleurs de chaque coté, entouré de feuillages).

BNF : 8° Yth. 17636; 8° Yth. 17637; 8°Yth. 17638. Arsenal: Rf. 5517 (rf); Rf. 5518 (rf); Rf. 5519 (rf); 8° BL. 13212 (1) (rf). Sorbonne: R. 677 (8°). CF : 1 TRO Boi. BM Caen: Rés. A 536 (rf). BM Toulouse: Fa D 76 (2) (rf).

153. Est comprise dans cette liste l'édition de 72 pages du *Port de mer* que nous avons évoquée plus haut.

B1

LE BAL / D'AUTEUIL , / ***COMEDIE*** **.** / De Monsieur B*** . / [fleuron - feuillages groupés en forme de triangle renversé] / A PARIS , / Chez PIERRE RIBOU , proche les Augustins , à la descente du Pont-neuf , / à l'Image S. Louis . / [trait] / M. DCCII. / *AVEC PERMISSION* .

A-F6, G1: page de titre + 2 pages non numérotées + p. 3-74 (texte). P. 74 (en bas de la page) : permis d'imprimer daté du 31 août 1702, signé M. Le Voyer d'Argenson.

Erreurs dans les titres courants : p. 16, 18, 46, 48, 62, 68: LE BAILLI D'AUTEUIL, et p. 36, 50: DU BAL D'AUTEUIL .

BNF : Yf. 8313; 8° Yth. 1639. Arsenal : Rf. 5517 (rf); Rf. 5518 (rf); Rf. 5519 (rf) ; 8° BL. 13212 (2) (rf). CF: 1 BAL Boi. BM Caen: Rés. A 536 (rf). BM Toulouse : FaD 76 (5) (rf) (exemplaire incomplet).

P1

LE / PORT / DE / MER, / ***COMEDIE*** **.** / [fleuron - vase de fleurs] / A PARIS, / Chés PIERRE RIBOU , proche les / Augustins , à la descente du Pont- / neuf, à l'Image S. Louis . / [trait] / M. DCCIV. / *Avec Permission* .

[â]2, A-D6, E4 : p. 1-56: texte. â[1] ro: page de titre; â[1] vo: blanc; â[2] ro: Permission; â[2] vo: Acteurs. Les pages 13 et 45 sont paginées respectivement 15 et 54. Le titre courant de la page 6 est imprimé LE POR TDE MER. Permis d'imprimer daté du 29 février 1704, signé M. R. de Voyer d'Argenson.

BNF : Yf. 12175; 8° Yth. 14466; 8° Yth. 14467. Arsenal : Rf. 5518 (rf). BM Caen: Rés. A 536 (rf). BM Périgueux: D. 6 508. BM Troyes: Z. 16. 3541 (édition de relance, datée de 1754; exemplaire incomplet). BM Toulouse: FaD 76 (4) (rf) (exemplaire incomplet).

P2

LE / PORT / DE / MER / ***COMEDIE.*** Edition sans date et sans page de titre. Au verso du faux titre: ACTEURS. Bandeau sur la page de départ du texte: vase de fleurs dans un cadre circulaire entouré de fleurs et de feuillages.

[â]1, A-D6: p. 1-46. P. [47] - [48]: approbation et privilège. Approbation pour 'les Pieces qui doivent composer le Theatre François', datée du 1er novembre 1704 et signée Pouchard. Privilège daté du 12 avril 1710 et enregistré le 11 juillet 1710, signé Delaunay.

BNF : 8° Yth. 14468 . Arsenal: Rf. 5519 (rf) ; 8° BL. 13212 (3) (rf). Mazarine: 36002 (rf). BM Toulouse: FaD 3099 (6) (rf)

[Saint-Pétersbourg, Bibliothèque Voltaire, n° 443: Paris, Ribou, 1713: même pagination que **P 2**, dans un *Recueil de pièce[s]*, t. II]

P3

LE PORT / ***DE MER*** **/ COMEDIE /** ***EN PROSE ET EN UN ACTE*****, / SUIVIE D'UN DIVERTISSEMENT. / Représenté pour la premiere fois le / Jeudi 29 Mai 1704.** / [s.l.n.d.]. La p.[1], signée A, porte la mention 'Tome I'. p.[2] = Acteurs. p.[3] = page de départ du texte, avec bandeau figurant urne sur table entourée de feuillages.

A-C12. p. [1] - 72. Signature A5 signée Avi. Erreurs de pagination: la page 39 est paginée 93, la page 69 est paginée 89, la page 70 est paginée 90. La page 28 est paginée 28 [*sic*] .

BNF: 8° Yth. 14469. CF : 1 POR Boi. B Versailles : Bibliothèque de la Reine 939.

ŒUVRES / DE / THEATRE / DE / M. BOINDIN./ NOUVELLE EDITION / *Revûe & Corrigée* . / [fleuron] / A PARIS , / Chez PRAULT fils , / Libraire, Quay de / Conty, vis-à-vis la descente du Pont / Neuf, à la Charité / [trait double] /M. DCC. XLVI. / *Avec Permission.*

Contient: *Les Trois Gascons*, p.[1] - 56 (**T2**); *Le Bal d'Auteuil* , p.[57] - 143 (**B2**); *Le Port de mer* , p. [145] - [2]18 (**P4**).

â2, A-S 8/4. 2ff. non signées + p. [1] - 218.

L et N non signées. Erreurs de pagination : la page 137 est paginée 179; la page 141 est paginée 144; la page 169 est paginée 269; la page 218 est paginée 318. La page 131 porte le titre courant COMEDIEs [*sic*].

Sorbonne : L. F. [théta]198. BM Lyon: 314 043. BM Rennes : 71 488. BM Toulouse : FaD 2971.

ŒUVRES / DE MONSIEUR / BOINDIN ,/ *De l'Académie des Inscriptions & / Belles Lettres* ./ TOME PREMIER./ *Contenant ses piéces de Théâtre, & ses / conjectures sur le mérite d'Homere* ./ [fleuron - vingt ovales rangés en carré entouré de feuilles] / A PARIS, / Chez PRAULT, fils, Quai de Conti, vis/ à-vis la descente du Pont-Neuf à la/ Charité./ [trait]/ M. DCC. LIII./ *Avec Approbation & Privilége du Roi.*

Le tome I contient : l'Avertissement de l'Editeur, p. i-v; le Mémoire sur la vie et les ouvrages de M. Boindin, p. vi-xxiii; les comédies : *Les Trois Gascons* , p.[1]-56 (**T3**); *Le Bal d'Auteuil* , p.[57]-143 (**B3**); *Le Port de mer*, p.[145]-218 (**P5**); *Le Petit Maître de robe*, p.[219]-276 (**M1**).

La page 237 est paginée 372.

Approbation datée du 11 février 1752, signée Gibert. Privilège daté du 20 mars 1752, signé Sainson (tome II).

BNF: Z. 27525. Arsenal: 8° NF. 37 434, Rf. 5520; 8° BL. 13213; 8° BL. 13214; 8° 13215. CF: 2 BOI. O. 1753. Mazarine: 21856 Y-Z. Sorbonne: L. F. [pi] 17. BHVP: 948 428. BM Angers: Belles Lettres 3112. BM Avignon [ ]. BM Besançon: 205 337. BM Caen : A 3280 / 1. BM Chalons-sur-Marne : Gt 4387 (1). BM Dijon: 8314 et

Virely I 373. BM Lille: 88729 - 1. BM Lyon: 302146 et 349062. B Méjanes (Aix-en-Provence): C. 1905. BM Montpellier: 53 683 (1). BM Nantes: 28669.BM Orléans : 8° D 2147. BM Reims: P. 2339. BM Rouen: Montbret p 3873 et O. 2925. BNU Strasbourg: CD 113 589. BM Versailles : F.A., in-12, E 51 g, et Rés. C. 436.

Autres œuvres de N. Boindin.

[An.], *Harangue de Monsieur Boindin à sa rentrée au café de Procope le 12 janvier 1744*, [s.l.n.d.]. (BHVP: 103 833).

[An.], *Lettres historiques sur tous les spectacles de Paris*, Paris, Prault, 1719.

Mémoire pour servir à l'histoire des couplets de 1710 attribués faussement à Monsieur Rousseau, Bruxelles, Foppens, Eugène-Henry Fricx, 1752.

BIBLIOGRAPHIE

Manuscrits

Paris.

Archives de la Comédie-Française:
Chronologie des pièces restées au théâtre et des acteurs d'original.
Manuscrit Ms. 52 : manuscrit de souffleur des *Trois Gascons*, copié par Lapierre[154].
Registres d'assemblées, 1701-1707.

Archives de l'Institut de France:
ms. Z. 201: 'Registre journal des assemblées et délibérations de l'Académie royalle des inscriptions et médailles; année 1712, 1ere partie'.

Bibliothèque Nationale de France :
ms. n.a.fr. 24444; ms. fr. Smith-Lesouef 105; ms. fr. 22158.

Bibliothèque de l'Arsenal:
ms. 3113 (t. 2) (rôle de Doutremer) ; ms. 3329, f. 64-65 (supplique au lieutenant criminel); ms. 6468 (t. 2), f. 221 (couplets satiriques); ms. 6712, f. 50 (document concernant les couplets de Rousseau); ms. Bastille 11463, f. 136 V (incident Rochart).

Imprimés

ABIRACHED, Robert, *La Crise du personnage dans le théâtre moderne*, Paris, Grasset, 1978.

ALASSEUR, Claude, *La Comédie-Française au 18e siècle, étude économique*, Paris et La Haye, Mouton & Co., 1967.

154. Parmi les variantes des *Trois Gascons*, le sigle Ms désigne celles qui proviennent de ce manuscrit.

ARGENSON, Marc-René de Voyer, comte d', *Rapports inédits du lieutenant de police, René d'Argenson (1697-1715)*, publiés par Paul Cottin, Paris, Plon, Nourrit et Cie. (Bibliothèque Elzévirienne), 1891.

- , *Notes de René d'Argenson, lieutenant général de police*, Paris, Voitelain, 1866.

ARGENSON, René-Louis de Voyer de Paulmy, marquis d', *Mémoires et Journal inédit du Marquis d'Argenson*, Paris, Jannet (Bibliothèque Elzévirienne), 1857, 5 vol.

- , *Notices sur les œuvres de théâtre*, publiées par H. Lagrave (Studies on Voltaire and the Eighteenth Century, 43-44), Genève, Institut et Musée Voltaire, 1966, 2 vol.

ATTINGER, Gustave, *L'Esprit de la Commedia dell'Arte dans le théâtre français*, Paris, Librairie Théâtrale et Neuchâtel, La Baconnière,1950.

BALLARD, Christophe, éd., *Recueil d'airs sérieux et à boire de différens auteurs, pour l'année 1702*, Paris, Christophe Ballard, 1702.

BALCOU, Jean, *Le Dossier Fréron, correspondances et documents*, Saint-Brieuc, Presses Universitaires de Bretagne, 1975.

BARBIER, E.-J.-F., *Journal historique et anecdotique du règne de Louis XV*, éd. A. de La Villegille, Paris, Renouard, 1846-1856, 4 vol ; II.

BEAUCHAMPS, P.-F. G. de, *Recherches sur les théâtres de France*, Paris, Prault, 1735, 3 vol.

BEAUMARCHAIS, Pierre Augustin Caron de, *Le Barbier de Séville*, in *Œuvres*, éd. P. Larthomas, Paris, Gallimard (Bibliothèque de la Pléiade), 1988.

BENABOU, Erica-Marie, *La Prostitution et la police des moeurs au XVIIIe siècle*, Paris, Perrin, 1987.

BENICHOU, Paul, *Morales du Grand Siècle*, Paris, NRF-Gallimard (coll. 'Idées'), 1967.

BERGSON, Henri, *Le Rire. Essai sur la signification du comique*, 273e édition, Paris, Presses Universitaires de France, 1969.

BLANC, André, *F.C. Dancourt (1661-1725). La Comédie-Française à l'heure du Soleil couchant*, Tübingen, Gunter Narr et Paris, Jean-Michel Place, 1984.

BLEGNY, Nicolas de (*dit*, Abraham du Pradel), *Le Livre commode des adresses de Paris pour l'année 1692*, éd. E. Fournier, Paris, Daffis ('Bibliothèque Elzévirienne'), 1878, 2 vol.

BOILEAU-DESPREAUX, Nicolas, *Œuvres complètes*, introduction par Antoine Adam, textes établis par Françoise Escal, Paris, NRF-Gallimard ('Bibliothèque de la Pléiade'), 1970.

BOISROBERT, François Le Métel, sieur de, *Les Trois Orontes*, Paris, Courbé, 1653.

BONNASSIES, Jules, *La Comédie-Française. Histoire administrative*, Paris, Didier, 1874.

BORDELON, abbé Laurent, *L'Ambigu d'Auteuil*, Paris, Vve Combe, 1709.

BRENNER, Clarence D., *A Bibliographical List of Plays* [...] *1700-1789*, New York, A.M.S. Press, 1979.

BROOKS, William et YARROW, Philip, *The Dramatic Criticism of Elisabeth-Charlotte, duchesse d'Orléans*, Lewiston, Queenston, Lampeter, Edwin Mellen Press, ('Studies in French Literature' 9), 1996.

CALAME, Alexandre, *Regnard, sa vie et son œuvre*, Paris, Presses Universitaires de France, 1960.

CALLIERES, François de, *Des mots à la mode (1692). Du bon et du mauvais usage dans les manières de s'exprimer (1693)*, Genève, Slatkine Reprints, 1972.

CANOVA, Marie-Claude, *La Comédie*, Paris, Hachette, 1993.

CHEVALLEY, Sylvie, 'Les Premières Assemblées des Comédiens Français', in *Mélanges Couton*, Presses Universitaires de Lyon, 1981.

CLAVILIER, Michèle, et DUCHEFDELAVILLE, Danielle, *La Commedia dell'Arte : le jeu masqué*, Grenoble, Presses Universitaires de Grenoble, 1994.

CLEMENT, Jean-Marie-Bernard et LA PORTE abbé Joseph de, *Anecdotes dramatiques*, Paris, Veuve Duchesne, 1775, 3 vol.

CLEMENT, Pierre, *La Police sous Louis XIV*, Paris, Didier, 2e édition, 1866.

COLLÉ, Charles, *Journal et mémoires*, éd. H. Bonhomme, Paris, Firmin Didot, 1868, 3 vol.

CUENIN, Micheline, *Le Duel sous l'Ancien Régime*, Paris, Presses de la Renaissance, 1982.

DANGEAU, Philippe de Courcillon, marquis de, *Journal du marquis de Dangeau*, publié [...] par Soulié *et al.*, Paris, F. Didot, 1854-1860, 19 vol.; t. VIII, XI, XVII.

DAVIDSON, Hugh M., 'La Vraisemblance chez d'Aubignac et Corneille; quelques réflexions disciplinaires', in *L'Art du théâtre, mélanges en hommage à Robert Garapon*, Paris, Presses Universitaires de France, 1992.

DEKKER, Rudolf M., *The Tradition of Female Transvestism in Early Modern Europe*, New York, St Martin's Press, 1989.

DEMERSON, M. L., *Histoire naturelle de la vigne et du vin*, Paris, Charpentier, 1826.

DEPPING, Georges-Bernard, *Correspondance administrative sous le règne de Louis XIV*, Paris, Imprimerie Impériale, 1850-1855, 4 vol.

DESNOIRESTERRES, Gustave Le Brisoys, *La Comédie satirique au XVIIIe siècle*, Paris, Perrin, 1885.

- , *Voltaire et la société au dix-huitième siècle* : 2e série : *Voltaire au château de Cirey*, Paris, Didier, 1871.

DESTOUCHES, Philippe Néricault, *L'Irrésolu*, éd. John Dunkley, Paris, Société des Textes Français Modernes (206), 1995.

- , *L'Obstacle imprévu*, Paris, Le Breton, 1718.

Dictionnaire de l'Académie Françoise, Paris, J.-B. Coignard, 1694, 2 vol.

Dictionnaire de biographie française, dirigé par M. Prévost et Roman d'Amat, Paris, Letouzy et Ané, 1954, t. VI.

Dictionnaire de la musique en France au XVIIe et XVIIIe siècles, publié sous la direction de Marcel Benoit, Paris, Fayard, 1992.

Dictionnaire encyclopédique du théâtre, éd. Michel Corvin, Paris, Bordas, 1991.

Dictionnaire universel, par Antoine Furetière, 2e éd., La Haye, A. et R. Leers, 1701, 3 vol. ; et La Haye, Pierre Husson *et al.*, 1727, 4 vol.

Dictionnaire universel français et latin, vulgairement appelé Dictionnaire de Trévoux, Paris, Les Libraires Associés, 1771, 8 vol.

Dix-huitième Siècle 22 (*L'Œil expert :* 'Voyager, explorer'), publié par la Société française d'étude du 18e siècle, Paris, Presses Universitaires de France, 1990.

DUBOIS, Jean, LAGANE, René et LEROND, Alain, *Dictionnaire du français classique*, Paris, Larousse, 1971.

DU BOS, Jean-Baptiste, *Réflexions critiques sur la poésie et sur la peinture*, Paris, Jean Mariette, 1719, 2 vol.

DUBU, Jean, 'La Condition sociale de l'écrivain de théâtre au XVIIe siècle', *XVIIe Siècle* 39 (1958), p. 149-183.

DUCKWORTH, George E., *The Nature of Roman Comedy, a study in popular entertainment*, Princeton, Princeton University Press, 1952.

DUFRESNY, Charles Rivière, *Amusemens sérieux et comiques*, éd. John Dunkley, Exeter, The University ('Textes Littéraires Français'), 1976.

DUNKLEY, John, 'Theatrical Censorship and Nicolas Boindin's *Le Bal d'Auteuil* (1702)', *Studies on Voltaire and the Eighteenth Century* 329 (1995), p. 185-196.

DUVIGNAUD, Jean, *L'Acteur, esquisse d'une sociologie du comédien*, Paris, Gallimard (Idées), 1965.

EMELINA, Jean, *Le Comique, essai d'interprétation générale*, Paris, SEDES, 1991.

- , *'Le Courrier facétieux'* , *Revue des sciences humaines* (1967), p. 523-544.

- , *Les Valets et les servantes dans le théâtre comique en France de 1610 à 1700*, Grenoble, Presses Universitaires de Grenoble, 1975.

Encyclopédie, ou dictionnaire raisonné des sciences , des arts et des métiers, Paris, Briasson, David, Le Breton et Durand, 1751-1770 (réimprimé : 'Compact Edition', New York, Readex Microprint Corporation, 1969, 5 vol).

FAIRCHILDS, Cissie, *Domestic Enemies ; servants and their masters in Old Regime France*, Baltimore et Londres, The Johns Hopkins University Press, 1984.

FORESTIER, Georges, *Esthétique de l'identité dans le théâtre français, 1550-1680: le déguisement et ses avatars*, Genève, Droz, 1988 ('Histoire des idées et critique littéraire' 259).

GACON, François, *L'Anti-Rousseau, par le poète sans fard*, (*Œuvres de Rousseau*, vol. III), Rotterdam, Fritsch et Böhm, 1712.

- , *Histoire satirique de la vie et des ouvrages de M. Rousseau en vers ainsi qu'en prose*, Paris, Ribou, 1716.

GAIFFE, Félix, *L'Envers du Grand Siècle*, Paris, Albin Michel, 1924.

GARAPON, Robert, *La Fantaisie verbale et le comique dans le théâtre française du Moyen Age à la fin du XVIIe siècle*, Paris, Armand Colin, 1957.

GASSIER Emile, *Les Cinq Cents Immortels, histoire de l'Académie française, 1634-1906*, Paris, Jouve, 1906.

GOUBERT, Pierre, *Histoire des étrangers et de l'immigration en France*, Paris, Larousse, 1992.

GOUHIER, Henri, *Le Théâtre et l'existence*, nouvelle édition, Paris, Vrin, 1980.

GRENTE, Georges, cardinal, *Dictionnaire des lettres françaises. Le XVIIIe siècle.* Edition revue et mise à jour par François MOUREAU, Paris, Fayard, 1995.

GRIMM, Friedrich Melchior, baron, *Correspondance littéraire, philosophique et critique*, éd. M. Tourneux, Paris, 1877-1882 ; 16 vol. ; t. I, II, VI, XI.

GUTTON, Jean-Pierre, *Domestiques et serviteurs dans la France de l'Ancien Régime*, Paris, Aubier Montaigne, 1981.

HAASE, A., *Syntaxe français du XVIIe siècle*, nouvelle édition traduite et remaniée par M. Obert, 4e édition, Paris, Delagrave, 1935.

HALLAYS-DABOT, Victor, *La Censure théâtrale*, Paris, Dentu, 1862.

HERRMANN-MASCARD, Nicole, *La Censure des livres à Paris à la fin de l'Ancien Régime (1750-1789)*, Paris, Presses Universitaires de France, 1968.

HOWELLS, Robin, 'The Rise of the rococo', *Studies on Voltaire and the Eighteenth Century* 302 (1992), p. 95-115.

- , 'Rococo and carnival', *Studies on Voltaire and the Eighteenth Century* 308 (1993), p. 187-221.

ISAMBERT, DECRUSY et TAILLANDIER, *Recueil général des anciennes lois françaises depuis l'an 420 jusqu'à la Révolution de 1789*, Paris, 1821-1833, 29 vol. ; t. XVIII, XX.

JAEGER, Gérard, *L'Aventure maritime; corsaires, flibustiers, pirates et Barbaresques. Synthèse d'une légende*, Paris, Diffusion Université Culture, 1986.

- , *Pirates, flibustiers et corsaires. Histoire et légendes d'une société d'exception*, Avignon, Aubanel, 1987.

JAL, Auguste, *Dictionnaire critique de biographie et d'histoire*, 2e édition, Paris, Plon, 1872.

JOANNIDES, A., *La Comédie-Française de 1680 à 1920. Dictionnaire général des pièces et des auteurs*, Genève, Slatkine Reprints, 1970.

- , *La Comédie-Française de 1680 à 1920 ; tableau des représentations par auteurs et par pièces*, Paris, Plon, 1921.

KARSTAN, David, *Roman Comedy*, Ithaca et Londres, Cornell University Press, 1983.

KORS, Alan C., *Atheism in France, 1650-1729*, Princeton, Princeton University Press, 1990.

LACROIX, Paul, *Catalogue de la bibliothèque dramatique de Monsieur de Soleinne*, (Paris, Alliance de Arts, 1843-1845). Réimprimé: Graz, Akademische Druck- u. Verlagsanstalt, 1969, 3 vol.

LA BRUYERE, Jean de, *Les Caractères, ou les moeurs de ce siècle*, in *Œuvres*, éd. M. Servois, Paris, Hachette, 1865-1878, 3 vol., t. I.

LA CHESNAYE DESBOIS et BADIER, *Dictionnaire de la noblesse*, 3e édition (Paris, 1870), Nendeln / Liechtenstein, Kraus Reprints,1969 ; t. XVI.

LAFONT, J. de, *Les Trois Frères rivaux*, Paris, Ribou, 1713.

LAGRAVE, Henri, *Le Théâtre et le public à Paris de 1715 à 1750*, Paris, Klincksieck, 1972.

- , 'Le Costume de théâtre: approche sémiologique', *Messages* 4 (1973), p. 33-45.

LALANNE, Ludovic, *Dictionnaire historique de la France*, Paris, Hachette, s.d.

LA MOTTE, Antoine Houdar de, *La Matrone d'Ephèse*, Paris, Ribou, 1702.

LANCASTER, Henry C., *The Comédie Française, 1680-1701, plays, actors, spectators, finances*, Baltimore, The Johns Hopkins Press et Londres, Oxford University Press, 1941.

- , *The Comédie Française, 1701-1774, plays, actors, spectators, finances*, Philadelphia, The American Philosophical Society, 1951.

- , *Sunset; a History of Parisian Drama in the Last Years of Louis XV, 1701-1715* (1945). Réimprimé Westport (Conn.), Greenwood Press, 1976.

LARTHOMAS, Pierre, *Le Langage dramatique* (1972), Paris, Presses Universitaires de France, 1989.

LOTTIN, Auguste-Martin, *Catalogue chronologique des libraires et des libraires-imprimeurs de Paris, depuis l'an 1470*, Paris, J.-R. Lottin de Saint-Germain, 1789.

LOUGH, John, *Paris Theatre Audiences in the Seventeenth and Eighteenth Centuries* (1957), Londres, Oxford University Press, 1972.

LURCEL, Dominique (éd.), *Le Théâtre de la Foire au XVIIIe siècle*, Paris, Union Générale d'Editions, ('10/18'), 1983.

LYONNET, Henry, *Dictionnaire des Comédiens français (ceux d'hier) ; biographie, bibliographie, iconographie* (1904). Réimprimé Genève, Slatkine, 1969, 2 vol.

MARTIN, Henri-Jean, *Livre, pouvoirs et société à Paris au XVIIe siècle, 1598-1701*, Genève, Droz, 1969, 2 vol.

MAURY, Alfred, *Les Académies d'autrefois* ; 2e partie : *L'Ancienne Académie des Inscriptions et Belles-Lettres*, Paris, Didier, 1864.

MAZA, Sarah C., *Servants and Masters in Eighteenth-Century France. The uses of loyalty*, Princeton, Princeton University Press, 1983.

MAZOUER, Charles, 'L'Eglise, le théâtre et le rire au XVIIe siècle', in *L'Art du théâtre* (*Mélanges Garapon*; voir Davidson, *supra*).

- , 'Le Gascon dans le théâtre comique sous Louis XIV', in *L'Image littéraire du Gascon ; IIe colloque de littérature régionale*, publié par 'Les Cahiers de l'Université de Pau et des pays de l'Adour' 21, 1984, p. 85-108.

MELESE, Pierre, *Répertoire analytique des documents contemporains d'information et de critique concernant le théâtre à Paris sous Louis XIV, 1659-1715*, Paris, Droz, 1934.

- , *Le Théâtre et le public à Paris sous Louis XIV, 1659-1715*, Paris Droz, 1934.

MINOIS, Georges, *Censure et culture sous l'Ancien Régime*, Paris, Fayard, 1995.

MOLIERE, Jean-Baptiste Poquelin, *Œuvres complètes*, éd. G. Couton, Paris, NRF-Gallimard ('Bibliothèque de la Pléiade'), 1971, 2 vol.

MOREL, Jacques, *Agréables mensonges. Essais sur le théâtre français du XVIIe siècle*, Paris, Klincksieck, 1991 (*Mélanges Morel*).

MOUHY, Charles de Fieux, chevalier de, *Tablettes dramatiques*, Paris, S. Jorry, 1752-1753.

- , *Abrégé de l'histoire du théâtre français*, Paris, L'Auteur, Jorry, Mérigot jeune, 1780, 4 vol., t. I.

MOULINAS René, 'Le Conseil du roi et le commerce des Juifs d'Avignon en France', *Dix-Huitième Siècle* 13 (1981), p. 169-179.

MOUREAU, François, *Dufresny, auteur dramatique (1657-1724)*, Paris, Klincksieck, 1979.

- , *Les Presses grises. La Contrefaçon du livre (XVIe-XIXe siècles),* textes réunis par François Moureau, Paris, Aux Amateurs des Livres, 1988.

- , voir: GRENTE.

- , 'Du côté Cour, la Princesse Palatine et le théâtre', *Revue d'Histoire du théâtre*, 1983, 3, p. 275-286.

- , 'Le petit-maître intrigué: espaces du libertinage au théâtre jusqu'à la Régence', *Eros philosophe. Discours libertins des Lumières*, éd. F. Moureau et A.-M. Rieu, Paris, Honoré Champion, 1984, p. 119-135.

NAUDÉ DE MOUTIS, Jean-Pierre, *Auteuil-Passy, demeures et jardins, XVIIIe et XIXe siècles*, Paris, Aux Editions d'Art des Anciennes Demeures Françaises, 1982.

NYROP, K. R., *Grammaire historique de la langue française*, Copenhague, Glydendalske Boghandel Nordisk Forlag, 1925 ; t. V.

OEXMELIN, Alexandre-Olivier, *Histoire des aventuriers, des flibustiers et des boucaniers d'Amérique*, Paris, La Sirène, 1920.

ORLEANS, Elisabeth Charlotte, duchesse d', *Correspondance de Madame, duchesse d'Orléans* [...], traduction et notes par Ernest Jaeglé, 2e éd., Paris, Bouillon, 1890, 3 vol.

PARFAICT, François et Claude, *Dictionnaire des théâtres de Paris*, Paris, Lambert, 1756, 7 tom., t. I.

- , *Histoire du théâtre français depuis son origine jusqu'à présent* (Paris, Le Mercier et Saillant, 1745-1749, 15 vol.). Réimprimée Genève, Slatkine, 1967, 3 vol.

PASQUIER, Pierre, *La Mimèsis dans l'esthétique théâtrale du XVIIe siècle. Histoire d'une réflexion*, Paris, Klincksieck, 1995.

Petite Bibliothèque des théâtres, Paris, Belin, Brunet, 1787, t. XII .

PEYRONNET, Pierre, *La Mise en scène au XVIIIe siècle*, Paris, Nizet, 1974.

PIRON, Alexis, *Œuvres inédites de Piron*, éd. H. Bonhomme, Paris, Poulet-Malassis et de Broise, 1859.

PITOU, Spire, 'The Comédie-Française and the Palais Royal Interlude of 1716-1723', *Studies on Voltaire and the Eighteenth Century* 64 (1968), p. 225-264.

PLUCHON, Pierre, *Nègres et Juifs au XVIIIe siècle. Le racisme au Siècle des Lumières*, Paris, Taillandier, 1984.

REGNARD, Jean-François, *Œuvres de Regnard*, éd. E. Fournier, Paris, Laplace, Sanchez et Cie., 1876, 2 vol.

ROUGEMONT, Martine de, *La Vie théâtrale en France au XVIIIe siècle*, Paris et Genève, Champion-Slatkine, 1988.

ROUSSEAU, Jean-Baptiste, *Le Café, Le Capricieux, Le Flatteur*, in [*Pièces de théâtre*], Rotterdam, Fritsch et Böhm, 1712, 3 vol., t. II.

ROZIERE, Eugène de, et CHATEL, Eugène, *Table générale et méthodique des mémoires* [...] *de l'Académie des Inscriptions et Belles-Lettres,* Paris, A. Durand, 1856.

SAINT-EVREMOND, Marguetel de Saint-Denis, sieur de, *Sir Politick Would-Be,* éd. R. Finch et E. Joliat, Paris et Genève, Droz ('Textes Littéraires Français' 250), 1978.

SCHERER, Jacques, *La Dramaturgie classique en France*, Paris, Nizet, 1950.

SEDAINE, Michel-Jean, *Le Philosophe sans le savoir*, éd. John Dunkley, Egham, Runnymede Books, 1993.

SEGUIN, Jean-Pierre, *La Langue française au XVIIIe siècle*, Paris, Bordas (Etudes) 1972.

SMADJA, Eric, *Le Rire*, Paris, Presses Universitaires de France ('Que-sais-je?'), 1993.

STACKELBERG, Jürgen von, 'Quelques Réflexions méthodologiques sur l'histoire du théâtre français au XVIIIe siècle', *Œuvres et critiques*, II, 2 (1978), p. 75-85.

STREICHER, Jeanne (éd.), *Commentaires sur les 'Remarques' de Vaugelas*, Paris, E. Droz, 1936, 2 vol.

TISSIER, André, *M. de Crac, gentilhomme gascon. Etude de la formation littéraire et des transformations d'un «type populaire» [...]*, Paris, Didier, 1959.

TRUCHET, Jacques (éd.), *Théâtre du XVIIIe siècle*, Paris, NRF-Gallimard ('Bibliothèque de la Pléiade'), 1972-1974, 2 vol.

- , *Thématique de Molière*, Paris, SEDES, 1985.

UBERSFELD, Anne, *Lire le théâtre*, 4e édition, Paris, Editions Sociales, 1982.

VAN BEVER, A., *Contes et conteurs gaillards au dix-huitième siècle*, Paris, Daragon, 1906.

VAUGELAS, Claude Favre de, *Remarques sur la langue françoise*, éd. J. Streicher, Paris, Droz, 1934.

VIGIE, Marc, *Les Galériens du roi, 1661-1715*, Paris, Fayard, 1985.

VITTU, Jean-Pierre, 'Public et folies dramatiques ; la Comédie-Française (1680-1716)', in *Problèmes socio-culturels en France au XVIIe siècle*, Paris, Klincksieck, 1974, p. 89-145.

VOLTAIRE, François Marie Arouet de, *Correspondence*, éd. T. Besterman, Genève et Banbury, The Voltaire Foundation, 1968-1977, 51 vol., t. II, XII, XIII, XXXII.

- , *Notebooks*, I (*Complete Works*, LXXXI), Genève, Institut et Musée Voltaire et University of Toronto Press, 1968.

- , *Le Siècle de Louis XIV*, in *Œuvres historiques*, éd. R. Pomeau, Paris, NRF-Gallimard ('Bibliothèque de la Pléiade' 1957.

- , *Le Temple du goût*, in *Œuvres complètes de Voltaire*, éd. L. Moland, Paris, Garnier, 1877-1885, 52 vol., t. VIII.

- , *Le Temple du goût*, éd. E. Carcassonne, 2e éd., Genève, Droz, et Lille, Giard, 1953.

VOLTZ, Pierre, *La Comédie*, Paris, Armand Colin, 1964.

WITHERELL, Anne L., *Louis Pécour's 1700 'Recueil de dances'*, Ann Arbor, UMI Research Press ('Studies in Musicology' 60), 1983.

LES

TROIS GASCONS

COMEDIE

PERSONNAGES

Mr ORONTE pere de Lucile

LUCILE amante d'Eraste

ERASTE amant de Lucile

MARTON suivante de Lucile

Mr DE SPADAGNAC Gascon [a]

JULIE amante de Mr de Spadagnac

FRONTIN, valet de Mr de Spadagnac

LA ROZE, valet de Mr Oronte

TROUPE de Basques & de Gasconnes [b]

La Scène est à Paris chez Mr Oronte.

---

[a] Ms Gentilhomme Gascon

[b] Ms accompagnez de Hautbois

LES

TROIS GASCONS,

COMEDIE

SCENE PREMIERE.

MARTON, FRONTIN.

MARTON

Que me dis-tu là, Frontin? quoi, ton maître est en chemin? & l'on n'a pû le retenir à Bordeaux?

FRONTIN

Au moins, Marton, ce n'est pas ma faute: tu sçais que j'avois écrit à Julie [1], de ne le point laisser partir [2],

1. Sur l'utilité de la culture écrite pour la promotion sociale des serviteurs, voir J. Emelina, *Les Valets et les servantes*, p. 421-426. Les serviteurs lisaient plus facilement qu'ils n'écrivaient, et ceux qui écrivaient le faisaient généralement assez mal ; voir C. Fairchilds, *Domestic Enemies*, p. 117-118.

2. Le pronom objet se plaçait normalement entre les deux éléments de la négation au XVIIe siècle ; voir A. Haase, *Syntaxe française*, § 156 D, rem. II.

& qu'il ne venoit ici qu'en fraude de leurs engagements; mais il lui est échapé malgré toutes nos mesures![a]

MARTON

Voila donc Lucile enlevée à nôtre barbe?

FRONTIN

Que veux-tu? j'en suis fâché pour elle, & pour Julie; mais en tout cas, si mon maître épouse Lucile, il faudra bien m'en consoler avec toi! aussi bien ai-je déja fait, par son ordre, tous les aprêts de sa nôce, & par-dessus le marché, ceux de la nôtre!

MARTON

Tu comptes donc bien sur moi, Frontin?

FRONTIN

Oh, je te l'avoüe; j'ai bû de l'eau de la Garonne: je suis fait à l'espérance.

MARTON

Boi de l'eau de la Seine; tu ès trop vif.

FRONTIN

Oh, tu ne sçaurois t'en dédire: je t'ai vûë, tu m'as plû,

---

[a] Ms MARTON Et Julie ne l'a pas fait suivre?
FRONTIN Si fait, vrayement ; Elle me mande quelle [sic] s'est mise elle mesme en campagne ; mais qu'il auroit pris les deuants, et qu'il vient en poste.

je te l'ai dit. Je te plais sans doute. Tu ne m'as pas dit le contraire. Voila des raisons de reste pour t'épouser. En doutes-tu encore? Veux tu des arrhes?

MARTON

Tout beau, Monsieur Frontin! Si Monsieur de Spadagnac épouse Lucile, il n'y a point de Marton pour vous.

FRONTIN

Mais, Madame Marton, mon maître ne vous doit point de gages; vous ne songez pas que son mariage me pouroit payer des miens? & s'ils manquent, je vous avertis que je ne suis pas un trop bon parti: je n'ai encore reçû que des coups depuis que je le sers!

MARTON

Ne t'embarasse point de tes gages: je t'en répons, je les vaux bien.

FRONTIN

D'accord; mais, Madame Marton, que deviendra le petit divertissement que nous avions préparé pour Monsieur de Spadagnac?

MARTON

Ce qu'il poura, ne t'en mets point en peine!

FRONTIN

A la bonne heure; mais, Madame Marton...

MARTON

Ho! plus de mais, Monsieur Frontin! il faut rompre ce mariage, vous dis-je, & travailler ensemble à celui d'Eraste: Marton est à ce prix.

FRONTIN

Hé bien[a] , travaillons: je ne demande pas mieux: mais le voici tout à propos[b] .

SCENE II

ERASTE, MARTON, FRONTIN.

ERASTE

Hé bien, ma chere Marton! que puis-je espérer?

MARTON

Rien, Monsieur; tout est perdu!

ERASTE

Comment?

MARTON

Monsieur de Spadagnac arrive incessament.

---

[a] Ms *omet* Hé bien.

[b] Ms Mais le voici tout a propos *attribué à Marton*

ERASTE

Quoi! ce Gascon[3] qu'on destinoit à Lucile?

MARTON

Oüi, lui-même, il vient l'épouser!

ERASTE

Et tu ne sçais aucun moyen de parer ce coup?

MARTON

Moi? non!

ERASTE

Il faut donc que je me coupe la gorge avec lui!

MARTON

Si nous pouvions cependant faire en sorte...

ERASTE

Ah, ma chere Marton, tu me rends la vie!

MARTON

Non, je n'imagine rien encore...

---

3. Gascon. 'Fanfaron, hableur, querelleur. Cet homme se vante de bien des bravoures, mais c'est un *Gascon*, il hable' (Furetière). Sauf indication contraire, nos références au *Dictionnaire universel* de Furetière se rapportent à la seconde édition (1701).

ERASTE

Tu me replonges dans le desespoir.

MARTON

Attendez... ne m'avez-vous pas dit que Lucile vous avoit permis de tout entreprendre pour l'obtenir?

ERASTE

Il est vrai.

MARTON

Que vous l'aviez même fait demander à son père, par Monsieur vôtre oncle?

ERASTE

J'en conviens.

MARTON

Et que son père content de vos biens, & de vôtre famille, n'avoit trouvé d'autre obstacle à vôtre bonheur, que la parole qu'il avoit donnée à Monsieur de Spadagnac[a] ?

ERASTE

Hé bien?

---

[a] Ms la parole qu'il auroit donné à son frere pour Mr de Spadagnac

MARTON

Hé bien! le bon homme ne vous connoît point: il n'a jamais vû vôtre rival: il faut vous présenter ici pour lui.

ERASTE

Mais encore, sur quelle apparence veux-tu que je passe à ses yeux pour Monsieur de Spadagnac[a] ?

MARTON

Ne vous mettez point en peine; nous avons des ressources. Voila son Valet que j'ai déja[b] mis dans vos intérêts, & qui vous présentera pour lui à Monsieur Oronte. C'est moi qui vous en répons.

ERASTE *à Frontin*

Quoi! tu voudrois bien...

FRONTIN

Moi? je ne dis pas cela. Comment! puis-je en conscience...

MARTON *à Frontin*[c]

Je te le conseille, vraiment, de me mettre en compromis[4] avec ta conscience!

---

[a] pour mon Rival

[b] T2 , T3 *omettent* déjà

[c] Ms *omet cette didascalie et la suivante*

4. Mettre en compromis. 'On dit [...] qu'on ne se doit point mettre en *compromis* avec ses inférieurs, pour dire, avoir des paroles ou des querelles avec eux' (Furetière).

FRONTIN

Quoi! je trahirois mon Maître de guaïeté de cœur? je n'en ferai rien!

MARTON *à Frontin*

Comment! que dis-tu là?

FRONTIN *s'éloignant de Marton*

Laisse-moi; ne vien point me corrompre.

ERASTE

Ah, Monsieur Frontin! laissez-vous attendrir: il n'y a rien que vous ne deviez espérer de ma reconnoissance, si...

FRONTIN *le quittant brusquement*

Adieu.

ERASTE

Quoi! me quitter ainsi...

MARTON *à Frontin, en l'arrêtant*

Où vas-tu?

FRONTIN *à Eraste*

Bon, bon! ne vois-je pas où tout cela nous meine? vous seriez homme à m'offrir vôtre bourse; je suis fragile, je me connois: j'aime mieux ne point m'exposer.

ERASTE *en lui donnant sa bourse*

Ah Frontin! elle est à toi, & tu peux compter que c'est la moindre partie de ta récompence.

FRONTIN

Ne le disois-je pas? cette maudite bourse me fournit déja des raisons...[5]

MARTON

Comment! que dis-tu?

FRONTIN

Que cette bourse me fait souvenir de certains engagemens de mon Maître, avec une fille de Bordeaux, dont je me crois obligé de prendre les intérêts.

ERASTE

Eh! pourquoi donc hésiter...

FRONTIN

Comme vous m'avez ouvert l'esprit! Je crois à présent pour la sûreté de mon Maître, & pour la mienne, pouvoir tout entreprendre, pour rompre le mariage que vous craignez; car c'est une fille dangereuse que celle dont je vous parle, & qui pouroit bien nous joüer quelque mauvais tour!

---

5. Selon J. Emelina, la cupidité et la vénalité entraient dans les traits les mieux enracinés des serviteurs (comiques) de l'époque - selon la pensée des maîtres, bien entendu ; *op. cit.*, p.227-231.

ERASTE

Nous joüer quelque mauvais tour?

FRONTIN

Oüi, vraiment; c'est une héroïne, une Amazone[6] : moitié femme, moitié petit Maître; qui fait le coup de pistolet, & vous sangle[7] un coup d'épée, comme elle boiroit un verre de vin!

ERASTE

Comment diable!

FRONTIN

Au reste, généreuse, magnifique, qui n'a rien à elle, dès qu'elle aime une fois; mais aussi furieuse à proportion, dès qu'on l'abandonne; qui vous poignarderoit son amant, sa rivale, & elle-même, dans un besoin: fille à poursuivre un infidele au bout du monde; & à se faire aimer de peur par un perfide un peu poltron[a] !

ERASTE

Et sçait-elle les desseins de ton Maître?

---

a Ms à se faire épouser de peur par le perfide le plus determiné

6. Amazone. Furetière donne les deux sens du mot : 'Femme ou fille genereuse & guerriere' et 'femme courageuse capable d'une entreprise hardie' . Tous deux s'appliquent à notre personnage.

7. Sangler. 'Il lui a *sanglé* un soufflet, *sanglé* des coups de pieds au cu [sic], c'est-à-dire, donné de toute sa force' (Furetière).

FRONTIN

Oüi, vraiment; je n'ai pû me dispenser de lui en donner avis: car j'avois l'honneur de la servir, avant que d'être à lui; c'êtoit plus de souflets, plus de coups de pied au cul[a] [8] ! ho, je ne doute point qu'elle ne nous vienne faire ici quelque coup de sa tête!

ERASTE

Et quelle espèce d'homme est ce que ton Maître?

FRONTIN

Oh, pour lui, c'est un esprit bizare, qui n'aime que les choses extraordinaires: un homme revenu des plaisirs & des passions communes; qui s'est usé le gôut de bonne heure, & qui ne donneroit pas cela, d'une femme toute unie[9] .

MARTON

Lucile n'est donc pas son fait. Mais ne nous amusons pas[b] d'avantage: allez repasser vôtre rôle; il n'y a point de temps à perdre.

---

[a] Ms dans le cul

[b] Ms point

8. Les maîtres possédaient le droit et le devoir d'infliger à leurs domestiques des punitions corporelles, mais non de les brutaliser. Les abus étaient fréquents ; voir S. Maza, *Servants and Masters*, p. 173-174.

9. Uni(e). Mot familier pour désigner une personne 'sans façon, simple de goûts et de manières', selon le *Grand Dictionnaire universel du XIXe siècle*, XV (1).

FRONTIN

Il est vrai; mais si mon Maître arrivoit, aurois-je le front de le renier en face[10] ? cela est un peu violent, Marton!

ERASTE

Point de scrupules, Frontin; il ne tient qu'à toi d'étre à moi, dès ce moment: je suis ton Maître, su tu le veux; tu ne dépens plus de mon rival.

FRONTIN

J'accepte volontiers la condition; mais encore, Monsieur mon Maître[a], faudroit-il quelque chose qui pût vous faire passer avec quelque[b] vrai-semblance, pour Monsieur de Spadagnac?

ERASTE

Que cela ne t'embarasse point; tu sçais qu'on lui envoya le portrait de Lucile! j'en fis tirer une copie dans le temps; & j'en ai même fait imiter jusqu'à la boëte: il n'en faut pas davantage, avec les manières & l'accent du païs!

FRONTIN

C'est vôtre affaire; pour le déguisement, c'est la mienne: je lui ai fait faire ici des habits que j'ai fait

---

[a] Ms : Monsieur mon Maître ; textes imprimés : Monsieur Maître.

[b] Ms un peu de

10. Jeu verbal d'un type que Boindin affectionne.

voir à Monsieur Oronte; cela n'aidera pas mal à le tromper, & vous voila plus d'à moitié son gendre: c'est à Lucile à faire le reste!

ERASTE *en l'embrassant*

Ah, mon cher Frontin! comment pourai je reconnoître...

FRONTIN *se tirant*[a] *d'entre ses bras*

Tout beau, Monsieur! vous m'étoufez de joïe! que je te le rende, Marton?

MARTON

Point de bagatelles! j'entens du bruit; ce pouroit être Monsieur Oronte.

FRONTIN

Il seroit dangereux qu'il nous vît, retirons nous[11].

SCENE III

Mr ORONTE, LUCILE, MARTON.

Mr ORONTE

Non, vous dis-je, c'est une affaire arrêtée; & à laquelle il faut que vous vous disposiez.

---

[a] T3 *se retirant*

11. Cette scène et le début de la suivante ne trouveraient-ils pas un lointain écho dans les scènes 2, 3 et 4 du premier acte du *Barbier de Séville*?

LUCILE

Quoi, vous croyez, mon pere, que je puisse oublier Eraste, pour vôtre Monsieur de Spadagnac?

Mr ORONTE

Oüi, vraiment; ne vous l'ai-je pas ordonné ainsi? il seroit beau que vous fussiez rebelle aux ordres d'un pere!

LUCILE

Mais, mon pere, tient-il à moi de regler comme il vous plaît, les mouvemens de mon cœur?

Mr ORONTE

C'est bien à vôtre cœur[a] à avoir des mouvemens! je ne vois rien de plus impertinent que la jeunesse qui ne sçait ce qu'il lui faut, & qui se mesle de vouloir!

LUCILE

Ah! si j'ose former quelques desirs, ce n'est point pour aller contre vos volontés; & je vous les expose comme à un pere tendre, qui ne voudroit pas me marier pour mon malheur.

Mr ORONTE

Attendez! on vous marira pour vôtre plaisir! le mariage est une affaire de toute la vie; il y faut consulter l'honneur & l'intérêt: Monsieur de Spa-

---

[a] Ms à vous à avoir

dagnac se pique d'être d'une des meilleures[a] maisons de Gascogne; mon frere souhaite qu'il soit son neveu; & la succession de mon frere est considérable: ces raisons sont sans replique.

LUCILE

Elles doivent être bien foibles, mon pere, contre le désespoir où vous me voyez: de grace, laissez-vous attendrir; je vous conjure à genoux de ne me point réduire aux dernières extrémités.

Mr ORONTE

Mais, mais voyez un peu la petite opiniâtre! Marton, que dis tu d'une pareille desobéïssance?

LUCILE

Ah, mon pere! je[b] m'en raporte à elle; si elle me condamne, je me rends.

Mr ORONTE

Elle a trop de raison pour ne le pas faire.

LUCILE

Oüi, mon pere, elle a toute la raison possible, & je consens qu'elle décide entre vous & moi: parle, ma chere Marton, parle, je t'en conjure; est-il juste que je me sacrifie...

---

[a] Ms premieres

[b] T2, T3 si je m'en raporte

MARTON

Oüi, il est juste que Monsieur soit le Maître; & c'est à vous de trouver vôtre amant dans l'époux qu'il vous destine.

LUCILE

O Ciel! Marton me trahit!

MARTON

Marton ne vous trahit point, elle vous sert: & je sçais mieux que vous-même ce ce qu'il vous faut.

LUCILE

Ah mon pere! n'écoutez point ses[a] discours; & laissez-vous toucher par mes larmes.

MARTON *à Mr Oronte*

Tenez bon, Monsieur, point de féblesse[b] .

LUCILE

Ne me condamnez point à un engagement si funeste; & laissez-moi plutôt demeurer fille toute ma vie.

MARTON

Hé mort de ma vie[12] ! est ce que cela se peut?

---

[a] T2, T3 ces

[b] Ms faiblesses

12. Mort de ma vie. 'On dit innocemment et populairement *Mort* de ma vie, *Mort* non pas de ma vie' (Furetière).

LUCILE

Pouriez-vous m'envier la douceur de passer mes jours auprès de vous? Songez que vous n'avez qu'une fille.

MARTON

Hé que diantre! avez vous plus d'un pere? Mais courage, Monsieur; vous molissez, je pense?

Mr ORONTE

Je ne molis point, Marton; & je n'ai jamais êté si ferme dans mes résolutions.

LUCILE *à Marton*

Ah, cruelle! c'est de toi que j'attendois du secours, & c'est toi qui me désespères!

MARTON

Vous me faites pitié, je l'avoüe; mais l'avenir me rassûre; & quand vous connoîtrez celui que nous voulons[a] vous donner...

LUCILE

Ah! je n'ai que faire de le connoître! je suis sûre de le détester toute ma vie... mais mon pere, voyez Eraste; ses biens & sa famille vous convenoient: sa présence vous détermineroit peut-être.

---

[a] Ms qu'on veut

MARTON

La présence de Monsieur de Spadagnac vous déterminera, vous.

LUCILE

Ah! ce nom seul est un coup de poignard pour moi!

MARTON

Hé bien! nous le nommerons Eraste, s'il ne tient qu'à cela!

LUCILE

Tu redoubles encore mon aversion pour son[a] rival!

MARTON

Tant mieux, mort de ma vie[b], tant mieux.

Mr ORONTE

Comment donc, tant mieux?

MARTON

Oüi, Monsieur, la voila dans les plus hûreuses dispositions du monde pour être mariée!

Mr ORONTE

Mais, mais tu n'y penses pas?

---

[a] T3 un rival (T2 *imprime* on.)

[b] Ms Tant mieux, morbleu

MARTON

Si fait[13], vraiment, j'y pense; & c'est l'horreur qu'elle paroît avoir pour ce que vous lui proposez, qui me fait juger du plaisir qu'elle en aura.

Mr ORONTE

Mais encore une fois, je crois que tu perds l'esprit!

MARTON

Ho! ne vous y trompez pas! en fait de sentiments, & de sentiments de mariage sur tout, j'en juge toujours contre l'aparence, c'est le plus sûr. Mais on entre, c'est le Valet de Monsieur de Spadagnac.

SCENE IV

Mr ORONTE, LUCILE, MARTON, FRONTIN.

FRONTIN

Bonnes nouvelles, Monsieur, bonnes nouvelles! j'ai trouvé mon Maître, en vous quittant: je vous l'anonce; il vient sur mes pas.

Mr ORONTE

J'en suis ravi, Frontin; & nous allons le recevoir avec joïe.

---

13. Cette locution, qui revient souvent dans le discours des personnages de Boindin, est caractérisée, avec *Si est*, *Si ferai* et *Si ferai-je*, comme des 'façons de parler basses [...], dont on se sert quand on répond en affirmant', par Furetière ('Si').

LUCILE

Non, je ne puis attendre sa présence...

Mr ORONTE

Demeurez, s'il vous plaît, Lucile.

FRONTIN

Elle tremble pour son cœur! oh cadédis[14] ! elle a raison; il ne tiendra pas long-temps devant mon Maître!

Mr ORONTE

Ne perdons point de temps, Frontin: va chercher le Notaire; & fais venir nos Musiciens.

LUCILE

Quoi, mon pere, vous auriez la dureté...

Mr ORONTE

Voyez, voyez avant que de vous plaindre: peut-être que Monsieur de Spadagnac... mais le voici, je pense.

---

14. Ch. Mazouer signale que 'd'entrée, le Gascon fait résonner quelquè «cadédis» ou quelque «sandis»', et que les jurons pullulent dans leurs discours, *loc. cit.*, p. 93.

SCENE V.

Mr ORONTE, LUCILE, ERASTE,
MARTON.

ERASTE *avec les habits de Mr de Spadagnac, & parlant Gascon.*

Ah! Monsieur Oronte! vous voyez un homme qui seroit vénu du bout du monde, pour être vôtre gendre! qué jé vous embrasse en cette qualité...

Mr ORONTE

Ah![a] de tout mon cœur...

ERASTE

Encore cette fois, pour Monsieur vôtre frere...

Mr ORONTE

J'ai reçû de ses nouvelles; il me mande[15] vôtre arrivée: ma fille, qu'elle contenance est ce là? saluez Monsieur de Spadagnac.

ERASTE

Mon accent lui fait peur peut-être? mais patience, nous lé perdrons bien-tôt en sa faveur.

---

[a] Ms *omet* Ah!

15. Mander. Faire savoir, annoncer ; 'Tu tiens ces nouvelles de mon oncle [...] à qui mon père les a mandées par une lettre?', Molière, *Fourberies*, I, 1 ; J. Dubois, R. Lagane et A. Lerond, *Dictionnaire du français classique* (ci-après, DFC).

LUCILE

Ah Ciel! que vois-je?

ERASTE

Je vous étonne, n'est-ce pas? je m'en doutois bien: on né vous a pas prévenuë; l'ajustement, la personne, tout vous surprend? là, là, remettez-vous[a] .

MARTON

On seroit surprise à moins, Monsieur; mais je répondrois bien que le plaisir passe encore la surprise.

ERASTE

Cette fille a dé l'esprit! elle est à vous? jé la veux payer dé sa galanterie: tien, mon enfant, choisi; prens cé diamant, ou qué jé t'embrasse.

MARTON *prenant le diamant.*

Je sçais trop mon devoir, Monsieur, pour ne m'en pas tenir à la moindre de vos offres. Hé bien, Mademoiselle? augurois-je mal de cette entrevûë?

Mr ORONTE

Qu'en dis-tu, Lucile?

LUCILE

Je vous avoüerai, mon pere, que je ne m'attendois à rien moins qu'à ce que je vois.

---

[a] Ms *omet* là, là, remettez-vous.

Mr ORONTE

N'est-ce pas?

LUCILE

Je m'êtois fait par une prévention dont je n'êtois pas la maîtresse, une idée afreuse de l'époux que vous me destiniez, & je craignois de détourner les yeux sur Monsieur, de peur d'y trouver dequoi irriter[16] mon aversion; mais toute cette horreur s'est bien dissipée à sa vûë, & vous me voyez confuse d'avoir été si long-temps rebelle à vos volontés.

Mr ORONTE

Ah, voila les sentiments que je demandois de toi!

ERASTE

Point dé déguisement, Mademoiselle; il a fallu donner[17] quelque chose au païs: mon accent, mes manières lui appartiennent; connoissez cé qui est à moi, mes sentiments: jé né veux point vous devoir à l'autorité d'un pere; si vous m'aimez, à la bonne heure, unissons-nous, vivons hûreux: si vous en aimez un autre, jé vous céde, & jé murs!

LUCILE

Je ne vous déguiserai point, Monsieur, que j'ai déja

16. Irriter. Exciter : 'Enfin épargnez-moi ces tristes entretiens, Qui ne font qu'irriter vos tourments et les miens' ; Corneille, *Polyeucte*, v. 544; DFC.

17. Donner. Attribuer : 'Et l'on pourrait donner à la nécessité, Ce qui n'est que l'effet de la légèreté' ; Corneille, *Pertharite*, v. 365 ; DFC.

senti une passion violente pour un certain Eraste, dont le respect & la tendresse m'avoient charmée.

Mr ORONTE *bas à Lucile*

Ne parle point de cela, ma fille...

LUCILE

Non, mon pere, Monsieur ne prétend pas que je lui déguise rien[18] ; & je suis sûre que ma franchise lui fera plaisir.

ERASTE

Oüi, oüi, comptez qué jé prends bien la chose.

LUCILE

J'aimois Eraste, nous nous êtions promis un attachement inviolable; & il avoit tout lieu de croire que rien ne pouroit jamais l'éfacer de mon cœur.

ERASTE

Vous mé charmez, Dieu mé damne! il mé semble être cet Eraste!

LUCILE

Mais tout ce que j'ai jamais senti pour lui, je le sens

18. Selon le DFC, le sens de 'quelque chose' subsistait dans les phrases négatives, dubitatives ou interrogatives, ce qui fait comprendre son emploi en même temps que la négation complète; cf. Vaugelas, *Nouvelles Remarques*, p. 69, 'Observation', et, pour une explication de son emploi avec la négation complète, A. Haase, *Syntaxe française*, § 51.

en ce moment pour vous, & je ne m'aperçois pas même en cela que je change: je vous aime comme si j'êtois dans l'habitude de vous aimer; & je jurerois n'avoir jamais que vous.

ERASTE

Oh, vous n'y perdez rien, jé vous jure: & jé défierois cet Eraste même de vous aimer plus que jé le fais.

Mr ORONTE

Ils m'attendrissent, Marton!

ERASTE

Au reste, Monsieur Oronte, je vous démande Lucile tout de nouveau; point d'égards, en me l'accordant: comptez que jé n'ai jamais vû Monsieur vôtre frere, que jé ne suis point de la famille des Spadagnacs[a] ; détachez-moi de tout, isolez-moi: mé voulez-vous pour gendre?

Mr ORONTE

Ah, Monsieur, je n'envisage que vôtre personne; & vous me faites trop d'honneur...

ERASTE

Bien donc! un Notaire, & nous serons tous contents.

---

[a] Ms Spadagnac

Scene VI

Mr ORONTE, LUCILE, ERASTE
MARTON, LA ROZE[19]

LA ROZE

Monsieur de Spadagnac, Monsieur.[a]

Mr ORONTE

Comment! Monsieur de Spadagnac? hé, le voila!

LA ROZE

N'importe, Monsieur, c'est encore lui.

MARTON *à la Roze*

Va, va, dis-lui qu'il se trompe.

LA ROZE

Vous lui direz vous-même[20] , Madame Marton.

---

[a] Ms ajoute : ERASTE *bas*, Ah Marton !

19. La pratique qui consistait à 'rebaptiser' les domestiques en leur donnant un nom tiré du domaine botanique était courante à l'époque ; voir S. Maza, *Servants and Masters* , p. 176.

20. Selon A. Haase, le pronom de la troisième personne à l'accusatif servant de complément direct, et précédant un autre pronom au datif (le plus souvent celui de la troisième personne), pouvait être omis dans l'ancienne langue, qui considérait le nom qu'il remplaçait comme suffisamment présent à l'esprit ; *op. cit.*, § 4.

MARTON *à Mr Oronte*

Vous verrez que c'est quelque flaireur de dot qui voudroit vous escamoter[a] celle de Lucile!

Mr ORONTE

Il y a bien de l'aparence, Marton.

MARTON *à Eraste*

Au moins, Monsieur, ne vous déconcertez point; soutenez la gageure.

SCENE VII

Mr ORONTE, LUCILE, MARTON
ERASTE, Mr DE SPADAGNAC

Mr DE SPADAGNAC *en bottes*

Vous estes Monsieur Oronte? serviteur; & le cur mé dit que c'est là Lucile? son valet: allons, beau pere, point de rétardement; il faut que je l'epouse en bottes[b21] .

Mr ORONTE

Il est inutile...

---

[a] Ms vouloit vous excroquer

[b] Ms retardement, épousons.

21. Précipitation burlesque tout à fait contraire aux usages traditionnels complexes qui marquaient le mariage réel au dix-huitième siècle : voir F. Lebrun, *La Vie conjugale sous l'Ancien Régime*, p. 37-48.

Mr DE SPADAGNAC

Comment inutile! non, dé par tous les diables, les amours Gascons sont pressés: Concluons.

Mr ORONTE

Il est inutile, vous dis-je, de continuer ce personnage; vous venez un peu trop tard, pour nous surprendre[a].

Mr DE SPADAGNAC

Qu'est-ce à dire?

MARTON

Que vous estes un fourbe, un fripon dont on sçait des nouvelles, & pour qui il ne fait pas bon icy[22] .

Mr DE SPADAGNAC

Comment donc? fourbe, fripon! beau pere, où sont vous fénêtres?

ERASTE

Crains qu'on né té l'aprenne, l'ami: tu pourois bien né pas sortir par ailleurs.

Mr DE SPADAGNAC

Ah, jé reconois lé stile! hé donc, mon païs[23], apren moy qui tu peux estre?

---

[a] Ms pour nous tromper

22. Il fait bon. Avantageux ; 'Vous voulez parler à un tel seigneur, il est seul, il y fait bon' (Académie, 1694), cité DFC.

23. Païs. Compatriote (terme familier ou régional).

ERASTE

Jé suis l'amant de Lucile, j'en suis aimé, je l'épouse; voila mon nom, ma noblesse, & ma fortune.

Mr DE SPADAGNAC

Ah, j'entens, beau pere! vous couriez deux gendres à la fois?

Mr ORONTE

Je n'y comprens rien, Marton!

MARTON *à Mr de Spadagnac*

Eh, ne devinez-vous pas, Monsieur l'imposteur, que c'est là Monsieur de Spadagnac à qui vous prétendiez escamoter[a] Lucile?

Mr DE SPADAGNAC

Vous riez?

MARTON

Je ne ris point[b] .

Mr DE SPADAGNAC

Luy, Spadagnac?

MARTON

Oüy, luy-même.

---

[a] Ms enlever

[b] Ms *Les deux dernières répliques n'y figurent pas.*

Mr DE SPADAGNAC *à Eraste*

Eh, qui diable, mon amy, t'a fouré dans nostre famille?

ERASTE

Jé ne me compromets plus[24] : Monsieur mé connoît; & jé puis m'épargner la peine de té confondre.

Mr ORONTE

Ma foy, Messieurs, cette avanture me confond moy-même; car enfin l'un de vous deux est un fripon, & l'autre doit estre mon gendre: vous trouverez bon, s'il vous plaît, que j'aprofondisse les choses.

ERASTE *tirant un portrait de sa poche*[a].

Soit, Monsieur Oronte, & puis qu'il vous faut des preuves: connoissez-vous ce portrait?

Mr ORONTE

C'est celuy que j'envoyay à Monsieur de Spadagnac.

Mr DE SPADAGNAC *en tirant un autre.*

Eh donc! cette peinture! que sera-t-elle?

Mr ORONTE *les regardant tous deux.*

C'est la même chose; la boëte & le portrait[b], tout est semblable: je ne sçais que croire...

---

[a] Ms *Cette didascalie et les deux suivantes n'y figurent pas.*

[b] Ms le portrait et la boete

24. Se compromettre. S'abaisser ; le DFC cite l'exemple apparenté de l'Académie (1694) : 'Mettre la dignité, l'autorité de quelqu'un en compromis'.

Mr DE SPADAGNAC

Vous en croirez du moins le raport de Frontin? hola quelqu'un! qu'on me lé cherche.

Mr ORONTE

Comment! Frontin seroit-il aussi votre valet?

Mr DE SPADAGNAC

Non, c'est moy qui seray le valet de Frontin[25] ! Hé morbleu, n'est-ce pas par mon ordre qu'il est auprès dé vous?

Mr ORONTE

Je m'y perds, Marton!

ERASTE *à Mr de Spadagnac.*[a]

C'en est trop; sortons: C'est à nous dé montrer qui nous sommes.

Mr DE SPADAGNAC

Oüy, sors dé par tous les diables! sors; c'est ce que je demande.

ERASTE *en sortant.*

C'est assez.

---

[a] Ms *omet la didascalie.*

25. Adaptation burlesque de la formule de dénégation normale : 'je suis votre valet'.

Mr DE SPADAGNAC *à Mr Oronte.*

Il fait bien d'échaper! Est-il possible, beau pere, que vous ayez esté un moment la dupe de cet impostur?

ERASTE *revenant sur ses pas.*[a]

Quoi, lâche! tu ne mé suis pas?

Mr DE SPADAGNAC

Te voila encore, je pense? oh parbleu! tu sortiras mort ou vif!

Mr ORONTE

Point de desordre chez moi, Messieurs de Spadagnac: vous me devez au moins ce respect, sous le nom que vous prenez tous deux.

Mr DE SPADAGNAC

Non, dé par tous les diables! jé viens exprès de Bordeaux; on m'a donné des paroles: il faut que j'épouse.

ERASTE

Mon nom m'est moins cher que cé que j'aime; sois Spadagnac, si tu veux: mais sois sûr qu'on né peut obtenir Lucile, qu'après ma mort.

---

[a] Ms *omet la didascalie.*

SCENE VIII.

Mr ORONTE, LUCILE, MARTON
ERASTE, Mr DE SPADAGNAC,
FRONTIN.

Mr ORONTE

Ah! voici Frontin, tout à propos!

FRONTIN

Oüi, Monsieur, je viens de chez le Notaire[a]... mais que vois-je? mon maître!

Mr DE SPADAGNAC

Ah parbleu, Monsieur Oronte! vous allez avoir des preuves; j'en répond sur ses oreilles!

MARTON *à Frontin*

Ne nous trahi point, Frontin; il y va de moi.

Mr DE SPADAGNAC *le tirant à lui.*[b]

Vénez çà, Monsieur lé coquin, vénez çà[26].

FRONTIN

Hé bien, Messieurs! dequoi s'agit-il?

---

[a] Ms je viens de tout disposer ... mais

[b] Ms tirant à luy frontin [*sic*]

26. Çà. Ici ; cf. 'Oui, venez çà, avancez là' ; *Le Malade imaginaire*, II, 8.

Mr ORONTE

De m'apprendre sur l'heure qui des deux est ton maître!

Mr DE SPADAGNAC

Oüi, parle, pendart! ne mé servois-tu pas à Bordeaux? & n'est-ce pas par mon ordre, qué tu ès ici?

FRONTIN

Il est vrai, mais...

Mr DE SPADAGNAC *le menaçant*

Heïm!

FRONTIN

Je vous dis, Monsieur, que j'en conviens.

ERASTE *à Frontin*[a]

Comment, coquin! tu n'ès donc pas à moi?

FRONTIN *se sauvant vers Eraste*[b]

Si fait, vraiment: cela n'empêche pas; & c'est à vous de me deffendre.

Mr DE SPADAGNAC *le retirant à lui*[c]

Avouë, traitre, avouë! ne té dois-je pas encore tous tes gages?

---

[a] Ms *le tirant à luy*

[b] Ms *omet la didascalie.*

[c] Ms *le menaçant*

FRONTIN

D'accord, Monsieur; point de violence: je suis prêt à les recevoir.

ERASTE *à Frontin*

Et moi, maraut? ne t'ai-je pas payé les tiens d'avance?

FRONTIN

Il est vrai; me voulez-vous encore avancer quelque chose[27] ?

Mr DE SPADAGNAC *tirant l'épée sur lui*[a]

Oh, répons autrement, traitre! ou je té mutile[b]...

ERASTE *ayant aussi la sienne à la main*[c]

Oüi, décide maraut, décide; où je té rends nul[d][28]

---

[a] Ms *mettant l'epée a* [*sic*] *la main*

[b] Ms ou je t'estropie

[c] Ms *tirant aussi la sienne*

[d] Ms ou je te perce

27. Elégante caricature qui combine la lâcheté, la vénalité et la cupidité que la classe des maîtres associait normalement au personnage du serviteur ; voir J. Emelina, *op. cit.*, p. 226-227 et C. Fairchilds, *op. cit.*, p. 144-150.

28. Nul. 'Je suis *nul*, vous êtes *nul*, pour dire, nous allons perir' (Furetière).

FRONTIN *se jettant à genoux entre eux deux, & tournant la tête alternativement vers l'un, & vers l'autre.*[a]

Hé, de grace, Messieurs! je vous dis les choses comme elles sont: vous m'avez envoyé ici; je suis à vous: je vous attendois; je vous ai annoncé, j'ai fait préparer des habits pour votre mariage; & je viens de chez le Notaire pour vous. Il me semble qu'il n'y a rien de plus positif.

Mr ORONTE

Oh, je n'y puis plus tenir! Frontin! tu ès un extravagant, ou un fripon, ou le diable s'en mesle!

FRONTIN *en se relevant.*[b]

Que voulez-vous, Monsieur? le moyen de parler raison, devant des épées nuës?

MARTON *à Frontin.*[c]

C'est donc ainsi, scélérat, que tu fais ton devoir? tu n'oses t'expliquer ouvertement pour ton maître? va, ne me regarde plus; je ne veux point d'un traitre.

Mr DE SPADAGNAC *tirant encore l'épee.*

Mortbleu, c'est trop hésiter! il faut que j'éface cé maraut du nombre des vivants...

---

[a] Ms *... entre eux, et tournant tour a* [*sic*] *tour la teste vers l'un et vers l'autre.*

[b] Ms *se relevant.*

[c] Ms *omet cette didascalie et la suivante.*

FRONTIN *se sauvant derrière*[a] *Eraste.*

Miséricorde![b]

Mr DE SPADAGNAC

Tu m'échapes, pendart? mais jé t'aprendrai ton devoir!

FRONTIN

Mortbleu![c] je ne vous dois rien; c'est vous qui me devez.

Mr DE SPADAGNAC *courant à lui.*[d]

Quoi, je soufrirai qué mon valet...

FRONTIN *tenant Eraste par la basque.*

Votre valet, vous -même: je ne reconnois point d'autre maître que Monsieur, puis qu'il faut le dire; & je n'ai jamais rien reçû de vous.

Mr DE SPADAGNAC

Va, va, tu récévras, je t'en répons... mais Monsieur Oronte, c'est à vous que jé me prends de tout cé qui m'arive ici; & jé m'en vais vous chercher des gens qui vous aprendront qui jé suis[e].

---

[a] Ms *vers*

[b] Ms Ah miséricorde !

[c] Ms Morbleu Monsieur, je

[d] Ms *omet la didascalie.*

[e] Ms ce qui m'arrive icy, et vous aprendrez a [*sic*] respecter le nom de Spadagnac. *Les dernières répliques de cette scène ne figurent pas dans le manuscrit.*

ERASTE *feignant de le suivre*

A la bonne heure.

Mr DE SPADAGNAC

Quoi, tu mé suis encore? oh parbleu, choisi! céde moi la place, ou demeure ici.

ERASTE

Vous voyez bien, Monsieur Oronte, qu'il sé bat en retraite!

Mr ORONTE

Oüi, oüi, je vois bien que c'est un fripon; & je ne doute plus que vous ne soyez mon gendre.

SCENE IX[a]

Mr ORONTE, LUCILE, ERASTE, MARTON, FRONTIN, LA ROZE

LA ROZE

Encore un Monsieur de Spadagnac, Monsieur.

Mr ORONTE *lui donnant un souflet*[29].

Encore le diable qui t'emporte!

---

[a] Ms *Cette scène est biffée dans le manuscrit. La dernière réplique comporte une phrase qui ne figure pas dans T1* : point entrer : mais Marton, on nous joue Et [*sic*] il faut me vanger de tout cecy.

29. Violence habituelle dans les comédies de l'époque ; cf. sa fréquence dans le théâtre de Molière ; voir J. Truchet et A. Couprie, 'Inventaire thématique' § 507, 'Gifles', in J. Truchet, *Thématique de Molière*, p. 259.

LA ROZE

Dame, Monsieur! est-ce ma faute s'il s'apelle comme ça?

Mr ORONTE

Di lui qu'il en a menti, butor; & ne le laisse point entrer.

SCENE X [a]

Mr ORONTE, LUCILE, ERASTE, MARTON, FRONTIN, JULIE *en habit d'homme, & se donnant pour Mr de Spadagnac*

---

[a] Ms *La scène ix est suivie d'une 'scène dernière', partiellement biffée. Les personnages et la didascalie sont les mêmes que ceux qui figurent dans la scène x de T1* :

[*biffé*] LA ROZE, à Julie

Non non vous n'entrerez point, Mr de Spadagnac Mon Maistre menvoye vous dire que ce n'est point vous.

JULIE luy donnant un souflet

Tien, mon amy te voila payé de ta commission.

LA ROZE Ouy da, des souflets ; nous verrons.

JULIE luy donnant un coup de pied au cul

Ah tu n'es point content, prens encore.

Mr de SPADAGNAC a part

Ah ciel ! que vois-je ? c'est Julie !

Mr ORONTE Comment donc monsieur, en use ton ainsy

JULIE Ouy bon homme ; autant a gagner pour quiconque osera me contester le nom de Spadagnac.

Mr ORONTE Quoy ! vous osez soutenir que ce nom vous apartient ?

JULIE Sil m'apartient ! Ah ouy de par tous les diables Et je

LA ROZE *à Julie.*

Non, non, vous n'entrerez point, Monsieur de Spadagnac; mon maître m'envoye... vous dire que ce n'est point vous.

JULIE *lui donnant un souflet.*

Tien, mon ami, té voila payé dé ta commission.

Mr ORONTE *à Julie.*

Comment donc, Monsieur! en use-t'on ainsi?

JULIE

Oüi, bon homme, autant à gagner pour quiconque osera mé contester lé nom de Spadagnac.

ERASTE

Quoi! vous osez-nous soutenir que cé nom vous apartient?

JULIE

S'il m'apartient[30] ? ah oüi, de par tous les diables!

(suite a)
ne quitte [*sic*] qu'avec la vie : mon honneur en depend. [*Fin des ratures.*]

Mr ORONTE Mais enfin quel est votre dessein et que venez vous chercher icy ?

JULIE Un fourbe, un imposteur ... [*Ici le texte du manuscrit rejoint celui de la scène dernière de T1.*] ah te voila perfide, Il faut que je t'etrangle.

30. On aura remarqué que Boindin utilise très souvent la reprise des mots pour assurer l'enchaînement de la conversation.

j'en ai de bons titres; & c'est par moi sule qu'il doit s'éterniser.

Mr ORONTE

Mais enfin, que venez-vous chercher ici?

JULIE

Cé que j'y viens chercher? ah, demandez à Frontin.

FRONTIN

A moi, Mad...

JULIE

Oüi, parle, maraut! n'êtois-tu pas à moi? & n'est-ce pas sur tes avis que jé me suis renduë ici?

FRONTIN

Il est vray, Monsieur, j'en conviens.

Mr ORONTE

Oh pour le coup, Marton, je ne sçais plus où j'en suis.

ERASTE

Jé ne crois pas néanmoins, Monsieur Oronte, que vous balanciez un moment, entre moy & cet homme?

JULIE

Cet homme! on voit bien, mon ami, que tu ne sçais encore à qui tu parles! cet homme!

ERASTE

Va, qui que tu sois, éloigne-toi d'ici; & qu'il té suffise que tu n'es pas lé fait de Lucile.

JULIE

Je né suis pas son fait? hé qui diable, te l'a dit?

ERASTE

En tout autre lieu, jé té l'aprendrois au péril de ta vie.

JULIE

La Gasconnade en est? ah j'en suis ravie! hé, sçais-tu bien, mon ami, qu'on n'a jamais vaincu d'homme fait comme moi?

ERASTE

Nous lé verrions à l'épreuve, si nous n'êtions pas ici.

JULIE

Oh, ne mé pousse point à bout; tu ne mé connois pas encore: jé suis un diable!

FRONTIN *bas à Eraste.*

Autant vaut[31] , elle est femme... c'est nôtre heroïne de Bordeaux.

JULIE *à Frontin.*

Que lui dis-tu, maraut? qué lui dis-tu?

31. Entendre 'en quelque sorte' ; voir DFC, 'Valoir'.

FRONTIN *bas à Julie.*

Je vous dis que c'est là l'amant de Lucile; & que je le fais passer pour Monsieur de Spadagnac, afin de vous conserver le véritable qui vient de sortir d'ici.

JULIE

Ah parbleu, Monsieur Oronte! il mé vient une idée: cet homme vient pour épouser Lucile: Vous avez lieu de croire que lé même dessein m'ameine: hé cadédis! puisque cela la regarde, c'est à son cœur à décider.

ERASTE

Volontiers; c'est de son cœur que je veux ténir tous mes droits.

JULIE *à Lucile*

C'est donc à vous dé parler, la belle; né confions point vôtre sort aux armes: que sçait-on? peut-être que celui qui vous conviendroit le moins seroit lé vainqueur: né risquons rien, tout y est encore, choisissez!

Mr ORONTE

Non, non, il faut qu'elle épouse Monsieur de Spadagnac; & je veux connoître le véritable.

JULIE

Hé, qu'importe? est-ce un nom qu'il lui faut? c'est un homme, dé par tous les diables!

Mr ORONTE *à Julie.*

Franchement, Monsieur, vous m'avez bien l'air d'être un fourbe, & de vous entendre avec celui qui vient de sortir.

JULIE

Oh, vous vous trompez, jé vous jure; & jé veux l'attendre ici, pour lé confondre devant vous.

Mr ORONTE

Tenez, le voici qui revient tout à propos.

SCENE DERNIERE

Mr ORONTE, LUCILE, ERASTE,
MARTON, FRONTIN, JULIE,
Mr DE SPADAGNAC

Mr DE SPADAGNAC

Il faut que jé sois lé plus désastré[32] des mortels! je n'ai pû trouver personne... mais que vois-je? Julie!

JULIE *à M. de Spadagnac.*

Ah, té voila, perfide! il faut que jé t'étrangle!

Mr ORONTE *à Julie.*

Tout beau, tout beau, Monsieur! vous n'y pensez pas!

JULIE

Ecoutez, Monsieur Oronte, vous n'avez qu'à voir si vous avez top d'une vie; mais c'est fait de vous si vous acceptez cet homme pour gendre!

32. Entendre 'infortuné'.

Mr DE SPADAGNAC *à part.*

Ah Morbleu! quel contre-temps!

JULIE *à Lucile*

Et vous, la belle, vous n'avez qu'à vous pourvoir ailleurs; ou morbleu, point de quartier, vous aurez affaire[33] à moi[a].

FRONTIN *bas à Marton.*

C'est nôtre amazone, au moins[b].

JULIE *à Mr de Spadagnac.*

Et toi, né pense pas m'échaper, traître! Frontin m'a mandé tes desseins: j'ai crevé plus dé dix chevaux, pour les prévénir; & me voici[c] enfin pour mé vanger dé ta perfidie, ou t'obliger à mé rendre ta foi.

Mr ORONTE

Comment, sa foi!

Mr DE SPADAGNAC *à Julie.*[d]

Eh! qui diable té l'ôte? jé t'aime, jé t'adore, jé t'ido-

---

[a] Ms ... à moi. Je suis un diable.

[b] Ms *Phrase remplacée par* Autant vaut, elle est femme.

[c] Ms voila

[d] Ms *omet la didascalie.*

33. Le mot 'affaire' (ou 'affaire d'honneur') désignait normalement un duel à l'époque, mais le DFC note son emploi fréquent et son sens assez vague à la fin du dix-septième siècle ; *loc. cit.*, p. 15 B.

latre: entre amants délicats, s'embarasse-t'on du reste? je n'épouse, Dieu mé damne, que lé bien de Lucile!

JULIE

Quoi, lâche! l'intérêt té feroit trahir ta parole? non, né croi pas que je le soufre; ni que jé m'en tienne au dédit que tu m'as fait: avec une fille comme moi, point d'autre dédit, que la mort.

Mr DE SPADAGNAC

Point de dédit, Julie; mais donne-moi au moins lé temps...

JULIE[a]

Non, non, choisi sur l'heure: rend-moi ton cœur, ou défend toi! il faut que jé t'épouse, ou que jé te tuë!

Mr DE SPADAGNAC

Hé bien, touche là[b]; va, j'accepte ta bravoure pour dot; & je t'avoüe pour Madame de Spadagnac.

Mr ORONTE

Pour Madame de Spadagnac?

JULIE

Oüi, Monsieur Oronte, il n'est plus temps dé feindre; c'est là le vrai Spadagnac: demandez à Frontin.

---

[a] Ms JULIE *tirant lépée* [*sic*]

[b] Ms He bien a la bonne heure . va,

Mr ORONTE *à Frontin.*[a]

Que répons-tu à cela, maraut?

FRONTIN *montrant Eraste.*

Moi? je veux tout ce qu'on veut: demandez à Monsieur.

Mr ORONTE *à Eraste.*

Comment, c'est donc vous qui vouliez nous tromper?

ERASTE

Au contraire, Monsieur; & il suffit de vous dire que je suis Eraste...[b]

Mr ORONTE

Eraste?

LUCILE

Oüi, mon pere, c'est lui-même, & je vous conjure de ne vous point oposer à nôtre bon heur.

MARTON

Allons, Monsieur, cédez à l'amour paternel; aussi-bien Monsieur de Spadagnac dégage t'il vôtre parole?

---

[a] Ms *omet la didascalie.*

[b] Ms que je suis Eraste pour vous donner une autre Idée.
Mr ORONTE Quoy, ce seroit vous ...
LUCILE Oui, mon pere, c'est

Mr DE SPADAGNAC

Oüi, Monsieur Oronte; je vous abandonne à la roture: Voila celle que j'annoblis.

Mr ORONTE

C'en est donc fait, Monsieur Eraste, vous êtes mon gendre: envoyons chercher Monsieur vôtre oncle; & nous dresserons les articles.

JULIE.

Qu'on grifonne nôtre contract en même temps: vous lé voulez bien, Monsieur Oronte? allons, bonne chere, & dé la joye, pour mé délasser!

FRONTIN

Voici tout à propos nos Basques, & nos Gasconnes: nous n'avons qu'à nous divertir; & vous, Monsieur, qu'à payer; voici le mémoire?

Mr DE SPADAGNAC

Je né prens pas garde à ces bagatelles; dançons toujours!

DES BISCAYENS & DES GASCONES[a]

joüant du tambour de Basque[34], & accompagnés de

---

[a] Ms *Le divertissement n'y figure pas.*

34. Le tambour de Basque 'est un petit tambour qui n'est enfoncé que par un bout en forme de sas ou de crible, & qui a des sonnettes ou petites plaques de cuivre enchassées dans les fentes faites dans son corps pour faire du bruit. Les Bohémiens s'en servent en dansant leurs sarabandes' (Furetière).

haut-bois, viennent se joindre à la compagnie, & forment avec elle un divertissement coupé de dances & de Chansons. Après leur marche,

FRONTIN chante.

Vivent les bords de la Garonne,
La pépinière des Cézars!

Le Chœur repette.

Vivent les bords de la Garonne,
La pépinière des Cézars!

FRONTIN

On y brave tous les hazards,
Et de l'amour, & de Bellone[35] *:*
Vivent les bords de la Garonne,
La pépinière des Cézars!

Le Chœur

Vivent les bords de la Garonne,
La pépinière des Cézars!

FRONTIN

Tout Gascon est mignon de Mars;
Toute Gasconne est amazone:
Vivent les bords de la Garone,
La pépinière des Cézars!

---

35. Déesse romaine de la guerre.

Le Chœur

Vivent les bords de la Garone,
La pépinière des Cézars!

Les Basques & les Gasconnes dancent une entrée, après laquelle on chante les paroles suivantes.

Mr DE SPADAGNAC

Ma foi, lé mérite est un sot:
Chacun mé court, lé sexe me jalouse;
Et tous les cœurs sont du complot:
J'ai beau fuir, enfin jé mé blouse[36] *;*
J'aime, jé m'engage, j'épouse:
Ma foi, lé mérite est un sot.

LUCILE

Laissez gronder l'amour volage,
Contre le nœud qui vous engage:
L'himen seul a dequoi remplir tous vos desirs;
Et si l'amour a des plaisirs,
Il les dérobe au mariage.

JULIE à Mr de Spadagnac

Qu l'himen & l'amour se rassemblent pour nous:
Soyons encore amants, en devenant époux;
Nos desirs satisfaits doivent toujours renaître:
Brûlons toujours des mêmes feux;
Que le droit de nous rendre hûreux,
N'ôte rien au plaisir que nous aurons de l'être.

---

36. 'Se Blouser signifie figurément, se tromper, échouer, prendre mal ses mesures dans ses affaires, ou dans ses marchez, n'y reüssir pas : mais ce terme est populaire' (Furetière).

Julie dance ensuite un menuet, après lequel on chante les trois Airs suivants; le premier avec un accompagnement de hautbois; le second avec des simphonies Italiennes, & le troisième avec des pointes de trompettes.

FRONTIN

Après avoir blessé les belles,
L'amour est prêt à s'envoler;
Pour l'empécher de s'en aller,
L'himen doit lui couper les aîles.

LUCILE

Ardir' è speranza
Ci vuol' in amor';
Valor' è constanza
Debellann' un cor';
Ardir' è speranza
Ci vuol' in amor'...

JULIE

Point de quartier, il faut se batre;
Ou me promettre un cœur constant:
J'aime moi seule comme quatre;
Mais si l'on ne m'en rend autant,
Point de quartier, il faut se batre.

Les Basques & les Gasconnes dancent ensuite le branle, sur lequel on chante les couplets suivants.

FRONTIN

La Garonne n'a pas vû naître
Tous les Gascons qui sont ici;

En tous lieux il s'en fait connaître;
Et sur tout en ce païs ci:
La Garonne n'a pas vû naître
Tous les Gascons qui sont ici.

LUCILE

Tel de nos cœurs se dit le maître,
Que nous accablons de souci;
La Garonne n'a pas vû naître
Tous les Gascons qui sont ici.

FRONTIN

En fait d'amour, tout petit maître
Se pique d'en user ainsi;
La Garonne n'a pas vû naître
Tous les Gascons qui sont ici.

JULIE

Que de plumets on voit paraître,
Qui font leur campagne à Passi!
La Garonne n'a pas vû naître
Tous les Gascons qui sont ici.

FRONTIN au Parterre

Chacun se fait honneur de l'être;
Nous le sommes par fois aussi:
La Garonne n'a pas vû naître
Tous les Gascons qui sont ici.

FIN

LE BAL

D'AUTEUIL

COMEDIE.

ACTEURS

DU PROLOGUE

Mr MAIGRET Marchand,	Bourgeois d'Auteüil.
Mr DE LA FAQUINIERE,	

LE BAILLI d'Auteüil.

La Scène est dans le Parterre de la Comédie.

Le Théatre représente un Bal de Campagne. On voit d'un côté, des Païsans & des Païsannes; de l'autre des Scaramouches & des Arlequines: plusieurs groupes de masques en éloignement; & de part & d'autre, des violons, des hautbois, & des musettes sur des arbres.

PROLOGUE

DU BAL D'AUTEUIL.

SCENE PREMIERE.

LE BAILLI, & Mr MAIGRET.

Mr MAIGRET

Ah, ah! c'est vous, Monsieur le Bailli? eh que diable venez-vous donc faire ici?

LE BAILLI[1]

Eh, parsanguenne[2] , Monsieur Maigret, j'y viens voir ste[3] petite drôlerie qu'ils allont joüer sur le Bal de nôtre Village!

---

1. Diverses ordonnances royales avaient, depuis la Renaissance, réduit le pouvoir des baillis au point de ne leur laisser que des attributions illusoires. M. Marion les qualifie de 'juges minuscules [qui] prêtaient souvent à rire' et de 'glorieux impuissants' qui fournissaient une cible de la comédie du dix-huitième siècle (*Dictionnaire des institutions*, p. 31-32).

2. Selon le *Dictionnaire de Trévoux* (1771), *palsangué* et *palsanguenne* étaient des jurons caractéristiques des paysans et des personnes de basse condition. En revanche, *palsambleu* caractérisait le discours des comtes et des marquis (cf. I, 2).

3. J.-P. Seguin (*La Langue française*, p. 41, 47-48) indique,

Mr MAIGRET

Ah! je vois ce que c'est, Monsieur le Bailli! vous craignez qu'on ne réjoüisse le public à vos dépens? vous autres Habitans d'Auteüil, vous avez des femmes un peu égrillardes, & l'on en pouroit bien toucher quelque chose, oüi?

LE BAILLI

Non, non, Monsieur Maigret, on n'en touchera rien sur ma parole! prenez seulement garde à la vôtre! il y auroit, morgué, dequoy faire une bonne farce de l'avanture que vous eûtes avec elle, l'année passée!

Mr MAIGRET

Comment donc! quelle avanture? que voulez-vous dire?

LE BAILLI

Eh là... quand vous surprîtes ce billet qu'alle écrivoit à un de vos amis communs, pour l'avertir de se trouver au Bal, avec une certaine écharpe qu'elle luy envoyoit afin de l'y reconnoître?

Mr MAIGRET

Hé bien?

---

d'après Gille Vaudelin (voir *ibid.*, p. 37), que la prononciation populaire se maintenait aux alentours de 1700 et que la stabilisation de l'orthographe au dix-huitième siècle imposa graduellement la prononciation moderne.

LE BAILLI

Hé bian! vous fûtes au Bal vous avec st'écharpe que vous interceptites; vôtre femme ne manquit[4] pas de donner dans le panneau; vous voulûtes voir jusqu'au bout comme alle traitoit les amis de la maison; mais morgué, vous fûtes le sot du stratagême! & alle en fut quitte pour dire qu'alle vous avoit reconnu!

Mr MAIGRET

Bon, bon, Monsieur le Bailli, ce n'est là qu'une bagatelle! cela ne vaut pas à beaucoup près le tour que vous joüât vôtre ménagere[5] ; ce ne seroit, ma foi, pas le plus mauvais de la Comédie!

LE BAILLI

Laissons cela, Monsieur Maigret: si ma femme m'a joüé queuque tour, je l'ai morgué bian[6] rossée à mesure! nous ne nous devons rien; la Comédie n'a que voir à cela.

Mr MAIGRET

Ne seroit-il pas fort réjoüissant, par exemple, de voir aujourd'hui un Bailli épier sa femme au Bal, après avoir feint d'aller à Paris? La Baillive s'apercevroit

---

4. J.-P. Seguin évoque la difficulté qu'éprouvait la langue populaire à manier le passé simple et la fréquence des désinences en *-it* qu'elle imposait abusivement (*op. cit.*, p. 83-84).

5. Le substantif *ménager* désignait un organisateur, un sage administrateur (DFC).

6. Prononciation populaire aux alentours de 1700 (J.-P. Seguin, *op. cit.*, p. 47).

de la fraude, elle feroit doubler son déguisement par une commere qui donneroit le change au Bailli, pendant que le galant escamoteroit la Baillive!

LE BAILLI

Franchement, ça ne me plairoit guères!

Mr MAIGRET

Mais quel plaisir de voir le Bailli à la fin du Bal, découvrir son masque postiche! & demeurer aussi étonné à la vûë de la commere, que si les cornes lui venoient à la tête! j'en rirois, ma foi, de bon cœur!

LE BAILLI

J'éclaterois morgué bian à l'écharpe, moy!... mais il me semble pourtant que nous sommes tous deux de grands sots! ne vaudroit-il pas mieux ne rire ni l'un ni l'autre, & empêcher que mille badauts ne rissiont à nos dépens?

Mr MAIGRET

La réflexion est de bon sens, Monsieur le Bailli.

LE BAILLI

Tout Auteüil est intéresse à ça, voyez-vous? il n'y a morgué point d'honneur si entier qu'il n'y ait toujours queuque maille à redire[7] ! mais voici encore un de nos bourgeois fort à propos.

7. Entendre: une petite indiscrétion capable de susciter les médisances.

SCENE II

LE BAILLI, Mr MAIGRET,
Mr DE LA FAQUINIERE

Mr DE LA FAQUINIERE

Hé quoi! Monsieur le Bailli avec Monsieur Maigret? ah parsambleu! je ne voulois rien croire du bruit qui court: mais il n'y a plus moyen d'en douter!

LE BAILLI

Eh, quel est donc ce bruit qui court, Monsieur de la Faquiniere?

Mr DE LA FAQUINIERE

Oh pour cela, cela est trop drôle! on dit que tout le Village en allarme s'est assemblé sur[8] la petite piece d'aujourd'hui: que les femmes ont mis dans la tête aux maris qu'il y alloit de leur honneur d'en empêcher la representation, & qu'enfin vous êtes député, & même défrayé par eux, pour venir juger ici des intérets du corps.

LE BAILLI

Il est vrai, Monsieur de la Faquiniere; mais c'est principalement pour vous que je craignons; & je ne suis ici que pour empêcher qu'on ne vous joüe.

Mr DE LA FAQUINIERE

Me joüer! moy? me joüer! ah par la sambleu! je vou-

8. Entendre: à propos de ou à cause de ; DFC.

drois bien qu'un petit fat d'Auteur s'avisât de me tourner en ridicule!

LE BAILLI

Il n'y a, morgué, rien à tourner à ça! il n'y a qu'à vous prendre comme vous êtes! c'est du ridicule tout craché!

Mr DE LA FAQUINIERE

On dit aussi, mon pauvre Monsieur Maigret, que vous avez envoyé une écharpe à l'Auteur, pour l'engager à rayer la vôtre de sa piece?

Mr MAIGRET

Et ne dit-on point aussi quel présent Monsieur de la Faquiniere lui a fait, pour ne rien dire de sa derniere bonne fortune?

Mr DE LA FAQUINIERE

Comment donc! qu'entendez-vous?

Mr MAIGRET

Eh... là... cette femme de qualité avec qui vous familiarisâtes au dernier Bal un peu plus que de raison; & qui vous mena gratieusement au bois, où, pour derniere faveur, elle vous fit roüer de coups de bâtons[a], par ses gens qui l'attendoient?

---

[a] B2, B3 bâton

Mr DE LA FAQUINIERE

Vous plaisantez, Monsieur Maigret, vous plaisantez.

LE BALLI

Eh non, morguenne, il ne plaisante point! je le sçûmes dès le lendemain par les laquais même; & il y a assez long-temps que vous en gardez le lit, oüi? je crois morgué que vous n'en estes relevé que d'hier?

Mr DE LA FAQUINIERE

Conte tout pur, conte tout pur! mais j'aperçois là haut une Dame qui me fait des mines. il faut que je l'aille joindre! sans adieu.

ACTEURS.

M. VULPIN vieux garçon

M. CIDARIS frère d'Hortence

Mad. CIDARIS sœur d'Eraste

HORTENCE amante d'Eraste

ERASTE amant d'Hortence

MENINE }
}Maistresses de Mr Vulpin
LUCINDE }

MARTON suivante de Mad. Cidaris

FRONTIN valet d'Eraste

LUCAS Jardinier de Mr Vulpin

LE TABELLION

TROUPES de Masques

TROUPE de Violons

La Scène est à Auteüil, chez M. Vulpin.

LE BAL
D'AUTEUIL

COMEDIE.

ACTE I

SCENE PREMIERE.

ERASTE, FRONTIN.

ERASTE

Hé bien, mon enfant! dequoy[9] s'agit-il? pourquoi m'as-tu mandé de me rendre ici?

FRONTIN

Pour deux choses: premierement, pour mes intérets; & en second lieu, pour les vôtres.

ERASTE

Comment donc? parle! qu'as-tu de nouveau à m'aprendre?

---

9. Les éditions B2 et B3 adoptent systématiquement la forme *de quoi*.

FRONTIN

Que je ne puis plus rester chez Monsieur Vulpin: qu'il veut absolument épouser Mademoiselle Hortence; & que je me lasse d'être ici le garde de vos amours.

ERASTE

Quoi! tu pourois m'abandonner dans une si crüelle conjoncture? ah, mon cher Frontin, donne-moi au moins le temps...

FRONTIN

Ah, que diable, Monsieur, le moyen! courir tous les jours, de Paris à Auteüil, & d'Auteüil à Paris! avoir à servir deux maîtres à la fois! être Lolive pour l'un, & Frontin pour l'autre! morbleu, j'aimerois autant...

ERASTE

Mais dequoi peux-tu te plaindre? tes gages ne te sont-ils pas bien payés? & n'ès-tu pas le mieux du monde chez Mr Vulpin?

FRONTIN

Oüi, d'accord; grand'chere[10] ! bon vin! gros jeu! vie de garçon! mais c'est ce qui m'oblige d'en sortir.

ERASTE

Comment donc?

---

10. Vaugelas note que c'est l'usage seul qui règle l'élision de l'e muet de *grande*. Il cite l'exemple même de *grand'chère* (*Remarques*, p. 168).

FRONTIN

Mr Vulpin reçoit grand monde[11] : il m'a fait l'intendant de tous ses plaisirs; & j'ai tous les jours chez lui à faire[12] à tant de gens, que je crains à la fin d'y être reconnu pour un fripon.

ERASTE

Eh! ne crain rien, Frontin! & compte qui je ne te manquerai jamais; mais est-il possible qu'il songe à m'enlever Hortence?

FRONTIN

Oh, très possible: Monsieur vôtre beau-frere la lui a promise; & nous lui donnons même aujourd'hui, entr'autres divertissemens, un petit Bal de Campagne pour avant-goût de mariage.

ERASTE

Quoi! Mr Vulpin songeroit à l'épouser, lui qui est un homme de plaisirs?

FRONTIN

Hé oüi, justement; c'est un homme de joïe, & de bonne chere! un agréable débauché, qui a passe toute sa vie à duper des joüeurs, ou à se laisser duper par des Coquettes; & qui veut enfin avoir une femme à lui!

11. Cette expression pouvait autrefois s'employer dans des contextes autres que négatifs.

12. Entendre *affaire*.

ERASTE

Mais vouloir se marier à son âge!

FRONTIN

Eh que diable, Monsieur! n'a-t'il pas raison? il a goûté jusqu'ici dans le célibat, tous les plaisirs du mariage; & se marie enfin par bien-scéance, pour goûter dans le mariage toutes les douceurs du célibat! c'est dans l'ordre.

ERASTE

Et tu crois qu'Hortence consente à l'épouser?

FRONTIN

Oh pour cela, non: c'est elle qui m'a ordonné de vous en avertir; & de vous faire trouver dans le petit bois du jardin, pour prendre ensemble des mesures.

ERASTE

Ah, mon cher Frontin! tu me rends la vie!

FRONTIN

Mais je crains que vos affaires n'en aillent guères mieux à vous dire la verité; & que Mr Cidaris ne consente jamais à vôtre bonheur.

ERASTE

Il l'avoit néanmoins promis à ma sœur!

FRONTIN

Oüi, mais elle n'êtoit que sa maîtresse alors; & elle

est sa femme à present: je ne sçais même si je me trompe dans mes conjectures; mais je m'imagine qu'il a quelque affaire de cœur en ce païs: car il l'écarte depuis un temps de tous ses plaisirs; & l'oblige même aujourd hui de s'en retourner à Paris.

ERASTE

Il l'oblige de s'en retourner à Paris? ah Frontin! de qui tiens-tu ces nouvelles?

FRONTIN

De Marton, c'est elle même qui me l'a dit; mais j'entens quelqu'un, on pouroit nous surprendre: allez-vous en lui parler avant qu'elle parte; & ne manquez pas de vous trouver au rendez-vous.

SCENE II

Mr VULPIN, FRONTIN, LUCAS

Mr VULPIN

Ah! te voila, Lolive.

FRONTIN

Oüi, Monsieur, je viens de tout préparer pour le Bal; & d'ameuter[13] tous nos simphonistes au Dauphin[14] : vous les aurez ici dans un moment.

---

13. Terme de venerie : rallier les chiens.

14. Des recherches menées auprès de la Bibliothèque Historique de la Ville de Paris et du Musée Carnavalet indiquent qu'il n'existait aucune auberge de ce nom à Auteuil à cette époque.

Mr VULPIN

C'est bien fait; mais avec qui êtois-tu là?

FRONTIN

Eh... c'est un jeune homme de Paris qui a quelque intrigue en ce païs ci; & qui me demandoit des nouvelles d'un Valet qu'il y avoit laissé pour lui en rendre compre.

LUCAS[15]

Comment! d'un Valet qu'il y avoit laissé?

FRONTIN

Eh oüi, d'une espèce de Valet de chambre qui a eü l'adresse de s'introduire chez son rival, & qui doit aujourd'hui lui ménager ici une petite entreveuë, avec la personne qu'il aime.

Mr VULPIN

Une entrevûë chez moi? A mon inscûë?

FRONTIN

Eh non, Monsieur! c'est au Bal qu'ils se doivent voir! & vous voyez bien que je vous en avertis.

Mr VULPIN

Ah, c'est autre chose!

---

15. Le personnage du jardinier paraît chez Chappuzeau (*La Dame d'intrigue*) et Dancourt (*Le Charivari*, 1697, et *Colin-Maillard*, 1701) et illustre, par son entrée dans l'univers de la comédie, l'évolution sociale à la charnière du dix-septième et du dix-huitième siècle.

FRONTIN

Oh! c'est un lieu fertile en rendez-vous que le Bal d'Auteüil!

Mr VULPIN

Oh pour cela, je t'en répons; & il n'y a pas jusqu'à Mr Cidaris qui n'y en ait un dans les formes: mais il faut l'aller avertir que tout est prêt.

FRONTIN

J'y cours.

SCENE III

Mr VULPIN, LUCAS

LUCAS

Hé fi, parsangué, Monsieur! c'est une honte de bailler[16] le Bal à vôtre âge!

Mr VULPIN

Que veux-tu? Mr Cidaris me l'a demandé; je suis sur le point d'épouser sa sœur: je n'ai pû le lui refuser.

---

16. Le *Dictionnaire de l'Académie* (1694) note que *bailler* est vieilli : 'l'on se sert plus souvent de donner dans toutes les phrases même où l'on mettait *bailler*'. Le *Dictionnaire critique de la langue françoise* de Féraud (1787-1788) note son emploi chez Malherbe et Balzac et ajoute que 'depuis longtemps il n'est plus du bel usage'.

LUCAS

Bon, d'épouser sa sœur! c'est encore queuque mariage du bois de Boulogne! car vous êtes de ces gaillards qui n'épousont que la débauche!

Mr VULPIN

Non, Lucas, je fais divorce avec elle.

LUCAS

Quoi, morgué! vous renonceriez à la vie de garçon?

Mr VULPIN

Oüi, mon enfant, c'en est fait, j'épouse Hortence; & je songe aussi à te marier.

LUCAS

Oh parsangué, pour moi, ça ne presse pas: vous êtes noble, vous; vous voulez faire souche & vous n'avez point de temps à perdre[a] !

Mr VULPIN

Comment donc! qu'est-ce à dire?

LUCAS

Eh, c'est à dire tout franc, qu'ous êtes déja un peu vieux pour avoir des rejettons; mais ne vous boutez[17]

---

[a] B3 pardre

17. *Bouter* était déjà vieilli au temps de Boindin. Vaugelas suggère que *bouter*, employé pour contrevenir délibérément au bon usage dans la phrase 'boutez-vous là', avait des résonances plutôt vulgaires que réellement plaisantes (*Remarques*, Préface, § vii, 3).

pas en peine, allez: on ne vous en laira[18] , morgué, pas manquer!

Mr VULPIN

Mais sçavez-vous bien, Monsieur le Jardinier...

LUCAS

Oh morgué! je sçavons bian ce que je sçavons[19] ! & que les mariages de qualité sont ceux qui avont le plus de sauvageons! c'est une jeune plante qui est diantrement varte, que ste Mademoiselle Hortence!

Mr VULPIN

Il est vrai qu'elle est jeune; mais c'est une fille bien élevée; & qui a toujours été tenuë fort serrée!

LUCAS

Hé oüi; mais quand les orangers sortont de la terre, on y voit parfois la fleur & le fruit tout ensemble!

Mr VULPIN

Oh, je n'ai rien à craindre d'elle; & sa vertu...

---

18. Vaugelas se montre catégorique: '*Lairrois, lairray*. Cette abréviation de *lairrois, lairray*, en toutes les personnes, et en tous les nombres, pour *laisserois*, et *laisseray*, ne vaut rien, quoiqu'une infinité de gens le disent et l'écrivent' (*Remarques*, p. 119).

19. 'Le plus grossier et le plus remarquable de tous les défauts en matière de langue est celui d'une mauvaise construction des mots, causé[e] par l'ignorance des règles de la grammaire. Si par exemple un homme de qualité disait, *j'étions à Paris, et j'en partîmes pour Versailles*, il parlerait comme le menu peuple' (*Du bon et du mauvais usage*, p. 135).

LUCAS

Il n'y a morgué, vartu qui tienne! la vartu est antée sur la nature, voyez-vous? & quand l'abre est trop fort, & que la grèfe est trop foible, il n'y a pas moyen qu'alle profite, la sève l'étoufe.

Mr VULPIN

Oh, tu as beau dire; ce mariage est une affaire arrêtée; & j'espere en faire dresser ce soir les articles.

LUCAS

Et moi, je crains bian que Madame Lucinde, & Madame Menine n'y veniont mettre empêchement!

Mr VULPIN

Comment est-ce qu'elles sçauroient mes desseins?

LUCAS

Je ne sçais; mais on vient de m'aprendre au Dauphin, qu'alles y sont toutes deux déguisées; & je ne doute point que ce ne soit pour vous venir surprendre!

Mr VULPIN

En effet, je ne les ai point averties du Bal; elles pouroient bien se douter de ce qui se passe: mais gardetoi bien d'en parler à personne; C'est un secret que je confie à ta discrétion.

LUCAS

Oh parsangué, vous faites bian! je suis tout propre à garder un secret, moi! & je serois mille ans tout seul, que je n'en parlerois à personne.

SCENE IV

Mr VULPIN, LUCAS, FRONTIN.

FRONTIN

De la joïe, Monsieur! de la joïe! voici Mr Cidaris avec sa sœur; & tous nos instruments sont au salon: il ne leur manque que du vin, pour préluder.

Mr VULPIN

Hé bien, Lucas; va-t'en leur en faire donner.

FRONTIN

Oüi, cours les enyvrer; sans cela, ils ne pouroient jamais s'accorder!

SCENE V.

Mr VULPIN, Mr CIDARIS,
HORTENCE, FRONTIN.

Mr CIDARIS

Ah, Mr Vulpin! vous me voyez dans la dernière joïe! & voici ma sœur qui ne demande qu'à partager nos plaisirs.

Mr VULPIN

Quoi, Madame! je pourois me flater de vous y voir prendre quelque part?

Mr CIDARIS

Oh, assurément; c'est moi qui vous en réponds!

HORTENCE *bas à Frontin*

Ton maître est-il arrivé, Frontin? l'as-tu vû?

FRONTIN *bas à Hortence*

Oüi, Madame, il ne manquera pas de se trouver au rendez-vous.

Mr VULPIN

Assurez m'en donc aussi, Madame, & que j'aye le plaisir de l'aprendre de vous-même!

HORTENCE

Hé bien, Monsieur, j'y consens; & je vous avoüe que j'avois toute l'impatience du monde d'être ici.

Mr CIDARIS

Eh! ne vous disois-je pas bien que ma sœur n'avoit point d'autres sentimens que les miens?

HORTENCE

Oh pour cela, non, mon frere, nos sentiments ne sont point si conformes que vous pensez: vous croyez que c'est par devoir que je me rends ici; & je vous assûre que c'est par inclination.

Mr CIDARIS

Hé bien! je ne lui fais pas dire, comme vous voyez.

Mr VULPIN

Ah! je suis le plus hûreux des hommes! mais n'avons nous rien à craindre de Madame Cidaris?

Mr CIDARIS

Non, non, nous en sommes défaits; & je viens de la renvoyer à Paris.

FRONTIN

Oh, c'est fort bien fait!

Mr CIDARIS

Et j'ai été bien aise aussi d'écarter Marton; car c'est une coquine qui ne songeoit qu'à nous traverser[20] ; & qui avoit ici des intelligences avec un certain pendart[21] de Frontin...

FRONTIN *à part*

Comment diable! c'est de moi qu'il parle? il faut payer d'éfronterie.

Mr CIDARIS

On dit que c'est un maraut[22] qui triomphe en fait de fourberies[23] ; mais il sera bien fin, s'il m'atrape!

---

20. Entendre : contrarier, gêner. Voir DFC, 'traverser'.

21. Les substantifs *pendard* et *maraut* ne s'appliquaient généralement qu'à des serviteurs.

22. Furetière ('Maraut') note que maraut était un 'terme injurieux qui se dit des gueux, des coquins, des fripons, des bélîtres, qui n'ont ni bien ni honneur, qui sont capables de toutes sortes de lachetés'.

23. J. Emelina consacre des pages lumineuses à la fourberie des valets de comédie et au personnage de Frontin qui s'épanouit au théâtre après 1700 (*op. cit.*, p. 53-55 et 175-176).

FRONTIN

Oh pour cela, Monsieur, je vous répons!

Mr CIDARIS

Comment est-ce que tu le connoîtrois?

FRONTIN

Oüi, vraiment; C'est un maraut qui m'a donné bien de la peine en[24] ma vie!

Mr VULPIN

Quoi! tu aurois eü des affaires avec lui?

FRONTIN

De crüelles même; & dont j'ai été bien-hûreux de me tirer: C'est le plus grand fourbe!

Mr CIDARIS

Oh! l'on me l'a bien dit!

FRONTIN *à Mr Vulpin*

Tenez, Monsieur, c'est un coquin qui s'insinuë dans vos affaires, qui s'empresse de vous servir; que vous croyez dans vos intérets; & qui dans le fond, ne cherche qu'à vous attraper!

---

24. La langue classique employait *en* pour introduire un complément de lieu, là où nous mettrions aujourd'hui *dans*; voir DFC, 'en ; préposition', et A. Haase, *op. cit.*, § 126 E.

Mr VULPIN

Oh, je n'en doute point!

FRONTIN

Vous le voyez, vous luy parlez, il vous avertit luy-même de ses fourberies, que vous ne vous appercevez pas encore qu'il vous trompe, & qu'il se moque de vous! oh, c'est un maraut qui sçait bien son mêtier!

Mr CIDARIS

Oh, j'en suis persuadé; mais je ne crois pas qu'il ose se joüer à moi[25] .

FRONTIN

Oh, ne vous y fiez pas! c'est un pendart à vous affronter en face; & qui n'est jamais mieux masqué que lors qu'il se montre tel qu'il est: mais ne vous mettez pas en peine, allez; je me charge de vous le faire connoître, avant la fin du Bal.

SCENE VI

Mr VULPIN, Mr CIDARIS,
HORTENCE, FRONTIN, LUCAS.

LUCAS

Hé tatigué, Monsieur! venez donc mettre ordre à ça!

---

25. Entendre : s'attaquer à, s'en prendre à, se frotter à. Cf. Molière, *George Dandin*, I, 6: 'Je voudrais bien le voir vraiment que vous fussiez amoureux de moi ! Jouez-vous-y, je vous en prie, vous trouverez à qui parler ' (DFC, s.v. 'se jouer à').

vela une tempête de filles qui vient de fondre sur vôtre Bal; & qui l'avont fait commencer sans vous!

Mr VULPIN

Commencer, Lucas?

LUCAS

Oüi, voirement[26] ; & finir aussi, Mr Vulpin!

Mr VULPIN

Comment donc! que veux-tu dire?

LUCAS

Eh! je veux dire que ces enragées-là ont voulu dancer à queuque prix que ce fut; & qu'alles avont avec elles, un vrai lutin de fille qui ne vaut pas le diable à contredire; & qui a pris la simphonie à la gorge pour la faire commencer!

Mr VULPIN

Hé bien?

LUCAS

Hé bian! parce qu'alle a fait un faux pas, alle a prétendu que c'étoit la faute des violons; les violons l'ont traitée de je ne sçais qui; alle a traité les violons,

---

26. 'Adv[erbe] qui marque quelque réflexion. Mais *voirement*, pour dire, Mais à propos, mais quand j'y pense. Ce mot est bas' (Furetière). Le *Dictionnaire de Trévoux* note, en 1771, que le mot est *bas* et *provincial*, et qu'il est vieilli.

je ne sçais comment: enfin l'orage a crevé; & alle a baillé tant de coups de pieds dans le ventre à ces gros instruments, qu'alle en a fait sauter toutes les cordes; & que les Menestriers s'en allont en jurant qu'ils en auront raison; & qu'on ne brutalise point comme ça un Arquestre!

Mr CIDARIS

Eh mais, mais, Mr Vulpin! cela n'est point à soufrir.

Mr VULPIN

Non, vraiment, Mr Cidaris; il faut aller mettre ordre à cela!

HORTENCE

Allez, j'ay quelques ordres à donner à Lolive: je vous rejoins dans un moment.

SCENE VII

HORTENCE, FRONTIN.

HORTENCE

Hé bien, mon enfant! as-tu songé à nos affaires?

FRONTIN

Hé oüi, vraiment; j'y ai assez songé; mais je ne sçais encore par où m'y prendre.

HORTENCE

Il faut commencer par rompre le mariage de Mr Vulpin, & songer ensuite à faire celui d'Eraste.

FRONTIN

Si nous commencions plûtôt par faire celui d'Eraste? nous n'aurions plus à rompre celui de Mr Vulpin; ce seroit la moitié de la peine d'épargnée.

HORTENCE

Il est vrai; mais comment en venir à bout?

FRONTIN

Eh... mais... mais, mon Maître vous dira cela; il est au jardin qui vous attent: allons-nous-en le trouver.

Fin du premier Acte

ACTE II

SCENE PREMIERE

LUCAS *seul*

Vela, morgué, de belles chiennes de nôces! des violons qui ne voulont pas joüer d'un côté! des Masques qui voulont dancer de l'autre! au milieu de tout ça, une Maîtresse qui s'éclipse! car on ne sçait, morgué, ce que la future est devenuë, pendant tout ce grabuge; & je ne jurerois pas qu'on ne nous l'eût escamotée! mais on vient ici: ne seroit-ce point queuque escamoteur? hé morgué, c'est Madame Menine!

SCENE II

LUCAS & MENINE *en Cavalier*

MENINE

Oui, mon pauvre Lucas, c'est moi-même; & je t'aprendrai le sujet de mon déguisement: mais dimoi, me trouves-tu un peu l'air d'un homme?

LUCAS

Eh... oüida! à queuque chose près!

MENINE

Mais de bonne foi? si tu ne sçavois que je suis fille, n'y serois-tu pas trompé?

LUCAS

Bon! est-ce que les filles sont faites pour autre chose que pour tromper? on vous prendroit, morgué, pour un petit maître[27] ! & je gagerois que vous venez joüer queuque tour à Mr Vulpin?

MENINE

Justement, je venois lui enlever sa Maîtresse.

LUCAS

Hé fi, parsangué, Madame! ne faites point cet afront-là à vôtre sexe! on croiroit...

MENINE

Oh! je me moque de ce qu'on pouroit croire! & je lui aprendrois à me trahir, après m'avoir promis de m'épouser!

LUCAS

Bon! s'il avoit épousé toutes les femmes à qui il le promettoit; il en auroit, morgué, une pépinière!

---

27. A l'origine, le terme 'petit-maître' s'appliquait aux jeunes seigneurs acolytes du prince de Condé, ensuite aux jeunes élégants de la Cour. Parmi les attributs des petits-maîtres, habituellement tournés en ridicule par les écrivains et les moralistes, figurait un ajustement recherché (*Encyclopédie*, s.v. 'Petit Maître', vol. II, p. 1 357).

MENINE

Oh! je l'empêcherois pourtant bien d'en épouser une autre, si j'en avois envie; mais hûreusement pour lui, j'ay d'autres vûës.

LUCAS

Quoi! vous auriez déja queuque autre intrigue en ce païs ci?

MENINE

Oüi, mon enfant, je viens de voir un jeune homme, au Dauphin, dont les manières m'ont charmée; & qui m'a entierement dépiquée[28] de Mr Vulpin.

LUCAS

Oh parsangué, j'en suis ravi! mais le connoissez-vous? sçavez-vous qui il est?

MENINE

Non, je n'ai pû encore lui parler que des yeux; & son visage m'est tout-à-fait nouveau: mais ses mines m'ont assez répondu de son cœur; & il ne s'agit plus que de faire connoissance.

LUCAS

Hé morgué! ne seroit-ce point ce jeune étranger que des Mesdames de Paris amenont tous les jours au bois de Boulogne?

---

28. Le *Dictionnaire de Trévoux* (1771) approuve ce mot. Il figure dans *Des Mots à la mode* (3e édition, 1692, p. 28-29), où les illustrations démontrent un usage répandu mais imprécis. Le personnage du Commandeur se plaint que 'ce mot n'offre pas [...] clairement à l'esprit ce qu'il veut exprimer'.

MENINE

Je ne sçais; mais c'est le plus ensorcelant petit minois[29]! oh! je t'avoüe que je n'ai jamais vû d'hommes faits comme lui! mais le voici qui vient à nous.

LUCAS *à part*

Hé morgué, c'est Madame Lucinde! *à Menine* Ho tatigué! vous avez raison; il n'y a point d'hommes faits comme ça! *à part*, Il faut pourtant que je songe à les écarter d'ici.

SCENE III

LUCAS, MENINE & LUCINDE *en cavaliers*

LUCINDE *d'un côté du théatre*

Oui, justemement, c'est luy-même! mais je pense qu'il est avec Lucas. Eh, bon jour, mon pauvre Jardinier!

LUCAS

Hé morgué, Madame! dans quel équipage[30] vous vela! que venez-vous donc faire ici?

---

29. Furetière et l'Académie constatent tous deux que ce mot est bas et du style plaisant.

30. Entendre: costume. Cf.: 'Vous ne dites rien de tout mon équipage? / Ai-je bien d'un sergent le port et le visage?' (Racine, *Les Plaideurs*, v. 515). Voir aussi Regnard, *Le Joueur*, v. 718-720.

LUCINDE

J'y venois surprendre ton Maître; mais qui est ce jeune homme-là avec qui tu ès?

LUCAS

Eh... c'est un jeune homme de mes amis, qui est assez bien fait, comme vous voyez, & qui meurt d'envie de faire connoissance avec vous.

LUCINDE

De faire connoissance avec moy!

LUCAS

Hé oüi, morgué! c'est un petit rejetton de chevallerie, qui est sur le point de faire ses caravannes[31] ; mais ce seroit dommage que ça fit des vœux, n'est-ce pas?

LUCINDE

Oüi, vrayment, Lucas; il a tres-bon air, je le trouve fort joly homme[32] ; & je suis ravie qu'il ait du

31. L'expression signifiait 'les premières campagnes que les chevaliers de Malte font sur mer pour s'acquitter du service qu'ils doivent à leur Ordre, afin de parvenir aux Commanderies et dignités de la Religion' (*Dictionnaire de l'Académie*). En tant que religieux, les membres de l'Ordre étaient tenus au célibat (d'où les regrets de Lucinde et de Lucas). Pour l'histoire et l'organisation de l'ordre, on consultera l'*Encyclopédie*, vol. II, p. 756-757, et M. Marion, *op. cit.*, p. 410-412.

32. Expression à la mode en 1702. Elle est citée par Callières, *Des mots à la mode*, p. 8 et, plus longuement, par Dufresny, qui évoque un beau jeune homme dont la parure recherchée attire la curiosité des dames, mais dont la taciturnité inepte finit par les rebuter. (*Amusements sérieux et comiques*, p. 42-44).

goût[33] pour moy: mais ne se douteroit-il point que je suis fille?

LUCAS

Oh palsangué, non: ça est au plus loin de sa pensée; mais si vous voulez, je l'en avertiray.

LUCINDE

Non, non, garde-t'en bien: laisse-moy tirer avantage de son erreur, & m'assurer de ses sentimens, avant de me découvrir à luy.

LUCAS

C'est morgué bian dit. *à part.* Comme alle baille dedans! oh palsangé ça est trop drôle!

MENINE *de l'autre côté du théatre*

Eh, que luy disois-tu donc, Lucas? tu luy parlois bien familiairement! est-ce que tu le connoîtrois?

LUCAS

Eh oüi, vraiment: c'est un Marquis de ma connoissance, & c'êtoit de vous que je luy parlois.

MENINE

De moy? ah, tu m'auras trahie! tu luy auras appris qui je suis?

33. Entendre : sympathie. Mais, déjà en 1702, on passait de l'amour-passion à l'amour-goût, de Racine à Crébillon fils.

LUCAS

Eh non, morgué, tout à l'encontre[34] : je luy disois que vous êtiez tous Chevaliers dans vostre famille, & il ne tient qu'à vous d'être bons amis.

MENINE

Quoy, sérieusement... mais au moins, Lucas, n'y a-t'il point de risque?

LUCAS

Oh pour ça, non; c'est moy qui vous en réponds: *à part* La nature y a morgué mis bon ordre! *à toutes deux* Eh, allons, Messieurs, sans compliments, point de façons, commencez par vous embrasser.

LUCINDE *embrassant Menine*

Ah! de tout mon cœur!

LUCAS *à part*

Ce n'est, morgué pas ce qu'alle pense!

MENINE *embrassant Lucinde*

Je n'ay jamais rien fait avec tant de plaisir.

LUCAS *à part*

Oh, palsanguenne, oüy! vela un beau[a] chien de plaisir!

---

[a] B3 biau

34. Selon l'Académie, *à l'encontre* était surtout en usage au Palais.

MENINE *à Lucinde*

Et je veux me lier avec vous de l'amitié la plus étroite.

LUCAS *à part*

Il ne faut pas toûjours juger de l'arbre pas l'écorce!

LUCINDE

Mais par quel hazard nous trouvons-nous tous deux icy?

LUCAS *entr'elles*

Oh, pour ça tenez, c'est le même vent qui vous y pousse, c'est l'amour qui vous y ameine l'un & l'autre; il se trouve qu'on vous y trompe tous deux: Eh parsanguenne, il faut vous en consoler ensemble!

MENINE

Ah volontiers!

LUCAS

Je m'en vas[35] donc vous laisser icy; aussi bien ay-je queuque petite affaire à mon jardin: Sans adieu, Monsieur le Chevalier... jusqu'au revoir, Monsieur le Marquis... oh parsanguenne, il y aura bien à rire, quand elles[a] viendront à se reconnoître!

---

[a] B3 alles

35. Vaugelas préfère la forme 'je vais' parce que la différentiation des personnes du verbe élimine les équivoques et contribue à la beauté et à la richesse de la langue. Cependant, il constate aussi que 'toute la Cour dit, *je va*, et ne peut souffrir, *je vais*, qui passe pour un mot provincial ou du peuple de Paris' (*Remarques*, p. 27).

Scene IV.

LUCINDE & MENINE *en Cavaliers.*

MENINE

En verité, Marquis, plus je vous regarde; & plus je crois que Lucas m'impose: non, il n'est pas possible qu'une femme vous trahisse! eh pour qui vous trahiroit-elle?

LUCINDE

Ma foy Chevalier, une femme qui me troqueroit auroit ses raisons! le moyen de s'aimer quand on n'est pas fait l'un pour l'autre? mais par où justifier une perfide qui n'auroit pû s'en tenir à vous? eh, que pourroit-elle donc desirer dans un homme!

MENINE

Tout ce qui me manque, Marquis; je ne fais point le fat là dessus: j'ay beau m'examiner; je ne me trouve point dequoy fixer une femme!

LUCINDE

Parbleu, Chevalier! je me mets pourtant le mieux que je peux à la place d'une femme qui vous aimeroit! & je ne sçaurois m'appercevoir qu'il y ait quelque chose à redire en vous!

MENINE

Eh mon Dieu, Marquis! demeurez ce que vous estes, pour me trouver à vôtre gré! c'est diminuer du prix de vos sentimens pour moy, que de vous mettre à la place d'un autre: mais revenons à vôtre perfide; elle ne vous occupe guères[36], ce me semble? oh, je vois bien, Marquis, que ce n'est pas là vôtre premiere avanture!

LUCINDE

Vôtre infidelle ne vous tient guères plus au cœur, Chevalier? mais parbleu, touchez-là; je veux vous donner icy la connoissance d'une Dame qui vous aidera à vous en vanger!

MENINE

Et moy, Marquis, je veux vous en faire connoître une qui se fera un plaisir de faire vôtre bonheur!

LUCINDE

Oh! pour mon bonheur, Chevalier, il dépend de vous! les femmes ne m'ont jamais tantée!

MENINE

Oh! ce n'a jamais été mon foible, non plus! & il n'y a rien que je ne sacrifiasse à un ami tel que vous.

LUCINDE

Si vous connoissiez néanmoins celle dont il s'agit; peut-être ne vous seroit elle pas si indiférente?

---

36. Vaugelas acceptait indifferemment *guère* et *guères* (*Remarques*, p. 335). Ménage, qui soutient que le *s* final fut ajouté, et l'Académie se rangent à son avis (*Commentaires*, II, p. 564-565). Cependant Corneille préfère généralement l'orthographe sans *s* (*ibid.*, p. 497-498).

MENINE

Peut-être ne mépriseriez-vous pas non plus celle dont je vous parle, si elle vous êtoit connuë?

LUCINDE

J'ose du moins me flatter que la ressemblance qui est entre nous, vous previendroit en sa faveur!

MENINE

Oh pour la ressemblance, on n'en sçauroit voir de plus parfaite que la nôtre; & ce n'est que par les habits qu'on peut nous distinguer!

LUCINDE

Je consens donc de la voir pour vous faire plaisir; mais c'est à condition que vous verrez la mienne auparavant.

MENINE

Oh pour cela, non; mais nous les verrons ensemble si vous voulez?

LUCINDE

Volontiers; que la vôtre se rende ici dans un quart d'heure; la mienne ne manquera pas de s'y trouver... mais au moins, Chevalier, ne manquez pas d'y revenir avec elle!

MENINE

Oh! j'y suis trop intéressée! maison vient à nous; courons changer d'équipage.

LUCINDE

Allons-nous démarquiser[37] ... mais je pense que c'est Madame Cidaris, avec Marton!

SCENE V

LUCINDE *en Cavalier*, Mad. CIDARIS & MARTON *en habits de Bal & tenant un masque à leur main*

MARTON *appercevant Lucinde*

Ah, Madame, le joli cavalier! mais je crois que ce n'est que Lucinde?

Mad. CIDARIS *à Lucinde*

Eh, ma chère! pour quelle avanture viens-tu au Bal dans cet équipage?

LUCINDE

Ma foi, je n'en sçais rien encore; mais toi, ma charmante, qu'y viens-tu faire dans ces habits?

Mad. CIDARIS

Oh! ce n'est point la galanterie qui m'y ameine; c'est Mr Cidaris que j'y viens chercher.

---

37. Féraud, dans son *Supplément au Dictionnaire critique*, qualifie ce mot de 'burlesque'. Le Marquis du *Joueur* de Regnard est également 'démarquisé' par Madame La Ressource (v. 1666).

MARTON

Quoi, Madame! c'est pour venir trouver un mari au Bal, que vous avez pris tant de soin de vôtre petite personne?

Mad. CIDARIS

Oüi, Marton; & c'est pour moi que Mr Cidaris s'y rend aussi.

LUCINDE

Mais tu te moques, ma chere? cela ne se peut!

Mad. CIDARIS

Non, je ne moque point; c'est une partie concertée entre nous.

MARTON

Oh par ma foy, Madame, je ne vous comprens pas! vous êtiez ce matin indisposée; vous ne pouviez vous en retourner à Paris; Mr Cidaris vous en a fait une nécessité: vous vouliez l'emmener avec vous; il vous a dit qu'il êtoit obligé de se rendre à Versailles: cependant il est ici; vous vous y trouvez: & c'est une partie concertée entre vous?

Mad. CIDARIS

Oüi Marton; c'est un rendez-vous que nous nous sommes donné.

MARTON

Oh, pour le coup, Madame, expliquez-vous.

Mad. CIDARIS

Quoi! tu n'as pas eü l'esprit de connoître que cette indisposition n'êtoit qu'une feinte?

MARTON

Oh pour cela, je l'ai compris d'abord; & j'ay crû même, connoissant les manières doubles & dissimulées des femmes, & l'esprit contrariant des maris, que vous ne pressiez le vôtre de vous accompagner, que pour vous en défaire plûtôt: pour le reste, je vous avoüe qu'il me passe!

Mad. CIDARIS

Apren donc, mon enfant, que je me fis faire cet habit pour le dernier Bal qu'il y eut ici: que j'eus le plaisir de n'y être reconnuë de personne, & celui d'y trouver un galant, en la personne d'un mari.

LUCINDE

Quoi, ma chere! Mr Cidaris t'en vint conter?

Mad. CIDARIS

Oüi, le traitre vint me faire mille protestations d'amour; mais croyant me tromper, il se trahit lui-même; & passa toute la nuit à me convaincre de sa perfidie.

MARTON

Et vous vous séparâtes, sans lui faire aucune infidélité?

Mad. CIDARIS

Oh! ce ne fut pas sans peine! il vouloit à toute force m'emmener avec lui; & je ne pus m'en défaire qu'en lui promettant de me rendre à la première assemblée qu'il y auroit ici: mais je l'aperçois qui vient ici, laisse nous ensemble.

SCENE VI

Mr CIDARIS, Mad. CIDARIS
& MARTON *masquées*

Mr CIDARIS

J'ai beau chercher ma sœur, je ne la sçaurois trouver; & je crains bien que ce pendart de Frontin... mais n'est-ce pas là mon inconnuë? ah, Madame, que j'avois d'impatience de vous revoir! & que ma joïe seroit parfaite si ce masque...

Mad. CIDARIS

Ah, Monsieur! je crains trop de me montrer telle que je suis! c'est à vôtre erreur que je dois ma conquête; c'est à mon masque que je dois vôtre cœur: permettez...

Mr CIDARIS

Non, Madame, je ne puis plus vivre sans vous voir!

Mad. CIDARIS

Non, vous ne sçauriez me voir sans cesser de m'aimer; je vous connois mieux que vous ne pensez.

Mr CIDARIS

Ah! je vous jure...

Mad. CIDARIS

Ne faites point de sermens: ce sont de foibles liens pour les amans d'aujourd'hui; & vous m'en feriez mille, que je n'en deviendrois pas plus crédule.

MARTON

Oh, nous ne sommes point si sottes! Madame y a déja été attrapée!

Mr CIDARIS

Mais tenez-moi du moins quelque compte du temps que j'ai passé sans vous voir: si vous sçaviez tout ce que j'en ai soufert! tout ce que j'en ai fait ressentir à ma femme.

Mad. CIDARIS

Oh! je vous en dois beaucoup, j'en tombe d'accord; mais pour être encore mieux persuadée de vôtre fidelité, je voudrois bien sçavoir quels seroient vos sentiments, si Madame Cidaris alloit de son côté...

Mr CIDARIS

Ah, Madame, qu'elle fasse tout ce qu'elle voudra! rien ne peut plus me toucher de ma femme; & je vous réponds que sa conduite ne m'intéresse plus du tout.

MARTON *bas à Mad. Cidaris*

Prenez témoins de cela, Madame; cela peut servir dans l'occasion.

Mad. CIDARIS

Mais si ses charmes n'ont pû vous retenir, que dois-je espérer de mes foibles appas?

Mr CIDARIS

Oh! il y a bien de la comparaison! ma femme a-t'elle cette taille, ce port?

Mad. CIDARIS

Oh pour cela, je n'ai rien qu'elle n'ait avec autant d'avantage.

Mr CIDARIS

Et moi, je ne lui trouve rien d'aprochant, & toute sa personne me déplait.

Mad. CIDARIS

Ainsi, Monsieur, si j'avois le malheur de lui ressembler?

MARTON

Bon, Madame, voila une belle difficulté! Monsieur aimeroit en vous tout ce qui lui déplait en elle?

Mr CIDARIS *en lui prenant la main.*

Assurément, Madame!

Mad. CIDARIS

Ah, moderez vos transports[38] ! si mon mari nous surprenoit...

Mr CIDARIS

Quoi, Madame! vous êtes mariée?

Mad. CIDARIS

Oüi, Monsieur; & c'est pour me vanger d'un traitre, d'un perfide, que je veux vous ouvrir mon cœur: il est ici avec une personne qui n'a aucun avantage sur moi; & pour laquelle il me méprise! mais puisqu'il m'outrage; je veux m'en vanger.

MARTON

Oh pour cela, il n'y a point de plus douce vangeance que celle qu'on prend d'un mari! & je ne mourrai point contente, que je ne me sois vangée de deux ou trois!

Mad. CIDARIS

Oüi, traitre! j'aurai le plaisir de te confondre; & de te faire voir ta femme, où tu ne crois trouver que ta maîtresse! mais j'oublie que je suis avec vous... je confonds l'amant, & le mari... pardonnez ce transport.

---

38. Dans cette scène, truffée du vocabulaire hyperbolique de l'amour précieux, le mot de *transport* revient à trois reprises. Boindin l'emploie au sens fort courant à l'époque (manifestation d'une passion) qui ne subsiste que dans la métaphore vide *transporté de joie, de colère*, etc.

Mr CIDARIS

Ah, Madame! vous me percez l'ame! est-il possible qu'il y ait un homme assez brutal pour vous offencer?

MARTON

Oh, vous en jugerez vous-même!

Mr CIDARIS

Ah vangez-vous, Madame, vangez-vous! & me rendez le plus hûreux des hommes![39]

Mad.CIDARIS

Eh comment me vanger, & vous rendre hûreux?

Mr CIDARIS

En répondant à ma passion, Madame; en vous abandonnant à ma tendresse.

Mad. CIDARIS

Non, ce seroit vous tromper, & me trahir moi-même; car enfin quelque outrage qu'un mari nous fasse...

Mr CIDARIS

Quoi! vous voudriez encore ménager un homme qui vous méprise?

---

39. 'Lorsque deux impératifs sont coordonnés par *et* (*ou*, *mais* et parfois *puis*) le pronom peut alors se placer, selon l'usage primitif, devant le dernier. [...] Cet usage est généralement suivi jusqu'au XVIIIe siècle. [...] Au XIXe siècle, cette tournure paraît nettement archaïque' (K. R. Nyrop, *Grammaire historique*, V, § 85).

Mad. CIDARIS

Eh, croyez-vous que ses mépris me mettent en droit de lui être infidelle?

Mr CIDARIS

Oh, assûrément, Madame.

Mad. CIDARIS

Ah, gardez-vous de me le persuader! vous y êtes plus intéressé que personne; & vous me parleriez contre vous-même.

Mr CIDARIS

Non, non, Madame; vous méritiez d'être adorée éternellement; & vous m'aviez même fait espérer...

Mad. CIDARIS

Oüi, je vous avois promis de vous rendre hûreux; & je sens bien que ce que je dois à mon mari, ne m'empêchera pas de vous accorder tout ce que vous voudrez éxiger de moi.

Mr CIDARIS

Ah, Madame! vous me transportez!

Mad. CIDARIS

Mais il faut m'accorder une grace auparavant, pour m'assurer de vôtre cœur.

Mr CIDARIS

Eh, quelle est-elle, Madame? parlez.

Mad. CIDARIS

Je m'intéresse au bonheur d'un amant dont vous pouvez combler les vœux: Eraste aime vôtre sœur; vous la lui aviez promise: pourquoi lui manquez-vous de parole?

Mr CIDARIS

Je vous avoüerai, Madame, que c'êtoit pour la donner à Mr Vulpin; & pour avoir le plaisir de faire enrager ma femme: mais puisque vous vous intéressez pour Eraste, je vous promets...

Mad. CIDARIS

Oh, ce n'est point assez de me promettre; il faut le rendre hûreux dès aujourd'hui; & rompre le mariage de Mr Vulpin en ma présence.

Mr CIDARIS

Hé bien, Madame, allons le trouver: j'y consens.

MARTON

Et moi, j'aperçois Frontin: il faut que je le sonde sous ces[a] habits; & que je voye s'il ne seroit point aussi d'humeur à me faire quelque gasconnade[40] conjugale.

---

[a] B3: ses

40. Vu le contenu de la scène suivante, le mot de *gasconnade* (forfanterie, hâblerie, vantardise) est légèrement impropre ; c'est plutôt d'une *infidélité* qu'il s'agit. Il se peut que le terme de gasconnade rappelle la situation des *Trois Gascons*.

SCENE VII.

FRONTIN & MARTON *masquée.*

FRONTIN

Pendant que nos amants sont ensemble, cherchons aussi quelque tête à tête: mais quoi! une femme seule au Bal! voyons un peu ce que ce pouroit être.

MARTON *à part*

Il me lorgne! le pendart s'aviseroit-il de m'en conter?

FRONTIN *à part*

Elle m'œüillade![41] parbleu; faisons le petit maître; & brusquons l'avanture: mais non, ce pouroit être quelque masque de qualité; laissons lui faire les avances.

MARTON *en le salüant d'un air gracieux*

C'est Monsieur de Lolive, si je ne me trompe?

FRONTIN *à part*

Foin![42] Me voila dégradé! *à Marton* Fort à vôtre service, Madame, il ne tient qu'à vous que je ne vous rende mes respects en face.

---

41. Lancer des oeillades à (mot blâmé par Malherbe) et vieilli selon Furetière (DFC); cf. Th. Corneille, *Le Charme de la voix*, II, 2.

42. Interjection qui marquait le dépit, l'agacement, la répulsion (DFC); cf. Molière, *George Dandin*, I, 2.

MARTON

J'ai eü plus d'une fois le plaisir de vous voir avec Mr Vulpin; & ce n'est pas aussi[43] la première fois que je vous ai souhaité sa fortune.

FRONTIN

Ah, Madame! c'en est une au dessus de la sienne, que vous vous soyez donné la peine de souhaiter quelque chose pour moi!

MARTON

Monsieur de Lolive est toujours ingénieux! tout ce qu'il dit, & tout ce qu'il fait est plein de graces; & je me souviens que vous me versâtes un jour à boire, d'un air à me faire penser à toute autre chose!

FRONTIN

Vous vous moquez, Madame ! *à part.* Qui diable seroit cette connoisseuse-là?

MARTON

Vous cherchez à me déchifrer[44], Monsieur de Lolive?

FRONTIN

Franchement, Madame, j'ai quelque peine: vous avez

43. A. Haase constate que 'aussi, construit avec une préposition (*sic*) négative, signifie *non plus* en ancien français et conserve ce sens jusque dans le XVIIIe siècle' et il cite des exemples puisés chez Corneille, Molière, Bossuet, Fénelon, etc. (*op. cit.*, § 142).

44. Entendre : dévoiler. Le sens du mot était plus large au XVIIIe siècle (DFC).

l'air un peu équivoque! mais n'importe, je vous attraperai! oüi... non... si fait... ah, je vous tiens! vous êtes cette jeune veuve qu'on ne connoît presque encore que sous son nom de fille? là, c'est vous qui n'en déplaise à vôtre aînée, avez porté le talent de jolie femme à sa perfection? & je ne vous connoissois point encore, que je m'avisai de vous aimer à ne vous voir que sur un écran![45]

MARTON

Vous vous trompez, Monsieur de Lolive; loin d'être vôtre jeune veuve, je ne suis pas même encore sortie de fille[46] .

FRONTIN

Il faut donc que vous soyez quelqu'une de ces galantes de distinction, à qui l'on a ordonné l'air de la campagne? & qui ne faisant plus à Paris qu'un séjour clandestin, n'osent plus se montrer que sous le masque?

MARTON

Encore moins, je vous assûre. *à part* Hom! que je te froterois[47] de bon cœur!

---

45. Entendre : vous ayant vue seulement sous la forme d'une représentation artistique.

46. '[Sortir] se dit figurément en choses morales, du changement d'état, de profession, de condition : [...] il est sorti de minorité, il est devenu majeur' (Furetière).

47. Frotter : donner des coups à quelqu'un; battre : 'Que le galant alors soit frotté d'importance (Corneille, *L'Illusion comique*, v. 606) (DFC). Furetière donne l'exemple: 'Les ennemis

FRONTIN

Oh pour le coup, Madame, j'y suis; & voila un poing fermé qui vous décèle! vous êtes cette fille d'épée, ou si vous l'aimez mieux, ce petit maître à phalbala? car on ne sçait pas bien encore dans le monde à quoi s'en tenir sur vôtre chapitre; & je ne jurerois pas qu'il n'y eut de la tricherie, non: je vous ai vû soupirer aux pieds d'une belle, aussi déterminément que si vous êtiez sûre de vôtre fait!

MARTON

Monsieur Frontin est toujours en défaut!

FRONTIN

Comment, Mr Frontin: oh, tout beau[48], Madame! vous me connoissez un peu plus qu'il ne faut! je ne suis Frontin qu'*incognito*[49] ; & je serois perdu si l'on me découvroit ici pour tout autre que pour Lolive!

MARTON

Allez, allëz, je sçais vos intérêts: vous servez Eraste; & vous trompez ici Mr Vulpin, pour lui enlever

---

furent bien frottés au passage d'une telle rivière', et le *Dictionnaire de Trévoux* (1771) ajoute que le mot ne s'employait alors que 'figurément et bassement'.

48. Le DFC note qu'au temps de Corneille l'expression 'tout beau', au sens de 'doucement, modérez-vous' appartenait au style noble, mais qu'elle devint bientôt familière.

49. L'auteur du *Bon et du mauvais usage* fournit une ample explication de cette expression, jugée fort utile (*loc. cit.*, p. 103-105); Frontin serait 'un particulier sans caractère [...] arrivé dans un lieu où il est connu, [et qui] s'y cache' (p.104).

Hortence en faveur de son rival: mais je crains bien que vous ne fassiez tout ce manége, pour vous assûrer vous-même une certaine Marton...

FRONTIN *à part*

De la jalousie? bon, mes affaires avancent!

MARTON

Franchement, Mr de Lolive; cette Marton là me tient au cœur.

FRONTIN

Eh Madame! vaut-elle seulement la peine qu'on y songe? il est bien vrai qu'il s'est agi de quelque chose entre nous; mais cela n'êtoit encore qu'ébauché; & ce n'est point une femme à finir que cette creature là!

MARTON

Si l'on êtoit bien sûre de vos sentimens à son égard ...

FRONTIN

Eh, bon, bon, Madame! est-ce pour des Martons que les sentiments sont faits? il y a de certaines femmes qui ne doivent couter tout au plus que du verbiage! encore, y perdroit-on!

MARTON

Eh, qui me répondra, Mr de Lolive, que vous me destiniez une autre monnoïe?

FRONTIN

Les effets, Madame, les effets! tenez, j'avois conclu dans ma tête, le mariage d'Hortence & d'Eraste; je commence par le casser tout net s'il vous donne le moindre soupçon.

MARTON

Non pas, s'il vous plait, Mr de Lolive; tout au contraire: je vous ordonne de confirmer ce mariage, puisque vous le tenez pour fait ; & c'est même à ce prix que je prétens me mettre.

FRONTIN

Ah! vous me comblez de joïe, ma Princesse! de grace, laissez-moi vous en marquer ma reconnoissance; & jurer à vos genoux, de ne songer de ma vie à cette enragée de Marton!

SCENE VIII

FRONTIN, MARTON, LUCAS.

LUCAS *trouvant Frontin aux pieds de Marton*

Hé tatigué, Monsieur de Lolive! quelle posture est-ce là? tandis qu'on vous attent, vous vous amusez là[50] , à faire l'espalier auprès de Madame! est ce qu'ous n'avez pas envie que je commencions la nôce?

---

50. Entendre : vous vous attardez ; cf. 'Amusez-le du moins à débattre avec vous: faites lui perdre du temps' (Corneille, *Nicomède*, v. 1622).

FRONTIN

Non, mon enfant; voici une Dame de qualité, qui a intérêt de la rompre; & qui m'assûre ma fortune, si j'en viens à bout; il ne tient qu'à toi d'en être de moitié.

LUCAS

De moitié! hé mais morgué, comment entendez-vous ça? est-ce qu'alle seroit d'humeur à nous épouser tous deux?

FRONTIN

Oh pour cela, non, c'est un fait à part: mais il y va de ton intérêt de nous aider à rompre le mariage de Mr Vulpin.

LUCAS

Eh parsangué, je ne demande pas mieux! que faut-il faire pour ça?

FRONTIN

Donner avis de ce qui se passe, à Madame Lucinde, & à Madame Menine; & les engager à nous venir seconder.

LUCAS

Hé morgué, que ne m'avez-vous dit ça plûtôt: alles êtiont ici tout à l'heure!

FRONTIN

Il faut aussi lui rendre suspecte celle qu'il veut épouser; & l'avertir d' un rendez-vous qu'elle a ici avec son amant: mais courons l'en informer nous-même; & tâchons de les lui faire surprendre ensemble: c'est le meilleur moyen de l'en détacher.

ACTE III

SCENE PREMIERE

Mr VULPIN, LUCAS

LUCAS

Oui, morgué, je vous dis qu'alle est dans le petit bois avec un Cavalier; & qu'il ne tient qu'à vous de les y aller surprendre: eh, tenez, morgué! ne les voila-t'il pas[51] qui en revenont?

Mr VULPIN

Justement; mais ne les éfarouchons point: passons derrière cette palissade.

SCENE II

Mr VULPIN, LUCAS, HORTENCE, ERASTE

HORTENCE

Non, Eraste; rien ne sçauroit me faire changer; & je vous promets de n'être jamais qu'à vous.

---

51. Cette construction est attestée au XVIIe siècle chez Tallement des Réaux et chez Molière (M. Grevisse, *Le Bon Usage*, § 387, Hist.).

LUCAS *à part*

Hé bien, morgué! l'entendez-vous?

HORTENCE

Mais séparons-nous; je tremble qu'on ne nous surprenne ensemble!

ERASTE *en lui baisant la main*

Ah, soufrez du moins que je prenne à vos pieds ce gage de mon bonheur...

HORTENCE

Hé bien, Eraste, estes vous content!

LUCAS *courant se mettre entr'eux*

Hé, oüi, mais morgué je ne le sommes pas nous!

HORTENCE

Quoi, vous êtiez là?

LUCAS

Oh parsanguenne oüi, je vous écoutions!

HORTENCE

Hé bien, tant pis pour vous: vous connoissez mes sentiments; je ne vous aime point; vous l'avez entendu: c'est à vous de prendre vos mesures là dessus.

SCENE III

Mr VULPIN, LUCAS

Mr VULPIN

Ouais! voici bien de la franchise, pour une fille!

LUCAS

Elle n'en fait, morgué, pas de façons, comme vous voyez.

Mr VULPIN

Et elle en feroit encore moins, si elle êtoit ma femme; mais cours un peu voir ce qu'ils deviennent; & me laisse ici réver à ce que j'ai à faire.

SCENE IV

Mr VULPIN *d'un côté*, & LUCINDE *en femme de l'autre*

LUCINDE

Voici justement l'heure de nôtre rendez-vous; & je suis surprise de n'y point trouver le Chevalier: mais j'aperçois Mr Vulpin, il faut que je m'en vange sur lui.

Mr VULPIN

J'entens, ce me semble, quelqu'un. ah, c'est Lucinde! sauvons-nous!

LUCINDE

Le traitre m'échape; & je n'ose le suivre de peur de

manquer le Chevalier: ah! que je l'aurois rossé de bon cœur! mais j'entens marcher dans cette allée; voyons si ce ne seroit point le Chevalier.

SCENE V

MENINE *en femme*

C'est ici que le Marquis doit se rendre, & j'y suis néanmoins la première! mais cela est dans l'ordre; & puisque nous mettons les hommes sur ce pied là, nous ne devons pas nous en plaindre: il devroit cependant avoir un peu plus d'empressement pour une première entreveuë; & la nouveauté de l'avanture le devroit piquer d'impatience: mais que vient chercher ici cette Dame?

SCENE VI

LUCINDE & MENINE *en femmes*

LUCINDE

Oh pour cela, il faut avoüer que les hommes se relâchent terriblement de ce qu'ils nous doivent! mais à qui en veut cette Dame?

MENINE

Comment! je crois que c'est le Marquis!

LUCINDE

Eh! je pense que c'est le Chevalier!

MENINE

Non, je ne me trompe point!

LUCINDE

Oüi, c'est lui-même!

MENINE

Eh, mon cher Marquis! dans quel équipage estes-vous là? & qui vous a fait prendre ces habits?

LUCINDE

Un sujet assez naturel: mais vous, Chevalier! pourquoi ce déguisement?

MENINE

Oh, ce n'en est point un, je vous jure!

LUCINDE

Comment donc?

MENINE

Ce sont les habits de mon sexe; & c'êtoit pour moi que je voulois m'assûrer de vos sentiments.

LUCINDE

Quoi! c'êtoit de vous que vous me parliez?

MENINE

Oüi, de moi-même: mais vous sçavez ce que vous m'avez promis; & je crois pouvoir compter sur vôtre cœur.

LUCINDE

Oh, quelque chose qui arrive, ce ne sera pas par là que vous vous plaindrez de moi!

MENINE

Mon bon-heur sera donc parfait!

LUCINDE

Il y aura pourtant quelque chose à dire![52]

MENINE

Comment! est-ce que vous ne voudriez plus nous unir?

LUCINDE

Non, je ne suis point vôtre fait.

MENINE

Pourquoi donc? nos états seroient-ils si différents...

LUCINDE

Eh, mon Dieu, ils ne sont que trop semblables! car enfin... je suis...

MENINE

Hé bien?

---

52. Entendre : quelque chose à critiquer, ou quelque chose dont vous regretterez l'absence (DFC). Selon Furetière, '*dire* sert [...] pour exprimer ce qui manque tant à l'égard des personnes, que des choses'.

LUCINDE

Je ne suis point ce que vous pensez!

MENINE

Comment! seriez-vous marié?

LUCINDE

Eh, non! au contraire...

MENINE

Oh, expliquez-vous donc!

LUCINDE

Hé bien, je suis fille, puisqu'il faut vous le dire.

MENINE

Vous êtes fille?

LUCINDE

Eh oüi, vraiment; vous l'êtes bien, vous! il me semble que je puis bien l'être aussi.

MENINE

Oh, ce n'est pas moi qui vous empêcherai! cependant, si les effets eussent répondu aux aparences?

LUCINDE

En ce cas nous eussions peut être été aussi folle l'une que l'autre; mais c'est à ce maraut de Lucas que nous devons nous en prendre.

MENINE

En effet, c'est lui qui nous a trompées; voyez un peu à quoi il nous exposoit!

LUCINDE

Mais n'en auroit-il point eü les mêmes raisons? & ne serions-nous point ici toutes deux sur le compte de Mr Vulpin?

MENINE

Justement; c'est pour cela qu'il vouloit nous en écarter : mais le voici qui vient à nous.

Scene VII

MENINE, LUCINDE, LUCAS

LUCAS *acourant à Lucinde*

Hé parsangué, Madame, il y a deux heures que je vous cherche[a] ! qu'avez-vous donc fait de Monsieur le Chevalier?

MENINE *en le*[b] *retournant de son côté*

Ce qu'elle en fait, traitre?

LUCAS *à Menine*

Hé quoi! vous vela aussi redevenuë fille?

MENINE

Oüi; mais nous vous aprendrons à vous joüer de nous!

---

[a] B3 charche

[b] B2, B3 *se*

LUCAS

Oh pour ça, morgué, ce n'est pas à moi qu'il faut vous en prendre!

LUCINDE

Ce n'est pas à vous, Monsieur le maraut?

LUCAS

Eh parsangué, non; vous vouliez toutes deux être hommes: vous m'aviez défendu de vous faire connoître. Est-ce ma faute si vos desseins n'avont pas réüssi?

MENINE

Mais tu croyois par là favoriser ceux de Mr Vulpin?

LUCAS

Hé morgué, tout au contraire! je[53] sommes ici quatre ou cinq qui ne songeons qu'à les faire avorter; demandez plûtôt à Mr de Lolive.

SCENE VIII.

LUCINDE, MENINE, LUCAS
FRONTIN

FRONTIN

Oh pour cela, Mesdames, c'est la vérité; il ne tiendra

53. La leçon *je*, conforme à la grammaire populaire du personnage, est maintenue dans les éditions B2 et B3, quoique le sens de la phrase semble imposer le pronom pluriel.

qu'à vous de l'épouser: C'est Eraste qui épouse la sœur de Mr Cidaris.

LUCAS

Quoi! morgué! celui avec qui alle avoit ce rendez-vous?

FRONTIN

Oüi, mon enfant; & c'êtoit pour la lui ménager, que je m'êtois introduit chez Mr Vulpin: mais le voici lui-même avec toute la compagnie.

SCENE IX

Mr CIDARIS, Mad. CIDARIS, ERASTE, HORTENCE, FRONTIN, MARTON, Mr VULPIN, LUCINDE, MENINE, LUCAS, LE TABELLION.

Mr CIDARIS

Oui, oüi, Monsieur Vulpin, je sçais que vous l'avez surpris avec ma sœur; & qu'ils s'êtoient ici donné rendez-vous: mais je vous aprens que c'êtoit à lui que je la destinois; & que c'est là ce pendart de Frontin qui s'entendoit avec Marton.

Mr VULPIN

Quoi, Lolive!

FRONTIN

Oüi, Monsieur, pour vous rendre service; & voici

Madame Lucinde, & Madame Menine qui êtoient ici pour le même dessein.

Mr VULPIN

Ah, je suis trahi!

LUCAS *à Mr Vulpin*

Je vous disois, morgué, bian qu'alles viendront mettre empêchement à vôtre mariage!

Mr CIDARIS

Quoi, Mr Vulpin! vous aviez des engagements; & vous vouliez épouser ma sœur?

LUCINDE *à Mr Vulpin*

C'êtoit donc pour me joüer, scélérat, que tu me promettois de n'aimer jamais que moi?

Mr VULPIN

Eh, non, Madame! je vous aime uniquement!

MENINE

Et moi, traitre?

Mr VULPIN

Et vous aussi.

FRONTIN

Oüi, Madame! il vous aime toutes deux uniquement; & vous épousera même uniquement toutes deux, si vous voulez!

MENINE

Oh pour cela, non, je l'en dispence; & je l'abandonne à sa perfidie.

SCENE DERNIERE

Mr CIDARIS, Mad. CIDARIS, ERASTE, HORTENCE, FRONTIN, MARTON, VULPIN, LUCINDE, LUCAS & LE TABELLION.

LUCINDE

Et moi, je n'en serai point la dupe; & je prétens qu'il me change en contract la promesse qu'il m'a signée.

FRONTIN

En contract de mariage; ou en contract de constitution: allons, allons, Monsieur le Tabellion, c'est de la pratique pour vous.

Mad. CIDARIS

Oüi, mais qu'il commence toujours par nous donner le nôtre à signer.

Mr CIDARIS *signant le contract entre les mains du Tabellion.*

Ah, Madame, je vous obéïs aveuglement... hé bien, me refuserez-vous encore le plaisir de vous voir?

FRONTIN *prenant la plûme des mains de Mr Cidaris, & la présentant à Marton.*

Et vous, Madame, estes-vous toujours dans la disposition de faire mon bonheur?

Mad. CIDARIS *à son mari*

Non, je ne puis plus m'en deffendre; mais je crains bien que vôtre femme ne vous fasse changer de sentiments.

MARTON *à Frontin*

Oüi, je suis toujours la même; mais je crains fort que Marton ne vous rende infidele.

Mr CIDARIS *à sa femme*

Ah! que vous étes injuste, Madame! plût au Ciel que vous m'aimassiez autant que je la hais!

FRONTIN *à Marton*

Eh, ne craignez rien, Madame! je la hais autant que je vous aime!

Mad. CIDARIS *en levant son masque*

Autant que je la hais? perfide!

MARTON *en se démasquant*

Autant que je vous aime? traitre!

Mr CIDARIS

Ah, ce n'est que ma femme!

FRONTIN

Ah, ce n'est que Marton!

Mad. CIDARIS

Non, traitre, ce n'est que ta femme.

MARTON

Non, coquin, ce n'est que Marton.

Mr VULPIN

Quoi, Mr Cidaris! c'est avec vôtre femme qui vous aviez ce rendez-vous?

LUCAS

Quoi, morgué, Mr de Lolive! c'est là ste femme de qualité qui devoit vous faire vôtre fortune?

Mr CIDARIS *à sa femme*

Oh pour le coup, Madame, j'ai tort, je l'avoüe; mais il y avoit de l'étoile dans tout ceci.

FRONTIN *se jettant aux genoux de Marton*

Oh assûrément, mais il n'importe, va, je t'en demande pardon.

MARTON

Il n'y a pardon qui tienne; il faut que je te frotte comme tous les diables!

FRONTIN

Eh, dou... dou... doucement!

MARTON *en le prenant à la gorge*

Ah, je suis donc une enragée, Monsieur le maraut?

FRONTIN

Eh, non, non; mais je ne le suis pas non plus, moi! vous m'étoufez!

MARTON

Je ne suis donc point une femme à finir?

FRONTIN

Eh si fait, si fait, je vous finirai, je vous finirai!

MARTON

Touche donc là, sinon je recommence!

FRONTIN

Ah, tout coup vaille! j'aime autant être marié qu'étranglé!

Mr VULPIN

Allons ne songeons donc plus qu'à nous réjoüir!

LUCAS

Voici tout à propos les masques & les Menêtriers qui venont sous le berceau[a] ; allons, morgué, de la joïe!

---

[a] B3 barciau

PLUSIEURS BANDES DE MASQUES viennent se mêler à la compagnie; & forment avec elle un divertissement coupé de dances & de chansons.

FRONTIN chante après leur marche.

Venez fillettes du Village,
Venez sous ce charmant feüillage,
Y faire un époux d'un amant:
Qu'au plaisir vos cœurs s'abandonnent;
Dancez, dancez, que le Bal est charmant,
Quand l'himen & l'amour le donnent!

Le Chœur reprend.

Dançons, dançons, que le Bal est charmant,
Quand l'himen & l'amour le donnent!

LUCINDE sur le même air, à Mr Vulpin

Cessez, cessez d'être volage,
Une epouse est d'un doux usage;
Unissons-nous en ce moment:
Qu'au plaisir nos cœurs s'abandonnent;
Dançons, dançons, que le Bal est charmant,
Quand l'himen & l'amour le donnent!

Le Chœur repette.

Dançons, dançons, que le Bal est charmant,
Quand l'himen & l'amour le donnent!

Mr VULPIN répond

Unissons-nous, j'en suis content;
Mais qu'aucun nœud ne nous engage;
Il me faut pour être constant,
La liberté d'être volage:
Fuyons l'embaras & les soins;
L'himen est un triste esclavage:
Peut-être en nous épousant moins;
Nous nous aimerons d'avantage.

On voit ensuite une entrée d'Arlequines & de Scaramouches, après laquelle une Arlequine & un Scaramouche chantent les paroles suivantes.

Si toutes les femmes galantes
Faisoient mettre sur leurs habits,
Autant de couleurs differentes,
Qu'elles ont eu de favoris,
Ah! que de figures plaisantes,
Que d'Arlequines à Paris!

Si l'on obligeoit les coquettes
De porter pour leurs favoris,
Des robbes de veuves complettes,
Comme elles font pour leurs maris;
Ah! que l'on verroit de fillettes,
En Scaramouches à Paris!

On voit ensuite une Scaramouchette & un Arlequin dancer en écho une forlane[54] ; après laquelle Lucinde & Menine chantent les paroles suivantes.

---

54. La forlane était une 'sorte de danse commune à Venise, surtout parmi les gondoliers. Sa mesure est 6/8; elle se bat gaiement, et la danse est aussi fort gaie. On l'appelle *forlane*, parce qu'elle a pris naissance dans le Frioul, dont les habitants s'appellent Forlans' (*Encyclopédie*, II, p. 55).

Epoux qui sentez d'autres flâmes,
Que celle qui doit vous brûler;
Vous ne devez jamais aller,
Où vous pouvez trouver vos femmes.

Et vous, belles, dont le cœur tendre
Vole au devant des favoris;
Gardez-vous d'aller les attendre,
Où peuvent estre vos maris.

Une Dame Gigogne dance ensuite une entrée, après laquelle on chante les couplets suivants.

Masques, qui pour nous abuser,
Prenez tronc, calotte, & jaquettes;
Souvent, croyant vous déguiser,
Vous vous montrez ce que vous estes.

Coquettes en chauves-souris,
Qui cherchez nocturne avanture,
Que vous estes pour les maris,
Des oiseaux de mauvaise augure!

Afin d'empêcher pour toûjours,
Que la médisance ne grogne;
Ramenez, filles, de nos jours,
La mode de Dame Gigogne.

Et vous pour nous tirer d'erreur,
Apprenez-nous Scaramouchettes,
Qui des mines fut l'inventeur,
De Scaramouche ou des Coquettes.

On ne se masque ici qu'au bal;
Mais à Paris tout temps est carnaval.

Telle a déja bonne famille,
Qui va toûjours masquée en fille:
On ne se masque icy qu'au bal:
Mais à Paris tout temps est carnaval.

Enfin de Paris c'est l'usage,
On n'ose y porter son visage:
On ne se masque ici qu' au bal,
Mais à Paris tout temps est carnaval.

FIN

Permission

Permis d'imprimer, ce 31. Aoust 1702.

M. LE VOYER D'ARGENSON

BRANLE.

LUCINDE.

2. Tous les maris une Coquette,
Y prend le Masque à sa Toilette. On ne &c.

UN PAYSAN.

3. Entre Epoux souvent les caresses,
Ne sont que de feintes tendresses. On ne &c.

HORTENCE

4. Telle de pleurs fait étalage,
Qui rit sous crêpe du Veuvage. On ne &c.

Mr. HARPIN.

5. Que les sermens trompent de Belles,
C'est le Masque des Infidelles. On ne &c.

MENINE.

6. Telle a déja bonne famille,
Qui va toûjours masquée en Fille. On &c.

FRONTIN.

7. Enfin de Paris c'est l'usage,
On n'ose y porter son visage. On ne &c.

FIN.

LE

PORT

DE

MER

COMEDIE

A PARIS,

Chés PIERRE RIBOU, proche les Augustins,
à la descente du Pont-neuf, à l'Image S. Louis.

PERMISSION.

Permis d'Imprimer. Fait ce vingt-neuf Février mil sept cens quatre.

M R. DE VOYER DARGENSON.

ACTEURS,

M. SABATIN, Marchand Juif.

BENJAMINE, Fille de M. Sabatin.

MARINE, Suivante de Benjamine.

M. DOUTREMER, Armateur.

LEANDRE, neveu de M. Doutremer.

LA SALINE, Valet de Léandre.

HALI, Galerien Turc.

BRIGANTIN, Galerien François.

Quatre Matelots.

Deux Cantarines.

Deux Barcarolles.

Deux Australiennes.

Un Singe.

La Scene est à Livourne.

LE
PORT
DE MER.

COMEDIE

SCENE PREMIERE.

LA SALINE, MARINE.

MARINE

De l'amour tant qu'il vous plaira, M. de la Saline; mais point de badinage.

LA SALINE

Ta main du moins.

MARINE

Pas seulement le bout du doigt. Que ne te dépêches-tu d'assurer le bon-heur de ma maitresse? le mariage nous mettroit d'accord, je te l'ay promis.

LA SALINE

De quoy peux-tu donc te plaindre, Marine? il me semble que jusqu'icy nous y avons été assez bon train. A peine arrivons nous à Livourne[1] , moy & mon maitre, que nous devenons amoureux de toy & de ta maitresse. On nous aprend que M. Sabatin son pere la destine à un Pirate qui la rendra mal-heureuse; aussi-tôt par bonté de cœur, nous entreprenons de nous faire aimer pour la dérober à ce brûtal-là; soins, perils, dépenses, rien ne nous coûte. Vous nous aimez enfin: il y en auroit qui s'en tiendroient-là; mais nous sommes honnêtes gens, nous voulons épouser.

MARINE.

Que ne songes-tu donc à en venir à bout?

LA SALINE

Je ne songe à autre chose, depuis trois semaines que je me suis fait courtier de M. Sabatin; & je me creuse nuit & jour la cervelle, pour assortir mes fourberies à son humeur & à ses affaires.

MARINE

Hé bien, qu'as-tu tiré de ta cervelle?

---

1. L'importance commerciale de Livourne, en plein essor au temps de Boindin, datait du règne de Ferdinand Ier de Toscane (1587-1609). La ville abritait pour cause de religion, les réfugiés, tels que les catholiques anglais et les Juifs et les Maures espagnols et portuguais.

LA SALINE

Doucement, Marine. M. Sabatin destine un Pirate à Benjamine. Il est bien aise de lui tenir toute prête une petite banqueroute pour sa dot[2]. Nous attendons des Esclaves de Smirne.

MARINE

A quoy bon tout ce détail?

LA SALINE

Je veux dégouter le Pirate du mariage que nous craignons. Je prétens profiter de la banqueroute, pour retirer de nôtre Juif les pierreries que nous luy avons engagées. A l'égard des Esclaves, je compte...

MARINE

Je veux, je pretens, je compte! voila de beaux projets, mais l'execution?

LA SALINE

Tu és pour l'execution, toy! j'y viens. Je me suis déja assuré d'un bon nombre de personnes pour certain stratagême que je médite: le magazin du Juif suffira de reste aux déguisemens necessaires; & il ne me manque plus qu'une bagatelle[3] .

---

2. Abstraction faite du cadre pseudo-italien, la loi française (l'Ordonnance du Commerce de 1673, titre XI, article 12) prévoyait la mort pour la banqueroute frauduleuse (M. Marion, *Dictionnaire des institutions*, p. 36).

3. La majorité des fripiers de l'époque étaient juifs (Furetière, s.v. 'Juifverie').

MARINE

Quoy donc?

LA SALINE

De l'argent.

MARINE

C'est une bagatelle essentielle vraiment; mais n'importe; il ne te doit pas manquer ici: caisse, comptoir, écrin, coffre fort, tout est sous ta main, il ne te faut que de l'adresse & du courage.

LA SALINE

Oüi-da, oüi-da, Marine, mais la Justice n'apelle pas cela comme toy.

MARINE

Va, va, ne crains rien, la Justice ne va point en mer.

LA SALINE

Eh non[a] par tous les diables, elle n'y va pas, mais elle y envoye.

MARINE

Vraiment, voila de belles molesses! oh il faut qu'un amant ait plus de fermeté. Enfin je te laisse; fais comme tu l'entendras; mais songe à m'obtenir tandis que[4] je t'aime, on n'a pas toûjours le vent en poupe.

---

[a] P2, P4 Eh non pas par

[4] L'emploi de *tandis* comme synonyme de *pendant* et de *durant* était courant à l'époque. Selon le *Dictionnaire de l'Académie*, l'emploi de *tandis* était plus fréquent dans la poésie.

LA SALINE

Peste soit de l'amour! cette friponne-là me fera faire quelque sottise.

SCENE II

LA SALINE, BRIGANTIN.

BRIGANTIN

Au diable le chien de comité!

LA SALINE

Mais que vois-je? voicy une rencontre de mauvaise augure!

BRIGANTIN

Ah, ah, j'ay quelque idée d'avoir vû cette tête-là sur un autre corps!

LA SALINE

Je crois que c'est... oüi par bleu, c'est lui même.

BRIGANTIN

Plus je le confronte, plus... he c'est toy, mon cher la Saline?

LA SALINE

Quoy, c'est toy, mon cher Brigantin? que veut donc dire cet équipage?

BRIGANTIN

C'est un petit déshabillé de mer, comme tu vois, que je me suis fait faire pour mes exercices.

LA SALINE

Hé depuis quand donc és-tu dans la Marine?

BRIGANTIN

J'y suis de la derniere promotion.

LA SALINE

J'entens, j'entens.

BRIGANTIN

Et c'est le zéle que tu me connois pour le bien public, qui m'a procuré cet emploi-là.

LA SALINE

Comment?

BRIGANTIN

Tu sais que j'ai toujours été fort amoureux des Spectacles? Je m'êtois dévoüé de tout temps à y maintenir la paix & le silence, & pour cela, j'allois réguliérement à la Comédie, où le plus discretement qu'il m'êtoit possible, je m'emparois des Epées pour prévenir les querelles, & des Tabatiéres pour empêcher les éternuëmens.

LA SALINE

Tu rendois-là un vrai service au public!

BRIGANTIN

Je m'en serois assez bien trouvé, sans un petit malheur qui m'arriva.

LA SALINE

Quel malheur?

BRIGANTIN

Le jour d'une premiére représentation, un maudit animal, un Auteur qui avoit interêt que ce jour-là le Spectacle ne fut pas paisible, me fit interrompre dans mon exercice. La Justice prit mon zêle de travers, & avec quelque autre petite chose qu'elle interpretta aussi mal, elle alla jusqu'à me soupçonner de vollerie, & me fit expédier un petit ordre pour Marseille. Je n'y fus pas plûtôt arrivé, qu'il me fallut prendre le Colier de l'Ordre, & venir faire mes Caravannes sur ces Côtes.
Qui l'eut dit qu'un rivage, à mes vœux si funeste,
Dût présenter d'abord Pilade aux yeux d'Oreste?[5]

LA SALINE

Je vois vraiment que tu t'és fort orné l'esprit!

BRIGANTIN

O diable! les Spectacles font bien un jeune homme; mais toi tu brillois autrefois dans le monde? cet équipage-là t'éface diablement! ne me débroüilleras-tu point un peu de tout cela?

5. Racine, *Andromaque,* I, 1, v. 5-6 ; var: Présenterait. La scène offre des ressemblances avec *Monsieur de Pourceaugnac*, I, 2.

LA SALINE

Bon, ai-je jamais eu de réserve pour toi? & peux-tu douter que je ne sois toujours le même? l'amitié s'altere-t-elle, quand la vertu en est le fondement?

BRIGANTIN

Vous vous moquez, M. de la Saline.

LA SALINE

Ah, mon enfant, les honnêtes gens sont maudits de la Fortune! le zêle du bien public t'a perdu; une tendresse de conscience a ruiné mes affaires.

BRIGANTIN

Une tendresse de conscience?

LA SALINE

Oüi, je tenois une Caisse à Paris, dont je faisois valoir l'argent un peu vigoureusement. Cette chienne de conscience se souleva contre moi; je luttai quelque temps contre elle; mais enfin elle m'atéra: j'eus horreur de moi-même; & pour ne point rougir devant mes compatriotes, je m'exilai généreusement de mon païs. Il est vrai que j'emportai sans y penser, le fonds de la Caisse...

BRIGANTIN

On ne peut pas songer à tout.

LA SALINE

Mais je ne le portai pas loin. La Mer, l'avare Mer a

tout englouti; & je n'ai sauvé du naufrage, que mes scruples, & mon intégrité.

BRIGANTIN

C'est le principal. Que fais-tu donc à présent?

LA SALINE

Je suis réduit à servir un jeune homme dont l'amour me taille bien de la besogne; & cet équipage n'est qu'un déguisement pour servir sa passion.

BRIGANTIN

A qui en veut[6] donc ton Maître icy?

LA SALINE

A la fille d'un certain Juif, chez qui je me suis introduit.

BRIGANTIN

Son nom?

LA SALINE

Je n'en ai pû encore retenir que la moitié; Hazaël-Raka-Nimbrod-Iscarioth-Sabatin.

BRIGANTIN

Quoi! Benjamine, la fille de M. Sabatin?

---

6. Le sens moderne de 'en vouloir à' était déjà usuel au dix-septième siècle, mais ici le contexte éclaire le sens de l'expression.

LA SALINE

C'est cela même.

BRIGANTIN

Diable, la jolie fille, & le vilain pere!

LA SALINE

Tu le connois?

BRIGANTIN

Trait pour trait[7]. Tien, l'usure, la dureté, la défiance, la fraude, & le parjure, avec quelques régles d'Arithmétique, n'est-ce pas ce qu'on appelle ici M. Sabatin?

LA SALINE

Justement, mais en récompense, la générosité, la tendresse, la franchise, & la constance, avec une taille divine, le visage le plus gratieux, les yeux les plus brillans du monde, & mille autres menus attraits, c'est ce qu'on appelle ici Benjamine.

BRIGANTIN

La peste, quelle pâte de fille ![8]

---

7. Boindin joue sur le son des mots.

8. Pâte : 'on le dit [...] de l'esprit et des moeurs. C'est la meilleure *pâte* d'homme qui fût jamais, c'est-à-dire, un homme doux, accommodant, dont on fait ce qu'on veut. Cela n'est bon que dans le style simple et familier' (Furetière).

LA SALINE

Cette fille-là, comme tu vois, merite assez qu'on ne s'épargne pas à la tirer des mains d'un pere comme le sien, qui pour comble de dureté, la veut donner pour femme à un brutal d'Armateur, encore plus digne de nôtre indignation. Non, mon cher Brigantin; non, ne soufrons point cette injuste alliance, & que le sort ne nous ait pas rassemblez en vain.

BRIGANTIN

Tu n'as qu'à dire.

LA SALINE

Me voila déja Courtier de M. Sabatin, j'en ménage plus commodément les intérêts de mon Maître, & pour peu que tu me secondes...

BRIGANTIN

Volontiers, je suis tout à toi; qu'y a t'il à gagner?

LA SALINE

Ta liberté. Pourquoi secoüer la tête? si nous servons utilement mon Maître; crois- tu qu'il manque de credit, ou d'argent pour l'obtenir?

BRIGANTIN

Ce n'est pas cela.

LA SALINE

Quoi donc?

BRIGANTIN

Veux-tu que je te dise? j'ai pris mon parti: je commence à me faire au service; & d'ailleurs, il y faudroit toujours revenir.

LA SALINE

Si-bien donc que tu aimerois mieux ta liberté en argent?

BRIGANTIN

Sur ce pied là, il n'y a point de danger que je n'affronte.

LA SALINE

Voici mon Maître tout à propos.

BRIGANTIN

Ciel, c'est Léandre!

Scene III

LEANDRE, LA SALINE,
BRIGANTIN.

LA SALINE

Monsieur, voila un Virtuose que je vous presente.

LEANDRE

Eh c'est ce coquin de valet que j'avois à Paris!

BRIGANTIN

Fort à vôtre service, Monsieur.

LEANDRE

Ah Monsieur le fripon, vous me payerez du moins de vos deux oreilles le Diamant que vous me volâtes.

LA SALINE

Comment diable, un Diamant?

BRIGANTIN

Ah Monsieur, je vous demande pardon. (*Il se jette à genoux.*) Vous me voyez au desespoir... de la surprise... que le remords... de l'impuissance où je suis...

LEANDRE *luy surprenant la main dans sa poche.*

Comment, éfronté, que cherches tu-là?

BRIGANTIN

Un mouchoir, Monsieur, pour essuyer mes larmes.

LA SALINE

L'habitude!

LEANDRE

Je ne sçay ce qui me tient...

LA SALINE

Tout beau, Monsieur, ce bona-Voglie[9] nous est plus necessaire que vous ne pensez: je l'avois déja mis dans nos interests; & il va vous restituer le tout en belles & bonnes fourberies.

BRIGANTIN *en se relevant.*

Il me faut du retour.

LA SALINE

Ne te mets pas en peine.

LEANDRE

Ah mon pauvre la Saline, je n'ai jamais eu plus besoin de secours. Tout semble conjuré contre ma flame: mon oncle est icy.

LA SALINE

M. Salomin?

LEANDRE

Oüi, M. Salomin, les gens de mon équipage l'ont vû, comment faire?

---

9. Furetière (1701) définit ainsi le terme 'bonavoglie': 'Terme de marine. Galérien volontaire ; un homme qui se loue volontairement pour tirer la rame. Ménage écrit *Bonne vouille*'. L'édition de 1727 ajoute : 'On les appelle aussi Mariniers de rame'. Là, on estompe une distinction importante : que les mariniers de rame étaient des conscrits. En fait, Brigantin n'est pas un bona voglie, mais un criminel condamné aux galères. La Saline le présente de manière à passer ses crimes sous silence tout en expliquant sa tenue.

LA SALINE

Lever, l'anchre, Monsieur, & prendre le large.

LEANDRE

Abandonner Benjamine?

LA SALINE

Que voulez-vous, Monsieur? soutiendrons-nous la présence de vôtre oncle? il n'y a que six mois que vous lui enlevâtes ses pierreries: nous avons été obligés de les mettre à la Juifverie[10]. M. Salomin me croira l'auteur du desordre; vous me l'avez peint brutal. De grace, Monsieur, évitons l'orage, & ne m'allez pas briser contre ce rocher-là.

LEANDRE

Abandonner Benjamine! & tu me crois un cœur à m'y resoudre?

LA SALINE

Mais à quelle diable de manœuvre pretendez-vous encor m'employer? vous m'avez déja fait afronter mille écueils, depuis que j'ai l'honneur de conduire vôtre barque; & votre amour est furieusement orageux!

---

10. Juifverie : 'Quartier d'une ville où demeurent les Juifs. Les lieux où demeurent les fripiers s'appellent aussi en plusieurs lieux la *Juiverie*, parce que la plupart des fripiers sont Juifs' (Furetière).

BRIGANTIN

Laissez-moy faire, Monsieur, je veux vous servir, moy, contre vent & marée[11].

LEANDRE

Ah, tu me rends la vie, mon cher Brigantin! seconde son zele, mon cher la Saline.

LA SALINE

Il ne risque rien, lui.

BRIGANTIN

Tant pis, c'est un agrément de moins.

LA SALINE

Allons, Monsieur, l'émulation me gagne, il faut se sacrifier pour vous. J'imagine déja un moyen de vous dérober à la veuë de vôtre oncle, & de vous introduire chez le pere de votre maitresse.

LEANDRE

Chez M. Sabatin?

LA SALINE

Oüi le bon homme m'a confié ses affaires, & je pretens... mais je l'aperçois, allez tous deux m'attendre à la galere.

---

11. Furetière (s.v. 'Vent', *in fine*) note que : 'on dit [...] de celui qui a fait une entreprise mal à propos, qu'il va contre *vent* et marée'. Boindin, qui cherche à truffer son dialogue d'expressions maritimes, élargit ici le sens de la métaphore.

BRIGANTIN

Sans adieu, camarade.

LA SALINE

Cet honneur là ne m'appartient pas.

BRIGANTIN

Il t'apartiendra, il t'apartiendra.

Scene IV

M. SABATIN, HALI, LA SALINE.

LA SALINE

Ha Monsieur je vous trouve à propos; je viens de tout préparer pour l'arrivée de nos esclaves.

M. SABATIN

C'est bien fait; mais as-tu songé à nôtre banqueroute?

LA SALINE

Oüi vraiment, Monsieur, toutes nos mesures sont prises; & j'espere la conduire hûreusement à terme, pour peu qu'Hali me seconde.

HALI

Mi volir, signor, mi volir, ma star una petita dificulta.

M. SABATIN

Comment donc, quelle dificulté?

HALI

Habir qualchi scrupuli, e volir sapir che star gambarutta?

M. SABATIN

Ce que c'est qu'une banqueroute? bon c'est le fin[a] du commerce, tu n'y entendrois rien.

HALI

Oh dirmi[12], signor, non povir far niente, se non sapir.

LA SALINE

Que veux-tu? c'est une maniere honnête de profiter de la confiance des gens, & de partager à l'amiable le bien d'autrui.

HALI

Star questo? e comesi far gambarutta?

LA SALINE

Eh mais, on commence par établir son crédit, & quand on a pû atraper l'argent ou la marchandise des gens, on disparoit à propos! & l'on en est quite pour partager.

HALI

Per partagir?

---

[a] P3, P4, P5 la fin

12. De l'anglais: 'dear me' (hélas!).

M. SABATIN

Oüi, c'est la regle.

HALI

E non star friponaria?

M. SABATIN

Rien moins.

HALI

Ela justitiâ non impicar?

M. SABATIN

Au contraire, c'est elle même qui en fait le partage; & il n'y a point de bon pere de famille qui ne doive faire au moins une banqueroute en sa vie.

LA SALINE

Et qui n'y soit même obligé en conscience.

HALI

In conscienza? oh non habir piu di scrupuli, e star presto à la gambarutta.

M. SABATIN

Va-t-en donc m'attendre au magazin, & m'envoye ici Benjamine.

LA SALINE

La voici tout à propos avec Marine.

M. SABATIN

Pour toi va-t-en sur le Port, au devant de M. Doutremer.

SCENE V

M. SABATIN, BENJAMINE,
MARINE

M. SABATIN

Et vous, ma fille, préparez-vous à le recevoir comme il faut.

MARINE

Quoi Monsieur, vous songeriez encor à nous donner ce Corsaire là?[13]

M. SABATIN

Assûrément: c'est un brave Pirate d'un abord un peu brusque à la verité; mais qui a de grandes intelligences dans son art, & qui sait sa mer par cœur.

MARINE

Mais au moins devriez-vous consulter l'inclination de vôtre fille!

---

13. Un corsaire était un pirate mandaté par son gouvernement pour s'attaquer à la flotte marchande de ses ennemis déclarés (G.A. Jaeger, *Pirates, flibustiers et corsaires*, p. 12). La langue quotidienne n'observe pas les distinctions entre pirates, flibustiers et corsaires, et Furetière note que: 'en général, le mot de *corsaire* se prend pour un méchant, un scélérat, un homme dur, impitoyable ; qui profite de tout pour s'avancer, et pour s'enrichir'.

M. SABATIN

Inclination ou non, Marine, M. Doutremer a ma parolle, & je la lui tiendrai.

MARINE

Ma foi, je ne luy conseillerois pas de s'embarquer à l'étourdie; le mariage est une mer bien dangereuse, quand on y a l'amour contraire.

BENJAMINE

Non, non, Marine, mon pere ne me sacrifiera point à des vûës d'intérêt; & la nature...

M. SABATIN

La nature est une bête, ma fille, quand elle s'oppose à des établissemens solides.

MARINE

Oüi vraiment, voila un établissement bien solide qu'un époux flottant!

SCENE VI

M. DOUTREMER, M. SABATIN.
BENJAMINE, MARINE.

M. DOUTREMER *fumant*.

Serviteur, beau-pere, me voici arrivé, épousons au plus vîte, le port m'ennüie déja.

M. SABATIN

Allons, ma fille, saluez M. Doutremer.

M. DOUTREMER

Sans façons[a], M. Sabatin, achevons ma pipe, & nos affaires, à quand la nôce?

M. SABATIN

A demain, si vous voulez.

BENJAMINE

A demain, mon pere!

M. DOUTREMER

Elle a raison, pourquoi pas aujourd'hui?

BENJAMINE

Ah de grace, mon pere, ne précipitez pas tant les choses; acordez moi quelque temps pour calmer mes répugnances; & s'il faut que je me sacrifie à vos ordres, laissez moi du moins préparer mon cœur à cet effort.

M. DOUTREMER

Bon bon Mademoiselle! les vents entendent bien toutes ces raisons là! ils souflent, il faut voguer[14].

---

[a] P3, P4, P5 façon

14. *Voguer* signifiait *ramer*, mais ici on comprend plutôt 'suivre le courant'.

BENJAMINE

Vous pouvez voguer tout seul, pour moi qui ne suis point faite à la Mer...

M. DOUTREMER

Vous vous y ferez Mademoiselle, & je vous en garantis quitte pour quelque maux de cœur.

BENJAMINE

Je tâcherai de n'en avoir point à vous reprocher.

M. DOUTREMER

O parbleu nous verrons, vôtre pere m'a promis ce mariage là, & je prétens qu'il me le tienne.

M. SABATIN

C'est comme si les Notaires y avoient passé.

MARINE

Pas tout à fait.

M. DOUTREMER

Songez donc aux formalités, & à la cérémonie; je n'entens rien à tout cela; mais je me charge du reste.

MARINE

Plaisante maniere de faire l'amour!

M. DOUTREMER

Je ne m'en pique pas, Marine, ce n'est pas mon métier.

MARINE

Pourquoi vous mêlez-vous donc d'épouser?

M. DOUTREMER

C'est autre chose.

MARINE

Distinction de corsaire.

M. DOUTREMER

Ce n'est pas que je renonce à aimer ta Maîtresse, non; & si elle vouloit m'aimer un peu...

BENJAMINE *le repoussant.*

Ah vous m'empestez!

M. DOUTREMER

Quoi, ces délicatesses sur un port? quand vous seriez en pleine terre!

MARINE

Vous voyez bien que vous n'êtes pas faits l'un pour l'autre!

M. DOUTREMER

Bagatelle, je veux qu'en moins d'un mois, elle sache fumer comme un Janissaire; & nous n'aurons pas plûtôt fait un petit tour du monde ensemble... touchez là...

MARINE *lui donnant la main.*

Tenez, Monsieur, c'est comme si c'étoit ma maîtresse. Vous pouvez compter sur un aversion invincible; & que plûtôt que de vous épouser, nous nous jetterons toutes deux dans la Mer une pierre au col[15]. Vous nous pécherez si vous voulez.[a]

M. SABATIN

Vous êtes une insolente...

BENJAMINE

Oüi mon pere, ce sont mes sentimens, & je vous laisse le maître d'en faire l'épreuve.

MARINE

Vôtre servante.

SCENE VII

M. DOUTREMER, M. SABATIN

M. DOUTREMER

Franchement, M. Sabatin, nous aurons de la peine à revirer[16] cet esprit là!

---

[a] CF et D *ajoutent la réplique* : DOUTREMER Je ne vous repêcherai point.

15. On prononçait 'cou' ; voir Vaugelas, *Remarques*, p. 13.

16. *Revirer*: 'terme de marine. Tourner la pointe du navire vers quelque endroit' (Furetière, 1701). L'édition de 1727 ajoute : 'Il se dit figurément dans le style bas et burlesque'.

M. SABATIN

Ne vous mettez pas en peine, je sçaurai la reduire, il ne faut pas s'étonner si la Mer & vos manieres l'ont d'abord un peu effrayée.

M. DOUTREMER

Ma foi, beau-pere; je ne changerai pourtant ni de manieres, ni d'élément; vous n'avez qu'à voir!

M. SABATIN

Il faudra bien qu'elle s'y fasse.

M. DOUTREMER

Songez donc à l'y disposer: je m'en vais faire un tour à mon bord: & je reviens sur le champ.

M. SABATIN

Allez vous pouvez compter sur elle; & je vous répons encor de sa personne; au cœur près, qui poura venir.

M. DOUTREMER

Par bleu, qu'il vienne ou non, je l'en quitte[17]. Est ce qu'on regarde les filles par là?

M. SABATIN

Vous avez raison, le cœur n'est qu'un zero dans un mariage bien sensé.

---

17. Entendre : je l'en dispense. Cf.: 'Je vous quitte de la peine de me répondre, quoique j'aime infiniment vos lettres' (Sévigné, 21 novembre 1664) DFC.

SCENE VIII

M. SABATIN, MARINE.
LA SALINE en Marchand d'esclaves, avec
LEANDRE en more, BRIGANTIN en esclavonne,
& d'autres esclaves.

MARINE

Monsieur, voila une maniere de Turc, avec des façons d'esclaves, qui vous cherche[a].

LA SALINE

Ah Monsieur, soyez le bien trouvé.

M. SABATIN

Sans façon, Monsieur, que vous plait-il?

LA SALINE

C'est de la part de vôtre corespondant de Smirne qui vous envoye ces esclaves que vous devez vendre à la Foire, & vous en voyez un échantillon.

M. SABATIN

Voila vraiment un fort bel échantillon.

LA SALINE

Oh pour cette marchandise là, je défie qu'on soit mieux assorti! maïs il faut un peu vous montrer ce

---

[a] P2, P3, P4, P5 cherchent

qu'ils savent faire. Allons, cette Forlanne ? Je ne fais point de montre[18], vous allez voir.

Les Esclaves dansent

[a]LA SALINE

Hé bien, à quoy pensez vous?

M. SABATIN

Je songe à y mettre le prix un peu haut.

LA SALINE

Vous avez raison, on peut tenir bon sur cette marchandise là; mais, écoutez un peu celle-ci, elle chante joliment.

Une Esclave chante.

O Felice schiavo d'amor.
Frà catene d'une belta,
Goder sempre dev'il suo cor;
Nella leggiadra juventù,
Menò giova la liberta
Che l'amorosa servitù.

M. SABATIN

Fort bien.

---

[a] CF *supprime le texte jusqu'aux mots* : '... ces petits talens-là'.

18. Le mot montre comporte ici des idées de spectacle, de démonstration et d'étalage de marchandise; voir DFC.

LA SALINE

Ma foi, vous y ferez vôtre compte, sur ma parole; il n'y a rien qui rencherisse les filles comme ces petits talens-là.

MARINE *s'aprochant du More.*

Ce visage là me revient assez, il est d'un beau noir.

M. SABATIN

A quoy est-il bon? chante-t-il, danse-t-il?

LA SALINE

Il ne chante, ni ne danse, mais il ne laisse pas d'avoir son talent: tout More qu'il est ce maraut-là a de l'esprit comme un Singe; & c'est un animal à changer du noir au blanc dans l'ocasion.

M. SABATIN

Et cette autre Eslave, d'où est-elle?

BRIGANTIN

D'Esclavonie, Monsieur.

LA SALINE

Elle est jolie femme, oüi!

BRIGANTIN

Fi donc, fi donc, vous me faites rougir. Il est vray qu'un Bacha entre les mains de qui je tombai, me destina sur ma mine au Serail du grand Seigneur; mais il se trouva un petit obstacle. On n'entre point là qu'on ne soit fille, exactement fille; & par malheur, j'étois mariée depuis trois mois. Trois ans plutôt, j'êtois en passe d'être Sultanne favorite.

M. SABATIN

Elle est réjoüissante.

LA SALINE

Et utile de plus, tenez donnez-lui vôtre main, elle vous dira la bonne avanture à livre ouvert.

M. SABATIN *luy donnant sa main toute gantée.*

Voyons.

LA SALINE

Dégantez vous-donc.

BRIGANTIN

Ce n'est pas la peine, j'aperçois déja à travers vôtre gand, les aprêts de certaine banqueroute.

M. SABATIN

Paix, Paix, passons cet article. La peste quel Linx!

BRIGANTIN

Ah voici qui ne dit rien de bon. Vous avez des vuës pour vôtre fille, que ses inclinations ne secondent point du tout.

M. SABATIN

Il est vray.

BRIGANTIN

Vôtre main la menace de malheur; mais laissez moy faire, je ne veux que manier son esprit un moment, je luy insinuërai [19] des résolutions convenables; & je veux la rendre heureuse en dépit de cette main-là.

M. SABATIN

J'aime bien autant ceux-cy que les autres.[a]

LA SALINE

Cela se trouve le mieux du monde, mon maitre m'a chargé de vous les presenter de sa part, en reconnoissance des soins que vous prendrez du reste.

M. SABATIN

Je luy suis vraiment fort obligé, & je les veux garder pour l'amour de lui; mais vous plait-il d'entrer?

LA SALINE

Non, je m'en retourne à la rade; & nous débarquerons quand vous jugerez à propos.

M. SABATIN

Serviteur. *Il rentre*[b] *avec Leandre & Brigantin.*

---

[a] CF celle-ci que l'autre.

[b] CF *sort*

19. Entendre : 'faire pénétrer adroitement, glisser' (DFC).

[a]SCENE IX

MARINE, LA SALINE.

LA SALINE. *En quittant son habit de Turc.*

He bien, Marine, ne m'en suis-je pas bien tiré?

MARINE

A merveilles[20] , mais à quoy cela nous menne-t-il?

LA SALINE

A donner le tems à Leandre de s'expliquer avec Benjamine, pendant que je travaillerai de mon costé à faire échoüer M. Doutremer.

---

[a] CF supprime les scènes ix et ix et y substitue :

BENJAMINE, MARINE, SABATIN.

Benjamine
Ah ! mon Pere, voila ce coquin de Turc qui vous emporte vos pierreries.

SABATIN

Mes Pierreries ! Ah je suis ruiné !

MARINE

Ne perdez point de temps ; courez vîte au Port, de peur qu'il n'échappe.

20. La présence du *s* paraît indifférente ; cf. scène xi : *à merveille*.

Scene X.

M. SABATIN, LA SALINE, MARINE.

M. SABATIN

Ah je suis perdu! je suis ruiné!

LA SALINE

Comment donc Monsieur, qu'est-il arrivé?

M. SABATIN

Ce coquin de Turc qui vient de m'emporter mes pierreries.

LA SALINE

Vos pierreries? ah je suis volé!

MARINE

Ne perdez point de tems, courez viste au Port de peur qu'il n'échape.

Scene XI

BENJAMINE, MARINE

BENJAMINE

He bien, ma pauvre Marine, comment nous déferons-nous de ce Monsieur Doutremer?

MARINE

Ma foi, Mademoiselle, je ne sais pas; vôtre pere veut que vous épousiez ce Pirate là: franchement, nous sommes mal, il a le vent sur nous[21].

BENJAMINE

Et pour comble de maux, Leandre m'abandonne encor dans cette extremité.

MARINE

Leandre vous abandonne?

BENJAMINE

Qu'il est cruel, Marine! il y a près d'un jour que je n'ai eu de ses nouvelles.

MARINE

Vous moquez-vous? Je croyois tout perdu! Quoi, pour quelques moments employés sans doute à chercher des remedes essentiels, vous allez dabord aux invectives! Fi, Mademoiselle, faut-il avoir le cœur si ombrageux?

BENJAMINE

Juge par là de mon amour pour Leandre, & par cet amour comprends toute mon aversion pour son rival.

---

21. Furetière fournit de très nombreuses expressions du vocabulaire nautique qui concernent le vent. Le sens le plus proche est celui des expressions 'être au *vent* d'un vaisseau, passer au *vent* d'un vaisseau, monter au *vent*, lui gagner le *vent*, avoir l'avantage du *vent*, le dessus du *vent*, lorsque le *vent* porte un vaisseau sur un autre', qui désignent tous un avantage.

MARINE

J'entre dans tout cela à merveille, mais je ne vois pas par où en sortir.

BENJAMINE

Mais quelque dureté que mon pere affecte, crois-tu qu'au fond il ne conserve pas encore assez de tendresse...

MARINE

Que parlez-vous de tendresse? je ne vous connois qu'un pere Juif, je n'en sâche point d'autre.

BENJAMINE

S'il étoit bien convaincu du desespoir ou sa résolution me jette...

MARINE

Il n'en démordroit pas, vous dis-je; il a calculé ce mariage, & en a fait la preuve; il n'y a plus à revenir.

BENJAMINE

Malhûreuse!

MARINE

Mais en recompense, il vous destine pour present de nôces les deux plus aimables esclaves.

BENJAMINE

Ah ne me parle de rien qui ait raport à ce mariage-là.

MARINE

Patience, ils pouront bien étourdir[22] vôtre douleur, & vous tenir lieu même de vôtre amant.

BENJAMINE

Tu m'outrages!

MARINE

Vous verrez, vous verrez, il y a une Esclavonne qui vous sera bonne à mille choses, & le plus joli petit More... vôtre cœur m'en dira des nouvelles.

SCENE XII

BENJAMINE, MARINE,
BRIGANTIN, en Esclavonne.

BRIGANTIN *à part.*

Ne pourrai-je point trouver la fille de nôtre Juif?

MARINE

Tenez, voici l'Esclavonne.

BRIGANTIN

Ah Mademoiselle, je mourrois d'impatience de vous rendre mes respects; & je sais bon gré à l'esclavage...

---

22. 'On dit figurément, étourdir la douleur pour dire, l'endormir, empêcher qu'elle ne soit si sensible' (*Dictionnaire de l'Académie*, 1762). Furetière ne donne pas d'expression analogue.

Que le sort... dont l'agrément m'offre l'occasion... Je suis vôtre très humble servante, Mademoiselle.

MARINE

Le compliment est bien troussé!

BRIGANTIN, *à Marine dans sa voix naturelle.*

N'est-ce pas? *reprenant sa voix de femme.* Mais Mademoiselle est toute à ses chagrins, & il ne luy reste guere d'attention pour mon zele.

BENJAMINE

Comment voyez-vous, je vous prie, que j'aye des chagrins?

BRIGANTIN

Bon, Mademoiselle, je lis dans les cœurs tout courament! demandez si je n'ay pas lû tantôt tout vôtre pere, dés la premiere vuë.

MARINE

Jusqu'à la derniere syllabe.

BRIGANTIN

Vous êtes encore plus lisible, vous. Tenez: horreur d'un mariage qui vous menace, impatience de voir un amant que vous craignez de perdre, murmure contre un pere qui vous sacrifie à son avarice, n'est-ce pas là l'abregé de vôtre cœur?

BENJAMINE

Vous m'étonnez!

BRIGANTIN

Je ferai plus, je veux vous servir. Je sais ce qu'il en coûte à nôtre sexe de n'avoir pas ce qu'il aime. On soufre diablement!

MARINE

Je vous en répons.

BRIGANTIN

On a aimé quelquefois! Vous pouvez croire qu'on n'a pas déplu. Des monstres d'épouseurs sont venus à la traverse[23]. J'ai tant juré contre ces chiens de parens!

BENJAMINE

Il est vray qu'ils sont bien cruels!

BRIGANTIN

Cruels? ce sont de vrais Turcs! Il semble qu'ils nous fassent exprès là, pour nous faire enrager.

MARINE

Le beau plaisir!

BRIGANTIN

Que ne nous laissent-ils le soin de nous pourvoir! ne savons-nous pas ce qu'il nous faut?

---

23. Entendre : y faire obstacle; cf. Molière, *Les Précieuses ridicules*, sc. 4.

MARINE

Qui le sait mieux que nous?

BRIGANTIN

Mais les choses sont si mal réglées! l'amour soufle à droit[24], le mariage soufle à gauche, le courant de la nature nous emporte, la raison a beau ramer... L'orage se déclare... On perd la tramontane... Je ne sais si je m'explique, mais vous voyez bien que les parens ont tort?[25]

MARINE

C'est sans replique.

BRIGANTIN

Demandez, demandez, à mon camarade, il va vous confirmer tout cela.

SCENE XIII

BENJAMINE, MARINE
BRIGANTIN en femme Esclavonne.
LEANDRE, en More

LEANDRE

Eh qui pouroit, Mademoiselle, ne pas condamner les

---

24. La forme *à droit et à gauche* subsistait toujours à cette époque ; voir J.-P. Seguin, *op. cit.*, p. 90.

25. R. Garapon a noté la présence de la parodie du jargon professionnel dans le Théâtre Italien entre 1681 et 1697 (*La Fantaisie verbale*, p. 300-301). La Comédie-Française fait flèche de bois recyclé.

auteurs de vos chagrins? mais ce n'est pas assez de les plaindre, il faut vous en afranchir, trop hûreux si nôtre zele...

BRIGANTIN *bas à Leandre.*

Autant de perdû, vous l'éfarouchez!

LEANDRE

Ah! charmante personne, honorez-moy du moins d'un de vos regards; & faites grace à ma couleur en faveur de mes sentimens.

MARINE *à Benjamine.*

Il n'est pas si diable qu'il est noir.

BENJAMINE

Laissez-moy, je vous prie; c'est la seule preuve que j'exige de vostre affection.

LEANDRE

L'heureux Leandre sans doute est l'objet de cette inquiétude!

BENJAMINE

Que dites-vous de Léandre?

LEANDRE

Je sais, Mademoiselle, toute la part qu'il a dans vôtre cœur; & c'est en sa faveur que je vous prie d'agréer mes services: J'entre dans tous les transports que lui doit causer vôtre tendresse: & j'ose même vous remercier à vos genoux... *Il lui baise la main, & se découvre.*

BENJAMINE

Insolent!... ah, Léandre.

LEANDRE

Ah, Benjamine!

MARINE

Les pauvres enfans!

BENJAMINE

Quelle joïe! je tremble! cachez-vous vîte qu'on ne vous surprenne... que je vous voïe encore une fois... par quelle avanture êtes-vous ici?

LEANDRE

Vôtre pere attendoit des Esclaves de Smirne, La Saline les a prévenus[26], nous a supposez[27], je vous vois enfin, que nous importe le reste?

BENJAMINE

Vous savez que M. Doutremer est arrivé?

LEANDRE

Hé-bien, à quoi êtes-vous résoluë?

---

26. Entendre : devancés.

27. Supposer: 'Mettre une chose à la place d'une autre par fraude et tromperie' (Furetière).

BENJAMINE

Je ne savois pas bien encore; mais vôtre présence me détermine; & j'aimerois mieux mourir que de me souffrir à un autre.

BRIGANTIN, *dans sa voix naturelle.*

Vous ne mourrez point, Mademoiselle, c'est moi qui tiens le gouvernail, & je vous conduirai à bon port, sur ma parole.

BENJAMINE

Ce n'est point une femme!

BRIGANTIN

Je ne l'ai jamais été.

LEANDRE

C'est un de mes anciens valets que j'ai retrouvé ici, & qui doit vous servir auprès de vôtre pere, sous l'habit où vous le voyez.

BENJAMINE

L'honnête garçon! ne voudra-t-il pas bien garder cette montre pour l'amour de moi?

LEANDRE

Non, s'il vous plaît.

BRIGANTIN

Laissez, laissez, Monsieur, cela n'est pas inutile, en cas de fourberies, on ne sauroit prendre son temps trop juste.

MARINE

Ciel, voici vôtre pere!

SCENE XIV

M. SABATIN, BENJAMINE, LEANDRE, MARINE, BRIGANTIN.

MARINE

He bien, Monsieur, avez-vous des nouvelles de vôtre Turc?

M. SABATIN

Pas encore; mais je viens d'envoyer des Sbires[a] [28] après. Ah, ah, ma fille, que faites-vous ici? ne vous avois-je pas défendu de prendre l'air qu' à travers vos jalousies?

BRIGANTIN

Je lui contois en nous promenant la maniére dont je suis tombée dans l'esclavage.

M. SABATIN

Ce n'est pas pour vous que je parle; je suis ravi que vous l'entreteniez: Oüi, Benjamine, écoutez cette femme-là, elle est de bon conseil.

---

[a] CF envoyer La Saline après.

28. 'Nom qu'on donne aux archers en Italie' (*Encyclopédie*, III, p. 430).

BENJAMINE

Je tâcherai d'en profiter, mon pere.

BRIGANTIN, *faignant de continuër son histoire, & se mettant toujours devant Monsieur Sabatin, pendant que Léandre parle à Benjamine.*

Sur ce Port donc, où je vous disois que mes parens m'avoient mennée, je vis un certain homme de mer qui me vit aussi. Il fut touché de la délicatesse de mes traits: je fus charmée de son air marin, de sa voix brusque, & de la plus belle moustache du Levant.

M. SABATIN

Bon!

BRIGANTIN

Vous trouvez du caprice à cela, mais vous savez que c'est le défaut des belles! Bref... écoutez-moi donc.

M. SABATIN

Je vous écoute.

BRIGANTIN

Nous nous aimâmes: mes parens me destinoient un époux de terre ferme; mais néant, mon cœur étoit à flot. Vous ne m'écoutez pas?

M. SABATIN

Si fait, si fait.

BRIGANTIN

Enfin, j'épousai le Corsaire; & nous ne fûmes pas plûtôt mariez, que nous nous embarquâmes. Me suivez-vous?

M. SABATIN

Oüi, vous dis-je.

BRIGANTIN

Il me dit qu'il vouloit me faire voir toute la terre.

MARINE

Pouviez-vous vous résoudre à aller là?

BRIGANTIN

On va bien loin avec ce qu'on aime; mais le perfide!

MARINE

Hé-bien?

BRIGANTIN

J'ai le cœur si serré quand j'y songe!

M. SABATIN

Que fit-il donc?

BRIGANTIN

Le traître commença son voyage par m'aller vendre à un Bacha, avec qui il avoit fait marché pour toutes ses femmes. J'étois la treiziéme malheureuse qu'il achetoit de ce barbare-là!

M. SABATIN

La treiziéme!

BRIGANTIN

Hélas! plût au Ciel que je fusse la derniére: J'ai encore apris en arrivant ici, que mon boureau jettoit ses plombs[29] sur la fille d'un riche Marchand du païs, pour en faire, sans doute, le même usage.

MARINE

Monsieur! un Corsaire! la fille d'un riche Marchand! il faut approfondir cela.

M. SABATIN

Qu'est-ce donc que ce Corsaire?

BRIGANTIN

C'est un homme qui rôde de Port en Port, un certain Doutremer...

M. SABATIN

Doutremer!

MARINE

Monsieur!

---

29. 'En termes de marine, on dit, *jeter* la sonde ou le plomb, quand on veut savoir la hauteur de l'eau, ou s'il y a fond' (Furetière, s.v. 'Jetter', § 7).

BENJAMINE

Mon pere!

BRIGANTIN

D'où viennent donc toutes ces surprises? connoîtroit-on ici mon perfide?

MARINE

C'est justement celui que Monsieur vouloit faire épouser à sa fille.

BENJAMINE

Moi! je ne veux point être venduë!

M. SABATIN

Non, non, ma fille, cela ne sauroit être: je connois celui que je vous destine; & je vous répons qu'il n'a jamais été marié.

BRIGANTIN

Tenez, celui dont je vous parle, est un gros homme tirant[a] sur le matelot, qui a, comme je vous ai dit, l'air marin, la voix brusque, & le teint salé.

MARINE

Le voilà!

---

[a] P3, P4, P5 un homme tirant

BENJAMINE

C'est lui-même!

M. SABATIN

Seroit-il possible?

BRIGANTIN

Le scélérat! je voudrois le tenir ici, je le dévisagerois de bon cœur.

SCENE XV

M. DOUTREMER, M. SABATIN, BENJAMINE, LEANDRE, MARINE, BRIGANTIN.

M. DOUTREMER

Pour le coup, beau-pere, vous serez content de moi; & je défie Mademoiselle de tenir contre la petite fête que je lui ai préparée: Je suis morbleu galant, quand je m'y mets!

LEANDRE *à part*

Ciel, c'est mon oncle!

M. SABATIN

Vraiment Monsieur, j'aprens ici de belles nouvelles!

M. DOUTREMER

Qu'est-ce à dire belles nouvelles?

MARINE *bas à Brigantin*

Ne perds pas courage!

BRIGANTIN

Il est tout perdu!

M. SABATIN *à M. Doutremer*

Falloit-il jetter les yeux sur ma fille, pour de semblables perfidies?

M. DOUTREMER

Comment donc des perfidies? je ne m'attendois pas à cette bourasque-là; que voulez-vous dire?

M. SABATIN

Que c'est être bien inhumain que d'épouser ainsi de jeunes filles, pour les aller vendre à des Bachas.

M. DOUTREMER

Je veux être noyé, si j'y comprens rien! débroüillons un peu ceci, beau-pere, orientons-nous.

BRIGANTIN *bas à M. Sabatin*

Ne me commettez pas[30], c'est un brutal.

M. SABATIN *à M. Doutremer*

Vous ne pouvez que trop vous reconnoître & cette Esclave...

---

30. Entendre : 'Ne m'exposez pas à sa colère'.

BRIGANTIN, *à M. Sabatin*

Vous me perdez.

M. DOUTREMER

Hé-bien, cette Esclave?

M. SABATIN

N'est-elle pas la treiziéme de vos femmes que vous avez venduës?

M. DOUTREMER

Qui ose donc vous soutenir ces impostures?

M. SABATIN

Elle-même.

M. DOUTREMER

Comment impudente!

BRIGANTIN

Des injures! ah, j'aime mieux me retirer...

M. DOUTREMER

Non, non, ventrebleu, vous ne m'échaperez pas, fourbe que vous êtes; & je vais vous mettre à feu & à sang, si vous ne changez de langage.

BRIGANTIN, *dans sa voix naturelle.*

Ah, Monsieur, quartier! je vous prenois pour un autre.

M. DOUTREMER

Ah parbleu, Monsieur le fripon, vous ne nous aurez pas imposé[a] impunément!

BRIGANTIN ouv*rant son habit de femme & faisant voir celuy de galerien.*

Tout-beau, Messieurs! je suis un fripon privilégié, voila mes titres.

M. DOUTREMER

Eh, je pense que c'est ce maraut de Brigantin.

BRIGANTIN

C'est moi-même.

M. SABATIN

Le More est sans doute du complot? il faut qu'il nous débroüille tout ceci.

M. DOUTREMER

Oüi, par la sambleu, vous parlerez ou point de quartier; je vous traiterai tous deux de Turc à More[31] .

LEANDRE *se démasquant.*

Hé-bien, il faut donc se découvrir.

---

[a] P3, P5 vous ne nous en aurez pas imposé

31. 'On dit [...] traiter de Turc à More ; pour dire, à la rigueur et en ennemi déclaré' (Furetière).

M. DOUTREMER

Ciel, c'est Léandre!

LEANDRE

Oüi, mon oncle, vous voyez à vos genoux, un rival & un neveu; c'est à vous de voir ce que vous voulez être à mon égard: mais au moins ne me laissez pas la vie, si vous voulez encor m'aracher Benjamine.

M. SABATIN

Eh quoi, Monsieur Doutremer, seroit-ce la le neveu dont vous m'aviez autrefois parlé pour ma fille?

M. DOUTREMER

Je n'en ai point d'autre.

SCENE XVI

M. DOUTREMER, M. SABATIN, BENJAMINE, LEANDRE, MARINE, BRIGANTIN, LA SALINE.

LA SALINE

De la joie, Monsieur, de la joie, voilà vôtre Turc qu'on vous ameine!

M. DOUTREMER

Tenez, ce fripon là étoit encor de l'intelligence.

M. SABATIN

Quoi, maraut...

LA SALINE

Qu'est ce donc, Messieurs? fripon d'un côté! maraut de l'autre! que veut donc dire tout ceci?

LEANDRE

Que tout est découvert, mon pauvre la Saline, & que mon bonheur, ou mon malheur dépend à présent de mon oncle que tu vois.

LA SALINE

Vous, Monsieur Salomin?

M. DOUTREMER

Tais-toi, je ne suis Salomin qu'à Merseille [*sic*] , & je suis ici Doutremer. Je change de nom & de pavillon, selon mes interêts.

LA SALINE

Excusez-moi donc, Monsieur Doutremer, si je ne vous ai traité[a] que comme le rival de mon maître.

M. SABATIN

Trève d'éclaircissement. Quelle est vôtre résolution? vous voyez qu'ils s'aiment.

M. DOUTREMER

Je n'hésiterois pas à les rendre hûreux, sans certaines pierreries que j'ai toûjours sur le cœur.

---

[a] P3, P4, P5 de ce que je vous ai traité comme

LA SALINE

Que cela ne vous embarasse point; nous les avions confiées à Monsieur, & voila le fripon qui nous les a volées.

SCENE XVII

M. DOUTREMER, M. SABATIN, BENJAMINE, LEANDRE, MARINE, BRIGANTIN, LA SALINE, HALI.

HALI

No, no, mi non star friponne; mi far gambarutta.

M. DOUTREMER

Comment, comment, que veux-tu dire avec ta gambarutta?

HALI

Si, si, Signor, mi star un povero Turca che far Gambarutta in conscienza.

M. SABATIN

O! parbleu, je te ferai pendre avec ta conscience!

HALI

Hò, la justitia non impicar! ma sapir la regula, partagir[a] ?

---

[a] P3, P4, P5 partagir *est omis*.

M. DOUTREMER *lui arrachant des mains les Pierreries.*

Hé! donne, maraut, & va te faire pendre ailleurs!

HALI

A la forza, justitia, justitia!

M. DOUTREMER

Nous compterons, Monsieur. C'en est fait, Léandre, j'oublie tout; & j'en passerai par où M. Sabatin voudra.

M. SABATIN

Donnez-vous donc la main, mes enfans.

LEANDRE

Quel bonheur, Benjamine!

BENJAMINE

Je tremble que ce ne soit qu'un songe!

MARINE

La peste, que je connois de filles qui voudroient rêver de même!

LA SALINE

Il ne tient qu'à Monsieur, que tu n'en ayes le plaisir. *à M. Sabatin.* Je vous sers depuis trois semaines, donnez-moi mon congé, & Marine pour récompense.

M. SABATIN

Volontiers, nous voila tous contens.

M. DOUTREMER

Il n'y a que ce pauvre Brigantin, pour qui nous ne saurions rien faire.

BRIGANTIN

Ne vous mettez point en peine; je ne suis pas le plus à plaindre; on se fait aux galeres, & l'on se lasse du mariage: tout cela revient au même. Que je sois seulement de la nôce; & ne songeons qu'à nous divertir.

M. DOUTREMER

Allons, commencez donc vôtre petite manœuvre.

FESTE MARINE

Quatre Matelots avec deux Barcarolles, & deux Australiennes suivies d'un Singe qui leur porte un Parasol, forment une marche, & commencent la Fête.

[a]LA SALINE, *S'approchant des Australiennes, aprés qu'elles ont dansé.*

Voila vraiment de fort jolies danseuses; mais d'où sont celles-ci?

---

[a] CF *supprime le texte jusqu'à* UN MATELOT commence. / *Jeunes cœurs, venez aprendre*, etc.

M. DOUTREMER

Ce sont des Australiennes, dont je voulois faire present à Benjamine.

MARINE

Et ce Singe là qui leur sert de Page?

M. DOUTREMER

C'en est un qui entend la langue de leur païs.

MARINE

Comment, elles ne parlent donc pas François?

M. DOUTREMER

Si-fait vraiment, je ne fus pas plûtôt sur leurs terres, que tout le monde l'aprit jusqu'aux Péroquets, & cela en moins de huit jours.

BRIGANTIN

Huit jours! ces Peuples-là n'ont pas la mémoire courte, apparemment?

M. DOUTREMER

Si-fait, mais leurs jours sont longs, ils durent six mois.

LA SALINE

Des jours [de] six mois! par ma foi, M. Doutremer, le monde est une plaisante machine!

M. DOUTREMER

Tu és un vrai badaut, toi! tu n'as jamais vû que ton continent. Mais laissons continuer la Fête.

UN MATELOT commence

Jeunes cœurs, venez aprendre
La manœuvre des amours.

LE CHOEUR, répette

Jeunes cœurs, & c.

UNE BARCAROLLE.

Embarquez-vous dans vos beaux jours:
C'est perdre temps que s'en[a] *défendre:*

LE CHOEUR.

Jeunes cœurs, venez aprendre
La manœuvre des amours.

UN MATELOT.

Les yeux jaloux veillent toujours:
Veillez toujours pour les surprendre.

LE CHOEUR

Jeunes cœurs, venez aprendre
La manœuvre des amours.

---

[a] P3, P5 *que de s'en défendre*

UNE BARCAROLLE

L'Himen après de longs[a] *détours,*
Est le Port où son doit se rendre.

LE CHOEUR

Jeunes cœurs, venez aprendre
La manœuvre des amours.

[b] UN MATELOT & UNE BARCAROLLE dancent ensemble.

M. DOUTREMER chante ensuite.

Plus de commerce, Amour! Bacchus fait[c] *mon destin;*
Ton flambeau me plaît moins que ma Pipe allumée.
Mettre en fumant toujours, ma Bouteille à sa fin,
C'est l'unique plaisir dont mon ame est charmée:
Avec du Tabac, & du Vin,
Mes chagrins s'en vont en fumée.

UN MATELOT danse seul.

BRIGANTIN

Pour moi, j'en reviens toujours à nos Australiennes; celle-ci est toute jeune; je gage qu'elle n'a pas plus de quinze jours.

---

[a] P5 *vains détours*

[b] CF *supprime le texte jusqu'à* Les Matelots & les Barcarolles dansent le branle, sur lequel on chante les Couplets suivans.

[c] P2 *fais*

M. DOUTREMER

Bon!

BRIGANTIN

Quinze jours de leur païs, s'entend.

M. DOUTREMER

Te moques-tu? la plus jeune à ses soixante ans passez.

BRIGANTIN

Elles ne paroissent pas, ma foi, leur âge.

LA SALINE, *s'adressant à une des Australiennes.*

Si cette petite vieille-là vouloit s'établir ici, & qu'elle pût s'accommoder d'un enfant comme moi; qu'en pensez-vous?... Mais, morbleu, pourquoi nous tromper? Vous nous dites que ce sont des femmes, & elles ne parlent point!

M. DOUTREMER

C'est le défaut des femmes de leurs climats; on ne sauroit leur arracher une parole: Ce n'est pas qu'elles n'ayent la voix jolie; je veux vous en donner le plaisir, écoutez:

L'une des AUSTRALIENNES commence.

Nôtre bouche est toujours muette;
Mais nos yeux sont de grands parleurs:
Leur feu sincere est l'interprette
De celui qui brûle nos cœurs.

LA SALINE répond

Ici la bouche est moins discrette;
Et les yeux sont plus grands menteurs.

L'autre AUSTRALIENNE continuë.

Nôtre bauté, toujours nouvelle,
A soixante ans fait des jaloux;
La jeunesse ici dure-t-elle,
Aussi long-temps que parmi nous?

LA SALINE

On s'y dit jeune, on s'y fait belle,
Aussi long-temps qu'on l'est chez vous.

La 1re AUSTRALIENNE reprend.

On n'a point chez nous de méthode,
Pour bien arranger ses attraits,
La jeunesse les accommode,
Et la nature en fait les frais.

LA SALINE

Rien n'est ici moins à la mode,
Que les visages sans aprêts.

Les deux Australiennes dansent ensuite avec le Singe, sur un Air Chinois.

Une BARCAROLE chante.

Sopra'l mare d'amor,
Voga, voga, mio cor;
Dell' Amante in procella,
La sua face è la stella:
Sopra'l mare d'amor,
Voga, voga, mio cor.

Les Matelots & les Barcarolles dansent le branle[32], sur lequel on chante les Couplets suivans.

LA SALINE

Que sans craindre le naufrage,
Chacun s'embarque en ce jour;
On fait toujours bon voyage,
Quand on vogue avec l'Amour:
Mais qui cherche un heureux sort,
Sans l'avoir pour soi, risque fort
De faire naufrage au Port.

Une BARCAROLLE

Que sous l'amoureuse étoile,
Vos cœurs suivent leurs desirs;
Faites tous force de voile,
Vous touchez presqu'aux plaisirs:
Mais redoublez vôtre effort,
Un Amant perd tout, s'il s'endort;
Ne vous reposez qu'au Port.

BRIGANTIN

On dit que le Mariage
Est le seul Port de l'Amour:
Pour y finir son voyage,
Ce Dieu rame nuit & jour:

32. '*Branle*, en termes de musique, est un air ou une danse par où on commence tous les bals, où plusieurs personnes dansent en rond, et non pas en avant, en se tenant par la main, et se donnent un *branle* continuel et concerté avec des pas convenables, selon la différence des airs qu'on joue alors' (Furetière).

Mais par un bizare sort,
Souvent après tout son effort,
L'Amour fait naufrage au Port.

M. DOUTREMER

Avec le Dieu de la Tonne[33] *,*
Il vaut bien mieux s'embarquer[a]*;*
L'Amour du gros temps s'étonne,
Et Bachus aime à risquer:
Mais en buvant à plein bord,
La raison trouve un plus doux sort
Dans le naufrage qu'au port.

BRIGANTIN

Avant que d'être aux Galeres,
On n'aime point à risquer;
Il est certaines affaires
Où l'on n'ose s'embarquer:
Mais je ne crains plus le sort,
Je défie Archers & Record,
Ma chaîne est mon Passe-port.

---

[a] P5 *mieux bien s'embarquer*

33. Bacchus. Jeu de mots sur «Latone», allusion au célèbre bassin de Versailles qui représente l'héroine mythologique avec ses enfants. On citera la gravure de N. Bonnard, représentant Arlequin dans un tonneau et légendée : «Arlequin au ventre de sa mère La Tonne» (BNF., est.).

LA SALINE au Parterre

La Piéce a fait bon voyage,
Laissez-nous le croire ainsi,
Le vent de vôtre suffrage,
L'a conduite jusqu' ici:
Mais hélas! nous craignons fort,
Si vous n'en assurez le sort,
De faire naufrage au Port.

FIN

LE PETIT

MAÎTRE

DE ROBE,

COMEDIE.

EN PROSE ET UN ACTE,
suivie d'un Divertissement.

Pour le Théatre François.

ACTEURS,

LA COMTESSE, Tante d'Angelique.

LE PRESIDENT, Oncle d'Eraste & de M. Fatenville.

ANGELIQUE, Niéce de la Comtesse, Amante d'Eraste.

ERASTE, Neveu du Président, amant d'Angélique.

M. DE FATENVILLE, Conseiller, Neveu du Président.

NERINE, Suivante d'Angélique.

FRONTIN, Valet d'Eraste.

LA FLEUR Valet de M. Fatenville.

Une Actrice chantante.

Une Actrice dansante.

M. PASSEPIED, Compositeur de Ballets.

M. DU TREILLIS, Tailleur.

LUCAS, Paysan.

Acteurs du Divertissement.

L'AMOUR.
UN PLAISIR.
PREMIER AVOCAT.
SECOND AVOCAT.

La Scene est à Paris,
dans une Salle de la maison de M. Fatenville.

LE PETIT MAÎTRE DE ROBE,

COMEDIE

SCENE PREMIERE.

FRONTIN, NERINE.

FRONTIN

Oh çà, Nérine, tandis qu'Eraste & Angelique renouvellent leur tendresse, reprenons un peu le fil de nos amours... où en étions-nous restés?

NERINE

Tout-beau, M. Frontin; il me semble que la guerre vous a rendu bien familier.

FRONTIN

Ce n'est point familiarité, c'est passion; d'ailleurs,

nous arrivons en poste; la poste, comme tu sçais, a ses priviléges[1] .

NERINE

Laissons la bagatelle, & venons au solide.

FRONTIN

Au solide? Volontiers...

NERINE

Eraste est-il toujours bien amoureux?

FRONTIN

C'est donc-là ce que tu appelle le solide?

NERINE

Sans doute, & nos petits intérêts ne sont que les accessoires de ceux de ton maître & de ma maîtresse.

FRONTIN

Accessoires! Je crois, parbleu, que tu parles chicanne.

NERINE

Oui, vraiment, nous sommes devenues plaideuses depuis votre départ.

---

1. Boindin fait peut-être allusion à la *franchise postale* accordée aux Directeurs des Postes, qui se faisaient adresser du courrier sans payer.

FRONTIN

Comment donc?

NERINE

M. le Comte est mort, & Made. la Comtesse, la tante d'Angelique, nous a associées à ses procés; sa Nièce solicite les Conseillers, & moi les Sécretaires.

FRONTIN

Tu est Sous-solicitante.

NERINE

A peu près.

FRONTIN

Tu feras fortune dans la robe; mais, dis moi, par quelle aventure êtes-vous venues loger dans ce chien d'hôtel?

NERINE

Est-il de ta connoissance?

FRONTIN

Le maître est cousin germain d'Eraste, & neveu comme lui de M. le Président Oronte, dont ils attendent tous deux la succession.

NERINE

Quoi, M. Fatenville est ce cousin de ton maître, avec qui il s'est brouillé?

FRONTIN

Lui-même: n'est-ce pas un jeune fat, plein de distractions méditées, & de contretems étudiés? Conseiller le matin, & petit maître le soir?

NERINE

Le voilà trait pour trait.

FRONTIN

Je ne le connois cependant que sur le rapport d'autrui.

NERINE

Il loge dans cet appartement, comme nous dans l'autre; & c'est le voisinage du palais qui a attiré la Comtesse chez lui.

FRONTIN

Il seroit à souhaiter pour notre intérêt que vous en fussiez logées bien loin.

NERINE

Pourquoi?

FRONTIN

C'est que nous n'y pouvons venir qu'incognito, & cela est diablement génant.

NERINE

Pour la premiere fois, vous n'avez pas à vous en plaindre.

FRONTIN

Aussi avons-nous pris le tems que le Conseiller & la Comtesse sont au palais.

NERINE

J'entens un carosse, ce pourroit bien être l'un ou l'autre; jette-toi dans ce cabinet, & tire la porte sur toi.

FRONTIN

Et mon maître?

NERINE

Je prendrai soin de l'avertir.

FRONTIN

C'est, je pense, le Conseiller!

NERINE

C'est lui-même.

SCENE II

NERINE, M. FATENVILLE,
LA FLEUR[2].

---

2. Normalement, les maîtres rebaptisaient leurs domestiques en choisissant des formes abrégées pour les noms des filles (Elisabeth devenait Lisette) et des sobriquets pour les hommes. La botanique, de même que les noms de province, fournissait une source d'inspiration fréquente (cf. Lolive); voir S. Maza, *op. cit.*, p. 176-178, et surtout J. Emelina, *op. cit.*, 4e Part., ch. 2, p. 333-350.

FATENVILLE

Hola, hé laquais[3], qu'on me deshabille... Ah bon jour, ma chere Nérine, mille fois bon jour.

NERINE

Monsieur, je suis votre servante.

FATENVILLE

Encore un bon jour pour ton aimable maîtresse.

NERINE

Je vous en remercie pour elle.

FATENVILLE

Elle est vraiment fort jolie, ta maîtresse... Eh, mes chiens, laquais, mes chiens; les a-t-on amenés[4] ?

LA FLEUR

On n'en a point de nouvelles.

FATENVILLE

J'en suis presque amoureux.

---

3. Cette interpellation, quoique fréquente, était jugée vulgaire; voir C. Fairchilds, *op. cit.*, p. 102, n. 10.

4. Dans les commentaires sur de nombreux membres de la magistrature que les intendants adressaient à Colbert, une préoccupation excessive de la chasse revient assez souvent; voir F. Gaiffe, *L'Envers...*, p. 142-147, surtout les pages 144 et 145.

NERINE

De qui, Monsieur? de ma maîtresse, ou de vos chiens?

FATENVILLE

Eh non, c'est de... Mon tailleur n'est pas venu?

LA FLEUR

Pas encore.

FATENVILLE

Avoue, Nérine, que je suis bien malheureux d'avoir été sacrifié au soin pénible d'avoir des procés!

NERINE

Le parti de l'épée vous seroit peut-être mieux convenu?

FATENVILLE

Oui, l'épée, ma chere, l'épée, tu me prens par mon foible.

NERINE *à part*

Ciel, nous sommes perdus!

SCENE III

ANGELIQUE, ERASTE,
NERINE, M. FATENVILLE,

ANGELIQUE

Retirez-vous de grace, Eraste, je tremble qu'on ne vous trouve ici.

FATENVILLE

Oh, oh, Eraste avec Angelique?

ERASTE

Adieu, charmante Angelique, conservez-moi ces sentimens...

ANGELIQUE

Oh Ciel! voilà le Conseiller.

FATENVILLE

Je suis charmé, Mademoiselle, de vous voir dans ces heureuses dispositions pour ce petit Monsieur; je ne désespere pas de vous plaire à mon tour.

NERINE

Madame, voici une querelle.

ANGELIQUE

En vérité, Monsieur, vous avez des termes...

ERASTE

Eh, Mademoiselle, tout ce qu'il dit est sans conséquence.

FATENVILLE

Je vous trouve bien familier, Monsieur, de venir chez moi pousser la fleurette [5], vous pourriez mieux prendre votre terrain.

---

5. Fleurette 'se dit au figuré de certains petits ornements du langage, ou des galanteries, et des termes doucereux dont on se

ERASTE

Je me serois épargné la peine de vous y voir si des raisons invincibles...

FATENVILLE

Des raisons invincibles! on pourroit vous apprendre à les vaincre.

ERASTE

Il me paroît, M. le Conseiller, que le tems ne vous a point changé, vous êtes toujours vif.

FATENVILLE

Vous faites l'agréable; sçavez-vous, morbleu, que je n'entends point raillerie.

ERASTE

Vous vous échauffez? vos discours deviennent sérieux?

ANGELIQUE

Eh Messieurs, de grace...

FATENVILLE

Oui sérieux, & des discours, je pourrois passer aux effets.

---

sert ordinairement pour cajoler les femmes. C'est un diseur de *fleurettes*. Il conte *fleurettes* à cette dame ; c'est-à-dire, Il lui fait l'amour' (Furetière). Selon l'Académie (1694), 'il n'a guère d'usage que dans la poésie pastorale'.

ERASTE

Aux effets, vous, aux effets?

FATENVILLE

Oui, morbleu, aux effets; apprenez M. mon petit cousin, que ma robe ne tient qu'à deux boutons.

NERINE

Eh, Madame, arrêtez-les...

ERASTE

Apprenez M. mon grand cousin, que vous ne serez jamais qu'un fat.

FATENVILLE

Un fat, Madame, un fat! Ventrebleu...

NERINE

Hai!

ANGELIQUE

Messieurs, du moins par respect pour moi.

FATENVILLE

Oui, du respect, Mademoiselle, du respect; je me retiens par respect, vous m'en tiendrez compte au moins[6].

---

6. Le duel était une manière noble de vider les différends. Or, la magistrature de cette époque était considéré comme étant plutôt

NERINE *à part*

Voilà une gasconade de robe.

ERASTE

Adieu, Monsieur, je vais instruire M. le Président de vos petites manieres.

ANGELIQUE

Il faut avouer, Monsieur, que vous avez un procédé bien outrageant!

FATENVILLE

Le vôtre est touchant! Adieu, Madame.

SCENE IV

M. FATENVILLE, M. DU TREILLIS[7], LA FLEUR.

FATENVILLE

Hola hé! ne pourrai-je d'aujourd'hui avoir mon tailleur?

---

bourgeoise que noble en raison de ses activités *professionnelles*. Les bourgeois qui se provoquaient en duel étaient ridicules ; voir d'Argenson, *Notes*, p. 77-79. Depuis longtemps, le duel était défendu, et la plus récente législation prohibitive était l'ordonnance de 1679; voir H. Pierquin, La *Juridiction du point d'honneur*, p. 138-161, et Sedaine, *Le Philosophe sans le savoir*, éd. J. Dunkley, p. 24-38.

7. Boindin est friand de la dénomination propre. *Treillis* signifiait soit une toile teinte en noir qu'on employait pour les doublures ou les habits de deuil, soit 'une espèce de grosse toile, dont on fait des sacs, et dont les paysans et les manœuvres s'habillent' (Furetière).

LA FLEUR

Le voici.

FATENVILLE

J'aurai le plaisir... parbleu, M. Du Treillis est un négligent original. Ah! c'est vous? est-ce là mon habit?

DU TREILLIS

Oui, Monsieur, le voulez-vous mettre?

FATENVILLE

Apparament: croyez-vous que je veuille passer la journée en robe! allons qu'on m'ôte cet équipage; donnez...

Scene V

M. FATENVILLE, M. DU TREILLIS
M. PASSEPIED[8].

FATENVILLE

C'est vous, M. Passepied! que je vous embrasse, vous me négligez furieusement, M. Passepied.

---

8. Un 'passe-pié' était une 'sorte de danse fort commune, dont la mesure est triple, se marque 3/8, et se bat à un temps. Le mouvement en est plus vif que celui du menuet, le caractère de l'air à peu près semblable' (*Encyclopédie*, II, p. 1 271).

PASSEPIED

J'ai mille excuses à vous faire de n'être pas venu hier, il me fût impossible; je passai l'après midi chez une Duchesse, où la conduite d'un ballet rouloit sur moi.

FATENVILLE

Une Duchesse & un ballet, voilà deux bonnes raisons, M. Passepied.

PASSEPIED

Je sçais que vos bontés...

FATENVILLE

Vous êtes tout pardonné. Vous ne me dites rien de mon habit, comment le trouvez vous?

PASSEPIED

De très-bon goût.

FATENVILLE

A propos, m'a-t-on apporté ma lorgnette[9] ? Voyons, voyons, c'est fort bien, je distingue à merveille. Mais je ne suis pas content de mon habit, il me semble qu'il ne me va pas bien.

DU TREILLIS

Quand il seroit né sur vous, il n'iroit pas mieux; demandez.

---

9. Le mot semble dater de 1694. Fatenville emploie un objet de luxe moderne.

FATENVILLE

Je n'en suis pas content, vous dis-je.

DU TREILLIS

Le trouvez-vous trop long?

FATENVILLE

Non.

DU TREILLIS

Trop court?

FATENVILLE

Non, non.

DU TREILLIS

La manche n'a-t-elle pas une bonne tournure?

FATENVILLE

Si fait.

DU TREILLIS

La taille est-elle trop haute, ou trop basse?

FATENVILLE

Non, morbleu, non: mais je vous dis encore une fois que je n'en suis pas content.

DU TREILLIS

Si vous vouliez m'en dire la raison je pourois...

FATENVILLE

La raison? cela est plaisant, la raison! n'est-ce pas votre métier de la sçavoir?

DU TREILLIS

Mais Monsieur!

FATENVILLE

Oh, point de mais, Mr Du Treillis; on le portera pour vous faire plaisir.

DU TREILLIS

Vous plaît-il de jetter les yeux sur le compte?

FATENVILLE

Bon, le compte, je m'en raporte bien à vous; adieu Mr Du Treillis.

DU TREILLIS

Mais si vous vouliez...

FATENVILLE

Encore un coup, je m'en raporte bien à vous; vous êtes honnête homme, il suffit, adieu.

DU TREILLIS

Voilà tout ce qu'on en peut tirer.

FATENVILLE

Qu'on avance mon dîner.

PASSEPIED

Danserez-vous aujourd'hui?

FATENVILLE

Oui, dansons, il y a trois jours que je n'ai dansé. Qu'est-ce que c'est?

LA FLEUR

Un plaïdeur qui demande à vous parler.

FATENVILLE

Un plaideur, à moi, un plaideur! qu'on le renvoye à mon sécretaire... On ne sçauroit être un moment en occupation sérieuse sans être interrompu. Mais à propos, M. Passepied, eh, notre fête?

PASSEPIED

J'ai tout préparé pour ce soir, & comme ce n'est point aujourd'hui jour d'Opéra, je vous ai ménagé quelques Actrices.

FATENVILLE

Quelques Actrices! cela est bon, Mr Passepied, cela est bon. N'est-ce point encore quelque plaideur?

LA FLEUR

Non, Monsieur, c'est une plaideuse, c'est Madame la Comtesse.

FATENVILLE

Adieu, Mr Passepied, souvenez-vous des Actrices.

SCENE VI

Mr FATENVILLE, LA COMTESSE

LA COMTESSE

Ah, Mr le Conseiller, je suis morte, je suis au désespoir!

FATENVILLE

Ce n'est rien, Madame, ce n'est rien.

LA COMTESSE

Comment, ce n'est rien? nous venons de perdre un gros[10] procès.

FATENVILLE

Ce n'est rien, vous dis-je, il faut éloigner tout ce qui peut affliger.

LA COMTESSE

Ce n'est pas la perte du procès qui me choque, c'est la maniere de le perdre, & l'affront que je viens d'essuyer.

FATENVILLE

Après le petit divertissement que je vous ai préparé, vous n'y penserez plus.

---

10. Une affectation de l'époque consistait à employer *gros* au lieu de *grand* (une grosse affaire, une grosse distinction, etc.) (Callières, *Des mots à la mode*, p. 4-18).

LA COMTESSE

Vous sçavez de quelle conséquence étoit pour moi le procès que j'avois avec le fermier de mon mari?

FATENVILLE

Vous sçavez le goût que j'ai pour ces sortes de fêtes?

LA COMTESSE

Je l'ai perdu ce procès, & avec dépens, Monsieur, & avec dépens.

FATENVILLE

On doit m'amener des chanteurs, des danseurs, & des filles d'Opéra, Madame, & des filles d'Opéra.

LA COMTESSE

C'est mon raporteur[11] qui m'a joué ce tour-là.

FATENVILLE

C'est mon maître à danser sur qui tout roule.

LA COMTESSE

Mon mari afferme[12] une terre pour six ans, il meurt la

---

11. 'Celui des juges qui expose l'état d'une affaire qui doit être jugée' (DFC).

12. Furetière explique que le terme *affermer* signifiait 'donner, ou prendre à ferme quelque terre, quelques droits pour un certain temps et moyennant certain prix'. La ferme était 'un bail ou louage qu'on fait d'héritages ou de toutes sortes de droits, moyennant certains prix ou redevances qu'on paye tous les ans au propriétaire'. On donnait en même temps l'asurance de ne point expulser le fermier pendant le temps du bail.

seconde année, je suis commune, Monsieur, je suis commune...[13] vous ne m'ecoutez pas, Monsieur, vous ne m'écoutez pas.

FATENVLLE

Jamais fête ne fût plus galante; vous ne faites point d'attention à ce que je vous dis, Madame.

SCENE VII

Mr FATENVILLE, LA COMTESSE,
LA FLEUR, NERINE.

LA FLEUR.

Monsieur, on a servi.

NERINE

Croyez-moi, Madame, allons diner, & essayons de nous consoler.

LA COMTESSE

Me consoler, moi,. me consoler! Voyez un peu l'impertinence!

---

13. La Comtesse ne peut résilier le contrat établi par son mari, car, selon Furetière, 'on dit que par la Coutume de Paris, le mari et la femme sont uns et *communs* en biens ; pour dire, qu'ils ont contracté société ensemble, et qu'ils partagent le gain et les pertes l'un de l'autre'. Elle avait sans doute espéré rentrer en possession de la ferme (au sens littéral) et en expulser le fermier. La décision lui déplaît, certes, mais l'épithète *commune* la vexe davantage, car, placé aprés le substantif, *commun* voulait dire *ordinaire* (non pas vulgaire pourtant).

FATENVILLE

Mille pardons, Madame, on m'attend, pour une affaire indispensable.

Scene VIII

LA COMTESSE, NERINE.

LA COMTESSE

Yeût-il jamais une femme plus infortunée; perdre en trois mois deux procès & un mari!

NERINE

Il y a des années bien malheureuses.

LA COMTESSE

Oh, je sçais un moyen de me rendre la justice favorable. Je veux marier ma nièce à un homme de robe; & j'ai déja jetté les yeux sur le Conseiller.

NERINE

Votre nièce à un homme de robe? à Mr de Fatenville?

LA COMTESSE

Le caractere ne décide de rien, & j'aurai toujours l'appui du Président son oncle.

NERINE

Cela mérite réflexion.

LA COMTESSE

Allons qu'on se dépêche de me faire diner, je veux dès aujourd'hui en aller parler au Président.

SCENE IX

Mr FATENVILLE, FRONTIN,
LA FLEUR.

FRONTIN

Il est tems de sortir; mais j'entens du bruit, ha me voilà pris.

FATENVILLE

Ah, te voilà, mon enfant, comment se porte le Marquis?

FRONTIN *à part*

Le Marquis! il ne me reconnoît pas.

FATENVILLE

Au fait, au fait, sont-ils bien fatigués? La traite [14] est longue.

FRONTIN

Ils m'ont chargé de vous faire leurs complimens.

---

14. La traite était 'la distance d'un lieu à un autre. Il y a une bonne *traite* de la porte St. Jacques à la porte St. Denis' (Furetière).

FATENVILLE

Leurs complimens! des chiens?

FRONTIN

Je ne dis pas cela, je dis que Mr le Marquis...

FATENVILLE

Je t'entend, je t'entend.

FRONTIN *à part*

Cela est heureux, la peste m'étouffe si je m'entend moi-même.

FATENVILLE

Tu m'améne donc deux couples de chiens?

FRONTIN

Je crois qu'oui, Monsieur.

FATENVILLE

Et où sont-ils?

FRONTIN

Mon camarade les aménne; je vais l'avertir de se dépêcher.

FATENVILLE

Non, non, je quitte exprès mon diner, pour en aprendre des nouvelles. Comment se porte la petite fermiere? ah, tu m'entens bien?

FRONTIN

A merveille: toujours un pied en l'air[15].

FATENVILLE

Comment donc, elle étoit si triste, elle a bien changé... eh dis moi, Lucas... là... tu sçais bien ce que je veux dire?

FRONTIN *bas*

Le diable m'emporte si j'en sçais rien ; *(haut)* mais mon camarade tarde trop, & je vais...

LA FLEUR

Monsieur, voilà Monsieur votre Oncle.

FRONTIN.

La fâcheuse visite! qu'on dise que je n'y suis pas.

LA FLEUR

Le voilà, Monsieur.

SCENE X

M. FATENVILLE, LE PRESIDENT.
LA FLEUR.

FATENVILLE

Ah, c'est vous, mon cher Oncle, vous!

---

15. 'On dit d'une personne gaie, qu'elle a toujours un pied en l'air' (Furetière).

LE PRESIDENT

Oui, mon Neveu, c'est moi-même.

FATENVILLE

Quoi, coquin, maraut, ne vous ai-je pas dit cent fois de m'avertir avant que Monsieur descende de carrosse?

LE PRESIDENT

Trève de cérémonie, mon Neveu.

FATENVILLE

Vous vous portez à merveille, vous vivrez cent ans, je suis, parbleu, ravi de vous voir. Prenez-vous de l'Espagnol[16] ?

LE PRESIDENT

Eh, ne quitterez-vous jamais ces maniéres extravagantes?

FATENVILLE

Que trouvez-vous donc de si extravagant à mes maniéres?

LE PRESIDENT

Tout.

---

16. Fatenville offre du vin d'Espagne. L'*Encyclopédie*, qui fournit un inventaire détaillé de la production des vins espagnols, note qu'on les servait 'par régal' ; III, p. 1 043 ('Vin').

FATENVILLE

Tout? cela est fort.

LE PRESIDENT

Comme le voilà vêtu! ne le prendroit-on pas plutôt pour un Officier de dragons, que pour un Conseiller?

FATENVILLE

Vous ne me trouvez pas bon air?

LE PRESIDENT

Eh, vos airs deviennent tous les jours plus impertinens. Je ne désespére pas de vous voir au premier jour à l'audience en plumet[17]. Quelle conduite! n'aller au palais que pour s'y faire des affaires!

FATENVILLE

Quand on a du cœur...

LE PRESIDENT

N'en sortir que pour aller avec cinq ou six petits maîtres s'enyvrer grossiérement!

FATENVILLE

Grossiérement, avec du vin de Silleri[18] ?

---

17. *Plumet* 'se dit d'un jeune homme qui porte des plumes : et ordinairement il ne se dit en ce sens qu'en raillerie, ou par mépris' (*Dictionnaire de l'Académie).*

18. Silleri, ou Sillery était un vin blanc non mousseux de la Marne. Selon Demerson, c'était des vins 'blancs, légèrement

LE PRESIDENT

Ne quitter la table, que pour aller sur un théatre se donner en spectacle au public[19] !

FATENVILLE

Eh mais, mais, si vous vous emportez vous tomberez malade.

LE PRESIDENT

Voilà de ces airs impertinens qu'il faut que tout le monde essuie! n'avez-vous pas eû encore aujourd'hui l'impudence d'insulter Eraste dans votre maison?

FATENVILLE

Comment donc?

LE PRESIDENT

Que seroit-il arrivé, s'il n'eût été plus sage que vous?

FATENVILLE

Plus sage... oh pour cela, mon Oncle, vous êtes furieusement prévenu contre moi.

---

ambrés, très délicats, les meilleurs de tous les vins blancs' ; *Histoire naturelle de la vigne et du vin*, p. 133. Il avait peut-être d'autres qualités aussi, car on lit dans *L'Obstacle imprévu* de Destouches, l'assertion de Valère que ; 'Nous avons bu d'un vin de Sillery qui m'a bien donné de l'amour' (V, 3).

19. Petit-maître, Fatenville prend une des places sur la scène du théâtre (elles étaient les plus chères). Ces places furent supprimées en 1759, grâce aux efforts de Voltaire, de Lekain et du comte de Lauraguais, qui aboutirent à l'indemnisation des Comédiens.

LE PRESIDENT

Je n'entens point raillerie, je sçais comment la chose s'est passée, & je prétens que vous lui fassiez satisfaction.

FATENVILLE

Satisfaction! il se croit donc l'offensé? j'en suis parbleu charmé; j'avois sur le cœur certains termes dont il s'est servi, je l'oublie en votre faveur, je l'oublie.

LE PRESIDENT

Ne pensez pas en être quitte à si bon marché.

FATENVILLE

Il me semble pourtant que c'est se mettre à la raison.

LE PRESIDENT

Ecoutez, vous me ferez prendre des résolutions.

FATENVILLE

Eh, prenez, Monsieur, prenez, je vous abandonne à vos réflexions. (*Il sort.*)

LE PRESIDENT *seul.*

L'insolent! je ne sçais ce qui me tient... à qui en veulent ces femmes-là? c'est sans doute à mon Neveu.

SCENE XI

LE PRESIDENT, UNE ACTRICE CHANTANTE, UNE ACTRICE DANSANTE,

Qui entrent en chantant & en dansant.

L'ACTRICE CHANTANTE

Dans un si beau jour tout doit s'enflamer;
Le tems heureux des jeux, est le tems d'aimer.

Mr Passepied, Monsieur, nous a fait une si charmante peinture de votre belle humeur que nous avons crû ne pouvoir entrer chez vous de meilleure grace, qu'avec toute la gayeté qui convient à notre petit caractere.

LE PRESIDENT

Je l'ai bien prévû, ce sont des aventurieres qui se méprennent.

L'ACTRICE CHANTANTE

Que marmotez-vous là? Vous êtes tout occupé de votre cadeau, apparamment.

L'ACTRICE DANSANTE

Point de façons pour nous au moins, nous sommes femmes sans cérémonies.

LE PRESIDENT

Je le vois bien. (*Elles dansent.*) Sans façons donc, Mesdemoiselles, allez chanter & danser ailleurs, & laissez-moi, je vous prie, en repos.

L'ACTRICE CHANTANTE

Ah, ah, voilà parbleu un plaisant accueil! Mr Passepied ne nous l'avoit point noté sur ce ton-là.

L'ACTRICE DANSANTE

En effet, vous étes d'un bouru épouvantable.

L'ACTRICE CHANTANTE

Epouvantable au moins.

LE PRESIDENT

Eh oui, Mesdemoiselles, chacun ne fait pas profession de joie comme vous[20] ; & je vous prie encore une fois de me laisser ici à mes chagrins.

L'ACTRICE CHANTANTE

Un ton grondeur & severe
N'est pas un grand agrément.
Le chagrin n'avance guére
Les affaires d'un amant.

LE PRESIDENT

Quelle extravagance.

L'ACTRICE DANSANTE

Que dites-vous là?

---

20. Rappelons que l'expression «de joie» est équivoque pour désigner la profession de chanteuse.

LE PRESIDENT

Rien, Mesdemoiselles, point de conversation, s'il vous plaît; je vois bien que vous n'êtes pas faites pour entendre raison.

L'ACTRICE CHANTANTE

Le plaisir nous appelle
Il faut l'écouter;
La raison rebelle,
Veut y résister
Mais cette cruelle,
Que nous offre-t-elle,
Pour nous arrêter?

LE PRESIDENT

En vérité, vous vous oubliez, & vous portez les choses dans[21] un excès...

L'ACTRICE CHANTANTE

Un doux excès sied bien dans la jeune saison,
Pour être heureux, il faut qu'un cœur s'oublie.

LE PRESIDENT

Quoi, vous danserez & vous chanterez toujours?

L'ACTRICE DANSANTE

Quoi, vous ne chanterez ni ne danserez, vous? oh par-

21. 'La préposition *dans* s'emploie dans les sens où la langue actuelle se sert de la préposition *à*' (A. Haase, *op. cit.*, § 126, 3). Il cite de nombreux exemples.

bleu, Monsieur, Magistrature à part, vous danserez un passepied avec moi.

LE PRESIDENT

Mesdemoiselles...

L'ACTRICE DANSANTE

Allons, allons, vous voilà bien malade! il ne vous en coutera qu'un peu de gravité.

L'ACTRICE CHANTANTE

On n'en est pas toujours quitte à si bon marché.

Il faut souvent pour être heureux,
Qu'il en coute un peu d'innocence.

LE PRESIDENT

C'en est trop, Mesdemoiselles, & je pourois enfin m'offenser de votre méprise.

L'ACTRICE DANSANTE

Comment donc méprise? est-ce que nous ne parlons pas à Mr de Fat... Fatenville?

LE PRESIDENT

C'est un extravagant que je punirai de votre visite.

L'ACTRICE DANSANTE

Oh, oh, le plaisant *quiproquo!*

L'ACTRICE CHANTANTE

Oh, oh, oh, la drole de figure[22] !

LE PRESIDENT

Qu'est-ce donc, Mesdemoiselles, pourquoi ces éclats de rire?

L'ACTRICE CHANTANTE

Rien n'est si plaisant que de rire,
Quand on rit aux dépens d'autrui.

LE PRESIDENT

Insolentes! je voudrois sçavoir un peu qui vous êtes.

L'ACTRICE CHANTANTE

Nous sommes vos très-humbles servantes.
Elles sortent en chantant & en dansant.

Dans un si beau jour, tout doit s'enflamer,
Le tems heureux des jeux est le tems d'aimer.

LE PRESIDENT

Je suis outré... reconnoîtroit-on à ce qui se passe ici, la maison d'un Magistrat? Mais à qui en veut ce bon homme avec ses chiens?

22. 'On dit ironiquement d'un homme laid, mal bâti, mal habillé, Voilà une plaisante *figure*, voilà une vilaine *figure*, une affreuse *figure*' (Furetière).

SCENE XII

LE PRESIDENT, LUCAS *tenant en laisse des chiens*

LUCAS

A Monsieur de Fatenville, à qui Mr le Marquis m'a chargé de les amener; mais morgué, c'est à contre cœur que je m'aquitte de la commission.

LE PRESIDENT

Vous n'êtes pas content de Mr le Conseiller?

LUCAS

Non, morgué, & je ne suis pas le seul...

LE PRESIDENT

Que vous a-t-il donc fait?

LUCAS

Il m'a fait, il m'a fait, que s'il vient encore passer les vacances chez nous, je le ferai morgué haper par un gros dogue que j'ai façonné exprès à ça[23].

LE PRESIDENT

Cela est violent!

---

23. *Façonner*, dans le sens de *former* ou de *polir*, s'est toujours appliqué plutôt à des personnes qu'à des animaux, mais Lucas a des tournures particulières. La syntaxe 'façonner quelqu'un à quelque chose' est maintenant vieillie.

LUCAS

Eh parsanguène, n'ai-je pas raison? J'avois bouté mon amiquié à la fermiere de Mr le Marquis; je nous aimions comme deux tourterelles, alle & moi; mais depuis que j'avons vû Mr de Fatenville, j'avons toujours maille à partir ensemble. J'étions fiancés, je sommes encore à épouser.

LE PRESIDENT

Voilà de ses plaisirs!

LUCAS

Vous grondez quelque chose?

LE PRESIDENT

Je dis que le mariage racommodera tout cela.

LUCAS

Bon, ce Mr le Conseiller rebrouilleroit tout de plus belle; il amenne avec lui cinq ou six libartins qui se plaisent à mettre le désordre par-tout. Ils cajolent toutes les paysannes, ils rouont de coups tous les paysans; & ils disont pour toute raison, que c'est leur folie.

LE PRESIDENT

Belle société pour un homme de robe!

LUCAS

Ce sont morgué des drôles qui ne respectont rian. Il n'y a pas jusqu'à Mr le Bailli qu'ils bernirent trois heures dans une couvarture, parce que Mlle. la Baillive est assez gentille, & que Mr le Bailli ne veut pas qu'on lui fasse des meines.

LE PRESIDENT

Quelle insolence!

LUCAS

Passe pour stila[24], j'en devois au Bailli, & je sûs bon gré à Mr le Conseiller de quelques coups de canne qu'il me donnit, pour me faire tenir un des coins de la Couvarture.

LE PRESIDENT

Faut-il que j'aie un si ridicule Neveu?

LUCAS

Quoi vous êtes l'Oncle de Mr le Conseiller? ah morgué, qu'il nous a fait de bons contes de vous!

LE PRESIDENT

Quoi, l'impertinent...

LUCAS

Je ne sçais comme il agence[25] tout ça, mais il nous

---

24. Prononciation populaire de *cettui-là* (*cestuy-là*, etc.). Vaugelas note que *cettuy-cy* 'commence à n'être plus guère en usage' ; *Remarques*, p. 367.

25. Furetière définit ainsi le mot *agencer* : 'disposer [les choses] d'une certaine manière qui les rende agréables', et il note la prépondérance des emplois au figuré.

fait entendre qu'ous êtes le plus bouru robin qu'il connoisse, qu'ous passez toute la vie à le gronder & à lui amasser du bien; mais qu'heureusement vos réprimandes & vous, tirent tous deux à leur fin.

LE PRESIDENT

L'ingrat!

LUCAS

Tant y a, qu'il n'a pas grand foi à votre santé; il a déja fait marché d'une terre dans notre voisinage, qu'il a promis de payer dans six mois sur votre succession.

LE PRESIDENT

C'est assez, mon ami, va-t'en, & remméne ces chiens... C'est donc ainsi qu'un ingrat reconnoît mes bontés! C'en est fait, me voilà déterminé en faveur d'Eraste, & je veux faire son bonheur, en lui assurant tout mon bien, & en lui faisant épouser la nièce de la Comtesse. Ah! la voici tout à propos.

Scene XIII

LA COMTESSE, LE PRESIDENT.

LA COMTESSE

Eh, quel miracle de vous voir[26], Mr le Président!

26. Furetière qualifie cette expression d'*hyperbole*.

LE PRESIDENT

J'allois, Madame, passer dans votre apartement pour vous entretenir d'une affaire de conséquence.

LA COMTESSE

Et moi j'allois chez vous, pour vous communiquer un dessein qui m'intéresse infiniment.

LE PRESIDENT

Je suis ravi de vous en avoir épargné la peine.

LA COMTESSE

J'ai une nièce, M. le Président...

LE PRESIDENT

J'ai un neveu, Madame la Comtesse...

LA COMTESSE

Elle est jeune & bien faite, & a fort bien profité des soins que j'ai pris de son éducation.

LE PRESIDENT

Il est fort estimé dans le parti qu'il a pris, & passe pour galant homme chez tous ceux qui le connoissent.

LA COMTESSE

Le bien de ma nièce n'est pas fort considérable par lui-même, mais j'y supplérai.

LE PRESIDENT

Mon neveu a consumé une partie de son patrimoine, mais le bien que je lui destine réparera ce désordre.

LA COMTESSE

Ma nièce vous paroît-elle un parti convenable à votre neveu?

LE PRESIDENT

C'est ce que je venois vous proposer.

LA COMTESSE

Est-il possible?

LE PRESIDENT

Rien n'est plus vrai.

LA COMTESSE

Si cela est ainsi, il n'y a qu'à dresser le contract, je signerai tout ce que vous voudrez, & je vous répons du consentement de ma niéce.

LE PRESIDENT

Voulez-vous que dès aujourd'hui nous finissions cette affaire?

LA COMTESSE

Le plutôt[27] est pour moi le meilleur.

---

27. *Plus tôt* et *plutôt* étaient souvent confondus à l'époque ; voir DFC.

LE PRESIDENT

Je vais de ce pas chez mon Notaire.

LA COMTESSE

Je vous attens avec impatience.

SCENE XIV

LA COMTESSE, M. FATENVILLE.

LA COMTESSE

Venez, mon cher Conseiller, que je vous embrasse, je suis transportée de joie.

FATENVILLE

Et moi, Madame, je suis dans le dernier chagrin.

LA COMTESSE

Ce n'est rien, ce n'est rien.

FATENVILLE

Ce n'est rien, Madame! après les traitemens que je viens d'essuyer!

LA COMTESSE

Ce n'est rien, vous dis-je, ne songeons qu'à nous réjouir.

FATENVILLE

Mon Oncle a de petites manieres avec moi.

LA COMTESSE

Nous venons de prendre ensemble des résolutions qui vous doivent charmer.

FATENVILLE

J'ignore ce que c'est, mais j'en augure mal, s'il s'en est mêlé.

LA COMTESSE

Nous vous marions avec Angelique.

FATENVILLE

Avec Angelique! Ma foi mon Oncle a pris le bon parti, c'étoit le seul moyen de me ranger.

LA COMTESSE

La voici, faites-lui en votre compliment.

Scene XV

LA COMTESSE, FATENVILLE, ANGELIQUE.

LA COMTESSE

Ma nièce, Mr le Conseiller va vous donner des nouvelles qui vous feront plaisir.

FATENVILLE

Oui, Madame, je vous félicite; on nous marie.

ANGELIQUE

Ensemble?

FATENVILLE

Oui, vraiment, ensemble... hola, hé, la Fleur... oui, Madame, ensemble... va-t'en me chercher ce portrait que m'a renvoyé la Marquise...plus d'Eraste au moins... entens-tu? Il est sur ma table. Nérine ne dit mot?

NERINE

On perdroit la parole à moins; ceci nous surprend terriblement.

FATENVILLE

J'ai été surpris, moi; mon Oncle ne m'en a pas fait la moindre honnêteté[28], cela est un peu cavalier, oui! & pour toute autre, il en auroit, ma foi, le démenti.

ANGELIQUE

Je ne vous conseille pas de vous contraindre; aussi bien ai-je de mon côté une aversion pour le mariage, que je ne vous répons pas de vaincre si-tôt.

FATENVILLE

Bon, une aversion pour le mariage, c'est encore un sacrifice que je vous fais, moi. Je m'étois fait un plan de vie avec les femmes tout-à-fait dégagé du contract, je comptois fleurette aux unes, je brusquois les

---

28. Entendre: civilité, compliment.

autres, je les méprisois toutes, & j'étois bien résolu de n'en aimer aucune que pour avoir le plaisir d'en médire.

NERINE

Vous nous faites bien de la grace.

FATENVILLE

Je déroge[29] à tout cela pour vous, il ne faut plus répondre de rien... Ce maraut de Bourguignon est longtems... Je veux vous faire présent de mon portrait par préciput[30] .

ANGELIQUE

Vous pouvez le garder pour quelque autre, Monsieur, les choses ne sont point encore si avancées qu'il ne puisse survenir des obstacles...

FATENVILLE

Des obstacles? Vous êtes soupçonneuse? Oh je vous répond que je ne suis point encore hipotéqué[31]. Mon portrait est de bon goût au moins; je me suis fait peindre en cuirassier; je veux que vous voyiez cette tête-là sous un haussecol.

---

29. Comme terme de droit, *déroger* signifiait 'céder, relâcher de ses droits' (Furetière).

30. *Préciput* est 'un avantage que l'on stipule dans les contrats de mariage en faveur du survivant, qu'il doit prendre sur les biens du prédécédé avant le partage de la succession ou de la communauté. En droit à l'égard des femmes, on l'appelle *augment de dot*, ou *donatio propter nuptias*' (Furetière).

31. Entendre: promis à une autre.

NERINE

Il n'y a rien qui ressemble mieux à un rabat.

LA FLEUR

Je ne le trouve pas, Monsieur.

FATENVILLE

Tu ne le trouves pas!

LA FLEUR

Non, Monsieur.

FATENVILLE

Quoi, morbleu! ah je me remets... Je l'ai prêté à une petite Procureuse, pour quelques-unes de ses lettres; mais en rendant, rendant, que cela ne vous mette pas en peine.

ANGELIQUE *bas à Nerine.*

Quel extravagant, Nérine!

FATENVILLE

Que dit-elle, mon enfant?

NERINE

Elle vous traite déja en mari.

FATENVILLE

Vous me paroissez pourtant bien triste, pour un jour de nôce; mais je vais hâter une petite fête qui vous mettra en goût de plaisir. Sans adieu, mes futures[32].

SCENE XVI

ANGELIQUE, NERINE

ANGELIQUE

Quoi? je serois la femme ce ce fou-là? ah! je suis au désespoir!

NERINE

Je vous le pardonne, votre situation est des plus cruelles; si vous résistez à votre tante, il vous en coûte un Amant. Franchement l'alternative est désesperante.

SCENE XVII

ANGELIQUE, NERINE, FRONTIN.

FRONTIN

De la joie, Madame, de la joie, vous êtes la plus heureuse personne du monde.

NERINE

Que veux tu dire avec ta joie? nous sommes au désespoir.

---

32. Furetière note que cet emploi de *futur[e]* était du Palais.

FRONTIN

Vous êtes au désespoir de votre bonheur?

ANGELIQUE

Quel bonheur? explique toi mieux. As tu vû Eraste?

FRONTIN

Si je l'ai vû! c'est lui qui m'envoie vous apporter ces bonnes nouvelles.

NERINE

Et quelles bonnes nouvelles?

FRONTIN

Ne vous l'ai-je pas dit? que vous n'aviez plus rien à craindre, & que tout alloit le mieux du monde.

ANGELIQUE

Mais comment?

FRONTIN

Mais comment! Mais pourquoi! Eh que diable, faut-il tant de raisons pour se réjouir? Quand ce seroit pour vous chagriner, vous n'y prendriez pas plus de précautions.

SCENE XVIII

ANGELIQUE, NERINE, FRONTIN, ERASTE.

ANGELIQUE

Ah! Eraste, tirez nous d'inquiétude, que veut dire Frontin?

ERASTE

J'ai vû mon Oncle, belle Angelique, j'ai eû le bonheur de le rendre favorable à mon amour, & il m'a permis de ne rien négliger pour être heureux.

ANGELIQUE

Cependant, Mr de Fatenville vient de m'annoncer qu'il alloit devenir mon époux.

ERASTE

Lui, votre époux?

ANGELIQUE

Lui-même, & ma tante m'a fait entendre la même chose.

ERASTE

Votre tante! Vous m'étonnez. Mon oncle auroit-il sitôt changé de dessein? me joueroit-il[33] ? Mais non,

---

33. 'On dit [...] qu'on *joue* quelqu'un lorsqu'on le fait courir inutilement ; ou qu'on le trompe, qu'on l'amuse de belles paroles et de vaines promesses' (Furetière). La forme pronominale s'imposait au cours du siècle (J.-P. Seguin, *op. cit.*, p. 87).

il n'y a nulle apparence, mon cousin vous aura trompé, & vous aurez mal entendu votre tante.

NERINE

Il y a du pour & du contre dans tout cela.

ERASTE

Enfin j'attendrai ici le dénouement de cette intrigue, & s'il ne m'est pas favorable, j'empêcherai du moins que mon rival ne jouisse de mon malheur.

SCENE XIX

ANGELIQUE, NERINE, ERASTE,
FRONTIN, M. FATENVILLE.

FATENVILLE

Ah vous voila, Mr Eraste; vous me paroissez un peu désolé. Je vous prie de la nôce[34], au moins. Au reste ce n'est pas sa faute. Si vous n'êtes pas content de l'Amour, vous pouvez vous en plaindre à son parlement qui s'avance.

ERASTE

Voyons à quoi tout ceci aboutira.

UN PLAISIR

L'Amour vient avec sa cour se placer sur son tribu-

34. Furetière donne l'exemple 'On *prie* ses amis à la noce'. S'agit-il de l'omission des mots 'd'être' ?

nal, & donner audience, un Plaisir servant d'huissier, & tenant une liasse de placets, appelle les causes en chantant.

Amans qui d'une belle essuyez le caprice,
Vous belles, que pour prix d'un tendre sacrifice,
On immole à d'autres Amours;
Accourez, venez tous, on vous rendra justice:
L'Amour tient ici ses grands jours[35] .

DEUX AVOCATS se présentent & chantent.

LE PREMIER

Je parle pour Tircis.

LE SECOND

Je suis pour Célimene.

LE PREMIER

Un rendez-vous étoit concerté comme il faut,
Le fidéle Tircis attendoit l'inhumaine,
Mais helas, l'attente fut vaine,
Elle n'y vint pas assez-tôt.

---

35. Allusion aux Grands Jours des Cours Souveraines. Au dix-huitième siècle, les Grands Jours n'étaient plus que des commissions extraordinaires envoyées pour réprimer des désordres que la justice ordinaire ne pouvait ou ne voulait empêcher (M. Marion, *op. cit.*, p. 268).

LE SECOND

L'impatient Tircis est lui seul en deffaut,
L'Amour au rendez-vous fit courir Célimène,
Mais helas! sa course fût vaine,
Tircis étoit parti trop tôt.

L'AMOUR prononce

Ordonné que sans perdre tems,
Un nouveau rendez-vous finisse,
Les plaintes de ces deux Amans,
L'Amour en leur rendant justice,
Veut leurs plaisirs pour toute épice,
Et compense entre eux les dépens.

LES DEUX AVOCATS en quittant leur robe.

Connoissez sous cet équipage,
Les deux Amans jugés qui vous rendent hom-
[mage.
Ah! que cet arrêt a d'appas!
Non, nous n'en appellerons pas.

REQUETE

L'air des Robins déplaît aux Belles[36]*,*
Plaise à l'Amour les bannir d'auprès d'elles,
Mais si quelque Robin prenoit les airs exquis,
Du petit Maître, ou du Marquis,
Qu'il pousse à bout les plus cruelles!

---

36. Destouches illustra cette constatation, assez habituelle sur la scène contemporaine, dans des scènes qu'il ajouta à la version originale de son *Irrésolu* (éd. J. Dunkley, p. 197-204 (variantes)). Voir aussi Lafont, *Les Trois Frères rivaux*, sc. 2, pour une description et des sentiments analogues.

REPONSE

Soit fait ainsi qu'il est requis.

AUTRE REQUETE

Plaise à l'Amour qu'il soit permis,
De décreter sur les Maris,
Dont l'humeur est sombre & jalouse,
Le cœur d'une charmante épouse!

REPONSE

Soit fait ainsi qu'il est requis.

SCENE DERNIERE.

LE PRESIDENT, ET LES ACTEURS PRECEDENS.

LE PRESIDENT

Allons, Madame, voila le contrat tout dressé, faisons signer les parties... Mais que signifie tout ceci?

FATENVILLE

C'est un divertissement que je donne à la compagnie, il ne pouvoit venir plus à propos.

LA COMTESSE

Allons, Mr le Conseiller, signez donc.

LE PRESIDENT

Non, non, Madame, voilà le neveu pour qui le contrat

est dressé, & à qui je donne tout mon bien. L'autre est un libertin indigne de vos bontés & de mon estime.

LA COMTESSE

Je vous avoue, Monsieur, que je m'étois trompée; mais n'importe; votre alliance m'est toujours chere, je signe aveuglément...

FATENVILLE

Je suis donc trahi! Mr Passepied, suivez-moi.

FRONTIN

Ah, Mr. L'Amour, de grace, encore un jugement prononcez.

Qu'au milieu des jeux & des ris,
Nerine & Frontin soient unis,
Que Nerine soit bientôt mere,
D'un fils, dont Frontin soit le pere!

L'AMOUR

Soit fait ainsi qu'il est requis.

AU PARTERRE

Et vous, nos seigneurs du Parterre,
Si notre pièce a sçû vous plaire,
Que des soins que nous avons pris,
Votre suffrage soit le prix!

LE PARTERRE

Soit fait ainsi qu'il est requis.

TABLE DES MATIERES

SOCIÉTÉ DES TEXTES FRANÇAIS MODERNES (S.T.F.M.)

Fondée en 1905
Association loi 1901 (J.O. 31 octobre 1931)
Siège social : Institut de Littérature française
(Université de Paris-Sorbonne)
1, rue Victor Cousin. 75005 PARIS

La Société des Textes Français Modernes (S.T.F.M.), fondée en 1905, a pour but de réimprimer des textes publiés depuis le XVIe siècle et d'imprimer des textes inédits appartenant à cette période.

Pour tout renseignement et pour les demandes d'adhésion : s'adresser au Secrétaire général, M. Jean Balsamo, 22, rue de Savoie, 75006 Paris.

Demandez le catalogue des titres disponibles et les conditions d'adhésion.

LES PUBLICATIONS DE LA SOCIÉTÉ DES TEXTES FRANÇAIS MODERNES SONT EN VENTE AUX ÉDITIONS KLINCKSIECK
8, rue de la Sorbonne 75005 Paris

EXTRAIT DU CATALOGUE

(janvier 1997)

XVIe siècle.

Poésie :

4. HÉROËT, *Œuvres poétiques* (F. Gohin).
5. SCÈVE, *Délie* (E. Parturier).
7-31. RONSARD, *Œuvres complètes* (P. Laumonier).
32-39, 179-180. DU BELLAY, *Deffence et illustration. Œuvres poétiques françaises* (H. Chamard) *et latines* (Geneviève Demerson).
43-46. D'AUBIGNÉ, *Les Tragiques* (Garnier et Plattard).
141. TYARD, *Œuvres poétiques complètes* (J. Lapp.).
156-157. *La Polémique protestante contre Ronsard* (J. Pineaux).
158. BERTAUT, *Recueil de quelques vers amoureux* (L. Terreaux).
173-174, 193, 195, 202. DU BARTAS, *La Sepmaine* (Y. Bellenger), *La Seconde Semaine (1584),* I et II (Y. Bellenger), *Les Suittes de la Seconde Semaine* (Y. Bellenger).
177. LA ROQUE, *Poésies* (G. Mathieu-Castellani).
194. LA GESSÉE, *Les Jeunesses* (G. Demerson et J.-Ph. Labrousse).
198. SAINT-GELAIS, *Œuvres poétiques françaises,* I (D. Stone).
204. SAINT-GELAIS, *Œuvres poétiques françaises,* II (D. Stone).
208. PELETIER DU MANS, *L'Amour des Amours* (J.C. Monferran).
210. POUPO, *La Muse Chrestienne* (A. Mantero).

Prose :

2-3. HERBERAY DES ESSARTS, *Amadis de Gaule (Premier Livre),* (H. Vaganay-Y. Giraud).
6. SÉBILLET, *Art poétique françois* (F. Gaiffe-F. Goyet).
150. NICOLAS DE TROYES, *Le Grand Parangon des Nouvelles nouvelles* (K. Kasprzyk).
163. BOAISTUAU, *Histoires tragiques* (R. Carr).
171. DES PERIERS, *Nouvelles Récréations et joyeux devis* (K. Kasprzyk).
175. *Le Disciple de Pantagruel* (G. Demerson et C. Lauvergnat-Gagnière).
183. D'AUBIGNÉ, *Sa Vie à ses enfants* (G. Schrenck).
186. *Chroniques gargantuines* (C. Lauvergnat-Gagnière, G. Demerson *et al.*).

Théâtre :

42. DES MASURES, *Tragédies saintes* (C. Comte).
125. TURNÈBE, *Les Contens* (N. Spector).
149. LA TAILLE, *Saül le furieux. La Famine...* (E. Forsyth).
161. LA TAILLE, *Les Corrivaus* (D. Drysdall).
172. GRÉVIN, *Comédies* (E. Lapeyre).
184. LARIVEY, *Le Laquais* (M. Lazard et L. Zilli).

XVIIe siècle.

Poésie :

54. RACAN, *Les Bergeries* (L. Arnould).
74-76. SCARRON, *Poésies diverses* (M. Cauchie).
78. BOILEAU-DESPRÉAUX, *Épistres* (A. Cahen).
123. RÉGNIER, *Œuvres complètes* (G. Raibaud).
151-152. VOITURE, *Poésies* (H. Lafay).
164-165. MALLEVILLE, *Œuvres poétiques* (R. Ortali).
187-188. LA CEPPÈDE, *Théorèmes* (Y. Quenot).

Prose :

64-65. GUEZ DE BALZAC, *Les Premières Lettres* (H. Bibas et K.T. Butler).
71-72. Abbé de PURE, *La Pretieuse* (E. Magne).
80. FONTENELLE, *Entretiens sur la pluralité des mondes* (A. Calame).
135-140. SAINT-ÉVREMOND, *Lettres* et *Œuvres en prose* (R. Ternois).
142. FONTENELLE, *Nouveaux Dialogues des morts* (J. Dagen).
144-147 et 170. SAINT-AMANT, *Œuvres* (J. Bailbé et J. Lagny).
153-154. GUEZ DE BALZAC, *Les Entretiens* (1657) (B. Beugnot).
155. PERROT D'ABLANCOURT, *Lettres et préfaces critiques* (R. Zuber).
182. SCARRON, *Nouvelles tragi-comiques* (R. Guichemerre).
191. FOIGNY, *La Terre Australe connue* (P. Ronzeaud).
192-197. SEGRAIS, *Les Nouvelles françaises* (R. Guichemerre).
199. PRÉCHAC, *Contes moins contes que les autres.* Précédés de *L'Illustre Parisienne* (F. Gevrey).
209. *Anthologie des Nouvelles du Mercure Galant* (M. Vincent).
211. Mme d'AULNOY, *Contes I* (J. Barchilon – Ph. Hourcade).

Théâtre :

57. TRISTAN, *Les Plaintes d'Acante et autres œuvres* (J. Madeleine).
58. TRISTAN, *La Mariane. Tragédie* (J. Madeleine).
59. TRISTAN, *La Folie du Sage* (J. Madeleine).
60. TRISTAN, *La Mort de Sénèque. Tragédie* (J. Madeleine).
61. TRISTAN, *Le Parasite. Comédie* (J. Madeleine).
62. *Le Festin de pierre avant Molière* (G. Gendarme de Bévotte-R. Guichemerre).
73. CORNEILLE, *Le Cid* (G. Forestier et M. Cauchie).
121. CORNEILLE, *L'Illusion comique* (R. Garapon).
126. CORNEILLE, *La Place royale* (J.-C. Brunon).
128. DESMARETS DE SAINT-SORLIN, *Les Visionnaires* (H. G. Hall).
143. SCARRON, *Dom Japhet d'Arménie* (R. Garapon).
160. CORNEILLE, *Andromède* (C. Delmas).
166. L'ESTOILE, *L'Intrigue des filous* (R. Guichemerre).
167-168. *La Querelle de l'École des Femmes* (G. Mongrédien).

176. SCARRON, *L'Héritier ridicule* (R. Guichemerre).
178. BROSSE, *Les Songes des hommes esveillez* (G. Forestier).
181 et 190. DANCOURT, *Comédies* (A. Blanc).
185. POISSON, *Le Baron de la Crasse, L'Après-soupé des auberges* (Ch. Mazouer).
196. G. DE SCUDÉRY, *Le Prince déguisé. La Mort de César* (E. Dutertre, D. Moncond'Huy).
200. GHERARDI, *Le Théâtre italien*, I (Ch. Mazouer).
205. MARESCHAL, *Le Jugement équitable de Charles Le Hardy* (C. Griselhouber).
207. GHERARDI, *Le Théâtre italien,* II (R. Guichemerre).

XVIIIe siècle.

80-81. P. BAYLE, *Pensées diverses sur la Comète.* (A. Prat-P. Rétat).
87-88. VOLTAIRE, *Lettres philosophiques* (G. Lanson, A.M. Rousseau).
89-90. VOLTAIRE, *Zadig* (G. Ascoli).
91. VOLTAIRE, *Candide* (A. Morize).
131. DIDEROT, *Éléments de physiologie* (J. Mayer).
162. DUCLOS, *Les Confessions du Comte de N**** (L. Versini).
159. FLORIAN, *Nouvelles* (R. Godenne).
148. MABLY, *Des Droits et des devoirs du citoyen* (J.-L. Lecercle).
112. ROUSSEAU J.-J., *Les Rêveries du Promeneur solitaire* (J. Spink).
190. SEDAINE, *Le Philosophe sans le savoir* (R. Garapon).
201. MARMONTEL, *Bélisaire* (R. Granderoute).
203. BOUFFLERS, *Contes* (A. Sokalski).
206. NERICAULT-DESTOUCHES, *L'Irrésolu* (J. Dunkley).
212. BOINDIN, *Quatre comédies* (J. Dunkley).

XIXe siècle.

124. BALZAC, *Le Colonel Chabert* (P. Citron).
119-120. CHATEAUBRIAND, *Vie de Rancé* (F. Letessier).
129-130. CHATEAUBRIAND, *Voyage en Amérique* (R. Switzer).
127. MAUPASSANT, *Notre Cœur* (P. Cogny).
115-116. MICHELET, *La Sorcière* (L. Refort).
110. MUSSET, *Lorenzaccio* (et : *La Genèse de Lorenzaccio*) (P. Dimoff).
94-95. SENANCOUR, *Rêveries sur la nature primitive de l'homme* (J. Merlant et G. Saintville).

ACHEVÉ D'IMPRIMER
EN SEPTEMBRE 1997
PAR L'IMPRIMERIE
DE LA MANUTENTION
À MAYENNE
N° 272-97

Dépôt légal : 3e trimestre 1997